The Burning Library

The Burning Library

Writings on Art, Politics and Sexuality
1969–1993

Edmund White
Edited by David Bergman

Chatto & Windus
LONDON

First published in 1994

1 3 5 7 9 10 8 6 4 2

This edition and all previously unpublished material
© Edmund White 1994
Introductory matter © David Bergman 1994

First published in Great Britain in 1994 by
Chatto & Windus Limited
Random House, 20 Vauxhall Bridge Road, London SW1V 2SA

Random House Australia (Pty) Limited
20 Alfred Street, Milsons Point, Sydney,
New South Wales 2061, Australia

Random House New Zealand Limited
18 Poland Road, Glenfield
Auckland 10, New Zealand

Random House South Africa (Pty) Limited
PO Box 337, Bergvlei, South Africa

Random House UK Limited Reg. No. 954009

A CIP catalogue record for this book is available from the British Library

ISBN 0 7011 6168 X

Typeset by SX Composing Ltd, Rayleigh, Essex
Printed in Great Britain by Mackays of Chatham PLC, Chatham, Kent

Contents

III   The Nineties

Introduction

David Bergman

'No one has a slogan, no one even has an attitude, but something's brewing,' wrote Edmund White in a letter describing the riot that had broken out one warm Friday night in June 1969 in the West Village outside the Stonewall Inn, a gay bar that he sometimes patronized. His letter, to Ann and Alfred Corn, friends then living in Paris – a city he would later claim as his home – is filled with a youthful wonder and disbelief at being at the center of events. For White the police skirmish was the start of a revolution and the Stonewall Inn nothing less than 'that mighty bastille'. There he was, caught in the current of what one queen tartly dubbed, 'the swish heard round the world'.

The Stonewall Riots, which many see as the start of the gay liberation movement, were not a one-night affair. Clashes with the police went on all weekend. On the second night, Saturday, White returned to Sheridan Square to give 'stump speeches about the need to radicalize, how we must recognize we're part of a vast rebellion of all the oppressed'. His calls to arms were met not only by jeers and cheers, but also by the embrace of 'straight Negro boys', who now viewed him as a brother in the Struggle. Yet the most decisive result of his oratory was that it symbolically divided him from the 'dreary middle-class East-Side queens', who stood about disapproving yet unable to leave, 'torn between their class loyalties, their desires to be respectable, and their longing for freedom'.

In the Hollywood version of his life, in which White no doubt would be played by Tom Cruise, this scene – replete with burning buildings and howling squad cars, sadistic policemen in a 'paddy wagon as big as a school bus', scantily dressed hustlers toting parking meters and a 'mad Negro ... whirl[ing] like a dervish with a twisted piece of metal' – this scene of anarchy and devastation would become the site where the young gay writer is born. And indeed his novel *The Beautiful Room is Empty* concludes with this attack on 'Fort Disco'. But the truth is, as usual, more complicated and less cinematographic. By the time the Stonewall Riots occurred, White had virtually finished *Forgetting Elena*, his first published novel; he was already a veteran writer for Time–Life Books and was about to begin the first essay in this collection, 'The Gay Philosopher'. Yet the impact of the Stonewall Riots should not be underestimated. It brought dramatically to the surface the crisis of language with which Edmund White had been struggling, and also began a social/sexual movement he has spent over two decades participating in and chronicling.

Edmund White was born in 1940 in Cincinnati, 'that Valhalla of Republicanism', as he dubbed it, and he lived there off and on until he graduated from college. The impact of the midwest and Cincinnati cannot be underestimated. For all the cosmopolitan baggage he carries around, he still keeps a rucksack filled with the insular ethic of the Queen City. His novels are filled with small enclosed places – the island kingdom of *Forgetting Elena*, the island colony in *Caracole*, the Manhattan island of *The Beautiful Room is Empty*. All these imaginative spaces are informed by his knowledge of Cincinnati, where White first witnessed 'a grand Balzacian canvas of greed, corruption, competition and disappointment' as painted by his father, who knew, according to *States of Desire*, 'everyone's pedigree and pretensions, the scope of their infidelities and the true size of their bank accounts'.

The lyricism of White's prose hides the fact that his interests are sociological rather than psychological. He shows his disdain for psychology when he packs the pill-popping, brow-beating, insane Dr O'Reilly of *A Boy's Own Story* and *The Beautiful Room is Empty* off to the sanitarium for a dose of his own medicine. His particular strength is his ability to see how the material forces at work hold his characters in vital tension. Even in the make-believe world of *Caracole* where the ethos seemingly shapes the action, it is the pressure of the imperial forces that really holds this world together. Not that the characters are

marionettes, whose strings are pulled by the vulgar but economically superior conquering army. Rather the conquerors have
roped off the little island where the action takes place and turned
it into a fighting ring. It is not surprising, therefore, that one of
White's assignments as an editor for Time–Life Books was to help
write *The First Man*, a book of popular paleontology, in which he
could examine layer upon layer of human development. White's
fiction and non-fiction share this same vision of social dynamics.

White's apprenticeship with Time–Life Books reinforces an important point. If we now view Edmund White primarily as a
novelist, this was not how he first made his name. For a long time
he was better known as a journalist and editor – he was an editor
for both *Horizon* and the *Saturday Review* for brief periods.
(Forgotten is his experience as a playwright; his *Blue Boy in
Black*, about a black maid who gains control over a white family,
met with mixed reviews when it premièred Off-Broadway in 1963
as did *Trios* when it was staged in London in 1993.) Although
Forgetting Elena and *Nocturnes for the King of Naples*, his first
two published novels (1973, 1978), won him a literary reputation
among a small group of New York intellectuals, it was the publication (in 1977) of *The Joy of Gay Sex* (with Charles Silverstein)
and *States of Desire: Travels in Gay America* (1980), two works
of non-fiction, that brought him a large general readership. Even
after the success of his novels, White has continued to write non-
fiction, including his monumental biography of Jean Genet. The
essays collected in this volume represent almost a quarter century
of non-fiction writing.

The novelist career and the journalist career have always been
intertwined. As an essayist, White is at his best when he brings to
his subject a kind of novelistic color and texture. His best pieces
rely as much on atmosphere as on facts, on striking a general
point of view as much as establishing specific positions. And as a
novelist, he places plot and psychological depth second to evok-
ing a society in which the narrative is performed. In fact, his
novels seem closer to the imaginative ethnography of the nineteenth century than to modern American fiction; in his books he
often plays a dandified Melville jumping ship and living among
some mystifying but attractive tribe of strangely and barely clad
natives.

White has said that all his novels are about initiation, but the persona he develops in essays both early and late is the figure of the innocent – or rather of the flaneur eternally surprised by the world he thought he knew so well. He is the young man on the boulevard, observing with equal measures of cunning, curiosity, concern and amusement the society around him. Thus in 'Sexual Culture' he is surprised when a friend, a straight woman, asks him if gay men have friends. How could it be that she did not know this? he asks. He who had thought that he had been part of her culture, had assumed they shared the same assumptions, now must face the truth that he *never* really understood the world through which he moved with such seeming assurance. The point of view in 'Sexual Culture' is merely the reverse image of the point of view in *Forgetting Elena*, where the narrator has forgotten that *he* is the prince of the island, that rather than being the outsider he has all along assumed he must be, he is the insider, the one who sets the terms of social interaction. In his essays White constantly slides between being inside and outside, performer and observer, innocent and sophisticate. As in his fiction, the humor and force come from his ability to move rapidly between extremes.

One of White's longtime friends and co-workers warned me when I began work on this book, 'Don't trust anything Ed says.' It was good advice, advice that White himself frequently gives the reader, if somewhat indirectly, for many of these essays celebrate the value of irresponsibility. The reader of his essays must expect to be betrayed.

The two essays that take up the issue of the value of irresponsibility most explicitly were written far apart in time, but have a great deal in common. Robert Mapplethorpe is the first of White's irresponsible alter egos. White not only knew Mapplethorpe, but they worked together: Mapplethorpe photographed White's interviews with Truman Capote and William Burroughs. Yet it is not as a fellow workman that White regards Mapplethorpe. What White values about Mapplethorpe's photographs is their obscenity – their refusal to submit themselves to domestication, to the social framework of the good and useful. Although White does not use these words, what he finds most admirable, even moral in Mapplethorpe's art is that Mapplethorpe turns values on their head. Mapplethorpe's value is based on the fact that he was a racist and a fetishist, but not your usual racist and fetishist. He turned people into objects, not to make them commodities, but to transform them into holy relics of Dionysian potency. Mapplethorpe's classicism, although often cool – even icy – underscores his subjects' relationship to the pagan, the pre-Christian, the orgiastic. His black men, particularly, resist domestication, absorption into the social structure, because they are greater than what would contain or elevate them, whether the polyester suit or the Stickley table. For White, Mapplethorpe expresses 'not love in the sense of sustained social responsibility but love as passion, as appetite, as irrepressible yearning ... all the legal and social rules of marriage, of commitment and responsibility, cannot vouchsafe the life of passion. Art and passion live, thrive and die regardless of public utility and convenience; art and passion are the two supremely irresponsible modes of experience.'

A dozen years after his 1980 essay on Mapplethorpe, White once again addresses the issue of irresponsibility in his essay on the singer Prince. Like Mapplethorpe, Prince is also a highly erotically charged artist incapable of domestication. Like Mapplethorpe, his eroticism blurs the lines of gender while intensifying issues of race. The conjunction of race, eroticism, and art is extremely powerful, but as Susan Sontag argues, can be the wellspring of Fascism. It is the danger of Fascism that White addresses in his essay on Prince:

> The Fascist esthetic, as exemplified by the films of Leni Reifenstahl, the operas of Wagner and the plays of Robert Wilson, overwhelms and tranquilizes the critical intelligence. These works exalt the spirit and preclude humor or irony. To the degree they summon erotic energies, they disguise or transcend them ... Any shock, any laugh, any rupture would cause the hot-balloon to deflate and hurl us back to earth.
>
> By contrast, Prince's art thrives on shock, contrast, scandalous changes of direction, sudden hemorrhages of meaning.

Only when artists are being irresponsible of their culture, of their audience, of their very material do they keep the extremity of art from becoming Fascistic. White proudly described his essay on

Prince to me as 'over the top'. But it's just this over-the-top, excessive, irresponsible style that keeps his esthetic from becoming Fascistically unesthetic. Prince's vulgarity, just like White's vulgarity, just like Mapplethorpe's vulgarity, is his saving grace. Without such irresponsibility, without such impurity, the fetishism of these men would become Fascism.

White would not have to work so hard to establish the value of irresponsibility and betrayal, did dignity, propriety and duty not have so tight a grasp on his psyche. From his first essay, he expounds on the importance of friendship for gay men in general and for him in particular. Only because friendship is so important to him is its violation so revealing, exposing the betrayer and betrayed to the most penetrating and ruthless inspection. Because White aspires to make all affinities elective, he reserves the right to switch parties and demand another vote.

For White, the unseemly is a way of opening up the seamless. The Fascistic element of art and sexuality is the illusion of its seamlessness, of its naturalness, of the possibility of perfection. By ripping through this illusion White hopes not to eliminate power relations, but to make them more visible, so they can be altered. Perhaps that is why he often begins his essays through the eyes of straight people, usually straight women. In 'Sado Machismo', a heterosexual woman regards gay men as nice guys, 'sweet', 'sensitive'. Gay S and M puts the lie to that illusion, to the lie that sexuality can ever be divorced from relationships of power. But by theatricalizing that power relationship, White makes it visible, something to play with and alter.

The value of homosexuality is that it has the potential to assist the gay man not by stripping the trappings of life away, but by revealing the trappings in all their decorativeness. The homosexual knows the *illusion* of naturalness first hand, because he learns at an early age how to ape what other people believe is 'natural' and hears from all sides that what has come to him 'naturally' is 'unnatural'.

Of course, the eye-opening potential of homosexuality is rarely realized, or can be so abused as to fold in upon itself. Thus in a review of works by Pier Paolo Pasolini, White compares the radicalism of Pasolini with the neo-Fascism of Mishima. Whereas

Mishima obsessively represses the very forces unleashed by his insight back into the seeming 'naturalism' of ritual and feudal codes, Pasolini, in his self-consciously shocking film *Salo*, shows how Fascism takes the polymorphously perverse and through ritual naturalization turns it into something both disgusting and utterly boring.

Pasolini is the author of one of the recurrent themes of White's writing, repeated like a chorus throughout his long meditation on Juan Goytisolo, another of White's European touchstones. Pasolini argued that 'the body is always radical' not because it can be represented, but because it can never be fully represented, it always sticks out behind the representation draperies that would make it known. As a child I was fascinated by *The Invisible Man* whose presence could be known only when he was wrapped up. Clothes were clearly not the man, but the only way to make the body known. White shares that understanding. For White, the eternal admirer of beautiful bodies, the body is the only way we can have a sense of our being in the world, even as we recognize that bodily representations have failed to make us fully known.

His pleasure in the body – his attachment to the flesh and his dreams of transcending – plays itself out in his novels as well as in these essays, particularly in the remarkable valediction to Isherwood, 'Pools in Rocks by the Sea'. Isherwood, with Vladimir Nabokov, was one of the greatest influences on White's development. Like Isherwood, White is interested in Asian art and thought. (White majored in Chinese at the University of Michigan and his notebooks from college are filled with delicately traced Chinese characters, at odds with his scrawled, messy English penmanship.) White's initial attraction to Asian thought was his desire to escape desire, his sensuous need to rub against the disembodied. For White, Isherwood's fiction represents, among other things, 'the fertile contradiction . . . between the impersonal forces of cosmic energy and the patterns, unique as a fingerprint, through which that energy flows and that constitutes what we call the individual'.

The most radical consequence of the body for gay men in the last twenty years is, of course, AIDS. AIDS has become an excuse to turn against the body, no longer to elevate sensuous joys and erotic pleasures to the place they occupied in the 1970s and early 1980s. White rejects that strategy. For White, rather than pushing the body to the margins, AIDS places it in an even more intense spotlight. 'The body becomes central' since its ravages demand no less of our attention, admiration and participation than do the endowments of a youthful physique. White notes how Don Bachardy, in his portraits of the dying Isherwood – who succumbed to cancer, not AIDS – catches 'the skull under the face, reveals the relationship between bloated body and bony head, changes the inspired gaze of a seer into the angry grimace of a ruined old baboon'. The revolutionary impact of the AIDS body is its ability to stir, not desire, longing, nostalgia – although these too have the capacity to incite action – but anger, aggression, resentment. If Edmund White is less willing to storm the bastille of the National Institutes of Health or give stump speeches to join all the oppressed, it is not because he is any the less aware of, or more reconciled to the homophobia around him.

AIDS is perhaps the most obvious reason that these essays have been organized chronologically. Whatever the continuities of White's views on sexuality and society may be, there is a marked difference between the way he speaks about sexuality before the outbreak of the AIDS epidemic and after. In 'Fantasia on the Seventies' he speaks with disappointment at the growing conformity of gay life and its failure not to give full expression to the diversity of sexual impulses. As the epidemic increased, the importance of friendship – which was always present – is emphasized even more strongly as he mourns the loss of so many people close to him.

Isherwood influenced both White's style and content. Isherwood walked a tightrope between autobiography and fiction throughout his career, a tightrope drawn all the more tightly because his style seemed so styleless – a colloquial easiness of manner that belied its crystalline accuracy. Isherwood's manner weighed all the more on White because he was gay: he made his sexuality a central concern of his work, not because he was agonized by it, but because nothing else – death, love, spirituality, family, art or politics – could be addressed honestly and directly if one were silent about sex. The limpid simplicity and directness of Isherwood's style dictated his approach.

In many ways Isherwood is the extreme opposite of White's other great influence, Vladimir Nabokov. Where Isherwood is direct, Nabokov is labyrinthine; where Isherwood is colloquial, Nabokov is rhetorical; where Isherwood is plainly sincere, Nabokov is floridly parodistic; where Isherwood's fiction is a thin cover for the autobiographical, Nabokov's autobiographical allusions lead to wildly proliferating fictions; where one is quietly gay, the other is triumphantly hetero. A reader has the sense that Isherwood would like to strip off all masks (if one could) whereas Nabokov can't seem to find enough masks to put on. It is hard to imagine how a writer could be influenced by two such extremely different sensibilities. Yet, in White they come together. Isherwood's austerity is a way toward the carnivalesque cornucopia of Hindu beliefs and Nabokov's Baroque fantasies the winding road toward some blinding field of light. Both find in the erotic the key to imaginative energy and the most alluring obstacle to understanding. Finally, they both serve as a bridge between American culture and European culture – a transatlantic sensibility that seems to be White's destiny.

The literary essays, which make up the largest portion of this book, can be divided between those about American authors and those about European authors. Of these, the earliest are about American writers, usually gay American writers – Capote, Burroughs and Tennessee Williams – and White's gay American literary friends – the poets James Merrill, James Schuyler and the novelist-playwright Coleman Dowell. White is unusual among American novelists in being so influenced by poets, who often keep their distance from novelists. Yet their influence is clearly marked in his lyric style. Indeed, 'The Oracle', White's finest short story, in which a man is give advice by his dead lover through the intermediary of a beautiful Greek boy, owes not a little to Merrill's *Changing Light at Sandover*, in which Merrill speaks to the dead by means of a Ouija board. But I should emphasize that the American writers who most interest White tend to be transatlantic in their sensibilities, and the straight writers he has singled out – Harry Mathews and James Jones – are expatriates.

As White grew older and especially after his move to Europe, his roster of significant writers has included more Europeans.

Three stand out: Genet, Goytisolo and Pasolini, who come to represent the lyrically erotic, the formally experimental and the politically engaged points of White's sensibility. Indeed, these three strains cannot be separated from one another, and by aspiring to this merger, White clearly wishes to graft continental branches on to his American roots.

Emphasizing Edmund White's grounding in the gay literary and political movements in this way may make him seem a writer of parochial interests and limited relevance. In fact, the origins of many of the essays indicate their wide audience; most were written for mainstream journals – *Vanity Fair*, *New Republic*, the *Nation*, the *Times Literary Supplement* – while a few found their way into gay journals or publications on the fringe. But White has positioned himself quite clearly as either a gay man speaking to other gay men or as the intermediary between the gay and straight reading communities. Whether or not he wished to assume this position, the social and political forces in which he worked dictated that his writing should be viewed in this light. A writer of White's generation had one of two choices: either to stay in the closet or to be labeled a gay writer.

Yet even as he accepts the reality that gay and straight communities are frequently divided, he has sought to subvert this division. He sees the gay ghetto as both a limitation imposed on the homosexual and as a place of refuge sought by gay men. Most importantly, however, he sees it as a laboratory in which men have experimented in different ways of conducting their lives and whose pressurized atmosphere produces all sorts of interesting phenomena that may be studied, tinkered with, and analyzed. He assumes what goes on within the hermetic world is of interest to both gay and straight readers alike, and his discoveries are applicable to human interaction in a wide variety of circumstances. *Caracole* is his major novelistic attempt at applying his observation of the gay world to the straight one. Many of the pieces in this book are his essayistic attempts.

White's fiction is also riddled with allusions to the theatrical and his plays are filled with the novelistic; he is interested in the individual dynamics of each situation. His interests are the variables of power and language, and because these dynamics reach out beyond the frame of the narrative, they implicate the world. Consequently, he sets most of his narratives on small islands to impose a frame – a highly permeable frame – on what threatens to spill over the boundaries. As Neil Bartlett has pointed out, the 'queerest' way that White could depict homosexuality is by removing all references to homosexuality. White has become a central writer because he has placed the homosexual in the midst of the heterosexual, which, like a pointillist figure, gives the illusion of a clear boundary only at a distance. Up close, we see irresponsible messiness: but a messiness that contains, paradoxically, the purest truths and the most stringent morality.

The present collection contains a fraction of White's prose, but it includes all his important essays. As a journalist he produced articles on travel, home furnishing, interviews with movie stars and directors, and even, on one occasion, an account of visiting the Motor Vehicles Administration in New York. Charming and interesting as these articles were, their republication here would, we thought, dampen *The Burning Library*. Included here are articles that continue to be fresh and lively and those so deeply rooted in their moment that they shed important light on our recent cultural past. *The Burning Library* is a kind of flow chart – which its chronological arrangement is meant to reinforce – mapping not only White's intellectual growth and artistic maturation, but also changes in our social history. For example, 'The Personal is Political', the final essay of the volume, although taking its title from the feminist slogan of the 1970s, could not have been written at that time, nor would the first essay of the book, 'The Gay Philosopher', be written today. Including both these works marks how far White has altered and remained unchanged as a writer, thinker and man.

Since most of the pieces were written under the pressure of deadlines – and White's frequent assertions that he hates to take time from his domestic and social pleasure to write is belied by the sheer bulk of his production – they showed signs of stress. They have been modified for clarity, style, and to avoid repetition (like most busy writers White sometimes steals from himself). 'Thoughts on *White on Black*: Coleman Dowell' and 'Sweating Mirrors: A Conversation with Truman Capote' each interweave two essays. In both cases a critical analysis of the literary works was combined with a portrait of the author. One reason White is such a good biographer is that he has an uncanny knack of seeing where the literary life and the life of the literature intersect, and the combined essays are stronger than the essays separated. 'Two Eulogies' and 'Two Princes' bring together under a single rubric related pieces, but do not interweave the texts.

Acknowledgments

Several people need to be thanked. Kasey Edison was an invaluable assistant. Maxine Groffsky has been an indispensable agent. The staff at the Beineke Library, Yale University have been valiantly cooperative. Patricia Willis, the curator of the American Literature Collection at the Beineke Library, has given graciously of her time. I want to thank Towson State University for granting me a research grant which allowed me the time to work on this book. Finally Edmund White has been helpful and full of encouragement, all that an editor could wish for.

David Bergman, 1993

The author, editor and publishers are grateful for permission to reproduce the following articles, in whole or in revised form: 'On Reading: An Exaltation of Dreams' (1983), *Town & Country*; 'Fantasia on the Seventies' (1977), *Christopher Street*; 'On James Merrill' (1979), *American Poetry Review*; 'Sado Machismo' (1979), *New Times*; 'The Political Vocabulary of Homosexuality' (1980), from *The State of the Language*, ed. C. Ricks and L. Michaels, by permission of Faber & Faber Ltd and The University of California Press; 'The Irresponsible Art of Robert Mapplethorpe' (1980), from *Black Males*, Galerie Jurka, Amsterdam; 'A Sensual Man with a Spiritual Quest' (1980), 'The Emperor of Signs' (1982), 'Movies and Poems' (1982), 'The Woman Who Loved Memory' 1986), 'The Angel in the House' (1990), 'Black Like Whom?' (1992) and 'Marquerite Yourcenar' (1993), *New York Times Book Review*; 'The Politics of Gender' (1980), *Nation*;

'Sweating Mirrors' (1980/1988), *After Dark*, 1980 and *Times Literary Supplement*, 1988; 'This is Not a Mammal' (1981), *Soho News*; 'James Schuyler (1981), *Little Caesar*; 'Thoughts on *White on Black on White*' (1982/92), *Journal of Contemporary Fiction*, 1982, and the Introduction to *A Star-Bright Lie*, by Coleman Dowell, by permission of the Dalkey Archive; 'Paradise Found' (1983), *Mother Jones*; 'Sexual Culture' (1983), *Vanity Fair*; 'Nabokov: Beyond Parody' (1984), *New York Review of Books* and *The Achievement of Nabokov*, edited by G. Gibian and S. J. Parker, by permission of the Center of International Studies; 'Writer on a Hot Tin Roof' (1985), 'Keeping up with Jones' (1985), *New Republic*; 'Their Masks, Their Lives' (1986), *Review of Contemporary Literature*; 'Esthetics and Loss' (1987) and 'Pool in Rocks by the Sea' (1992), *Artforum*; 'Danilo Kiš: The Obligations of Form' (1987), *Southwest Review*; 'The Critic, the Mirror and the Vamp' (1987), *Times Literary Supplement*; 'Paris Review interview' (1988), *Paris Review*; 'Out of the Closet, On to the Bookshelf' (1991), *New York Times*; 'The Wanderer' (1991), *Voice Literary Supplement*; Introduction to Genet's *Prisoner of Love*, by permission of Picador Ltd, Wesleyan University Press and The University Presses of New England; 'Prince' (1985) and 'Richard Prince' (1992), *Parkett*; 'Hervé Guibert' (1993) *London Review of Books*; 'The Personal is Political' (1994), *Brick*.

On Reading: An Exaltation of Dreams

First published in *Town and Country*, May 1983

'There is no frigate like a book to take us lands away.'
Emily Dickinson

Recently Fate – a melancholy version of Fate with snaky locks, bistred eyes and Art Nouveau jewelry feeding on her pale wrists and paler neck – has seen fit to remind me of my reading. The books I read as a child, I mean, the ones that started me dreaming the unhealthy, exalted dreams of romance so long ago. These books have been resurfacing in my life, the very editions if not the actual volumes. Just the other day I was kept waiting in someone's office, and there was *Disenchanted* by Pierre Loti, the tale of women's liberation in turn-of-the-century Turkey that had so engrossed me when I was ten. It was the same book I remembered, with the gold letters on the raincoat-colored cover and the green-and-black ornament that at first looked like a flower but on second glance resolved itself into three butterflies, one spread-eagle and the other two in poised profile.

I'd always been reluctant to search out this absurd curiosity by the refined, blue-eyed traveler who specialized in tales of exotic harem girls or geishas in distress (Loti's *Madame Chrysanthème* had indirectly inspired Puccini's *Madame Butterfly*). I'd feared that to subject its period charms to adult scrutiny would – well, would induct me, too, into the ranks of the disenchanted, whereas what I longed for was to preserve at least in memory Loti's spell, my recollection (perhaps my invention) of the lean Frenchman in his white vested summer suit and blue-ribboned straw hat who enters the shadowy room above a dozing, sweating Istanbul for a forbidden interview at noon with three Turkish ladies.

Despite their veils and enveloping black robes, the ladies are able to expose to their sensitive friend their souls, which are cultivated, gentle, yearning for freedom (they speak French perfectly and they've all read Baudelaire).

With trepidation I opened the book – and I was off, exactly as though I'd unstoppered the crystal flask of Shalimar that always crowned my stepmother's vanity table in Cincinnati when I was a boy. Only a few sentences into the novel my eyes misted over as the past was phantomed in over wavering lines of type. I could suddenly see the 1920s pink stucco Spanish villa where we'd lived for a few years and where I'd sat on the patio beside a fountain of a boy (even younger and paler than I) who'd hoisted a dolphin on to his shoulder. As the dolphin drooled I eagerly turned the pages, no longer hearing the distant hum of the sweeper, not even noticing my leg had gone to sleep.

As I look at the book now I see that I had misremembered some of the details (the Frenchman adopts the fez and discards his boater, the season is chilly spring, not hot summer, the room is a humble harem in the shadow of a mosque and not high on a hill at all), but the essentials – the plight of three cultivated women with their intelligent, sea-green eyes under the triple veil and their citron-colored silk frocks from Paris under the black shroud of their 'elegaic' robes, the traditional *tscharchaf* – oh, this reality had impressed itself like a spring mold on the batter of my ten-year-old spirit, for wasn't I during that sweltering Cincinnati summer – without funds or friends or activities – wasn't I, too, a beautiful prisoner, caught between two traditions, the glittering French world of my imagination and the stifling harem confines of my family? Wasn't I, too, poisoned (as Loti puts it), 'by the deep pessimism which, in our day, is ravaging the harems of the Turk'?

At one point in *Disenchanted* the French hero asks his soul-sisters whether they wouldn't have preferred continuing to doze in the oriental twilight of old Ottoman ways, never to have awakened to the frustrating temptations of French emancipation, and I, too, might have been happier if my Ohio torpor had never been disturbed by echoes from another chamber. Mind you, I wasn't certain of the exact location of that resonant place. I had no sense of geography and could never have found on a map

Istanbul (or 'Stamboul,' as Loti called it). Nor had I a grasp on history. The year of the novelistic action, 1906, might just as well have been 1806. As for the French hero's function as a symbol of modernity, that only puzzled me, since I knew enough to know that only the U.S. stood for progress and that Europeans were backward, eclipsed, grinding their teeth in envious rage. No matter. In fact, all the better. 'France' became just as shadowy and exotic as Turkey, Paris as insubstantial and decayed as Stamboul, the hero as cut free from time as any fairy-tale knight. What was lost by way of thematics (idealistic companionate marriage on the new French model versus squalidly sensual polygamy) was well-lost on a ten-year-old, who had little use for sex but every possible need for romance.

In those days before television the world was altogether less visual than it is now, less visual and correspondingly more visionary, since children were obliged to imagine how characters in books bowed, dueled, swooned: the whole repertoire of mysterious but at the same time curiously unsurprising actions. If I had been asked to bow I wouldn't have acquitted myself with much conviction, but in my mental theater the characters never hesitated, unless the text read, 'Adolphe paused then, hand to heart . . .'.

When I was sick on a school day I'd be given cinnamon toast and permitted to listen to soap operas on the radio. The ominous musical bridges I soon learned to link with suspense or anguish or danger (only the darker emotions were rendered; there were no tripping *allegretti* to suggest joy). Doors creaked, footfalls echoed, gun shots rang out, a booming voice announced: 'The Shadow knows . . .'. They were all shadows, the casts of those serials, and each listener knew them differently, assembling Ma Perkins, say, out of the round face and gray curls of a grandmother and the dough-scented apron of our cook, who reduced my sister and me to hysterics by singing, again and again, 'Indian Love Call,' her thin soprano invariably losing its footing in the high mountain passes of the yodeled, 'I'll be calling you-ooo-ooo-ooo-ooo-ooo-ooo . . .'.

Music, the radio, books – those were the means by which emotion was conveyed in that stolid house where any more immediate outburst of feeling was forbidden or simply never displayed. Nor were we permitted to go to the movies, on the

strange theory that they were corrupting to the young. Perhaps
they were; they were certainly distressing. I'll never forget the
first film I saw, *Two Years Before the Mast*. I was six and it was
1946. Alan Ladd for some reason was stripped, bound and beaten.
Then salt was cruelly rubbed into his wounds. The lash and the
salt might just as well have been applied to me, so convulsed was
I by sobs and so stunned by pain, as a series of nightmares were
to attest for many weeks to come.

That movie had been chosen because it was "educational," that
is, based on a classic American book, but what such films and
books taught me may not have been the lesson intended. From
them I learned that "real life" is savage, full of breathless incident
and exotic locations – and at the same time imbued with an exacting moral refinement. Perhaps that's why the actual adult life I've
come to lead has seemed so imperfect to me, so lackluster, for
books taught me that a marriage can end over a subtle but fiercely
held principle, that friendship can triumph over tyranny (even the
tyranny of years), that a woman can rise in the world not solely
on the basis of beauty or wealth but also through spiritual
elegance, and that these ethical qualities sooner or later must
become apparent to everyone.

When I was in fourth grade I encountered the first volume (but
never the concluding second) of the 1890 edition of Hawthorne's
The Marble Faun, which that same melodramatic Fate, slinking
toward me with a lily in one hand, recently pressed on me with
the other – or rather, returned to me. I was in a used book store
on Greenwich Avenue in New York City; I opened the first
volume and strummed its pages, dipped in gold along the top
edges. When I lifted the ancient red-thread bookmark it crumbled
in my hand. The thinnest sheets of tissue, cut slightly smaller than
the pages themselves, modestly veiled the illustrative photogra-
vures ('In the Catacombs,' as one caption printed on the inner
side of the tissue read in reverse until I brushed it back to study
the vaulted room which resembled the basement in my childhood
home save for the two icons of haloed saints by the door where
the electricity and water meters should have been). I read at random: '"We artists purposely exclude sunshine, and all but a
partial light," said Miriam, "because we think it necessary to put
ourselves at odds with Nature before trying to imitate her."'

When I mused over assertions like this one as a child I accepted without question such startling truths as: there is a tribe of beings called artists; they all think alike; and they live in shadows in order to oppose and court this strangely capitalized entity called Nature. Elsewhere in the same book I learned that all Italians are beautiful, light-hearted, but childlike creatures, and that all women have an innate talent for needlework.

Home truths, perhaps, but rather far from *my* home. My father was a civil engineer who'd become successful during the war as a broker of chemical equipment. He reigned in silence over dinner as he studied his paper; he once threw a soup spoon across the table and hit me on the forehead when I dared to speak to my stepmother in a whisper. Later, when I was a teenager, a deb I was dating decided we should invite to dinner at my house a New York actor our age, someone who was playing the juvenile lead in *The Matchmaker* at our local tent theater and who she decided must be lonely. My stepmother went along with the plan but refused to tell my father exactly what sort of person would be our guest. Over drinks my father was affable enough in his grave, old-fashioned way, but by the middle of the meal when he knew he had an *actor* at his table, steam hissed out of his ears and he grew fearfully silent.

No need to go into the irate aftermath. I've suggested, I hope, that he was not the sort of man from whom I could have learned about the lighting of artists' studios much less the national characteristics of the Italian man or the Turkish woman. What I knew along those lines I had learned from books, which were doubly precious to me because my father hated to see me reading, which he rightly considered an unhealthy substitute for sports or yard work and which he rightly feared would fill my head with funny ideas. As James Merrill has written about matinees he attended at the Metropolitan when he was a boy:

> What havoc certain Saturday afternoons
> Wrought upon a bright young person's morals
> I now leave to the public to condemn.
> The point thereafter was to arrange for one's
> Own chills and fever, passions and betrayals,
> Chiefly in order to make song of them.

Whatever romances I've engineered or endured, whatever notions about the artist I've tried to live up to, whatever distant places I've traveled to or haunted in my imagination – they've all been footnotes to those pages I read as a child, for hasn't Merrill himself called our lives 'fiction in disguise'?

I

The Seventies

The Gay Philosopher

Written in 1969 but previously unpublished, this essay circulated in manuscript in the early 1970s and was quoted in Donn Teal's *The Gay Militants* (1971).

Obviously we should pity the poor Farm Boy or Motorcyclist for being saddled with so many questions. Of course, everyone, straight or gay, enjoys playing the parlor philosopher occasionally. But most people, I suspect, have worked out serviceable explanations of why they married one person instead of another, get angry then and not sooner or later and in general managed to avoid the faults and mistakes of their friends and neighbors. In private moments and important discussions, they may confess that they're confused as to their true motives, but fortunately for them such moments and discussions are rare.

Yet for the homosexual, his question cannot be laid aside for the brandy and cigars. His sexual orientation, which picks his lovers, threatens his job and influences (or perhaps is influenced by) his tastes in clothes, books, friends and politicians, is eternally at hand, and surely something so ubiquitous requires an explanation. I remember once having a silly discussion with a group at a bar. Someone said that homosexuality had been fashionable five years ago, but then gone out of favor. Another boy sensed it was coming back into style. A third, who was a bit more realistic, said, 'All I can say is that in my case, fashion had nothing to do with it. Whether it's in or out, it's a party I'm going to be attending every night.' We all laughed as we watched our whimsy evaporate. Once I recall someone else asking another group, 'Can any of you ever recall *choosing* to be gay?' No one could come up with such a recollection, though I've known a few borderline cases. One friend of mine, who seemed to me to be neither gay nor straight, but rather a genuinely contented celibate, was finally convinced by his analyst that he must be homosexual. He had never harbored any secret hankerings after men (or women), but he humored his doctor by buying the appropriate nitsy clothes and standing around at the appropriate bars and street corners.

Since he's quite attractive, the desired therapeutic results were quickly obtained. I knew a lot of men (usually, for some reason, either dancers or actors) who darted gracefully and mindlessly back and forth between the sexes. In group therapy I met a boring young man who had never been part of gay life but who had enjoyed, and later agonized over, dozens of five-dirty-minutes-in-the-dark encounters. After a great deal of discussion he finally 'went straight' and found a girl. Unhappily (for him and us) he was always jesuitically examining his conscience to determine whether, when his elbow grazed the barber's crotch that afternoon, he had enjoyed it or not. Just to complete the picture, I should mention that I've heard that some very decadent and sated older men take up homosexuality late in life, just as a novelty to refresh their jaded tastes, and that they enter the gay world quite deliberately and with malic aforethought; but I've never known anyone of the sort. And finally, I have three friends who've married quite successfully, but they've never entirely abandoned gay life. Of course we've all heard the extravagant claims of psychiatrists who've 'cured' scores of homosexuals. But I've never met one.

But I repeat, almost all the people I know feel they never *chose* to be either homosexual or heterosexual, and many gay men have chosen to be straight, but to no avail. I myself came out when I was twelve, but I was horrified at myself and I regarded this boy who laid elaborate traps to snare men as a stranger, a sleepwalker, someone else. Every morning I made a resolution not to look at men, and every night I broke it. I heard once of a boy who literally had a horn on his forehead that was growing *inwards*, that was driving its point deeper and deeper into his brain, slowly and methodically destroying his faculties one by one. I was that boy, as I watched my obsession with men overtake me.

At first I convinced myself that I was simply passing through the 'ordinary homosexual phase' of early adolescence. Then I argued that I was gathering material for a novel. When I was sixteen, however, I knew that my love of men was crowding out my affection for girls. I blamed my family and fled from high school in a panic and went away to boarding school. There I was going to start all over. I became intensely religious. I meditated for hours every night after lights out, hoping to master the passion I felt for an athlete, a teacher, for every man. I read Buddhist sutras and tried to control my breathing and my thoughts and longed for the complete exhaustion of longing. On one day I'd contemplate suicide, on the next I'd immerse myself in novels, music, art books – but then I'd get hung up on a photograph of Rodin's Belgian soldier, a statue so realistic that the sculptor was accused of casting it from life.

Finally I decided I had to be analyzed. My father refused to pay for it. I bombarded him with the most eloquent letter I've ever written and, when he still remained adamant, made my first appointment and told the doctor to start sending my father the bills anyway. My father paid, and I worked with extraordinary diligence. No matter how far-fetched or unflattering the interpretation that the psychiatrist presented to me, I was ready to believe it rather than accept that I was gay. In college a staff psychologist told me that we never expelled the 'virus' of a sickness we had contracted, we simply had to learn to live with it. I flew into a rage. He was restricting my freedom. I had to be free to make myself into whatever form I wanted.

Now I'm twenty-nine, and I've spent thousands of dollars and seven years with three different analysts, all to no avail. Naturally, anyone who finds himself in the midst of an odd condition that determines so much of his life but that he doesn't recall having chosen is bound to wonder where it came from. Was it nature or nurture? If nature, then was it an inherited form of madness, a glandular mutation, a biochemical botch? Could it be that all those horrible pundits have been right, and homosexuals are indeed the 'third sex'? Those who argue against the third-sex etiology of homosexuality point out that most male homosexuals display none of the expected secondary female characteristics, such as enlarged breasts and wide hips, and that lesbians similarly fail to show evidence of beards and broad shoulders. I'm not convinced. First of all, secondary characteristics may be very slight; recall the scarcely noticeable rough skin and extra height of men who have the extra 'criminal' X chromosome. Second, belonging to a third sex need not mean that one should resemble women, if one is a man, or men, if a woman; a third sex may be exactly that and possess characteristics all its own. Finally, generalizations about male homosexuals may not apply to lesbians. The two conditions may have nothing to do with one another. Perhaps only language and a spurious common sense link them.

If the cause of homosexuality is nurture, was it Mom's fault, or Dad's? Or should I blame Society, Other-Direction or my fifth-grade teacher? One theory has it that 'closely binding' mothers make their sons queer. If that theory's correct, then why don't all the classic Jewish Mothers produce gay boys? Why isn't Portnoy gay? (Gay folklore, for what it's worth, contends that Jewish men tend to be less, rather than more gay than gentiles.) Traditional India committed the boy to his mother's exclusive care until he reached adolescence, and yet that culture wasn't considered particularly homosexual. Another theory has it that sons whose fathers are quite shadowy, dead or distant, or too weak or (alternatively) too menacing, grow up to be homosexual. Such a theory seems to be so vague as to be completely useless. A variant holds that homosexuals are men who failed in their childhood efforts to compete with their fathers; their perversion is nothing but a way of avoiding competition with men over women. This theory has sometimes seemed to me to contain a grain of truth, but I've known dozens of gay men who were viciously competitive, and an equal number of passive straight men.

Although an individual may be able to piece together some sort of theory that covers himself, or seems to, he keeps meeting other gay men who have exactly the opposite sort of inheritance and upbringing. He meets gay orphans and gay men who grew up with only one parent, or homosexuals who loved their fathers fanatically and hated their mothers, or vice versa – in fact the home life of homosexuals seems to run the whole ordinary gamut. It may be that the homosexual family experience typically is concentrated at one point along a curve, but no research has been done on this question to my knowledge. Anyway, I suspect most men under thirty have been more affected by their contemporaries than by their parents.

Perhaps the sensible thing to do at this point would be to abandon all theorizing, but the mind, when presented with a question, abhors a question mark. The human ability to entertain ambiguity is sadly limited and at any given moment most people have at least a hypothesis, if not an iron-clad theory, that explains the things that matter most to them.

A homosexual should probably try to know as much as he can about which theory he's embraced. The 'theory' may be a myth, a metaphor, an old wives' tale, a confused assortment of contradictions, but whatever it is, he should try to make it as clear and explicit as possible, for it undoubtedly influences his behavior in important ways. In the lifelong romance each man has with himself, he should know which vows he's sworn.

The all-important theory of the day, of course, is the psychoanalytic, both the pure Freudian formulation and also the folk version of it that pervades novels, plays, films, and the Sunday supplement and that pops up in every conversation on the topic in America. The folk version considers the homosexual 'sick', a metaphor that is constantly reinforced by the fact that the therapist who promulgates it to his 'patient' is usually a medical doctor. That the therapist is a doctor is simply an accident of history. Freud might just as easily have been a prison warden or a priest, or any other sort of professional who deals with eccentrics, in which case the 'criminal' or the 'sinner' would be sent up the river or on retreats, and we would not be faced with the equally arbitrary spectacle of seeing 'patients' – that is, those who are in deep philosophical or spiritual travail – shunted off to hospitals where they are bedded down in the same building with people about to have their tonsils or gall stones removed.

Since Freud happened to be a doctor, however, the language of 'treatment' is riddled with words like 'mental illness', 'recovery', 'symptom', 'diagnosis', 'therapy' and so on, and the people undergoing 'treatment' announce that they are 'getting better'. Almost all the practitioners I have ever met or heard of regard homosexuality as a sickness. This verdict is generally presented as though it were purely descriptive, non-judgmental and 'scientific'. But anyone can see, after a moment's reflection, that 'sick' is always a normative word; it is bad to be sick.*

---

* In December 1973, after the composition of this essay, the governing board of the American Psychiatric Association recommended dropping 'homosexuality' from its list of diseases, a recommendation that was approved narrowly by its members in the following year. But a recent survey reveals that most practicing psychiatrists continue to regard homosexuality as a disturbed form of behavior.

By extension, the homosexual himself is bad, or at least is doing something unhealthy that should be corrected. If his 'disease' turns out to be 'incurable', it none the less remains something that in an ideal world would not exist, like cancer. Oftentimes the therapist will regard the patient's inversion as merely a 'symptom' of a still deeper 'disease' – both undesirable. A slightly different vocabulary would have it that homosexuality is an 'infantile arrestment' which the analysand will 'outgrow'. To be considered infantile, I should imagine, is scarcely more flattering than to be considered sick; both words suggest an anomaly that treatment will seek to remove. The only major branch of theory and therapy that I am acquainted with that approaches homosexuality with an open, speculative mind, that in fact tries to regard all behavior with the true spirit of scientific candor, is the client-centered therapy of Carl Rogers. (Curiously enough, Rogers is also one of the few psychological theorists who has actually tried to determine whether his method works, and has set up large experiments using control groups and the whole she-bang. Note also that he has abandoned the word 'patient' for the less prejudicial term 'client'.)

Obviously if homosexuals regard themselves as 'sick', and most of them I know do, that belief cannot help but have a disastrous effect on their self-esteem. The famous mordant gay humor, which always attempts to cancel the sting of any jibe by making it funny, has sought, I think unsuccessfully, to camp on the 'sickness' metaphor; you can often overhear one queen telling another, rather affectionately, 'You're sick, honey,' or 'My dear, I love you, you're a madwoman.' But this approach, no matter how charming, brings little relief. Most homosexuals persist in seeing their love affairs, attitudes, friendships – their entire experience – as diseased and inauthentic.

Why have gay men put up with this really pernicious judgment against themselves?

The main reason, perhaps, is that they are members of this age and culture as much as anyone else, admire the same things and embrace the same vogues. Before the Black Revolution got under way, Negroes were in the same position and defamed one another by espousing white prejudices. Like the anti-Semitic Jews or the nigger-hating Tom, the queer-baiting homosexual has swallowed the opinion of the majority towards himself and his friends.

8

Second, there are certain 'morbid gains', as Freud would have put it, for the homosexual who considers himself sick. In a limited way, the Freudian conquest of America did improve the status of the homosexual. Before gay men were considered 'sick', they were judged to be 'criminal' or genetically 'degenerate', and obviously the psychodynamic view was more humane. Even this small advance, however, has had a beneficial effect only on the way homosexuals are treated socially; legally, every state except Illinois at the time of this writing still has laws against all homosexual acts, and in one Southern state the penalty is capital punishment.*

Another reason homosexuals accept the sick label is that they themselves often blame *all* of their woes, quite indiscriminately, upon their homosexuality. Like the boy who didn't make Yale and who thereafter attributes to that one failing all of his post-college misfortune, so many homosexuals chalk up their job losses, their indigestion or the difficulty in housebreaking poodles to the fact that they (the men, not the dogs) are gay. Those rare men who have come out late in life after years of knowing what it's like to be straight seldom make this mistake. They realize that living involves a great deal of suffering for everyone, straight or gay.

Considering oneself 'sick' is also mildly appealing to one's vanity. Vain people relish the notion that they're ailing or evil. They can't bear the notion that their mind is really as ordinary as it seems to be. Far preferable is the suspicion that so much conscious blandness is slyly concealing an unconscious teeming with horror-movie monsters. As Norman Mailer once remarked, you can tell someone at a party that he wants to sleep with his mother and he'll be thrilled, but the same man would be horrified if you told him he was using the wrong fork.

Finally, the psychoanalytic interpretation has been so widely accepted because so many people still regard psychoanalysis as 'a science', and it basks in all the enormous prestige accorded scientific opinion in general. This isn't the place to examine the

---

* In the twenty years since the composition of this essay the legal status of gay people in the USA has changed, but not significantly, with only a half dozen or so states granting gay people protection from discrimination in housing and employment.

methodological failings of psychoanalysis, nor am I qualified to conduct such an examination, but I might point out, briefly, that unlike other scientists, psychiatrists conduct no controlled experiments, their 'findings' are based on their work with only a tiny sample and cannot be either verified or falsified by other investigators, and their major terms, like 'libido' or 'repression', cannot be defined adequately, much less quantified in the same way that terms like 'velocity' in physics, 'molecular activity' in chemistry or 'demand' in economics can be treated. Analysts, in defending themselves against such points, have argued that their 'science' resembles the makeshift, intuitive methods of other branches of medicine and cannot be compared to the physical sciences. But that argument ignores the fact that whereas there might co-exist for a short while two or three rival schools of endocrinology, nevertheless research, experience and methodological demands for simplicity, consistency and comprehensiveness will inevitably cause one school to triumph over the others. The rival schools of psychotherapy, by contrast, are all going strong, despite the fact that each school considers the others heterodox; in this regard they seem closer to the denominations of the Christian church than to the subdivisions of a science.

I don't deny that therapists have eased the suffering of thousands of people, and I have reluctantly recommended it to several friends in pain. It seems particularly useful to people who can't sort out their problems or who can't ventilate them to their friends. My own grudge against therapy (or analysis – I've undergone both and I'm afraid I've been a little sloppy in distinguishing between them), is that I never felt any of my three doctors could entertain for even a second the notion that homosexuality wasn't a disease. They all failed to respond to the specific ups and downs and intricacies of a given situation in my life; for them, being gay was never a given, but the problem itself. If a married couple came into group therapy because one partner wanted to do something kinky in bed and the other one demurred, my last therapist always sided with the swinger. Why was the recalcitrant partner being so 'uptight'? How could we rid that poor person of his or her 'hang-ups'? The same liberality was never extended to the homosexual patients, however, even if their sex life were the tamest, most respectable ritual imaginable. For a husband to screech around the house in his wife's underwear was dandy, but should the queer just want to do the old in-and-out one dreary time a week, he was sick. Similarly, the group would spin the most complicated webs of causation trying to trace the motivation behind some trivial act performed by a straight patient. For the queer patient, no one had to go to such lengths. His case was open and shut. Being gay explained everything.

Perhaps I was unlucky. Perhaps I should have gone to a gay therapist (some homosexuals have learned to hate themselves so much that as soon as they hear that a therapist is gay they're convinced he must be a charlatan. When I was a teenager I recall the same sort of intramural loathing extended to all public figures who were reputed to be gay: 'Oh, he's not a good conductor; he's gay.' Perhaps I'm moving in a more adult crowd now, or perhaps the times are changing, but for whatever reason I hear this sort of remark less often).

From a scientific and philosophical point of view, however, I'm certain that my animosity towards psychoanalysis is well-founded. Because analysts have staked out the entire area of psychosexuality as their own private claim, reputable investigators in other branches of science have stayed away from it. As a consequence, all theoretical thinking about homosexuality has come to a standstill.

I've already touched upon a few other metaphors for homosexuality. Two of them, which regard the homosexual as a sinner or a criminal, need not be elaborated upon except to mention that the first has driven thousands of gay parishioners out of the Catholic into the Episcopalian Church (where for some reason they are received far more graciously) and the second notion remains a potent, though seldom publicized force among the ignorant and the elected officials of this country. Another metaphor for the homosexual community is to consider it a social club, like the Shriners or Elks. Certainly there are many strays, midgets, cripples and fat boys and girls who pal around with gay kids simply because they're accorded among them a tough, humorous, affectionate welcome and get a chance to be *very* busy socially.

Yet another metaphor (and I don't claim that these metaphors are mutually exclusive or even wholly comparable) sees the homosexual as a member of a minority group, like the Jew or Negro or possibly the worker. Employing this metaphor can produce a whole range of fascinating insights. Homosexuals (and possibly women) are the last people whom progressive intellectuals in America can safely hate. Whereas the *Village Voice* or *Time* would never dare publish with approbation an article attacking niggers or yids, they think nothing of castigating fags (incidentally, it seems to me that whereas homosexuals use the word 'faggot', the shorter form, 'fag', is usually the straight progressive person's property; more retrograde straights must rely on 'queer'). The *Voice* prints without comment a long, patronizing piece about the inanity of homophile meetings, seeking, by a clever move, to place homosexuals firmly in the world of squares. Now I know as well as anyone else that homosexuality has its squares as well as its rebels, but the point of the *Voice* article was that the squares were *representative*, and the whole vice was a tired scene. In the nineteenth century, when people were shocked by something, they said they were shocked; in the twentieth, they say they're bored by it.

At the other end of the spectrum from the *Voice*'s murky bias is the brilliantly lit hysteria evinced by *Time*'s infamous essay, 'The Homosexual in America', presented in the 21 January 1966 issue. I'd like to quote this piece at some length, because it represents the considered opinion, based on voluminous research, of the nation's leading news magazine. Lest that opinion be dismissed out of hand as the statement of a notoriously conservative publication (the usual intellectual evaluation of *Time*), one should recall that in social, as opposed to political issues, *Time* has had a fairly good progressive record in supporting civil rights, the poverty program, the emergence of the black man and so on. Yet this essay blandly presents the homosexual as 'witty, pretty, catty', paints him as a neutered sash boy who dances attendance on dowagers and it announces with alarm that 'increasingly, deviates are out in the open, particularly in fashion and the arts'. Some psychiatrist named Edward Stainbrook is patted on the back for deciding that homosexual artists are 'failed artists, and their special creative gift a myth'.

The essay then proceeds to pillory homosexuals for fostering

'Pop' and 'camp'. 'Homosexual ethics and esthetics', it warns us 'are staging a vengeful, derisive counterattack on what deviates call the "straight" world. This is evident in "pop", which insists on reducing art to the trivial, and in the "camp" movement, which pretends that the ugly and banal are fun . . . It is evident in the theater, with many a play dedicated to the degradation of women and the derision of normal sex.' The notion that homosexuals are addicted to the inconsequential and decorative in art, and that gay playwrights delight in portraying women as castrating bitches, is unfortunately so widespread that it's been accepted as a truism. Readers of the *New York Times* were subjected a few years back to a tiresome tirade by the drama critic, Stanley Kaufmann, who asserted that homosexual playwrights were simply translating their neurotic experience with their male lovers into heterosexual terms; in other words, [Albee's] Martha and George are really two men. All of these charges seem wide of the mark. Pop Art was never intended as satire, nor have the most sensitive critics considered it to be that. As Andy Warhol once said in an interview, 'Pop Art is a way of liking things.' Discussions of who's gay and who's straight seem to me to be irrelevant to art, impertinent and possibly libelous, but for the record most of the great names in Pop are stolid, painfully sincere married men. 'Camp' has never been a 'movement' to my knowledge, nor is it sinister, as *Time* implied. Susan Sontag, who seems to have cornered the market on the whole sensibility, wisely remarked:

Camp taste is, above all, a mode of enjoyment, of appreciation – not judgment. Camp is generous. It wants to enjoy. It only seems like malice, cynicism. (Or, if it is cynicism, it's not a ruthless but a sweet cynicism.) Camp taste doesn't propose that it is in bad taste to be serious; it doesn't sneer at someone who succeeds in being seriously dramatic. What it does is to find the success in certain passionate failures. Camp taste is a kind of love, love for human nature. It relishes, rather than judges, the little triumphs and awkward intensities of 'character' . . . Camp taste identifies with what it is enjoying. People who share this sensibility are not laughing at the thing they label as 'a camp', they're enjoying it. Camp is a tender feeling.

As to the absurd charge that homosexual playwrights and dress designers are trying to present women in the most unattractive light possible, one can only point out that it's a buyer's market. If women and theater goers don't like the product, they don't have to buy it. What's more, gay dress designers may have flattened breasts at times, but at other times they've exposed them generously. The vagaries of fashion (and even of high art) never quite correspond (if at all) to the current moral and sexual attitudes of the culture at large. Who could have predicted that the most popular form of painting during the Eisenhower years would have been the extraordinarily mandarin, introspective non-objective movement? Pop *should* have been the art of the 1950s (art historians, of course, gifted with hindsight, can always cook up a reason why it should have been the way it was, but in many cases the arguments seem unconvincing). In fashion the constant need to be new, the economic exigencies (skirts rose after the First World War partly because of a shortage of fabric), and the thousands of complex forces and counter-forces *within* the fashion world account more for the changes of styles than does the general *Zeitgeist*. Similarly, the stylistic means that a playwright has at his disposal determine his choice of subject matter more often than does the mood of the nation. Since all literature contains at least the possibility of being reportorial, plays are perhaps more sensitive than painting or music to extra-artistic influences. Thus I would hazard a guess that if Albee chose to portray a bickering couple in *Who's Afraid of Virginia Woolf*, it was because he had reached the point in his artistic development where he was very impressed by Strindberg's dramas of intense marital conflict (Strindberg, by the way, who started the whole misogynist tradition, was a confessed heterosexual) *and* because he, like everyone else in this country, was aware that the divorce rate is rising and conventional marriages are pulling apart at the seams. Interestingly enough, the play ended on a note of 'optimism'; Martha and George seem determined to make their marriage 'work'. Tennessee Williams is also frequently cited as a writer who's brought the malign homosexual mind to bear on women and marriage. The truth is that his portrayal of the tender Laura, the confused Blanche and the lusty heroine of *The Rose Tattoo* are all paeans to femininity, remarkable for their range and compassion. His women are distinctly not men in drag; witness the rehearsal notes he passed to Elia Kazan during the production of *A Streetcar Named Desire*. They contain many shrewd observations about the delicate psychological adjustments that take place in women who become pregnant, and all reveal the insight of a master anatomist of feminine passions. If some lesser playwrights have shown women as castrating bitches, that's only due to the general anti-feminism of the fifties, a period when everyone was hearing the snip-snip of the maternal scissors, when parlor psychology was at its height and when men couldn't adjust to the economic rise of women that had occurred during the Second World War.

I've strayed from my subject: the *Time* essay as a typical example of the anti-homosexual bias that pervades progressive circles. The essay quotes with approval a psychiatrist, Edmund Bergler, who 'found' that homosexual conflicts 'sap so much of their inner energy that the shell is a mixture of superciliousness, fake aggression and whimpering. Like all psychic masochists, they are subservient when confronted by a stronger person, merciless when in power, unscrupulous about trampling on a weaker person.' Further on, the essay attacks Alfred Kinsey's humane statement: 'The only unnatural sex act is that which you cannot perform.' Then the essay cites several theologians who consider homosexuality sinful and winds up with the hilarious conclusion:

Even in purely nonreligious terms, homosexuality represents a misuse of the sexual faculty and, in the words of one Catholic educator, of 'human construction'. It is a pathetic little second-rate substitute for reality, a pitiable flight from life. As such it deserves such fairness, compassion [*sic!*], understanding and, when possible, treatment. But it deserves no encouragement, no glamorization, no rationalization, no fake status as minority martyrdom, no sophistry about simple differences in taste – and, above all, no pretense that it is anything but a pernicious sickness.

Such rancor doesn't begin and end with *Time*. Since I 'pass' fairly easily, I've had the pleasure of hearing straight professors and hippies and artists discuss with complete self-assurance the 'fag problem'. The intellectual leaders of white society may be hypocritical and ineffectual in their attempts to support the black community, but nevertheless, for at least twenty years, every responsible element in America has paid lip service to the idea that there is a valid Negro culture and that black goals should be fulfilled. The gay community has never even had the dubious benefit of that sort of respect. Bars in the Village post signs that read 'No fags allowed', politicians win votes by 'cleaning up' the city and ordering cops to raid gay bars or to arrest suspected homosexuals as vagrants, and straight people endlessly indulge in windy generalizations about the gay character. In the late eighteenth century it began to dawn on a few intellectuals that the until then popular sport of generalizing, usually negatively, about the national character of the French or the Italians was a pretty dopey activity. In the nineteenth century the enlightened stopped generalizing about the poor and began to study them. In the last fifty years we've discarded our preconceptions about the races and, to a small (too small) extent, about the sexes. But *still, still* our fear of the unknown, our intellectual laziness, our xenophobia, our love of easy categories, compels us to dismiss the huge homosexual segment of our population with a few empty phrases.

The Black Revolution has done us all a great favor, and I feel certain that women will next follow blacks by demanding their rights and in creating a new, more attractive self-image. Perhaps after feminism scores a victory, homosexuals will finally take up arms (I'm suggesting only a temporal, not a casual relationship between the two phenomena). If homosexuals did assert themselves, they would become worthy of my own favorite metaphor for homosexuality; they would become rebels. Until now they, or rather we, have all too often been martyrs.

Many things, however, stand in the way of gay power; unlike blacks, homosexuals do not represent a single social class with shared economic goals. The force behind most revolutions, at least until the idealistic 1960s, has been a common desire for material wealth, or at least a desire to escape from deprivation. The gay community, unfortunately, is comprised of every social element, and I suspect that in their political decisions most homosexuals revert to their original class loyalties. Even the rich gay men I've known who've dallied with poor boys still support the Establishment at the polls (a Kinsey Institute survey suggested that gay men in general tend to be even more conservative than the population as a whole). Moreover, unlike most Negroes, most gay men 'pass'. Homosexuals either work in gay industries like fashion, where they feel little or no discrimination, or they 'pass' in the straight business world and are terrified of being detected and fired.

None the less, these are definite, concrete objectives that cry for a militant gay group of activists. Police harassment on the community level must stop. Similarly, the Federal government must be forced to hire homosexual civil servants and remove its discriminatory clauses against accepting gay poverty program workers, soldiers and Peace Corps volunteers. Statutes barring the immigration of gay foreigners on the grounds of 'moral turpitude' must be revoked. States should institute laws assuring equal opportunity for gay employees in private business.

Why do such demands sound far-fetched? Why have homosexuals failed to win the status of a minority group? Even if the 'sick' metaphor is accepted, when did we come to believe that the sick deserved torment? Philanthropies urge us to hire the handicapped, wounded veterans, rehabilitated criminals, but the straight community remains hostile to the homosexual. I think most straights justify their belligerence by switching metaphors in midstream. In some situations they endorse the 'sick' metaphor, which certainly has as a concomitant the idea that homosexuals are not responsible for being what they are; but in other situations, straight people choose to think that gay men are literally 'perverse' and have wilfully chosen to affront them by deciding to be gay. Straight spinsters undoubtedly have a right to be bitter about the fact that many attractive bachelors are gay, and straight men might feel uneasy around homosexuals, but neither reaction accounts for the injustice that has been meted out to the gay populace. And this is precisely where the 'minority group' metaphor breaks down. Whereas everyone knows Jews and Negroes haven't chosen to be what they are, whereas the enlightened realize that workers or the poor have usually been born, through no fault of their own, into their station in life, most straight people still feel at the back of their minds that somehow gay people have elected their condition. But such reasoning is based on the worst sort of mixed metaphor, and must be clarified. Take another metaphor – dissident political parties, like the neo-Nazis or the Communists. The members of these groups in the United States have chosen to belong to these parties, but even so, most progressive people who care about civil liberties realize that the rights of dissidents should be protected no matter how violently one disagrees with their principles.

None of the metaphors I've suggested quite fits the homosexual. This failure should be instructive and a cause for celebration – and for new, more adequate myth-making. So much of the distress I've suffered and that I've seen my homosexual friends undergo has come from unsuccessful attempts to jam the homosexual experience into ready-made molds. For instance, many gay men are constantly trying to reproduce with their lovers a facsimile of straight marriage. One gay man plays the 'butch' while the other plays the 'femme'. Every infidelity is seen as a threat to the bond that links them, to the 'marriage'. Between affairs the intervening periods of promiscuity are regarded as proof that 'the homosexual' is 'infantile' and incapable of forming lasting relationships.

Sexual role-playing between members of the same sex seems futile to me. That it can be momentarily exciting I don't doubt, but the humiliation and exaggeration that are necessarily involved are too high a price to pay for the pleasure of mindlessly imitating a straight folkway. Why need promiscuity be considered 'infantile'? Although such words strike me as meaningless, I can see good reason for regarding casual love-making just as easily as extraordinarily 'adult'. In straight life the economic necessity for marriage which prevailed during the agricultural period of our history when farmers needed wives to perform household services and children to work the fields – this necessity is no longer operative in urban society; in fact, marriage is now an economic burden, and the only reason anyone marries (or should) is out of love. But love, at least in my experience, is rarely an enduring thing. For gay men who have no family pressure to stay together, no social responsibility to raise a family, why should they struggle to create a lasting affair? Perhaps the promiscuity of many gay men is a vanguard experiment, a sort of trial run for the rest of the society. Most of the gay men I know have passionate, long-lasting friendships that provide the continuity and warmth that all human beings seem to need. Since friendships are not based on the highly explosive and whimsical appeal of sex, but rather on more enduring affinities such as shared interests and lifestyles, friendships seem destined to become the mainstay of lonely humanity should the marital bonds of the Age of the Pill break down. I have no antipathy to either gay or straight love affairs. All I'm suggesting is that it's about time homosexuals evolved metaphors that fit the actual content of their lives and that authenticate, rather than denigrate, their experiences.

On Becoming a Model for Male Smut

Previously unpublished, this essay was written in the early 1970s.

A couple of weeks ago I answered a personal ad in the *East Village Other*: '50 YOUNG male figure models for professor photographer. No experience necessary. $10.00 per hour.' I assumed that 'professor' meant 'professional', though I did entertain for a moment the picture of a black, Eastern European beard projecting from below an old, curtain-over-the-head camera and fifty, count them fifty, bare-assed nudes grinning into the flash of phosphorus. It wasn't the money that attracted me – although I could always use the money – but the chance to see if my efforts at body building would pay off in the competitive marketplace of skin.

A nice, motherly woman's voice answered when I called the number that had been printed; she took my name and number and told me I'd hear from – I'll call him Bill St Regis – as soon as he returned to the 'studio'. When Bill finally called four days later I had forgotten all about the ad; in fact, it was early in the morning and I was still asleep. A rather cultured, young, urgent voice was asking me if I could make a 'shooting' on the following Saturday of an hour-long film. 'Film!' I replied. 'But what sort of film? I don't want to be in a film, I don't think.'

'Oh, I see! There's really nothing to it. It takes an hour, you just walk around nude with five other fellas, no touching or anything, and they pay you twenty-five dollars!'

'Well, I thought from your ad you wanted someone for still pictures.'

'We do, we do,' Bill assured me. 'We're just starting up our own agency, we're actually going to be taking and selling pictures of our own, but we've found this movie job. You see the man who makes these movies is one of the oldest and most established figures in the industry and can be very helpful for a young model in getting launched.'

'Oh, I wasn't exactly wanting to be launched; I just thought I'd pick up a quick buck and satisfy my vanity, I guess.'

'Well,' Bill said, doubtfully. 'I'll put your name on my inactive list and if I get any calls from a private photographer – or, I know, why don't you think it over and call me back this evening?'

Bill's tact proved very clever; by the time I had come home from work the shock of the word 'movie' had worn off and I was, in fact, quite intrigued. I called him and he told me to go to a Forty-Second Street book shop at two on the following Saturday. On Saturday morning I ran to the gym and got all pumped up and hurried to the address, feeling at once cheap and tough, a real Forty-Second Street tough. In fake Brooklynese I said to the man behind the cash register, as Bill had instructed me to do, 'I'm here for the movie.'

The cashier answered in authentic Brooklynese, 'The movie's been called off. The photographer's sick and the producer's out of town. Sorry. Bill should have told you.'

I called Bill and asked him what was going on and he apologized for about ten minutes: 'You know, we have these troubles, I tried to get you but you weren't in, but next Saturday, next Saturday, I promise.'

Next Saturday was the same story – no movie. Another model, however, was there this time, a tall, thin, thirtyish type with bad teeth and a slow drawl. 'Damn,' he said to me. 'I really needed the money. I'm not like some of those creeps who are in this for kicks, I just need the money. I was going to go down to the Village Squire and buy some new clothes and also a bucket of paint so I could finish decorating my room.'

'Do you think it's definitely called off?' I asked him.

'Well, they're not really sure. Stick around. It seems they didn't get their shipment of film, but maybe it will come through.'

A blonde, short, plump girl with heavy but badly applied eye make-up came up to us with a vague smile on her face, a clipboard in her hand, just as though she were a Hollywood script girl, and an open black imitation leather handbag over her arm. 'Hi,' she said vaguely. 'I'm Betty. Sorry about the mix up.'

'Why can't they just run out and buy some film at a camera store?' I asked.

At the word 'film' an old man who was standing nearby reading *This Spanking World*, a magazine with a drawing of a woman in leather tights on the cover, looked up. Beside him two other men were plunking quarters into hand-cranked nickelodeons that showed striptease shots.

'They get it wholesale for two hundred dollars; if they bought it retail it'd cost twice as much,' she said. 'I'm really sorry about this. Look, I'm going to call Bill and see what he says.'

Betty climbed up on the raised platform at the front of the store, squeezed past the cashier and called on a private line. As she chatted, she idly flipped through the latest illustrated lesbian books, casting over them a disinterested, professional eye, occasionally scrutinizing a page to read the photographer's credit, if there was one. After a while she put the other model on to talk to Bill, and then me. 'They're doing something fishy up there,' Bill said. 'I haven't figured it out yet. I'm terribly, terribly sorry about all this, but I've told them that if they can't treat my models with respect, I'm just going to have to cut off the supply.'

The other model told me that he was going down to meet Bill. I asked if I could come along and he said sure. He mentioned that he didn't want to spend the subway fare and was going to walk all the way down to Chelsea; I told him I'd stand him a ride. On the way to the station, he looked at the hustlers and panhandlers all round us and said, 'This street's really gone down hill. These people are the dregs.' He told me that he lived in a hotel room on the West Side and was a cashier at a restaurant: 'The great thing about that job is, although they don't pay anything, you can eat all you want, and I eat three full meals in an eight-hour period. I'm originally from Mississippi, but I've been here five years. Why I'll never know.' I asked him if he thought Betty was going to be in the film, if and when it was ever made. He said he hoped not, he didn't go in for that.

We found Bill in a fourth-floor walk-up. That voice that had sounded so youthful and sophisticated on the phone came from someone with shoulder-length silver hair, wire-rim glasses, pale, somehow *painted* skin, a black beard, and a black tricot sweater and black hip-hugger pants that were gathered about him in a way that suggested – or at least *something* suggested – he had a hunchback or a partial paralysis. He had unbolted the door and opened it all in one violent gesture almost as though he thought we were the fuzz; I half expected to see a gun or a hypodermic in his hand. He led us into an incredibly dirty and disordered two-room apartment. The first room was the kitchen, the floor covered with torn-up, dirty linoleum, the breakfast table littered with used cotton wads; he placed a thermometer on the table and passed on into the larger living room. In both rooms the walls were crammed from ceiling to floor with a Baroque gallery of paintings, big primitive canvases done in colors right out of the tube, showing nude men with long, tubular penises and women with perfectly triangular *montes veneris*, if that's the plural. The figures were standing singly or in heterosexual pairs; a few women were odalisques. In one painting a photograph had been pasted into the composition; it was of Bill, without the hair and the beard and so much younger and less decadent that I had to ask him who it was. 'All of them were done by Betty. She's the sort of painter who needs big backing. As you can see, she's a big talent, and we're trying to get some real financial guns on our side. We were quite surprised to learn that the art racket is a strictly commercial matter and has nothing to do with talent. It's really appalling. Now, I suggest we go across the street to our other apartment. I think we'll be more comfortable there.'

Picking up a black purse, much smaller and newer than the one Betty had been carrying, Bill led us out into the street. In the daylight I was able to see that he was wearing some sort of pan-cake make-up and that his hair was more blond than white. An old woman looked at him curiously, but he seemed not to notice. I glanced at the other model, who was lagging behind; he pointed at Bill and tapped his head.

The other apartment was precisely like the first, except larger. Bill emptied one ashtray into another, kicked a slip under the chair and explained that the place was still a mess from last night's party. 'But I can't help tidying up a bit, I'm like that, I guess,' he added apologetically. He indicated for me to sit down on the couch, which was virtually like sitting on the floor since all the springs had gone and it dragged its belly like one of those dach-shunds with back trouble. I picked up a photograph of Betty lying on her back, a nude man sprawled on top of her. 'We want to make posters of those,' Bill said. 'No genitals are showing and technically they're within the law for posters although we all know what they're doing, don't we?' He showed us another picture, this one of Betty in a black bra that covered only one breast; the other breast was so large that it appeared to have popped out of the bra of its own accord. 'Another poster idea,' Bill mentioned.

'Now let me tell you kids all about who we are and what we're doing,' he said brightly. As he spoke, his voice became louder and higher and assumed the tone of amiable aggressiveness that some of the Quiz Kids on radio used to adopt – a sweaty, Bronx High School of Science, supercompetitive voice that was seeking to mask its frantic eagerness to give the right answer with a few oddly placed laughs and a few democratic 'you knows' tossed in. 'Betty and I have only been in this business since August and though we're not making any money yet, we hope to clean up soon. Originally I had an Establishment job, but I hated it and got out, or rather, they never let me in, so then Betty and I turned to smut. I call it smut, but eventually we would like to sneak art into our work by the back door. Take my books, for instance. Smut books used to be merely titillating in the old days. You'd say things like "his virility" or "his aroused manhood". When I came into the business, I thought that was what they still wanted and I wrote a book with "his virility" in it. I'm lucky, I guess! I can write a book in four or five days, I'm just fortunate in being a very fast writer. But the publishers all said it was too timid. *Now* I know the formula – you must use one four-letter word on every page, so that no matter where the reader opens the book he sees something of interest. But then, and this is my point, after I mastered the formula and started selling my manuscripts, I tried to do some books of a slightly higher, more artistic quality, which I would sign with another name and present to the publisher – actually, Betty gave it to him, he was hot for her – and she'd say, "You might be interested in this. A friend of mine wrote it. It's rather literary, but . . ." That's how we get art in by the back door.'

The longer Bill spoke, the more I realized that he was a born talker and intellectual performer, so enraptured with what he was saying that he was quite unaware of his surroundings, his listeners or even his own body. The same vague smile Betty had worn descended on him, and he raised his pale face as though he were hearing music. 'There's a great deal of money in this racket. Our plan is to set up a fair deal for the models. You see, if you had made this movie today they would have paid you twenty-five dollars, but they would have printed a thousand or more copies of the film and sold them for eight dollars each. They have distribution outlets in Chicago and San Francisco as well as New York. *Plus*, while you're posing for the film, another photographer will be shooting stills of you which they'll sell in a package for three dollars each; they'll easily clear ten thousand dollars, and all you've gotten is twenty-five. Now we want to set up a royalty system, sort of, and pay models a percentage of the profits. We'll be the first honest producers. But, until we can start making our own films, we want to get our models jobs so they can build up a reputation, make a little money and stay healthy.

'The book industry is also a racket. Look, I get five hundred for a manuscript, but they sell at least two thousand copies for about two dollars fifty each. There's one famous book, the *Song of the Loon* which is a gay book about love between cowboys and Indians, and the author only got the standard five hundred bucks for that, but it was such a big best-seller – it may be one of the great best-sellers of all time, nobody checks up on this stuff – anyway, the publisher, I heard, paid the author twenty-seven thousand dollars to write a sequel, so you can figure *they* must be making about a hundred thousand. Now the books all have nude photos inserted into them, and they're selling like wildfire.

'The publishers are such strange ducks. The real problem I faced when I started out was finding out who they were or where to send my stuff; they don't usually give a publisher's name or address on the title page, or at least they didn't used to. Betty and I would go to parties and approach people and turn the talk to publishing but –' he started laughing so hard I couldn't quite follow him – 'they'd say they were hetero publishers and I'd say that's what I did, and Betty would run from one to another, and he'd say he only did gay sadism. Oh, those parties. We were running, running.'

Bill stopped laughing and asked us if we were interested in

hearing more. We assured him we were. 'The biggest man in smut publishing', he said, 'has been in it for thirty-odd years and he's terrified. Simply terrified. He's afraid to show nudes even now or print hard-core pornography. I really think the big thrill for these guys is to think they're always just on the verge of being arrested. "Whew!" they must say, "I made it safely through another year." And they never usually *see* their authors or anybody *deviant*, you know, just deal through the mail. Well, I actually went to see this old, established publisher. I met three paunchy, bald, terrified, businessmen. I usually wear full make-up when I'm not ill and I keep my hair dyed blond – it probably looks white now, I generally go down once a week to the beauty shop on the corner. So, looking as I do at my best, I walked into their office and said real tough, "I got a homo book for you." They nearly died! Their eyes widened, as though I was Satan landed on earth and was about to drop a hot coal in their hands.'

Bill leaned back and said in a wise, board-meeting way, 'Everything changes. The times are changing, and the old publishers are being superceded by the times. Of course they've got endless files that keep them going. They have files of photographs that go back twenty years which they still use. They take a new picture of a boy or girl in the latest hat or boots – something obviously up-to-date – and put it on top of some old pictures and then seal them all in cellophane. The customer opens the packet when he gets home and discovers that all the pictures underneath are twenty years old of models in wool bathing suits pulled up to their chests.'

At that moment a young man in his early twenties opened the front door and came in with two girls who must have been about fourteen or fifteen at the most. One of the girls, who was wearing tight cotton pants covered with microscopic flowers said, 'All boys? Oh, I'm getting out of here.' The young man, who was tall, thin, had long hair and was quite handsome (could he be the man in the picture with Betty?) said to the girl, 'Relax. We're not going to rape you.' The girl snapped back, 'Aw, phooey, why not?' and she and her friend dissolved in giggles. Bill suggested that they come back in fifteen minutes, when they could have the apartment to themselves; the young man nodded and left with his little band.

'He's simply fantastic,' Bill told us after the door closed. 'He always has a new hang-up. This month it's little girls. Last month he was doing something strange with women's breasts. He's quite intriguing because he's so methodical about sex; I've never seen anyone so methodical. He'll try out something he's read about but which doesn't particularly turn him on. Nothing really turns him on itself. Then he studies everyone's reactions, and if we like the new hang-up, then he'll like it. Now it's these little girls.'

The other model asked Bill if the hang-up always involved girls. Bill smiled and said, 'Yes, he's quite straight. He's actually very sensitive about any slurs, too. For instance, in that picture where he's doing it with Betty, he didn't like the shot because he thinks his ass looks too effeminate. He wanted me to take a shot of his chest or something. He's so methodical – even while he's having sex, he's telling me how to take the picture. But he likes gay men. You see, when he was a little boy his older brother did something unspeakable to him, which he's never forgotten or forgiven. But all the same he's quite wistful about gay life, almost as though he wants to be liked by men who are like his brother. He'll stand in the center of the room at a gay party and drive all the guests wild because it's so obvious that he's just begging for attention from them. I told him that that wasn't fair. He should explain to every gay man he meets all about his brother and the unspeakable thing, you know, reveal that he's looking for an *analytic* sort of love, not a physical one. It's funny, but everyone in our little circle explains all their behavior by digging up some childhood trauma. Take my friend Paula. It seems she necked with a boy for two years and then they finally had sex, and he cut out on her the very next day and was never seen again. That, she says, is why she chooses the lovers she chooses now, and boy, are they far-out. And the worst of it is that she always insists that we like whoever it is at the moment. And that can be pretty tough when you have to spend a whole weekend with one of them. Betty and I are trying to tell Paula that we can still love her without necessarily loving all her lovers. I just don't know; it may not be possible to *relate* to Paula much longer unless her taste in lovers improves. They're not bad men, her lovers. Just selfish, or rather wilful, domineering. Like, if we all want scrambled eggs and he wants pancakes, he'll start cooking pancakes and to hell with the rest of us. Now tell me about yourselves.'

The other model related his problems in breaking into posing for smut magazines. 'I went to a top photographer and paid him a fortune to shoot a whole portfolio of me dressed in cowboy boots and a ten-gallon hat. Nude pictures. But now it turns out that there's no market for Western photos. You may ask me why I don't try other costumes but, heck, I really am from out West and I *like* that look. Now all they want is action shots. You've got to be sledging a bell with a hammer or jumping on a horse, or skiing in the nude. Action shots, action shots, that's all I hear.'

As we were leaving I asked Bill to explain a huge painting on the wall, obviously one of Betty's; it showed a woman fully dressed playing a lute and a man riding on a swan. 'Oh, that's one of Betty's illustrations to *The Lord of the Rings* by J. R. R. Tolkien; he's a writer. It's one of a series of thirty-two panels. Poor Betty. She did a painting of some adorable boy throwing a discus. He practiced and practiced to get the pose just right. But the painting was so big that the only way Betty could fit it in the same room with the model was to turn it on an angle and now the finished painting only looks right if viewed from the right angle. I told her that I'm going to explain it all in my diary or otherwise art critics in future centuries are going to think she was embodying some new *theory* of perspective.'

As he showed us out, Bill assured the other model and me that he would call us 'towards the beginning of the week', which I figured meant Tuesday, and confirm with us arrangements for making the movie. On the way down I got a glimpse of the young man with the methodical hang-up rough-housing with the girl in flowered pants; the other girl had disappeared. When he saw the other model and me, he pushed the girl away, eyed us nervously and ran a hand through his long hair.

Bill called me Thursday evening and said that he had had a big fight with the movie producer. Apparently the producer wanted to drive eight of Bill's models to a studio on Staten Island and film each one of them separately for an hour each. 'I refused, of course,' Bill said. 'The big men in the industry are all old and can't adjust to the idea that my models are decent people who want to be shot under decent circumstances. In the old days the movie producers would just go out and pick up a sailor and get him drunk and shoot him. You know, these men are even indignant about paying models at all. They regard all women who pose as sluts. It's really a matter of the conflict of generations. Today lots of hippies are posing for smut because they regard their bodies as beautiful and they want them to be photographed beautifully. Beauty is the key word.'

'Can these big producers get models on their own?' I asked.

'Not enough. You see, in the old days Z-sets – '

'What's a Z-set?'

'A packet of six nude shots. Z-sets used to be sold under the counter, and the volume of sales was much smaller. If a dirty old man could get up his courage to buy one he was happy, he treasured it, and didn't hope to ever have another. Now the sets are sold legally and sales have gone up enormously, it's incredible, it's fantastic. The stores have big problems. They have to put out new sets every three weeks, and they refuse to share because reputations are based on their Z-sets.'

Bill took a deep breath and said, 'So, the movie may be off for right now. But, don't worry. Do you have any money? I can write you a check if you want to come up for it. I don't have any cash.'

I assured him that wasn't necessary. I was in the whole thing more out of vanity than for money.

'I don't think vanity is a fair word, this word "vanity" you're using,' Bill said. 'Let's say you're interested in the artistic experience. I don't mind telling you that I'd like to shoot you myself. I could see that you have a very sensuous quality, a certain . . . sensuous quality. In fact, I'd like to make a poster of you – I'd pay you twenty-five dollars and then a percentage on all sales over a certain point. I've already worked out the pose. You'd be lying on a couch – the concept's very Renaissance – on your side with one arm thrown back and various rich fabrics flowing over you. It's a pose you see in many medieval paintings. You're the sort of vibrant model we want. Betty and I are very big models ourselves and big photographers, but we got fed up with the whirlpool, the whirlpool is really phenomenal. Studios and agents put you under contract and farm you out to this one and that one and keep you tied up for years and you can't do freelance. It's really terrible and most of the young people – the warm, emotional, younger generation – have gotten out of the business. The only young people left in it are very bland types who get no excitement out of being photographed.'

'Speaking of excitement,' I said, 'I've looked at some of the pictures in that store and some of the men are quite abnormally endowed and, well, I don't think I'm much more than normal in that respect.'

'Oh, you mean their "virility"?' He laughed. 'Don't worry about that. This business is subject to fads like any other. For a while big penises were the whole thing. A friend of mine got an assignment to shoot only really big ones. I sent many of my models to him, and these were men who were quite well hung, and the photographer would ask them to drop their pants and then reject them. I called him and asked him what was up. I said, "Look, Jack, you're not gay but you're worse than me, asking those boys to drop their pants." Well, we finally found – actually a girl we know found him – a boy who had the biggest one any of us had ever seen. Betty couldn't believe it. But the rest of him! He was about four feet tall, wrinkled, horribly emaciated with a deformed face, and we couldn't decide whether to shoot him or not. We finally did, made a Z-set, and it was a big hit. In my books I got into the fad, too. I wrote this thing about a guy who's so well hung he asphyxiates his girlfriend. I took thirteen pages to describe it; it's chapter twelve of my new novel. It made all of my friends sick. Well, now, I've got to be going. Paula's bringing her new lover; Betty and I are keeping our fingers crossed that he won't be a loser like the others. If only she didn't bring them along for the whole weekend. I'll be calling you any day to set up an appointment for the poster idea. I can see you on a couch, with all those rich fabrics, dripping, dripping all over you.'

I am still eagerly awaiting Bill's call.

The Joys of Gay Life

A talk given to a university group in Washington, D.C., 1977.

Having written something called *The Joy of Gay Sex* with Charles Silverstein, I thought it might be amusing to talk about the joys of gay life, at least of my own gay life, since that is the one I know best.

I'm thirty-seven, I came out when I was twelve, so I have a quarter of a century of gay life under my belt now. Certainly not all of it has been joyful. Throughout my teens and early twenties I was so guilt-struck about being gay that I spent a lot of my parents' money going to straight psychoanalysts and attempting to be cured. Through a great deal of this period my predominant mood was not depression but rather deep despair.

Even so, even when considering those years, I can find things to look back on with pleasure. Not everyone in this audience, I'm sure, will understand how such experiences could be counted as pleasures, and perhaps many people here will think of them more as sufferings that should be goading me to rail against straight society.

I am by no means a stranger to gay militancy, and I have spoken out sharply against the oppression of gays by straight society. Nevertheless, even if society were changed radically today or tomorrow and gays would suddenly find total acceptance, we would still have to deal with our pasts, we would still have to come to terms with all those years we spent in real inner and outer conflict. And it is my contention that in those conflicts can be seen some unexpected but very real blessings.

The record is complex, fragmentary and far from logical, but nevertheless certain realities can be teased out of the confusions of memory. For instance, at a very early age I became extraordinarily sensitive to what I imagined to be the experience of blacks.

I'm not claiming that this sympathy was a virtue nor that I developed this feeling in order to be virtuous. Nor can I say that my concern ever helped a single black. No, the only person my feelings helped was me. I was born in Cincinnati, Ohio, which is right across the Ohio River from Kentucky, and Cincinnati is itself in many ways a Southern city. My parents are both Southerners and my father is quite racist. His father was a well-known, even a notorious racist who wrote and published racist books – joke books with such titles as *Chocolate Drops from the South* and *Let's Laugh* – that are a blot on our family name. The situation, then, was set up for me, too, to become a bigot.

But in fact I drifted towards blacks at an early age. My best friend in grade school was black, a boy named David who gave me the first novel I ever read all the way through – *Lazarre*, about the lost dauphin. After meeting David, I always had close black friends despite my father's stern disapproval. We always had black maids, and I was highly aware of their anger and humiliation. This feeling of closeness culminated in a play I wrote that was produced off-Broadway – *The Blueboy in Black*, starring Cicily Tyson and Billy Dee Williams. It was about a black maid and gardener who set out to destroy the white family they work for. It was produced in 1964, at the height of the civil rights era, and its presentation of black anger puzzled white members of the audience – and thrilled black theatergoers.

I'm aware I may sound like one of those racists who say 'Some of my best friends are black', but I assure you that the only reason I mention this moment in my life is to establish one point – that I think my gayness, something I perceived even when I was a child – that this sense of being different made me feel as though I were a member of a minority group and that I shared something with other minorities. Given my Republican, Southern background, I was slated to become a bigot. If I escaped that particular form of spiritual impoverishment, it was because I was gay. Of course I recognize there are plenty of gay reactionaries, but I'm not speaking for them.

This early sense of being different, vulnerable, suspect, drove me inwards – and opened up for me the world of books. I can remember viscerally the sensation of learning to read – it was as though a door in a stuffy room had been opened. But all the arts appealed to me, and every week I imagined I would become a genius in a different art. For a long time the stage was my deepest love. I who was so shy otherwise became a fearless show-off once a spotlight was trained on me. From second grade on, as I moved around the country with my restless, newly divorced mother, I always managed to write the class play and to star in it. When I was twelve my interest turned to painting, and the smell of oils (something seldom smelled in this day of odorless acrylics) still brings back to me in a rush my labors over ships tossed under a cloud-obscured moon and over one handsome Spartan warrior, all helmet, plumes and cheekbones. When at age fifteen I finally settled down to write full-time, it was to compose my first novel – an impassioned work about my homosexuality. I called it *The Tower Window*. It was not an honest book because I was not honest with myself. It attempted to blame my turning gay on a girlfriend who had jilted me – a girl named Sally Gunn, whom I had dated only once. Nevertheless, the pain and guilt and fear I experienced about my homosexuality did drive me to sit down in my dormitory room (by that time I was living in a boarding school) and write two hundred pages of pure (or rather impure) anguish.

What I'm saying is that homosexuality forced me to confess, to express myself, to attempt to keep pace in my writing with the despair and confusion threatening at every moment to swamp me. Now I am less anguished, perhaps normally happy and unhappy, but I still enjoy the fruits of that early anguish – that is, whatever ability I have to write. And along the way I picked up lots of in-cidental information about the other arts. I took three classes in modern dance and one on the harp, I studied the harpsichord for a year, the recorder for a month, the piano for five years or so. I wrote part of an opera, words and music, which I even started to orchestrate. The opera was named *Orville*, after a handsome young farmer I'd met on the train. I no longer remember its plot, but I recall it was a dour tale of rural incest and madness. I took singing classes from an old gay man at the Cincinnati Conserva-tory of Music, a man who spent most of our classes discussing his own illustrious genealogy and an ancient Spanish diva who had been his teacher ('As the Señora would say, "The round tone is the gold in the mountain, the brightest of jewels"'). When he wasn't discussing these matters, he was chasing me around the piano.

Yet another joy of being gay is the philosophic turn of mind you are forced to develop. Whereas heterosexuals can, conceivably grow up without questioning their goals, their motivations, every homosexual must think everything out from the bottom up. We are forced to become reflective. We have no idea (neither do the scientists) why some people are gay and others are straight, yet we feel impelled to ask the question. And that question leads us to others concerning the nature of sexuality itself, the nature of love, the nature of child–parent relationships – and virtually every other Big Question that might interest an adult mind. Other people may dabble in such questions; we are forced to scrutinize them. Our meditation is complex, endless, self-revising – and that may explain why we are so naturally adapted to the social sciences and why we are peculiarly suited to be therapists, doctors, thinkers and teachers.

One of the things we are forced to re-examine is relationships. Unlike straight people we do not have church weddings, we are not often enrolled in the PTA, we are not clear on who is the breadwinner and who is the homemaker. We don't have relatives clucking over us, urging us to be faithful and fertile and upstanding. Our relationships have little social or legal reality. As a result, we must invent love all over again. Gay lovers must work out contracts or agreements that suit them. Household chores, money matters, social obligations – these things must be decided and assigned. Sex roles in bed, gender-linked behavior out of bed (who cooks, who mows the lawn, who pays the bills) – these things must be arbitrated. And fidelity, the thorniest question of all, must be arranged. Is tricking outside the relationship to be permitted? If so, under what terms? Shall the lovers describe the outside adventures to one another or stay discreetly silent? One couple might decide that each partner can trick but only during separate vacations or when apart. Or they might say there's one night a week for tricking out. Or they might say only three-ways are permissible. The variations are endless. My point is that convention does not govern us; we create new conventions for ourselves. Today more and more straight couples are deciding that traditional marriage doesn't work. The feminist revolution, a new emphasis on self-fulfilment, the entry into the job market of more and more married women, the weakening of traditional religious bonds, a new sexual permissiveness – all of these factors are forcing straight people to re-examine the institution of marriage. I would contend that we gays have been facing these painful questions for years – and that in a sense we represent a vanguard. Straight people might well learn something from us, since we have already sorted out the issues, even if we haven't arrived at solutions that will suit everyone.

Similarly, we know more about single life than most straights. Let me just take one aspect of the question. My friendships with a handful of men and women have had an importance for me that friendship doesn't seem to have for most straight people. I've known one of my best friends since I was sixteen, and I still see her constantly. My old lovers have become close friends. I have loved one man, another writer, for seven years with an almost romantic passion although we have never been to bed together. Such loving, chaste devotion would strike many straight people as adolescent; at least, I've been told it is adolescent. If so, I can be only grateful I've never outgrown it. What I observe is that for many gay people, especially single gays, friendship has assumed an importance seldom observed among straight adults. We gays derive spiritual sustenance and emotional continuity from our friendships – and that is what allows us to weather things so well. Some psychological studies have suggested that gays are, all in all, better adjusted than straights, and I think it is our gift for friendship that makes us so seaworthy.

I don't want to sound like a complete Pollyanna. I recognize that being gay has many disadvantages. Self-hatred and guilt are surely two of the worst curses. The sense that we should not be too conspicuous, that we should not run too many risks, sometimes holds us back on our jobs. I've observed that at the highest levels of corporate life, for instance, there are few gay men, though there are some gay women. This is just an impression, of course, but I do feel that sometimes we hang back in our careers out of a sense of social insecurity and a fear of being conspicuous. There are undoubtedly many ways that being gay is difficult. I am not conventionally religious, but I suspect that for Catholics and orthodox Jews and for many Protestants, it must be excruciating to deal with a sexuality that is considered sinful.

The point I was trying to make, however, is that there are advantages to being gay and that one of these advantages is that we are introspective about such basic things as love, sex and friendship. The exigencies of our lives, the fact that we *become* gay in a way that other people do not become straight, make us all reflective. We have the advantages of the outsider, of the foreigner and of the pioneer. As pioneers we learn how to innovate behavior – and this is useful training in a society that is changing so rapidly that everyone must sooner or later change his ways to survive. This is the country of mobility, and we as gays have always been on the road emotionally.

I've mentioned some of the big and perhaps important blessings of being gay – our understanding of other minority groups, our need to express ourselves in the arts, our ability to think out in fresh terms such crucial things as love and friendship, our skill at surviving in a changing world. There are also some minor blessings I can think of that are true for me, at least.

One of these is that through gay life I've met such an amazing and delightful assortment of people, people I never would have known if I'd married and stayed behind in Cincinnati. My novel, *Forgetting Elena*, found its way to Random House, where it was published, through the kindness of a Pulitzer prize-winning poet I met at a gay bar – the old Stud in the Village. A gay college friend introduced me to his relatives in Italy when I went to live in Rome for a year, and these people let me see the old Roman bourgeoisie at close quarters – a world ordinarily closed to foreigners. Living in New York, I have met gay composers, writers, publishers, critics, actors, directors, painters, poets. Oftentimes I get to know a group through meeting one of its members in the baths, on the street, at a bar. As a gay man I've met gypsies in Spain, hustlers in Morocco, an old baron in Paris who invited me to Neuilly for the most elegant dinner party I've ever been to – twelve men all in black tie who switched to perfect English whenever the servants entered the room. Through our multifarious contacts we learn the latest dance steps, the latest fashions, the latest slang. We hear stock-market tips, we hear about Washington scandals, we meet accountants from New Jersey and botanists from Harvard and *trompe-l'œil* painters from Connecticut and gymnasts from San Juan. Wherever we go we immediately plunge into a whole rich life in any given city or country. We are never sad tourists stranded behind the high walls of the Hilton compound. If you want to find us, look for us dancing upstairs at the tiny Café de Paris in Malaga in southern Spain; there you'll find us in the embrace of a Moroccan man who works on the ferry-boat from Tangier. We never become stiff in the joints. And by the end of the week we know a few words in Mahgrebi, the local Arabic dialect.

Fantasia on the Seventies

One of a series of articles about changes in the gay community over the decades, *Christopher Street*, 1977.

For me New York gay life in the seventies came as a completely new beginning. In January 1970 I moved to Rome after having lived in the Village for eight years. When I returned ten months later to the United States, an old friend met me at the airport, popped an 'up' in my mouth, and took me on a tour of the backroom bars. In Rome there had been only one bar, the St James, where hustlers stood around in fitted velvet jackets; the only sex scenes had been two movie theaters, where a businessman with a raincoat in his lap might tolerate a handjob, and the Colosseum, where in winter a few vacationing foreigners would cluster in nervous shadowy groups. For real sex in bed I had to rely on other Americans and upper-class Italians, the only ones who didn't regard love between men as ludicrous. (I had an affair with an impoverished Florentine baron who was writing his dissertation on William Blake.) On the streets, even when shopping or going to lunch, I dressed in a fitted velvet jacket and kept my eyes neutral, uninquisitive. Today, of course, Italy has an active gay liberation party, large annual gay congresses that choke on Marxist rhetoric, and articles in *Uomo* about gay fashions that purport to be without any historical precedent (actually they're just overalls or unironed shirts). But when I lived there Rome was still a bastion of the *piccolo borghese* and miniskirts were considered scandalous.

I have a disturbing knack for doing what used to be called 'conforming', and by the end of my Roman holiday I was hiding my laundry in a suitcase (to avoid the disgrace of being seen – a man! – carrying dirty shirts through the streets), and I was even drifting into the national sport of cruising women. My assimilation of heterosexuality and respectability made the new New

York all the more shocking to me. My friend took me to Christopher's End, where a go-go boy with a pretty body and bad skin stripped down to his jockey shorts and then peeled those off and tossed them at us. A burly man in the audience clambered up on to the dais and tried to fuck the performer but was, apparently, too drunk to get an erection. After a while we drifted into the back room, which was so dark I never received a sense of its dimensions, although I do remember standing on a platform and staring through the slowly revolving blades of a fan at one naked man fucking another in a cubbyhole. A flickering candle illuminated them. It was never clear whether they were customers or hired entertainment; the fan did give them the look of actors in a silent movie. All this was new.

At another bar, called the Zoo or the Zodiac (both existed, I've just confused them), a go-go body did so well with a white towel under black light that I waited around until he got off – at 8 a.m. In the daylight he turned out to be a bleached blond with chipped teeth who lived in remotest Brooklyn with the bouncer, a three-hundred-pound man who had just lost fifty pounds. I was too polite to back out and was driven all the way to their apartment, which was decorated with a huge blackamoor lamp from Castro Convertible.

For the longest time everyone kept saying the seventies hadn't started yet. There was no distinctive style for the decade, no flair, no slogans. The mistake we made was that we were all looking for something as startling as the Beatles, acid, Pop Art, hippies and radical politics. What actually set in was a painful and unexpected working out of the terms the sixties had so blithely tossed off. Sexual permissiveness became a form of numbness, as rigidly codified as the old morality. Street cruising gave way to half-clothed quickies; recently I overheard someone say, 'It's been months since I've had sex in bed.' Drugs, once billed as an aid to self-discovery through heightened perception, became a way of injecting lust into anonymous encounters at the baths. At the baths everyone seemed to be lying face down on a cot beside a can of Crisco; fistfucking, as one French savant has pointed out, is our century's only brand-new contribution to the sexual armamentarium. Fantasy costumes (gauze robes, beaded headache bands, mirrored vests) were replaced by the new brutalism: work

39

boots, denim, beards and mustaches, the only concession to the old androgyny being a discreet gold earbob or ivory figa. Today nothing looks more forlorn than the faded sign in a suburban barber's shop that reads 'Unisex'.

Indeed, the unisex of the sixties has been supplanted by heavy sex in the seventies, and the urge toward fantasy has come out of the clothes closet and entered the bedroom or back room. The end of role-playing that feminism and gay liberation promised has not occurred. Quite the reverse. Gay pride has come to mean the worship of machismo. No longer is sex confused with sentiment. Although many gay people in New York may be happily living in other, less rigorous decades, the gay male couple inhabiting the seventies is composed of two men who love each other, share the same friends and interests, and fuck each other almost inadvertently once every six months during a particularly stoned, impromptu three-way. The rest of the time they get laid with strangers in a context that bears all the stylistic marks and some of the reality of S and M. Inflicting and receiving excruciating physical pain may still be something of a rarity, but the sex rap whispered in a stranger's ear conjures up nothing but violence. The other day someone said to me, 'Are you into fantasies? I *do* five.' 'Oh?' 'Yes, five: rookie–coach; older brother–younger brother; sailor–slut; slave–master; and father–son.' I picked older brother–younger brother, although it kept lapsing into a pastoral fantasy of identical twins.

The temptation, of course, is to lament our lost innocence, but my Christian Science training as a child has made me into a permanent Pollyanna. What *good* is coming out of the seventies? I keep wondering.

Well, perhaps sex and sentiment *should* be separated. Isn't sex, shadowed as it always is by jealousy and ruled by caprice, a rather risky basis for a sustained, important relationship? Perhaps our marriages should be sexless, or 'white', as the French used to say. And then, perhaps violence, or at least domination, is the subtext of all sex straight or gay; just recently I was reading an article in *Time* about a psychiatrist who has taped the erotic fantasies of lots of people and discovered to his dismay that most of them depend on a sado-masochistic scenario. Even Rosemary Rogers, the author of such Gothic potboilers as *The Wildest*

Heart and *Sweet Savage Love* is getting rich feeding her women readers with tales of unrelenting S and M. The gay leather scene may simply be more honest – and because it is explicit less nasty – than more conventional sex, straight or gay.

As for the jeans, cowboy shirts and work boots, they at least have the virtue of being cheap. The uniform conceals the rise of what strikes me as a whole new class of gay indigents. Sometimes I have the impression every fourth man on Christopher Street is out of work, but the poverty is hidden by the costume. Whether this appalling situation should be disguised is another question altogether; is it somehow egalitarian to have both the rich and the poor dressed up as Paul Bunyan?

Finally, the adoration of machismo is intermittent, interchangeable, between parentheses. Tonight's top is tomorrow's bottom. Like characters in a Genet play, we're all more interested that the ritual be enacted than concerned about which particular role we assume. The sadist barking commands at his slave in bed is, ten minutes after climax, thoughtfully drawing him a bubble bath or giving him hints about how to keep those ankle restraints brightly polished.

The characteristic face in New York these days is seasoned, wry, weathered by drama and farce. Drugs, heavy sex, and the ironic, highly concentrated experience (so like that of actors everywhere) of leading uneventful, homebodyish lives when not on stage for those two searing hours each night – this reality, or release from it, has humbled us all. It has even broken the former tyranny youth and beauty held over us. Suddenly it's OK to be thirty, forty, even fifty, to have a streak of white crazing your beard, to have a deviated septum or eyes set too close together. All the looks anyone needs can be bought – at the army-navy store, at the gym, and from the local pusher; the lisped shriek of 'Miss Thing!' has faded into the passing, over-the-shoulder offer of 'loose joints'. And we do in fact seem looser, easier in the joints, and if we must lace ourselves nightly into chaps and rough up more men than seems quite coherent with our softspoken, gentle personalities, at least we need no longer be relentlessly witty or elegant, nor need we stand around gilded pianos bawling out choruses from *Hello, Dolly!*, our slender bodies embalmed in youth, bedecked with signature scarves, and soaked in eau de cologne.

My enthusiasm for the seventies, as might be guessed, is not uninflected. Politically, the war will not take place. Although Anita Bryant has given us the temporary illusion of solidarity, gay liberation as a militant program has turned out to be ineffectual, perhaps impossible; I suspect individual gays will remain more loyal to their different social classes than to their sexual colleagues. The rapport between gay men and lesbians, still strong in small communities, has collapsed in the city, and this rupture has also weakened militancy. A general American rejection of the high stakes of shared social goals for the small change of personal life (study of the self has turned out to be a form of escapism) has left the movement bankrupt.

But in the post-Stonewall decade there is a new quality to New York gay life. We don't hate ourselves so much (although I do wish everyone would stop picking on drag queens; I at least continue to see them as the saints of Bleecker Street). In general we're kinder to our friends. Discovering that a celebrity is gay does not automatically lower him now in our eyes; once it was enough to say such-and-such a conductor or pop singer was gay for him to seem to us a fake, as inauthentic as we perceived ourselves to be. The self-acceptance of the seventies might just give us the courage to experiment with new forms of love and camaraderie, including the *marriage blanc*, the three- or four-way marriage, bi- or trisexuality, a community of artists or craftsmen or citizens from which tiresome heterosexual competitiveness will be banished – a community of tested seaworthy New Yorkers.

On James Merrill

First published in *American Poetry Review*, September/October 1979.

James Merrill bears many resemblances to Marcel Proust. Both were dismissed early in their careers as mere esthetes; Merrill's *First Poems* held as little promise of what was to follow as did Proust's *Pleasures and Days*. In both volumes the objects of meditation (swans, princesses) are, by consensus, already beautiful and in no need of the alchemy of art. Both are static, frozen works. Similarly, neither writer fits the stereotype of the fierce young man on the make, booted and bearded, uncouth yet driven to disclose Great Truths. Quite the contrary: Proust was the pampered, asthmatic son of a rich doctor and in his youth danced attendance on the ladies of the Faubourg St Germain, chronicling their doings in his social notes. Merrill, the son of the stockbroker magnate, might have been expected not to talk at all, so full was his mouth of silver spoon. And indeed, for those readers who distrust a drawl and believe in the great academy of the streets, Merrill's cultivated accent and *Water Street* (his first important book) will seem irritating.

Both Proust and Merrill have transformed the loose change of their lives into the thick bank rolls of high art. In both cases the transformation has required the suppression of some details, the mitosis or meiosis of others, the highlighting of still more – the whole bathed in an intellectual warmth, a tender analysis that makes absurd any attempt ever again to contrast heart and mind. Neither writer had an exciting life in the Jacqueline Susann sense; they have had to make do with solicitous mothers, stern fathers, favorite governesses, a few trips, a few romances, and the sustained intrigue with art. Both are possessed of a sovereign intellect though neither is a trained intellectual (in fact one senses each clings to his amateur status, is ruled by enthusiasm alone, the

43

alternately careless and acute tourist through the museum of mind, as likely to stop to nurse sore feet as to weep or discourse before a masterpiece).

And both (I promise I'll wriggle in a moment out of the strait-jacket of this comparison) chose a curiously old-fashioned tone. After Rimbaud, Mallarmé, even the gem-encrusted, testudinal Huysmans, no one would have been prepared for the sweeping periods of Proust's prose – certainly no one would have called them modern. Proust's style manages to catch up in its folds every crumb of thought dropped on to its soft, thick, capacious damask. What *is* modern about Proust (in the sense of original) is his method of slowly revolving his character to catch, facet by facet, the light of his consciousness. The musical form of this book (more discussed as an ideal than observed as a reality), the excursions into the psychology of memory or jealousy, the circumambient analysis (so like the interstellar ether in the old astronomy, that medium for conveying gravity) – all these are in-novations, but only because they are familiar strategies carried to extremes.

In Merrill's verse there is also something curiously old-fashioned – at least at first glance. In his wielding of poetic forms, Merrill is masterful. His ordinary verse measure is iambic pen-tameter, usually blank verse but breaking easily into rhymed couplets. Scattered throughout the texts are other forms – villan-elles, sonnets, *terza rima*, irregularly accented lines of fourteen syllables and so on. Like his mentor Auden, Merrill can be so conversationally civilized in these forms that only half-way through them does the reader suspect the strictness of the design. The rhyming is always ingenious ('forgets' is paired with 'lun-cheonettes', 'all this' with 'Genesis', 'come to grief' with 'Gurdjieff'). Off-rhymes and slant-rhymes enliven many a page with their delicate finger cymbals ('bore' is twinned, fraternally, not identically, with 'Emperor', 'races' with 'caprices', 'slaves' with 'sleeves'). In poems that are hundreds of lines long, Merrill has wisely varied his technique and muted his natural brilliance.

Here's another way in which Merrill is old-fashioned: he never courts obscurity. In reading *Divine Comedies* (which is com-posed of nine separate poems and the ninety-page 'The Book of Ephraim'), I was struck by how tidily stage-managed this crowded tableau is. One is never at a loss as to which of the many characters is speaking nor what is being said – a still greater feat in *Mirabell*, the sequel to 'Ephraim', in which sometimes five voices are alternating dialogue about abstruse mystical and scientific matters. These are books of *ideas* (as well as of feelings, visions, people and personages), and the ideas are comprehensible. Whereas Eliot's ideas about tradition or Pound's economic theories are stated in clear, no-nonsense formulations only in their essays, the poetry acting as a dramatization (sometimes a fragmentation) of the thought, Merrill's epics are as straightforward as Pope's *Essays*. Nor are the cultural or scientific allusions in Merrill obscure. The phrases from other languages are usually translated or paraphrased, the debts to Dante or Wagner or Wallace Stevens are acknowledged, the presentation of scientific speculation is crisp. Of course Merrill is *playful* in the way we might say Mozart is playful – alternately noble and funny, disarmingly unrhetorical but never afraid of true grandeur.

Speaking more generally, I'd say Merrill has more trust in the transcendental power of language than almost any other contemporary poet. He believes that words do convey messages, that a line is a mix-and-match ensemble pieced together out of reliable signifiers. Other poets, perhaps fed up with the aural racket of our country, the booming emission of television, the press and advertising, have come to distrust (perhaps despise) discursive language. They prefer to hover like entranced oracles over the intoxicating fumes of the unconscious and to jot down its spare, suggestive but elusive utterances, to trace in the dust the faint outlines of their nether selves. Still others, more advanced, seem to be more interested in the syntax of thought than in the content of *a* thought. The speaker in John Ashbery's work, for instance, tells us nothing paraphrasable. His is not a sociable voice, he's at home neither with language – nor with us. Rather, Ashbery manipulates, in always less predictable ways, our verbal expectations – which he invariably frustrates. After I have finished reading a poem by Ashbery (whom I intensely admire), I have the feeling that Dr Penfield has run an electrode over various cells of the exposed cortex and that flickers of old memories, submerged sights and sounds, have been lit up in odd combinations. Merrill has nothing in common with such contemporary tendencies. For him words bear meanings, much as the messengers in his two prophetic books bear us news of the cosmos.

Since the triumph of structuralism, critics seek poems that exemplify their preoccupation with the verbal autonomy of the 'text in progress'. Undoubtedly Merrill's poetry will be dragooned into this fashionable activity, but in fact it is ill-suited to such an exercise. For indeed to hear the full resonance of this work depends upon a belief in every element of the old model of communication – writer, reader, the page, the world out there capable of being described and the reader's imagination, capable of being instructed. Of course I recognize that there are those who believe all literary communication is impossible, who have an epistemological theory (or at least prejudice) that makes literature into a solipsistic pursuit. Fair enough (though privately I wonder why literature is *especially* disabled, for surely the same objections can be lodged against *all* language, including the language of the critic, not just literary language). No matter. My point is that for readers to 'get' Merrill they must believe (or pretend to believe) in conventional communication. Only so can they enjoy or even understand his strategies – his habit of breaking off a thought once it's become obvious, his skilful manipulation of readers' sympathies, his direct address to the reader, his speculations about the 'real' meanings that underlie the words of his informants, his unearthing of the wisdom stored up in puns (Merrill once said that the 'collective unconscious of the race is the O.E.D.') – his complete faith, in short, in the transmitting and recuperative powers of language. The paradox that such realism is applied, in 'Ephraim' and *Mirabell*, to the occult in no way detracts, I think, from my argument. Indeed, these books can be read as subtle propaganda, inducting the skeptical reader into heavenly mysteries. The process of this induction, this overcoming of doubt, would not exist if there were no scandal (heaven in this case) to be passed off, if there were no subtle apologist (Merrill), no doubting Thomas (the reader) and no means of seducing the skeptic (poetry). The *action* of these books, in fact, is the seduction of the reader (speaking secularly) or his initiation (speaking religiously).

The action begins at the beginning. The first lines of 'The Book of Ephraim' disarm the reader's objections to a long, narrative poem full of events, information and the strange concourse with the supernatural:

> Admittedly I err by undertaking
> This in its present form. The baldest prose
> Reportage was called for, that would reach
> The widest public in the shortest time.

An urgency of tone (this is worth reading) is joined to a simplicity of statement. This introduction also serves as a shrugging, diffidently American approximation of the invocation to the muse. For all its becoming directness, however, this first section introduces us to Merrill's wit, which is his knack for saying the truth in surprising formulations. For instance, he tells us that he would have preferred to write a legend peopled by stock figures:

> The kind of being we recall from Grimm,
> Jung, Verdi, and the commedia dell'arte.

That conjunction of names makes perfect sense, though its impudence shocks us into laughter, as does his remark that the writers of the French New Novel have been 'suckled by Woolf not Mann...' When Merrill and his companion David Jackson come into contact through the Ouija board with Ephraim, a Greek Jew born in AD 8 and a favorite of the Emperor Tiberius, Merrill is the first to object to Ephraim's 'reality':

> The question
> Of who or what we took Ephraim to be,
> And of what truths (if any) we considered
> Him spokesman, had arisen from the start.

Just as we were succumbing to nasty, wise-guy suspicions that perhaps Ephraim is nothing but the ghost of Merrill's and Jackson's affection for each other, this cozy bit of second-guessing is brought out into the open. Merrill has a psychiatrist say,

> Harmless; but can you find no simpler ways
> To sound each other's depths of spirit

Than taking literally that epigram
Of Wilde's I'm getting damn
Tired of hearing my best patients parrot?

The epigram, we learn, is 'Given a mask, we'll tell the truth.' Throughout the long narrative of the two books, Merrill experiences our doubts and Jackson feels our fears; together they express and mold our own reactions.

At this point I'd like to summarize the wisdom, the message, of the two books. By taking the content out of context I run the risk of making it sound a bit absurd, perhaps – but surely no more so than a précis of *Paradise Lost* might sound. Before starting, however, I should mention that the revelations in 'Ephraim' come primarily from that eponymous speaker, whereas in *Mirabell* the main source is 741, a bat-like creature who transforms himself into the peacock Mirabell. Mirabell's information about the creation, about energy, God, nature, biology, and so on substantially revises and corrects Ephraim's partial knowledge. In the third volume, still unpublished, the angels will be the speakers and will presumably still further refine our data.

The Ouija board (a homemade cardboard one in this case) is divided into the letters of the alphabet, the arabic numerals, the words 'yes' and 'no', and (on the Merrill board) several punctuation marks. 'Ephraim', accordingly, is divided into twenty-six sections, each beginning with a letter, and *Mirabell* is headed by the ten numerals. Perhaps the final book will alternate between 'yes' and 'no'.

In 1955 Merrill and Jackson first started playing around with the board. After receiving bits of cosmic gibberish, they came in touch with Ephraim. It was Ephraim who told them that every living person on earth is a 'representative' of a 'patron' in heaven. Neither hell nor purgatory exists, though heaven has nine stages in its spiritual hierarchy. Patrons are forbidden, with rare exceptions, to intervene in earthly doings save 'in the entre-acte between/One incarnation and another'. Ephraim reports on the doings of the recently deceased and tells Merrill and Jackson of their own prospects. More surprisingly, we learn that heaven depends on earth; if earth were destroyed by nuclear holocaust, heaven itself would vanish. Heaven 'is the surround of the living'.

Earth faces two potential disasters: overpopulation and nuclear devastation.

In section U of 'Ephraim' strange, violent creatures wrest the transmitting cup away from the suave Greek. In *Mirabell* we learn these creatures are bats, eager to communicate with the living. They are the sons of Cain, the fallen angels *and* the negative force within the atom. Whereas 'Ephraim' contains relatively few revelations, and those few are subjected to Merrill's personal, elaborate musings, *Mirabell* bristles with supernatural news. The messages tapped out on the board are reproduced in capital letters, and the pages sometimes resemble tickertape transcripts.

I leave it to others to summarize Merrill's heavenly hydraulics and his references to bats, Atlantis, centaurs, atomic energy and the injection of human souls into new creatures. I prefer to concentrate on his cosmology.

The universe is ruled by God Biology, who is constantly at war with chaos. God Biology is history and the earth itself, in addition to a guiding intelligence. Whereas human beings derive their energy from electric charges coursing through the body, God Biology's source of energy is nuclear – solar energy, in particular. By meddling with nuclear energy the bats fell, and by experimenting unwisely with it man faces doom. Mankind is like Prometheus seeking to steal God's solar flame.

The world is ruled by rigid determinism – at least, everything that happens can be said to serve a purpose. 'No accident' is the rule of the universe. How such determinism is reconciled with human free will, of course, is the problem every religion must expand.

The old religions served their purpose, but they have been superceded by the reign of pure reason – not in a dry, logic-chopping sense but as an instrument of wisdom aided by the imagination; as the board taps it out:

PURE REASON
NOT IN THE VOLTAIREAN SENSE BASED ON KNOWLEDGE MERELY
BUT REASON RUN THRU THE FIRES OF MAN'S CLONED SOUL.

The three new faiths, appropriate to our day, are music, science and poetry. Underneath pure matter is pure mind, and these three faiths are most closely in tune with the mental. The scribe is, seemingly, the high priest of the new religion, since humanity rules through culture, which is based on language, and the scribe is the supreme repository and manipulator of language. Homosexuals are best suited to lead these new faiths of poetry and music, which are nonsexual or unisexual, as are all expressions of pure mind. Although the scribe reaches only a few readers, those readers form an elite leadership. The scribe's mission is to issue warnings against overpopulation and the nuclear holocaust.

I should make it clear right off that these do not necessarily represent the opinions of James Merrill. Apparently he 'received' them from the board, and they will undoubtedly be further revised in subsequent dictees in the third volume. Nor are these ideas stated so directly – or so drily. Indeed, the centerpiece of the book is a charming collaboration formed of two living speakers (Merrill and Jackson), their two dead friends (Auden and a Greek woman, Maria Mitsotaki) and the fifth – the bat, 741, who transforms himself into the peacock Mirabell. In fact, just as heaven depends on earth, in the same way Mirabell is a sort of emblem of the love the four friends bear for one another; as Merrill puts it:

Bon. We will try to remember that you are not
A person, not a peacock, not a bat.
A devil least of all – an impulse only
Here at the crossroads of our four affections.

Moreover, every revelation in *Mirabell* can be read analogically or metaphorically. Thus the black holes in space, the reservoirs of antimatter, correspond to a will to nothingness in mankind. Similarly, the lattice-like crust world created by the bats over Atlantis corresponds to the cortex in the human brain. God Biology is both a deity – and the accumulated wisdom in our cells. The bats are eerie intelligences, agents in competition and collaboration with nature – and also aspects of the atom.

Nor does *Mirabell* lack emotion or dramatic tension. Revelations are teased out of the bats and vouchsafed in tantalizing morsels. A sub-plot about Akhnaton's first disastrous nuclear experiment is told twice, for instance, and the second time around the complex narrative can be condensed and played for all its shocking, lyrical value. But perhaps the most tension in the book is generated by disclosures about Maria Mitsotaki. Her death is recent and the poet is still intimately attached to her. In her life she had been a fierce amateur gardener, an aristocratic, eccentric recluse – and a mother to Merrill (if any relationship so full of respect and affection can be considered familial). Before her death from cancer she had been subjected to cobalt treatments and, at one point in *Mirabell*, the poet fears the rays may have destroyed her soul, a suspicion seemingly confirmed when he learns she is to be reborn as a plant. Recalling the garden scene of *Parsifal*, Merrill asks:

> Was this your garden path?
> Was I, beguiled there, the Pure Fool
> Who mistook antimatter for a muse?

Maria's eventual salvation and transfiguration is the most touching drama of the book.

The suave art of Merrill's earlier work, which reaches its apotheosis in *Divine Comedies*, lies in his ability to unearth the casual correspondences that link seemingly disparate things, to discover (as in 'Yanninia' in *Divine Comedies*) that a visit to a town fair in Greece where in one booth a woman is sawed in half 'rhymes' metaphysically with the two sorts of women (pure and passionate) most men desire – the two wives of the town's nineteenth-century ruler, Ali Pasha, say, who in turn becomes a stand in for the poet's own much-married father. The last stanza of this remarkable poem is a breathtaking condensation of such far-flung associations, and we feel that Merrill himself is the magician who cuts us in half only to heal us whole. Throughout the glowing pages of 'The Book of Ephraim' we watch, heart in mouth, as Merrill swings airily from one distant point to another, his only net the wonderfully pliable and resilient interconnections of words. Thus a Japanese landscape instantly materializes in the spoonerism, 'Swirls before pine', the cliché 'small wonder' is freshly cut and inked, and a trilingual pun, like a Gogolian smile, generates a memorable miniature:

To touch on these unspeakables you want
The spry nuances of a Bach courante
Or brook that running slips into a shawl
Of crystal noise – at last, the waterfall.

Or Merrill enchants us with a wittily disconcerting line break *and*
a versatile homonym in this glimpse of nuclear holocaust as a version of *Götterdämmerung*:

While heavy-water nymphs, fettered in chain
Reaction, sang their soft refrain Refrain.

Here traffic grime eating into classical ruins is called 'the arch-
consumer', there 'sunrise' and 'hangfire' rub against each other in
the same line – and strike sparks! Here 'D Minor' is off-rhymed
with 'demeanor'. And, at the end of a section a tranquil leak
taken on a frosty morning's walk turns ominously into an atomic
explosion:

The droplets atomize, evaporate
To dazzlement a blankness overdusts
Pale blue, then paler blue. It stops at nothing.

Even Dante's *'gente nova'* transforms itself in the same line into
'a population explosion'.

Never do these verbal games stop or stump us; were we to
ignore them the flow of thought and sentiment would still
devolve with the same fine momentum. Take these bravura lines:

Jung says – or if he doesn't, all but does –
That God and the Unconscious are one. Hm.
The lapse that tides us over, hither, yon,
Tide that laps us home away from home.

Every syllable is melting under us but never gives way until we,
like little Eva, have crossed the ice. In this way, as in so many
others, Merrill recalls Vladimir Nabokov. He, too, knew everything and never resisted a joke, but his wit was not even visible to
the careless or uninformed eye. The sense rushes us along, but

should we pause we would notice the nine-tenths of the sub-merged myth, the frosty arabesques of detail, the glistening, blinding, shifting perspectives.

In all his mature work, and especially in 'Ephraim', Merrill is most at home in the Heraclitean elements of change: fire and water. Lights flame forth from mirrors or scorch the evening sky, tears rise to the eyes and shimmer, waterfalls plunge, window-panes catch fire – this is the characteristic moment in Merrill when, as he has it in an earlier poem, 'The world beneath the world is brightening.' In this moment, as in the alchemy of a pun or the stored energy of a 'deadwood' expression, things lose their solidity, flow or flame into something else, vanish only to show up elsewhere – the fast-motion film of decay and rebirth, the physicist's view of the conservation of energy joined to the naturalist's view of random and ever-proliferating variation. This alertness to transubstantiation is the religious impulse behind Merrill's verse.

In *Mirabell* the poet has turned away to some extent from the allure of language – an allure he has always suspected. In *Nights and Days* he had hoped his memories of voyages would not be 'wholly undermined / By fluent passages of metaphor.' In 'Ephraim' he breaks off a splendid passage with the weary self-condemnation, 'Unrelenting fluency'. His very ease, which he glories in but half-despises, is finally crowded out by something real – or rather unreal: the messages of the Ouija board. At last his own voice – sociable, irreverent, playful and tender – has been drowned out by heaven's steely tap-dance. Were we, just for a moment, to suppose that those messages are not words from the *au delà* but rather blueprints to the machines behind the stage that have always contrived the illusionistic dissolves, triumphs and transformations, then we might find in the dense pages of *Mirabell* the secret behind Merrill's art. The proscenium crumbles and flies and pulleys are exposed. Merrill has long been aware that the past figuratively inhabits and animates the present: in *Mirabell* we see the past literally projected forward into the future as souls, like actors 'between engagements', prepare for their next lives. The looming, troubling fathers who stand behind their sons are now regulated into a system of patrons and repre-sentatives. The bats, like inspiration, abject the density of a soul and create new substances out of familiar materials. Merrill has always had an agile imagination open to analogy; in *Mirabell* analogue becomes anagoge. Sudden shifts of scale, previously performed on the level of wit (a ring on his grandmother's hand is like 'the mosque of Suleiman the Magnificent' in 'The Thousand and Second Night'), now take place in the realm of the spirit when we learn God is the size of 'A MERE FINGER' who 'WEARS US AS A RING'. As Merrill says of these microcosm–macrocosm relationships,

> Given such crystalline
> Reversibility, the toy spyglass teaches
> That anything worth having's had both ways.

Even the moral atmosphere of the previous poems – at once humane and exacting – is codified in *Mirabell*, not always comfortably. Just as Nabokov contrasts his aristocratic, passionate characters with a troupe of fools, prudes, psychologists, villains and spoilsports and the resulting effect is both romantic and satiric, in the same way Merrill's verse is electric with the alternating currents of sympathy and scorn. In *Mirabell*, however, the scorn can become cruel, the snobbishness no longer temperamental but political, the affection smug – the only fault *I* can find in this work, a fault, mind you, that has characterized almost all the great poetry of this century. And to be fair I should point out that the fault lies not in Merrill but in his bats; *they* are the ones who portray the hierarchical system. He is merely their scribe.

Together 'The Book of Ephraim' and *Mirabell* form the first two-thirds of the most ambitious poem of our day, one that attempts to restore to verse the subjects, public and private, that an adult mind actually thinks about: our place in the universe, our fate, our origin, our virtues and sins. 'Ephraim' is the culmination of what Merrill has called his poetry of 'love and loss', a vast summa of his themes and techniques. As David Kalstone has written in *Five Temperaments*, the most acute essay we have on Merrill, 'The Book of Ephraim' is a compendium of voices – individual and social, emulated, sometimes feared and discarded. It suggests ways in which the apparently random material of our lives and reading, history, gossip – the rational and irrational bombardments – are somehow absorbed and selected for our experience. Echoes and re-echoes tease us with patterns whose existence we suspected but whose details were not yet clear.

Mirabell marks a new turn in Merrill's work, a translation of personal history and verbal ingenuity into history and cosmic engineering. He has written 'poems of science' and indeed established the poetic equivalent to the scientific picture of the universe in which time and space are relative, in which energy and mass are convertible into one another, in which the microcosm mirrors the macrocosm, in which nothing, not even the smallest wave or particle, is ever subject to a stable description but all, all plunges outward in a shift towards red – to *be* read.

Sado Machismo

New Times, 8 January 1979; published during the height of Anita Bryant's anti-homosexual campaign in Florida and in the midst of the Briggs Amendment campaign in California.

A strange thing is happening among gay men in the United States. These creatures – or rather we creatures – are moving, month by month, toward sado-masochism. A straight woman whom I've known for years insists on regarding the gay men she likes as sensitive, gentle, poetic, vulnerable; as Art Deco figurines; pairs of youths with dreamy eyes, sad mouths, slender figures, their fingers slightly linked, their bodies in *contraposto* as they wander into the sunset to the strains of Fauré. 'He's a lovely guy,' is her comment. 'Sweet. Sensitive.'

But the scandal is that the lovely guy on his way home picks up a trick whom he insults and penetrates with a fist or a dildo as big as a fist. The dreamy eyes are narrowed into slits of hatred, and the sad mouth barks out jeering obscenities to a 'slave' whose wrists are handcuffed and whose head is encased in a black leather mask. What would she say if she knew the whole horrible truth? If she recognized that Fred and Bob – those charmers who've redecorated her house in Bernardsville, who sent her to James Robinson for the best reproductions of antique silver and to a wizard on Long Island for expert marquetry work – that one of those charmers (Fred) spends hours at home in the stocks while Bob feeds him from a dog dish?

I ask the question in a straight magazine with some trepidation. Homosexuality may be trendy on college campuses, at beach resorts, in discos, but it is also subject to renewed legal oppression. All too many straight people are unaware of the fact that homosexual acts, even between consenting adults, are illegal in thirty-five out of fifty states. While hip straights are socializing with gays and coyly hinting that they themselves might have 'tendencies', that they, too, might swing, gays in small towns are losing their jobs and being ostracized for their sexual orientation.

And so it may seem a bit ill-timed on my part to bring up the unassimilable new fact of gay sado-masochism. Most of the straight people I know, especially women, are revolted by it. Unbridled gay promiscuity, a trick a night, seems hard enough to deal with, not to mention the queasy-making thought of two men having it off together, no matter how gently and affectionately they perform the act. As for gay S and M, it is as disturbing for heterosexuals to contemplate as was the thought of fair Celia on the potty for Jonathan Swift.

If it didn't sound too much like gay chauvinism, I'd suggest that gays have often pioneered the frontiers of urban single life. Gay fashions quickly become Fashion, and gay sado-masochism may portend yet another trend among straights, at least those living in this decade rather than some more comfortable time past. The dirty book stores are already crowded with magazines for heterosexual sadists and masochists (Barbarella in stiletto heels whipping a supine man in a French maid's mobcap and starched white apron). Not long ago, one New York leather bar for gay men experimented with setting aside Tuesdays for straight S and M couples, and one woman prostitute I know makes a killing pissing on male commodities brokers. Even the S and M boutiques attract timid straight couples asking to examine that, uh, restraint harness . . .

So if an *entente cordiale* is being formed between sophisticated straights and gays, both parties should know what they're getting into. And more and more gay men (though by no means the majority) are finding themselves drawn toward the trappings, the aura, the threat – if not always the reality – of sexual violence. And these trappings are increasingly in evidence on the streets as leather-clad men, cock-rings instead of hearts on their sleeves, trudge through the city at night. In San Francisco a gay bath house has fantasy rooms devoted to bondage, water sports, pain. Customers state their preferences on a bulletin board; no one need waste time with an uncongenial partner, nor can anyone complain later that he didn't know what was in store. In Los Angeles the police are so repressive that gays must lie low. Most of the men resent this tyranny, but one gay restaurant, the Academy, has all the waiters dressed as cops.

In New York a motorcycle club rents a three-deck ship for its annual party. Hundreds of paying guests board the ship near Wall Street late at night and are sailed through autumn mist up the Hudson. On the lowest deck beer and fried chicken are served. The middle deck has been converted into a disco, and serious sadists are faced with the difficult question as to how abandoned they can be on the dance floor and still maintain their menacing image; a lumbering roll from boot to boot is the self-conscious compromise. On the top deck the lights have been doused: the orgy floor. A porno flick casts light from the screen on to one kneeling figure sobbing in his chains, on another stripped and bent forward to service two masters at once, one fore, the other aft. Two enterprising souls have set up shop beside a quart can of Crisco; by the time the ship returns to port they have received a thorough proctological exam from at least half the other passengers.

But on any night of the week such sights can be observed in the Village at a private club. Four dollars at the door buys drink and admission to the huge painhouse. As your eyes adjust to the gloom, you see one guy whipping another. Over there someone who checked all his clothes in the coatroom is hoisted aloft in a leather swing. Those men are pressed to the wall, facing it. A punishment? No, the wall, you discover, has been pierced with crotch-high 'glory holes', and on the other side of the partition someone even now is being covered in glory. In the basement two stoned men are kissing under black light. Absurdly, touchingly, anachronistically romantic, they are unaware of everyone around them, their fluorescent white shirts gleaming eerily like Baudelaire's swan bathing its wings in the dust.

The oldest and dumbest joke about S and M has the masochist saying 'Beat me', and the sadist replying 'No'. What's all wrong about the joke is that it assumes sadism is the same thing as psychological cruelty. A playwright who's known to be a sadist is presumed to be cruel to his audiences ('No wonder that play went on so long'). Of an English poet whose verse follows strictly traditional forms, some wiseacre remarks, 'But of course the forms are strict. If you'd seen him in his saturnine leathers you'd understand his craving for discipline.'

So thoroughly corrupted are we by the Freudian parlor game that such interpretations have become the ordinary stuff of conversation; we are all rabbis, and life is the copious Talmud awaiting our narrow exegesis. The hermeneutics convince us that a life – my life, your life, anyone's life – is all of a piece. He's cruel in bed and cruel at work. Proust tortured mice for fun and tortures us by going on and on in his Big Book.

But what if each of us is not unified, but piecemeal? What if the parts oppose rather than duplicate one another? Sam the sadist is a loyal and loving son, a beneficent employer; and the motorcycle club he heads sponsors an annual benefit for handicapped kids. The playwright is famous for his own work with the disabled, the poet for his long hours of patient advice to his students; and Proust was a proverb of kindness (when he found 200 mistakes in twenty-three galley pages, he begged the proofreader not to take the discovery of these errors 'for a reproach').

More to the point, sadism itself is not cruel. Those gay 'top men' I've quizzed have admitted, somewhat sheepishly, that they seldom inflict much pain beyond a few slaps and light licks with a belt. So theatrical (or filmic) is sado-masochism that even the blows are designed to look and sound more violent to the (usually imaginary) audience than they actually are; the belt is doubled, the punishing hand is cupped.

Marijuana, poppers, mescalin and beer stimulate the imagination to such a fever that by merely standing over the cowering slave a master is able to suggest an assault. At every point the experienced master can judge whether his slave wants more or less pain. And sometimes the sadist will ask *sotto voce* if things are getting too heavy. Naturally there are some sadists who, like Sade himself, can be aroused only by inflicting pain, but these are in the minority. Ankle restraints are plush-lined; the paddle is *commedia dell'arte* slapstick.

The violence resides almost entirely in the language. One man licking another's Frye boots would be hilarious were the act not labeled 'humiliation'. Someone once remarked that in adolescence pornography is a substitute for sex, whereas in adulthood sex is a substitute for pornography; the S and M rap (that muttered or shouted stream of abuse, obscenity, military commands) is the conflation of pornography and sex, the marriage of signifier and signified, an act of extraordinary semiotic condensation. So essential is language to sado-masochism that a fully satisfying leather scene could be the most humdrum sex accompanied by a really filthy soundtrack. The parts of the body become fetishized through talk, exalted by four-letter words to a paradise of brutality. And one man performing fellatio on another is transported far from his high-rise eyrie to the heartache and longing of his childhood by having to call his dominant partner 'Daddy'.

The popularity of sado-masochistic sex has introduced new words into the gay vocabulary – as well as their domesticated, more casual variants. The original terms, such as slave and master, must have seemed too absurd, too theatrical, not quite plausible, too ... well, embarrassing. It is socially awkward to ask a stranger if he wants to be your 'slave' for the night. The word evokes dungeons, chains, pornographic novels of the eighteenth century – a sort of period claptrap. As a result, 'sado-masochism' has become 'S and M' or, more recently and innocuously, 'rough stuff'. 'Sadist' and 'masochist' are now 'top man' and 'bottom man'. The way to ask someone to be your slave, therefore, is 'Are you into a bottom scene?' Sexual aggression kept on the level of fantasy is a 'head trip', whereas to crave physical abuse is to be 'into pain'. And the 'dungeon' has become the 'game room'.

Why is S and M erupting now, precisely when gays presumably have been liberated from role-playing stereotypes and may at last be on the verge of integration into straight society? Could it be that gays don't want to go respectable, that S and M is a nostalgia for the criminal past? Could it be that liberation has given gays permission to stop being sissies and to become the he-men forbidden by the typology of the past?

One book published recently condemns gay S and M as an expression of self-hatred. Like those Jews in concentration camps whom Bruno Bettelheim claims impersonated Nazi officers, sado-masochists may be identifying with the oppressor. The sadist who torments his slave by calling him a 'faggot' is only, according to this interpretation, buying the denigrating terms of heterosexual society and, by repeating them, assuring himself of his own 'normality'.

But if S and M were really a way of identifying with the straight oppressor, we would expect the typical leather man to be older rather than younger, closety rather than overt, conformist rather than blatant. We'd expect him to be from the conventional, guilt-prone lower middle class, and we'd guess that S and M must have been more prevalent in the pre-liberation 1950s than in the 1970s. In fact, however, the S and M crowd is composed of all age groups, and it's aggressively gay and exists defiantly outside ordinary society, even ordinary gay society. Edgar Gregersen, a New York professor of anthropology who is preparing a study of straight and gay S and M, has interviewed scores of leather men and discovered that they are generally college-educated WASPs from the middle and upper classes. And gay S and M is definitely more popular since the advent of the homosexual liberation movement. The leather man, far from hiding in a business suit, is the most conspicuous figure on the streets. Garbed in chains and skin-tight cowhide, he has the nerve (so like that of the despised drag queen) to wear openly the badge of his fantasies. Leather is always a sexual statement, as much as a prostitute's high-rise wig and six-inch heels. Would someone who hates his own homosexuality proclaim it so loudly?

There's another theory: that gay S and M is a safe outlet for throttled rage. Sadism is, presumably, a way for uptight men to release their thunderbolts under the guise of passion. The masochist has indicated his readiness to be punished, and to abuse him seems to be simple compliance, almost charity. Still better, the anger can always be disavowed and laughed off later as just part of a game.

Some of Gregersen's findings support this interpretation. Leather men he's interviewed report that they are or have been vegetarians or pacifists. If not always liberal, many are at least libertarian in their politics, averse to authoritarianism of every stripe and hell-bent on defending individual rights.

If one rather cynically assumes that pacifism, vegetarianism, humaneness toward animals and libertarianism are indicative of repressed urges towards violence, then a case could be made for the theory that links S and M to contained rage. To me, however, these beliefs and character traits are more readily attributable to an active imagination, to empathy, to what Keats called 'negative capability' – the power to project oneself into another creature's skin. Such a capacity makes S and M itself possible; no one would be drawn towards the drama of domination (nor would he be good at it) unless he could project himself into the mind of the dominated.

Perhaps the leather man, far from being a stunted, diminished person, is in fact a privileged being. Perhaps his confidence, freedom and imagination allow him to dramatize social tensions that fascinate everyone. He may not fully grasp the conflicts he acts out, but he at least may have the courage to live them rather than just observe them.

These tensions are largely political. Like Marie Antoinette's milkmaids or those Spanish ladies who dressed up as *majas*, the gay sado-masochist, though himself a member of the elite, impersonates working men – truck drivers, construction workers, telephone linemen. When I've asked leather guys whether they'd rather make it with a real Con Ed man or a lawyer who looks like one, the question baffles them. It lies outside the system of their fantasies. In their hearts they may know that the lawyer would be the more adventurous and uninhibited lover, but their passion demands he at least appear to be a worker.

Of course, why shouldn't lawyers masquerade as laborers? The children of the middle class grew up without seeing any signs of sexuality emanating from their daddies, those corporation drudges in bulky suits who never whistled at women or scratched their deodorized crotches. The only bare chests were those of construction workers; the only tight clothes were those of Hollywood cowboys; the only images of male raunch were of Marlon Brando astride his bike or caterwauling for Stella. There is no middle-class sexual style for men. What would it be based on? Golfing? Discussing stock options? Attending church? Downing highballs?

But I think the impersonation of working people goes beyond borrowing their real or fancied sex appeal. I think it's a way of drawing the poisons from the body politic.

In 1919 Freud, unable to explain why children, war victims and many psychoanalytic patients deliberately re-created earlier traumatic experiences down to the last painful detail, formulated a new theory, the repetition compulsion. Earlier he had considered the pleasure principle to be the governing drive in unconscious behavior, but now he placed the repetition compulsion 'beyond the pleasure principle'. The child who relives with her dolls the frightening fights her parents are waging daily is attempting to master disturbing reality by stage-managing it. The fact that the fights remain acrimonious even in play doesn't matter; what's important is that the child, rather than being a passive observer, is now manipulating what threatens her.

The repetition compulsion seems an elegant model for sado-masochism, in which both partners, functioning under the benign dispensation of make-believe, re-enact not their own private troubles but rather our society's nightmarish preoccupations with power, with might. No acute person can fail to respond to the gross economic exploitation, the subtle oppression, the alienation and inauthenticity of modern life. Even if we insulate ourselves behind minute personal ditherings and distractions, we are still haunted by the arrival of the ghost at the banquet. Everywhere we see the results of racial bias, of sexism, of a self-perpetuating power elite. The same scramble after status rages through the family, the university, the corporation. Even those who have made it to the top know how precarious their perch is. And old age brings all careers to an ignominious end. No one is safe – ever, anywhere.

This miserable reality, fueled by greed, fear and intimidation, is so real we cannot bear to look at it; as Simone Weil put it, 'Unless protected by an armor of lies, man cannot endure might without suffering a blow in the depth of his soul.' Most Americans today dismiss social problems as 'dull' or drop a tired curtsy towards such issues in the form of a quip or rueful joke. Endless jokes – yet never a sober word about the scandal of power that ruins our sleep.

These hidden maneuvers after money and status are revealed in sado-masochism. Whereas ordinary social interactions are characterized by the joke, humor has always been inimical to sadism, just as light is to vampires. This humor that defuses outrage (no matter how justified) and dampens indignation (no matter how righteous) is just another name for surrender. Sado-masochism rejects the laugh that paralyzes social conscience. Within the charged space surrounding the master and his slave, true deeds are performed. One man does submit to another. One man does humiliate another. The same relief we experience in watching a Shakespeare play, the relief of participating in action devoid of irony and freighted with clear values, is the release offered to the sadist and masochist. The couple perform the mysteries of domination, of might, that obsess our cultures. As Gilles Deleuze and

Felix Guattari have said in *Anti-Oedipus*, 'Class struggle goes to the heart of desire.' For these writers there is no distinction between psychic and money economy, between the libido and other forms of energy; nor are the domestic dramas, the agonies of the Oedipus complex, divorced from the larger social struggles outside the home. Unlike the Freudians, Deleuze and Guattari would not believe the Germans worshipped Hitler because they were afraid of their fathers. Quite the reverse. They feared Dad because he expressed and passed on the totalitarianism of his society. And this fear is invested with sexuality.

The anger and brutality that the child glimpses in his duplicitous parents, that the boss senses in his wisecracking employees, that the middle class attributes to working people – this anger and brutality are exorcised in S and M. Sex becomes an act born of the repetition compulsion, an Aristotelian drama with its definition of character through action; the drama recapitulates the incoherent and far more frightening violence of our society. S and M has always surfaced at times when a crushing power structure is beginning to topple – at the end of the Roman Empire, at the outbreak of the French Revolution, and now. The unbearable suspense of awaiting revenge and resolution is reduced to the narrow limits of a sexual encounter. The fact that that encounter is by its very nature primarily linguistic allows it to tap the verbal reality of might; the sadist's commands and insults belong to the code of power ordinarily disguised by jokes. Instead of fencing with shadows, the sado-masochist encompasses in an hour a lifetime of pain and redemption. The dangers of class hatred are scaled down to the ritualized perils of the waif Justine, that career victim, and the lordly Count Bressac. Sado-masochism is a futile effort to reduce ubiquitous cruelty to the comprehensible scope of sex.

If nothing else, this theory of sadism as a premonition of socialism has the virtue of already having been satirized. A character in Thomas Pynchon's *Gravity's Rainbow*, a sinister fellow named Thanatz, asks why our capitalist masters have taught us to feel shame whenever the subject of S and M comes up.

Why will the Structure allow every other kind of sexual behavior but that one? Because submission and dominance are resources it needs for its very survival. They cannot be wasted in private sex. In any kind of sex. It needs our submission so that it may remain in power. It needs our lusts after dominance so that it can co-opt us into its own poor game. There is no joy in it, only power. I tell you, if S and M could be established universally, at the family level, the State would wither away.

Even I can chuckle over that one. In fact, it would be absurd for me not to express my own misgivings about S and M. All too many leather men become so addicted to the scene that they won't venture into jobs or social situations where they can't wear their costumes; the fantasy of power has confined them to the gay ghetto. In order to continue inhabiting their waking dream they may become quite literally addicted to booze or drugs. The demands of sexual illusion speed many leather men on from one partner to another, though quite a few guys into S and M are able to sustain long-term relationships.

More seriously, Susan Sontag, in her essay on the Nazi film director Leni Riefenstahl, has said that the fantasy behind sado-masochism is death and that the Hitler years have provided the sado-masochist with 'a master scenario available to everyone'. Pasolini's last film, *Salo*, spells out the supposed relationship between S and M and Fascism in stomach-turning detail. Four petty tyrants in the last days of the Fascist regime round up a group of teenage girls and boys and confine them to a villa, where they are subjected to the horrors of coprophilia, torture and death. Throughout these gory and melancholy rites the imaginations of the sadists are fired by stories recited by aging female 'narrators' done up in sequins and boas and given to melodramatic intonations and literary euphemisms. Almost always the sadists are dressed formally, and their revels take place not in dungeons at midnight but in cool, spacious rooms invaded by the clear light of day. The sounds of approaching warfare can be heard, but the sadists ignore their crumbling power and devote themselves to their ghastly rituals.

I was sickened by the film. Is this where S and M leads? Could it be that my fine theories might be justifying actual cruelty?

I think not. Hitler was not, I have heard, Eva Braun's master;

he was not a sadist in bed. The concentration camps were not sexual playgrounds but scenes of real, not make-believe, genocide. Actual gay sado-masochism, as practiced by some of Ernst Roehm's followers, was exterminated by the Nazis; perhaps, to paraphrase Pynchon's Thanatz, submission and dominance were too important to the Nazis to be wasted in private sex. *Salo* is Pasolini's translation of Sade into contemporary terms, not a matter of historical fact. The film may even be an expression of Pasolini's gay self-hatred, the very factor that led him to pick up the straight boy who murdered him. In any event, the film is not the least bit sexy.

The confusion arises from our double use of the word sadism to mean both criminal, brutal acts of non-sexual violence and harmless erotic games. They are not the same thing. The obscenities of war are not equivalent to the eccentricities of the bedroom. Indeed, totalitarian regimes, whether on the Right or the Left, have always suppressed sexual deviations of every sort, including sado-masochism. Political oppression feeds on sexual repression; S and M is too anarchic to serve the designs of Fascists.

'Go tell it to the Marines,' you might well be saying by now, dear reader, *mon semblable, mon frère* – and so I would were the Marines not better acquainted with the real sadism of our society than either you or I could ever hope to be.

II

The Eighties

The Political Vocabulary of
Homosexuality

From *The State of the Language*, edited by Christopher Ricks and
Leonard Michaels, 1980.

Gay liberation is a new phenomenon, yet it has already transformed attitudes among homosexuals and modified the ways in
which they speak. In June 1969, a group of lesbians and gay men
resisted a routine police raid on the Stonewall, a popular dance
bar in Greenwich Village. Opposition to police harassment was
unusual enough to signal a quickening sense of solidarity. Soon
after the Stonewall Resistance gay organizations and publications
were springing up across the country and, by now, gay liberation
has become both a national and an international movement.

I was present at that original event and can recall how the participants cast about for political and linguistic models. Black
power, feminism, resistance to the war in Vietnam and the New
Left were all available, and each contributed to the emerging gay
style and vocabulary. Discussing the beginning of the movement
in this way, however, makes it sound too solemn and deliberate.
Our recognition that we formed an oppressed minority struck us
as *humorous* at first; only later did we come to take ourselves
seriously.

I can remember that after the cops cleared us out of the bar we
clustered in Christopher Street around the entrance to the Stonewall. The customers were not being arrested, but a paddy wagon
had already hauled off several of the bartenders. Two or three
policemen stayed behind, locked inside with the remaining members of staff, waiting for the return of the paddy wagon. During
that interval someone in the defiant crowd outside called out
'Gay Power', which caused us all to laugh. The notion that gays
might become militant after the manner of blacks seemed amusing
for two reasons – first because we gay men were used to thinking
of ourselves as too effeminate to protest anything, and second

because most of us did not consider ourselves to be a legitimate minority.

At that time we perceived ourselves as separate individuals at odds with society because we were 'sick' (the medical model), 'sinful' (the religious model), 'deviant' (the sociological model) or 'criminal' (the legal model). Some of these words we might have said lightly, satirically, but no amount of wit could convince us that our grievances should be remedied or our status defended. We might ask for compassion but we could not demand justice. Many gays either were in therapy or felt they should be, and the words *gay liberation* would have seemed as preposterous to us as *neurotic liberation* (now, of course, Thomas S. Szasz in the United States, R. D. Laing in Britain and Felix Guattari on he Continent have, in their different ways, made even that phrase plausible enough).

What I want to stress is that before 1969 only a small (though courageous and articulate) number of gays had much pride in their homosexuality or a conviction that their predilections were legitimate. The rest of us defined our homosexuality in negative terms, and those terms isolated us from one another. We might claim Plato and Michelangelo as homosexuals and revere them for their supposed affinities with us, but we could just as readily dismiss, even despise, a living thinker or artist for being gay. Rich gays may have derived pleasure from their wealth, educated gays from their knowledge, talented gays from their gifts, but few felt anything but regret about their homosexuality as such. To be sure, particular sexual encounters, and especially particular love relationships, were gratifying then as now, but they were explained as happy accidents rather than as expected results.

Moreover, the very idea that sexual identity might demarcate a political entity was still fairly novel. Minority status seemed to be vouchsafed by birth, to be involuntary. One was born into a race or religion or nationality or social class – that was the way to become a member of a real minority. One could also be born a woman, though the large claims advanced by feminists still struck many people then as preposterous. Women, after all, formed a majority and they scarcely seemed to have much in common. Did an upper class WASP woman from Boston share a perspective with a poor chicano Catholic woman from Waco? The same question could be asked about gays: what was our common bond? This 'category confusion' assailed us and may have been one source of our laughter upon hearing the phrase *gay power*.

Then there was the problem about how people become gay. If they're born that way, they may represent, depending on the point of view, a genetic mistake or an evolutionary advance or a normal variation. If, on the other hand, they choose to be gay, then their rights seem less defensible; what has been chosen can be rejected. A third possibility is that the environment makes people gay against their will – but this etiology, because of conventional associations if not logical arguments, again smacks of pathology and suggests gays should seek to be 'cured'.

I raise these issues not because I propose answers (the whole discussion strikes me as politically retrograde, since at this point any etiology would disguise a program for prevention). I bring up the matter only because I want to demonstrate what a strange sort of 'minority' homosexuals belong to and why we were reluctant to embrace the political vocabulary (and stance) that had been useful in securing the civil rights of other groups.

Nevertheless, because the black movement was highly vocal and visible at the time of Stonewall, slogans such as 'black is beautiful' were easily translated into 'gay is good' and 'black power' became 'gay power'. Some of the resistant even dubbed themselves 'pink panthers', but that name did not catch on. These derivations, I should hasten to point out, were not approved of by black militants who, like most young white leftists, regarded homosexuality as 'decadent' and 'bourgeois'. In 1971, I believe, H. Rap Brown did propose a coalition between blacks and gays, but that suggestion was not very popular among his constituents.

A less obvious imitation of the black movement by gays was the elevation of the word *gay* itself. Just as *Negro* had been rejected as something contaminated because it had been used by (supposedly hypocritical) liberals and the seemingly more neutral *black* was brought into currency, in the same way *homosexual*, with its medical textbook ring, was dismissed in favor of the more informal and seemingly more innocuous *gay* (I say 'seemingly' because these words, *black* and *gay*, do have complex etymologies).

No one I know has any real information about the origins of

the word gay; the research all remains to be done. Those who dislike the word assume that it is synonymous with *happy* or *lighthearted* and that its use implies that homosexuals regard heterosexuals, by contrast, as 'grim'. But gay has had many meanings, including 'loose' and 'immoral', especially in reference to a prostitute (a whorehouse was once called a 'gay house'). In the past one asked if a woman was 'gay', much as today one might ask if she 'swings'. The identification of gay with 'immoral' is further strengthened by the fact that *queen* (a male homosexual) is almost certainly derived from *quean* (the Elizabethan word for prostitute).

In American slang at the turn of the century, a 'gay cat' was a younger, less experienced man who attached himself to an older, more seasoned vagrant or hobo; implicit in the relationship between gay cat and hobo was a sexual liaison. Yet another slang meaning of gay is 'fresh', 'impertinent', 'saucy' (not so very distant from 'immoral'). In French *gai* can mean 'spicy' or 'ribald'. My hunch (and it's only a hunch) is that the word may turn out to be very old, to have originated in France, worked its way to England in the eighteenth century and thence to the colonies in America. It has died out in Europe and Britain and is now being re-introduced as a new word from the United States. But this is only speculation.

If the exact etymology is vague, no wonder; the word served for years as a shibboleth, and the function of a shibboleth is to exclude outsiders. Undoubtedly it has had until recently its greatest vogue among Americans. In England, the standard slang word has been *queer*. In Bloomsbury *bugger* was the preferred term, presumably because it was salty and vulgar enough to send those rarefied souls into convulsions of laughter. One pictures Virginia Woolf discussing 'buggery' with Lytton Strachey; how they must have relished the word's public school, criminal and eighteenth-century connotations.

Today heterosexuals commonly object to gay on the grounds that it has ruined for them the ordinary festive sense of the word; one can no longer say, 'How gay I feel!' It seems frivolous, however, to discuss this semantic loss beside the political gain the word represents for American homosexuals. An English novelist visiting the States, after boring everyone by saying she felt gay life was actually sad (an observation she presented as though it were original), proceeded to call gay men 'queer', which I presume is less offensive in Britain than in America (a few older Americans use the word).

Many homosexuals object to gay on other grounds, arguing that it's too silly to designate a life-style, a minority or political movement. But, as the critic Seymour Kleinberg has mentioned in his introduction to *The Other Persuasion: Short Fiction about Gay Men and Women*, 'For all its limitations, "gay" is the only unpompous, unpsychological term acceptable to most men and women, one already widely used and available to heterosexuals without suggesting something pejorative.' Gay is, moreover, one of the few words that does not refer explicitly to sexual activity. One of the problems that has beleaguered gays is that their identity has always been linked to sexual activity rather than to affectional preference. The word gay (whatever its etymology) at least does not sound sexual.

In any event, gay is so workable a word that in the last ten years it has shifted from being just an adjective to being both an adjective and a noun. One now says, 'Several gays were present,' though such a construction sounds awkward to older American homosexuals. Just as Fowler in *A Guide to Modern English Usage* objects to *human* as a noun and prefers *human being*, so many homosexuals still prefer *gay person* or *gay man*.

The connection between feminism and gay liberation has been strong for a decade, though now it has broken down. Because of this break, the word gay now generally refers to homosexual men alone. Homosexual women prefer to be called *lesbians*, pure and simple. Most lesbian radicals feel they have more in common with the feminist movement than with gay liberation. Since political lesbians tend to resent a male spokesman, I have confined most of my remarks in this essay to the gay male experience which, in any event, is more within my range of competence and understanding.

This fairly recent rupture, however, should not obscure the debt that gay liberation owes to feminism. The members of both movements, for instance, regard their inner experiences as political, and for both gays and feminists the function of consciousness-raising sessions has been to trace the exact contours of their oppression. Women and gay men, as the argument goes, have been socialized into adopting restricting roles that are viewed with contempt by heterosexual men (despite the fact that these very roles reinforce the values of a virilist society). Accordingly, at least one aim of feminism and gay liberation has been to end the tyranny of stereotyped behavior. Much of this stereotyping, of course, is perpetuated by the victimized themselves. Many women have a low opinion of other women, and many gays are quick to ridicule other gays.

For example, political gays have fought the use of the feminine gender when employed by one homosexual man of another. In the past a regular feature of gay male speech was the production of such sentences as: 'Oh *her*! She'd do anything to catch a husband . . .' in which the 'she' is Bob or Jim. This routine gender substitution is rapidly dying out, and many gay men under twenty-five fail to practice it or even to understand it. This linguistic game has been attacked for two reasons: first, because it supposedly perpetuates female role-playing among some gay men; and second, because it is regarded in some quarters as hostile to women. Since one man generally calls another 'she' in an (at least mildly) insulting context, the inference is that the underlying attitude must be sexist: to be a woman is to be inferior.

Following the same line, a large segment of the lesbian and gay male population frowns on drag queens, who are seen as mocking women, all the more so because they get themselves up in the most *retardataire* female guises (show girls, prostitutes, sex kittens, Hollywood starlets).

This rejection of transvestites has been harsh and perhaps not well thought out. As long ago as 1970 Kate Millett in *Sexual Politics* saw the drag queen in quite another light – as a useful subversive

> as she minces along the street in the Village, the storm of outrage an insouciant queen in drag may call down is due to the fact that she is both masculine and feminine at once – or male, but feminine. She has made gender identity more than frighteningly easy to lose, she has questioned its reality at a time when it has attained the status of a moral absolute and a social imperative. She has defied it and actually suggested its negation. She has dared obloquy, and in doing so has challenged

more than the taboo on homosexuality, she has uncovered what the source of this contempt implies – the fact that sex role is sex rank.

Anyone familiar with drag knows that it is an art of impersonation, not an act of deception, still less of ridicule. The drag queen performing in a night club, for instance, is often careful to reveal his true masculinity (deep voice, flat chest, short hair) at some point in his performance; such a revelation underscores the achievements of artifice. Since, in addition, most gay transvestites are from the working class and many are either black or Puerto Rican, discrimination against them may be both snobbish and racist. The greatest irony is that the Stonewall Resistance itself and many other gay 'street actions' were led by transvestites.

As to why drag queens have singled out prostitutes and show girls to imitate, the explanation may be at least partially historical. In Jonathan Katz's *Gay American History*, one discovers a clue. Testimony given to the New York police in 1899 has this to say of male prostitutes: 'These men that conduct themselves there – well, they act effeminately; most of them are painted and powdered; they are called Princess this and Lady So and So and the Duchess of Marlboro, and get up and sing as women, and dance; ape the female character; call each other sisters and take people out for immoral purposes.'

Obviously, then, many of the early drag queens actually were prostitutes. Others may have found that the world of the theater and prostitution was the only one where overt homosexuals were welcome. Or perhaps the assertive make-believe of such women, purveyors of sex and fantasy, seemed naturally related to the forbidden pleasures of gay men. Or perhaps the assault on convention staged by prostitutes and performers appealed to gay men because it was a gaudy if ambiguous expression of anger. In any event, this legacy can still be faintly heard in gay speech today, though less and less often ('Don't be such a cunt', 'Look, bitch, don't cross me', 'Go, girl, shake that money-maker', and in a vagueness about proper names and the substitution of the generic *darling* or *Mary*). Much more hardy is a small but essential vocabulary derived from prostitute's slang, including: *trick* (a casual sex partner as a noun, to have quickie sex as a verb); *box* (the crotch); *trade* (one-sided sex); *number* (a sex partner); *john* (a paying customer); *to hustle* (to sell sex); *to score* or *to make out* (to find sex) and so on. Few young gays, however, know the origins of these words, and certain locutions borrowed from prostitutes have been modified in order to obscure their mercenary connotations. For instance, few homosexuals still say, 'I'd like to turn that trick.' Instead, they say, 'I'd like to trick with him.' That homosexual slang should be patterned after the slang of prostitutes suggests that in the past the only homosexual men who dared talk about their sexual tastes and practices either were prostitutes themselves or lived in that milieu. Curiously, that vocabulary has flourished among gay men who have never dreamed of selling sex.

In the past, feminization, at least to a small and symbolic degree, seemed a necessary initiation into gay life; we all thought we have to be a bit *nelly* (effeminate) in order to be truly gay. Today almost the opposite seems to be true. In any crowd it is the homosexual men who are wearing beards, army fatigues, checked lumberjack shirts, work boots and T-shirts and whose bodies are conspicuously built up. Ironically, at a time when many young heterosexual men are exploring their androgyny by living with women in platonic amicability and by stripping away their masculine stoicism and toughness, young gays are busy arraying themselves in these cast-offs and becoming cowboys, truckers, telephone linemen, football players (in appearance and sometimes also in reality).

This masculinization of gay life is now nearly universal. Flamboyance has been traded in for a sober, restrained manner. Voices are lowered, jewelry is shed, cologne is banished and, in the decor of houses, velvet and chandeliers have been exchanged for functional carpets and industrial lights. The campy queen who screams in falsetto, *dishes* (playfully insults) her friends, swishes by in drag is an anachronism; in her place is an updated Paul Bunyan.

Personal advertisements for lovers or sex partners in gay publications call for men who are 'macho', 'butch', 'masculine' or who have a 'straight appearance'. The advertisements insist that 'no femmes need apply'. So extreme is this masculinization that it has been termed 'macho Fascism' by its critics. They point out that the true social mission of liberated homosexuals should be to break down, not reinforce, role-playing stereotypes. Gay men should exemplify the dizzying rewards of living beyond gender. But they have betrayed this promise and ended up by aping the lost banal images of conventionally 'rugged' men – or so the anti-macho line would have it.

In the heady early days of gay liberation, certainly, apologists foresaw the speedy arrival of a unisex paradise in which gay angels, dressed in flowing garments and glorying in shoulder-length, silken hair, would instruct heterosexual men in how to discard their cumbersome masculinity and ascend to the heights of androgyny. Paradoxically, today it is the young straights who wear their hair long and style it daily, who deck themselves out in luxurious fabrics and gold filaments, who cover their bodies in unguents, dive into a padded conversation pit and squirm about in 'group gropes' (in which, mind you, lesbianism may be encouraged for its entertainment value to male spectators but never the swains shall meet). Simultaneously but elsewhere, crew-cut gays garbed in denim and rawhide, are manfully swilling beer at a Country and Western bar and, each alone in the crowd, tapping a scuffed boot to Johnny Cash's latest.

Another objection to the masculinization of gay life is that it has changed a motley crew of eccentrics into a highly conformist army of clones. Whereas gays in the past could be slobs or bohemians or Beau Brummels or esthetes striking 'stained-glass attitudes' or tightly closeted businessmen in gray flannel suits, today this range of possibility has been narrowed to a uniform look and manner that is uninspiredly butch. The flamboyance and seediness and troubling variety of gay life (a variety that once embraced all the outcasts of society, including those who were not gay) have given way to a militant sameness.

This argument, I think, ignores our historical moment. In the past gay men embraced the bias of the oppressor that identified homosexuality with effeminacy, degeneracy, failure. To have discovered that this link is not necessary has released many homosexuals into a forceful assertion of their masculinity, normality, success – an inevitable and perhaps salutary response. Moreover, the conformism of gay life, I suspect, is more on the level of appearance than reality. The butch look is such a successful get-up for cruising that some sort of 'natural selection' in mating has made it prevail over all other costumes. But this look does not preclude the expression of individuality, of tenderness and zaniness, in conversation and private behavior.

Yet another thought occurs to me. In the past many homosexuals despised each other and yearned for even the most fleeting and unsatisfactory sexual (or even social) contact with straight men. Some gays considered sex with other homosexuals pointless and pitiable, a poor second best, and thirsted for the font of all value and authenticity, a 'real' (i.e. straight) man. Today, fortified by gay liberation, homosexuals have become those very men they once envied and admired from afar.

The apotheosis of the adult macho man has meant that the current heart throb in gay pornography – and in actual gay cruising situations – is no longer the lithe youth of nineteen but rather the prepossessing stud of thirty-five. The ephebe with hyacinthine curls has given way to the bald marine drill sergeant, and Donatello's *David* demurs to Bernini's.

The change has affected the language of approbation. In the past one admired a 'boy' who was 'beautiful' or 'pretty' or 'cute'. Now one admires a man who is 'tough' or 'virile' or 'hot'. Perhaps no other word so aptly signals the new gay attitudes as *hot*, whereas *beautiful* in gay parlance characterizes the face first and the body only secondarily, hot describes the whole man, but especially his physique. One may have a lantern jaw or an asymmetrical nose or pockmarked skin and still be hot, whereas the signs of the beautiful face are regular features, smooth skin, suave coloring – and youth. The hot man may even fail to have an attractive body; his appeal may lie instead in his wardrobe, his manner, his style. In this way 'hotness' is roughly equivalent to 'presence' with an accent on the sexy rather than magisterial sense of that word. In addition, hot can, like the Italian *simpatico*, modify everything from people to discos, from cars to clothing. Gay chartered cruises promise a hot vacation and designers strive after a hot look. If an attractive man strolls by, someone will murmur, 'That's hot.' The 'that' in place of 'he' may be an acknowledgment that the person is as much a package as a human being, though more likely the impersonal pronoun is a last echo of the old practice (now virtually abandoned) of referring to a one-time-only sex partner as an 'it' (as in, 'The trick was fine in bed, but I had to throw it out this morning – couldn't get it to shut up.')

Gay male culture, as though in flight from its effeminate past, is more and more gravitating towards the trappings of sado-masochism. The big-city gay man of today no longer clusters with friends around a piano at a bar to sing songs from musicals; now he goes to a leather and Western bar to play pool and swill beer. Gay men belong to motorcycle clubs or engage in anonymous sex in backrooms, those dimly lit penetralia behind the normally sociable bar.

Sado-masochistic sex has introduced new words into the gay vocabulary [as described in the previous essay], and interestingly, gay men, usually so fastidious about staying *au courant*, are willing to utter outmoded hippy words from the drug culture of the 1960s such as *scene*, *trip* and *into* if those words enable periphrases that stand in for the still more ludicrous vocabulary of classical sadism.

I have tried to point out that gay male culture and language have registered a shift in taste away from effeminacy to masculinity and from youth to maturity. But now a larger question might be posed: has the status of – and the need for – a private language itself become less important to homosexuals?

I think it has. In the past homosexuality was regarded with such opprobrium and homosexuals remained so inconspicuous that we faced some difficulty in detecting one another. A familiar game was to introduce into an otherwise normal conversation a single word that might seem innocent enough except to the initiated ('I went to a very lively and gay party last night'.) If that risk was greeted with words from the same vocabulary ('I'm afraid the party I went to was a real drag; everyone acted like royalty,' i.e., 'queens'), a contact was established. Two businessmen could thus identify themselves to one another in the midst of a heterosexual gathering.

But the value of a private language was not merely practical. It also allowed gays to name everything anew, to appropriate experience in terms that made sense only to the few. Sailors became 'sea food', 'chicken' (always singular) were teenage boys and so on – there is a whole book, *The Queen's Vernacular*, that lists these words. Equally amusing and subversive was the pleasure of referring to a revered public leader as 'Miss Eisenhower', or to oneself (as Auden does at the end of an otherwise serious poem) as 'Miss Me'. When gay frustration had no outlet in action, it could find expression only in language. But even in language the impulse had become sour and self-destructive through long suppression; its target was more often other gays than straights or in the fiction that respectable straights were actually outrageous queens. In self-satire lies the reflexive power of thwarted anger. Gay identity, now rehearsed nightly in thronged discos and in a myriad of gay bars, was once much more tenuous. It was an illegitimate existence that took refuge in language, the one system that could swiftly, magically, topple values and convert a golf-playing general into a co-conspirator in a gingham frock and turn a timid waiter into a drag queen for a night – or at least into the Duchess of Marlboro.

Now that homosexuals have no need for indirection, now that their suffering has been eased and their place in society adumbrated if not secured, the suggestion has been made that they will no longer produce great art. There will be no liberated Prousts, the argument goes, an idea demonstrated by pointing to the failure of *Maurice* in contrast to Forster's heterosexual novels. A review of my novel, *Nocturnes for the King of Naples*, claimed that it was not as strong as my earlier, 'straight' *Forgetting Elena* precisely because I no longer needed to resort to the pretense of heterosexuality.

This position strikes me as strange and unexamined. Proust, of course, *did* write at length about homosexual characters – in fact, one of the complaints against his novel is that so many characters implausibly turn out to be homosexual. *Maurice*, I suspect, is a failure not because it is homosexual but because it is a rather exalted, sentimentalized masturbation fantasy. When he wrote *Maurice* Forster had even less knowledge of the homosexual than of the heterosexual world, and he was forced back on his daydreams rather than on his observations from life. It is not for me to judge the merits of my own books, but what strikes me as most 'homosexual' about *Nocturnes* is not the content so much as the technique, one that uses endless dissolves of time and geography, as though the same party were being reassembled over decades and on different continents, something like that 'marvellous party' in the Noël Coward song. Anyone who has experienced the enduring and international links of gay life will recognize how the technique is a formal equivalent to the experience.

Unless one accepts the dreary (and unproved) Freudian notion that art is a product of sublimated neuroses, one would not predict that gay liberation would bring an end to the valuable art made by homosexuals. On the contrary, liberation should free gays from tediously repetitious works that end in madness or suicide, that dwell on the 'etiology' of the characters' homosexuality (shadowy Dad, suffocating Mum, beloved, doomed, effeminate Cousin Bill) and that feature long, static scenes in which Roger gently weeps over Hank's mislaid hiking boot. Now a new range of subject matter has opened up to gays, much of it comic; Feydeau, after all, would have loved gay life, since every character can cheat with every other and the mathematical possibilities of who may be hiding under the bed (if not in the closet) have been raised geometrically. Still more importantly, gay liberation means that not so many talentless souls need to continue lingering about in the sacred precincts (i.e. the gay ghetto) of high culture. Finally they are free to pursue all those other occupations they once feared to enter – electrical engineering, riding the range, plumbing. The association between homosexuals and the arts, I suspect, suited some of us but not most; the great majority of gays are as reassuringly philistine as the bulk of straights.

The Irresponsible Art of Robert Mapplethorpe

Introduction to *Black Males*, the catalogue for an exhibition of Mapplethorpe's photographs at the Galerie Jurka, Amsterdam in 1980.

Blacks have told me that they study whites with far more attention and curiosity than whites study blacks. Many blacks can perform quite detailed parodies of white speech, mannerisms and social attitudes – detailed and seemingly funny; Richard Pryor is alarmingly accurate as a redneck bigot. But whites scarcely see blacks at all. When a white looks at a black, the act is an anxious one.

The frank anthropological curiosity of the past is no longer permissible, at least not in the United States. One black American told me that when he hiked through Scotland a few years ago, little children in villages would run out to surround him, touch him with awe, ask to feel his hair, tease him by asking if his mother had fallen down a chimney or if his father was a dustman.

But, of course, this sort of innocence has long since died in America. To be sure, in the 1920s and 1930s a much more sophisticated but equally benign mode flourished among such whites as Nancy Cunard, Carl Van Vechten and Ronald Firbank in America and Britain – a mode that saw blacks as elegant Art Deco figurines ('The allegro Negro cocktail shaker', as Edith Sitwell said; or, as Firbank wrote: 'All iris in the dusk, a few loosely-loinclothed young men had commenced dancing aloofly among themselves'). This is the exotic and esthetic mode of the Josephine Baker era; some of Robert Mapplethorpe's pictures slyly allude to this period of sinuous lines and gleaming 'African' masks.

Today the considerably less ingenuous ways of looking at blacks across class barriers as inferiors, as thugs, psychotics, killers or rapists – these ways of looking, alas, are all too prevalent, but they scarcely count as *looking* at all. Rather, these are forms of blindness. Prejudice is a visceral not a visual process.

Fear promotes fight or flight; a frightened eye-witness sees nothing but his own preconceptions – he has no eye and witnesses not a thing. Certainly racism is something that cannot be photographed. The camera, by its very specificity, its rendering of the actual moment, cannot accommodate a thought too abstract to be seen, a bogus thought that is always defeated and erased by the particular.

When Robert Mapplethorpe looks at black men, he sees them in two of the too few modes of regard available to a white American today: he sees them either esthetically or erotically. Esthetically, Mapplethorpe turns his subjects into antique bronzes. When he photographs the wonderfully articulated back of a man sitting on a pedestal, or when he shows us a white-haired young man in *profil perdu* staring off into a stylized distance, or when he anatomizes the abstract shapes of body parts – a head from which the face has been cropped, or an open, rising hand beside a leg, or the great lyre of muscled legs and buttocks – in these pictures Mapplethorpe looks at the black male body as a thing of beauty. One aspect of that beauty is its very eroticism ('All iris in the dusk'), an allure one can no longer dare mention but that the eye can't help but see.

Political prohibitions may silence all discussions of black hair, luster, anatomy, but the camera can and must see these attributes. In these 'esthetic' pictures, bodies and body parts are rendered 'purely', i.e. in their least functional, least personally expressive, least psychological way. These shapes have been isolated and abstracted in order to tranquilize anxiety; we lapse into serene silence after we have 'looked and looked our infant sight away' (a phrase from Elizabeth Bishop that reminds us that 'infant' means 'speechless').

But the moment a face and eyes are introduced into a photograph, the esthetic strategy no longer obtains. The black man is looking at you. The look may be an assault, an invitation, an inquiry, an appraisal or a mere acknowledgment, but whatever the expression may be it is not a neutral or distanced artistic fact but rather a social event (a rupture). Nothing could persuade us to consider any of these faces as a still life or as a structure of hues, lines and planes. All faces speak to us, tell us stories, and black faces challenge or reproach us . . . Or so we might say, anxiously seeking words to describe these expressions or more likely to describe our own response (everyone is quite certain what these faces mean and everyone has a different interpretation: 'This one's very arrogant, isn't he?' 'Not at all, terribly vulnerable I would have thought.') But it is precisely this idle curiosity, this fatuous speculation about blacks that has come to seem so offensive, so unappetizing, impossible.

Sexual attraction, however, is inarguable (or 'incorrigible' as British philosophers say). Who feels comfortable telling someone he *may* not lust after someone else? To say he may not is only one step away from saying he *does* not – which is nonsense. Whoever feels desire feels it and is the best – the only! – judge of the matter. The religious may prohibit the *expression* of some forms of desire, but even they do not presume to say that desire does not exist or is evil in itself. The camera records what exists.

There are those liberationists, of course, who would say that whenever a white desires a black, some sort of 'racism' is occurring, just as supposedly whenever someone older longs for someone younger he must be guilty of 'agism'. But such assertions, fine and ringing as they may sound as parade-ground rhetoric, never stand up to the individual case. Because sexual desire, finally, is a form of love – of wanting to possess, explore, probe, taste, invade and inhabit an alien body if only for a moment. Not love in the sense of sustained social responsibility but love as passion, as appetite, as irrepressible yearning. Oddly enough, passion, like art, is always irresponsible, useless, an end in itself, regulated by its own impulses and nothing else. Just as a vast and expensive establishment (a museum or an academy or a Lincoln or Kennedy Center) may be built to house an art, but the size and expense are no guarantee that the art will actually *live* in these houses, in the same way all the legal and social rules of marriage, of commitment and responsibility, cannot vouchsafe the life of passion. Art and passion live, thrive and die regardless of public utility and convenience; art and passion are the two supremely irresponsible modes of experience. No wonder that they are the only two innocent and honest modes left by which the races can look at each other. And no wonder that they are the modes of regard chosen by Robert Mapplethorpe, who has always, thank the gods, been shockingly irresponsible in his work

– irresponsible towards the *idées reçus* of society but tremblingly responsive to the images flickering across the retina of his perverse and generous imagination.

A Sensual Man with a Spiritual Quest: Christopher Isherwood

Review of Isherwood's *My Guru and His Disciple*, New York *Times Book Review*, 1 June 1980: White was currently working on *A Boy's Own Story*.

In *Ramakrishna and His Disciples*, a biography of the nineteenth-century Indian saint, Christopher Isherwood distinguishes between two religious approaches: discrimination and devotion. Discrimination eschews the loving worship of deities and concentrates instead on a more disciplined meditation on the unity that underlies experience. Devotion, by contrast, is more relaxed, more human, more homespun; as Isherwood puts it, 'Devotion comes more naturally to the great majority of mankind ... For most of us it is the easier and safer path, because discrimination demands a most powerful will and strict austerity, and its occupational risk is pride.'

My Guru and His Disciple is a contemporary work of devotional literature, but not in the dry, hagiographic sense. Rather, it is a sweetly modest and honest portrait of Isherwood's spiritual instructor, Swami Prabhavananda, the Hindu priest who guided Isherwood for some thirty years. The book is also about the often amusing and sometimes painful counterpoint between worldliness and holiness in Isherwood's own life. Sexual sprees, all-night drinking bouts, a fast car ride with Greta Garbo, script-writing conferences at MGM, intellectual sparring sessions with Bertolt Brecht alternated with nights of fasting at the Vedanta Center, a six-month period of celibacy and sobriety and the pious drudgery of translating (in collaboration with the Swami) the *Bhagavad-Gita*. Seldom has a single man been endowed with such strong drives toward both sensuality and spiritually, abandon and discipline; out of the passionate dialectic between these drives, *My Guru and His Disciple* has been written.

This is a book uniquely devoid of pretension, either literary or personal – as though Isherwood at seventy-five has finally achieved the dissolution of egotism that is the goal of Vedanta, the philosophy of the ancient Sanskrit texts, the Vedas. Isherwood's method is to punctuate the long meditative passages written today with terse diary entries from his youth. This bifocal approach allows him to see both close and far and to spot his own vanity or good-heartedness through either the lens of the past or the present. Like all truly honest people, he is as ready to praise as to blame himself.

What emerges is a record of a religious adventure that would have delighted Kierkegaard, for Isherwood rejects conventional piety – all the humdrum apparatus of worship – in favor of a direct, even jaunty appreciation of how preposterous, certainly precarious, spirituality can be today. No other writer I'm aware of has so accurately rendered what it would be like to sit down one day on the floor to meditate – to be a clever, upper-class Englishman, a socialist and a skeptic, a handsome party boy, a celebrated novelist who sits down and begins to meditate for the very first time. A few of us, I suppose, have had highly colored fantasies of abandoning our lives and entering a Zen or Trappist monastery, but our daydreams seldom get beyond the dramatic renunciation scene and the frozen *tableau vivant* of the praying monk or nun on the rice mat or prie-dieu. What Isherwood has detailed in precise stages are his four decades of actually trying to put this dream into action.

In 1939 Isherwood emigrated from England and settled in Los Angeles, where he worked as a film writer and continued to turn out novels (those he discusses in this memoir are *Down There on a Visit* and *A Meeting by the River*). Los Angeles during the war years, of course, was the artistic and intellectual capital of the world thanks to such expatriates as Mann, Stravinsky, Schoenberg, Brecht and Adorno. Through two of his brilliant fellow expatriates, Aldous Huxley and Gerald Heard, Isherwood became acquainted with Swami Prabhavananda, a priest who had been sent by his monastery in India to Los Angeles as a missionary. At first their relationship was tentative, but over the years it became a true father–son bond. The quality of his guru's love – undemanding and never varying – was what became most useful to Isherwood. As he writes:

I personally am a devotee first and a Vedantist second. I flatter myself that I can discriminate – bowing down to the Eternal which is sometimes manifest to me in Swami, yet feeling perfectly at ease with him, most of the time, on an ordinary human basis. My religion is almost entirely what I glimpse of Swami's spiritual experience.

Isherwood's devotion to his teacher, however, never obscures his vision of the Swami's faults and foibles – his chain-smoking, his occasional laxness about monastic discipline, his fiery Indian nationalism and his moments of preening over his famous disciples. But even these shortcomings sometimes seem to be glimpses of the playful, childlike, even irresponsible nature of divinity – the boy Krishna sporting in the river with his maidens.

At times I found this book too enamored of its own plain style; although a seeker after wisdom may free himself of the senses, the writer mustn't. As Sartre once said, 'In the eyes of God, Who cuts through appearances and goes beyond them, there is no novel, no art, for art thrives on appearances.' Similarly, I sometimes longed for Isherwood even in this work of non-fiction to describe his characters and settings more fully. On another level, I wanted Isherwood to relate his religion to his politics. He has certainly been active throughout his life in various progressive movements from socialism to pacifism and gay liberation, but I kept wondering how he reconciled such activities with his otherworldly beliefs. India itself, with its sanctity and its suffering, seems a very symbol of this contradiction.

Nevertheless, I am grateful to this book for its candor and sincerity. In these pages Isherwood has re-invented the spirit of devotion for the modern reader. If I had to propose a candidate for canonization, Isherwood – wry, self-conscious, scrupulously honest – would get my vote.

The Politics of Gender: Michel Foucault

Review of Foucault's *Herculine Barbin*, translated by Richard McDougall, *Nation*, 7 June 1980.

One of the complaints lesbians sometimes make about the patriarchy is that it doesn't take sex between women seriously, as though intimacies into which a phallus doesn't raise its ugly head aren't real or important enough to be noticed. *Herculine Barbin* is a curious historical document that lends unexpected credence to this complaint. As the subtitle tells us, the book is 'The Recently Discovered Memoirs of a Nineteenth-Century Hermaphrodite', and it recounts in often lachrymose detail the story of how an orphaned child raised in convent schools and employed as a teacher in an exclusive girls' academy learns she is not a female (as she had always considered herself), but a male, who must live the rest of her life out as a man. So long as Herculine was considered to be female, her ardent erotic attentions toward other women were accepted as the forgivable excesses of a girl. But once she was discovered to be a hermaphrodite and was reclassified officially as a man, his sexuality was taken seriously enough to be rejected.

This volume consists of four parts: an introduction by Michel Foucault, the author of *Madness and Civilization* and *The History of Sexuality*; a dossier of documents of the period that relate to the case (including medical reports about the hermaphrodite's body); the memoir (which is incomplete, since the recollections of the hermaphrodite's last years are missing); and the text of a late nineteenth-century story, *A Scandal at the Convent*, a licentious tale written by Oscar Panizza that is loosely based on the memoirs, though the author uses the hermaphrodite's revealed identity as a way of capping a story of lesbian titillation.

In his introduction, Foucault argues that the civil and legal status of hermaphrodites has changed over the centuries, a development that reflects more general attitudes toward gender. In the Middle Ages and the Renaissance, Foucault asserts, hermaphrodites were free to choose in early adulthood which sex they wanted to join. 'The only imperative was that they should not change it again but keep the sex they had been declared until the end of their lives, under pain of being labeled sodomites. Changes of option, not the anatomical mixture of the sexes, were what gave rise to most of the condemnations of hermaphrodites.'

With the rise of administrative control in modern nations, however, the indeterminate individual was no longer free to choose his or her gender. 'Henceforth, everybody was to have one and only one sex,' as Foucault writes. 'Everybody was to have his or her primary, profound, determined and determining sexual identity; as for the elements of the other sex that might appear, they could only be accidental, superficial, or even quite illusory.'

In the modern world, gender is strictly assigned and the sexual conduct associated with each sex by convention has been raised to the level of an imperative of nature. As a result, sexual irregularities – the 'passive' man, the 'virile' woman, the lesbian or the homosexual – are perceived as chimeras, errors, false identities that run contrary to natural law. And such chimeras are not mere eccentricities, mere white lies, but deep deceptions, because gender is now regarded as the deepest truth about the individual, the *fons et origo* of individuality. As Foucault observes, 'It is at the junction of these two ideas – that we must not deceive ourselves concerning our sex, and that our sex harbors what is most true in ourselves – that psychoanalysis has rooted its cultural vigor.'

From a socialist perspective one might find it significant that this insistence on nature, on human nature, appeared simultaneously with the triumph of the bourgeoisie. As so many thinkers, from Engels to Adorno, Gramsci to Barthes, have argued, capitalism attempts to obscure its rather recent historical origins and to justify its arbitrary social arrangements by appealing to nature ('You may think our system is cruel, but after all it simply reflects human nature; things have always been this way.') Since nature by definition is unitary and unvarying, thanks to it the bourgeoisie is able to universalize and eternalize its own behavior. Sexuality, as presumably the most basic, animal and irrational aspect of our psychology, becomes the very center of the bourgeois notion of the static natural self. As Foucault has pointed out, Victorian prudishness (and the Victorian urge to classify sexual 'disorders') paradoxically served to deploy a consciousness of sexuality into every corner of experience. Whereas art, customs, the economy and language are all visibly evolving, the cornerstone of society – human nature, i.e. human sexuality – must appear to be immutable. Since so much emphasis is suddenly placed on sexuality (and, by extension, on gender), the system cannot sustain ambiguities. Herculine Barbin cannot be permitted to occupy a shadowy zone between the sexes; she or he must have a 'true' sex, an essential gender that holds true despite misleading surface clues. Herculine must be a 'pseudohermaphrodite'.

The medical reports of the period leave us with no doubt that Herculine (or Alexina, to use the real name behind the pseudonym) was in fact a genuine hermaphrodite: a penis (or clitoris) two inches long when flaccid that was not perforated with an opening and that was partially sheathed in a fold of skin; a vagina two and a half inches deep into which male seminal ducts drained, no womb and no menstruation; a female urethra, and two testicles (one undescended). The secondary sexual characteristics were mostly masculine: flat chest; abundant pubic hair; a few beard hairs; and narrow hips. The voice, however, was that of a woman. One might hazard a guess that after puberty Herculine gradually shifted toward a more masculine appearance since his body development was being shaped by testosterone secreted by the testes (no ovaries were discovered during the autopsy, though two vulvovaginal glands were detected).

In spite of this perfectly clear evidence of mixed gender, the two examining doctors insisted that Herculine's 'true' sex was male. One of them wrote:

Is Alexina a woman? She has a vulva, labia majora, and a feminine urethra . . . She has a vagina. True, it is very short, very narrow, but after all, what is it if not a vagina? . . . Yes, but Alexina has never menstruated . . . Her tastes, her inclinations, draw her toward women. At night she has voluptuous sensations that are followed by a discharge of sperm; her linen is stained and starched with it. Finally, to sum up the matter, ovoid bodies and spermatic cords are found by touch in a divided scrotum. These are the real proofs of sex. We can now conclude and say: Alexina is a man, hermaphroditic, no doubt, but with an obvious predominance of masculine sexual characteristics.

Inclinations, voluptuous sensations and testes – these make a man even out of a creature with a vagina. How fascinating that this definition leans much more on behavior than on anatomy.

The memoir itself tells a simple, moving story, presented in a style that ironically seems 'feminine' for that period: appeals to the reader for mercy and understanding; a liberal use of exclamation marks; and heavy doses of sentiment that alternate with moralizing.

Alexina's youth was 'passed in the delicious calm of religious houses'. At age seven she was admitted as a charity student into a convent school for rich girls: 'Thus between them and myself there was a natural line of demarcation that the future alone was able to break.' In this passage the 'natural line' is that of wealth, not gender. She repeatedly tells us she was unusually intelligent though clumsy in handicrafts – prophetic signs she has planted to warn us of her latent if not yet manifest masculinity.

When she was fifteen, Alexina became a lady's maid, 'although I did not possess *all the qualifications* for my position...' (italics mine). Throughout her narrative, Alexina does two things: (1) she falls in love with the wealthy girls and women she is placed among; and (2) she professes the most orthodox religious and political views. When her sex is reclassified, she asks anxiously, 'Didn't this abrupt change, which was going to reveal me in such an unexpected way, offend all the laws of conventional behavior?' Amorousness and conventionality balance each other neatly and blend together in the figure of the beloved, a girl who is always both obliging and virginal, receptive and angelic.

The crisis came when Alexina confessed her unusual bodily conformation to a 'wise' bishop, who in turn sent her to his doctor. Once the 'error' was discovered, the doctor in a panic rectified Alexina's civil status and changed his gender in the public records. One day Alexina appeared at church dressed as a man. The scandal was so great that he was no longer permitted to teach at a girls' school; he was torn away from the young women whose bed he had shared so happily for many months. He was sent to Paris to seek his fortune, where he obtained a job as a railroad clerk. Alexina laments his fate as he looks back upon his first visit to the bishop: 'I possessed happiness, true felicity, and with gaiety of heart I was going to sacrifice all that – for what? For an *idea* . . .' (italics mine). By the time he was thirty Alexina was so in despair that he committed suicide.

His despair was fueled by the very rejections he received from women in Paris. As a woman living a cloistered life with other women, Alexina was quite successful in making amorous conquests. She was bright, upright, strong-minded, sympathetic – a perfect companion. As a woman among women, her sexual relationships with them were free precisely because they occurred outside economics; there was no question of an economic transaction. But as a man, he was a poorly paid clerk with no prospects; a major part of the 'idea' of being a man is the ability to provide a comfortable income to one's dependents. In *Down and Out in Paris and London*, George Orwell recalls how women who had flirted with him when he was prosperous literally didn't *see* him when he became poor.

Curiously, Alexina found one of the chief impediments to be the years he'd lived as a woman:

> I, who am called a man, have been granted the intimate, deep understanding of all the aptitudes, all the secrets, of a woman's character. I can read her heart like an open book. I could count every beat of it. In a word, I have the secret of her strength and the measure of her weakness, and so I would make a detestable husband for that reason. I also feel that all my joys would be poisoned in marriage and that I would cruelly abuse, perhaps, the immense advantage that would be mine, an advantage that would turn against me.

Remarkably, plumbing the secrets of a new-found world of men in Paris did not impress Alexina. Perhaps he found no secrets. But the secrets of women he is privy to – what are they? Could they be the hidden resentments, the feigned pleasures, the hypocrisies, fake compliments, simulated piques, pouts and ecstasies that wives, forced into economic submission, have had to resort to in order to achieve some of their own wishes and to defend a modicum of freedom? Alexina was always in love with women, but in becoming a man he entered a new relationship with them. There is a George Eliot story called 'The Lifted Veil' in which someone penetrates the membrane sealing off the future and comes back into the present, despairing. Alexina penetrated the barrier between the sexes and died with his awful knowledge of their shared humiliations, their mutual bondage. Tiresias had to be blind to survive.

Sweating Mirrors: Truman Capote

This version of 'Sweating Mirrors' combines the interview published in *After Dark*, 1980, with a review of *The Capote Reader* in the *Times Literary Supplement*, 13 May 1988.

It was 99 degrees in New York, not a breeze stirring, the air yellow and poisonous. Strangers on street corners actually stopped each other to comment on the weather as though it were the first rumblings of an earthquake. That's how menacing the hot smog seemed – not a torpid ambience but an active agent. Cycling through my brain on a loop were the words 'What a despairing day'.

I was looking forward to the frigid embrace of Truman Capote's apartment in the United Nations Plaza, but when I stepped off the elevator he was standing barefoot in the hallway with a torn pink palmetto fan in hand and a drenched white T-shirt, and he told me that his air conditioner was on the blink. He was thin-lipped and cheerless and so faint that his voice was nearly inaudible as he led me into a small sun room that looked out on the steaming East River and the UN Secretariat, which today looped up more like a static tornado than a building. The huge windows of the sun room were sealed shut, and the only air came from tiny vents ajar below them.

We sat at opposite ends of a large Victorian couch ('My grandmother's,' he said) and looked at the larger adjoining sitting room and its mirrored wall; even the mirror was fogged and perspiring.

I congratulated Capote on his new *Music for Chameleons*, his first book in seven years. It contains a sort of pendant to *In Cold Blood* called 'Handcarved Coffins', a short story, 'Mojave', and, best of all, effervescent non-fiction portraits of Marilyn Monroe and of a char ('A Day's Work'). In both of these portraits he himself appears as a fully fleshed character – gossipy, elfin, compassionate, doomed. In the introduction to the book he explains that he'd sought a way to employ all his technical skills at once. One might add that the most dazzling 'technique' is the stunning personal candor, one that sheds the same mordant brilliance that Nabokov achieved in a quite different way, by contrasting passionate tenderness toward the beloved with patrician contempt for everyone else.

When I read 'A Day's Work' in Andy Warhol's *Interview*, it was so good I called up a dozen friends to tell them about it. In this small masterpiece of journalism, Capote follows his maid, Mary Sanchez, as she goes from one cleaning job to another. The lives of the clients can be deciphered instantly from their apartments: the divorced executive's pigsty piled high with bottles of vodka; the tidy quarters of a young woman with a position in publishing whom Mary, against her Catholic principles but in accordance with the dictates of her heart, had helped during the woman's recovery from an abortion ('from having a baby murdered', as Mary puts it); and finally the overstuffed apartment of Mr and Mrs Berkowitz, where Capote and Mary, high on grass and gorged on sweets, dance around the living room until they are discovered by the irate master and mistress of the house.

Truman Capote's entire *œuvre* is a shrewd staging of a fairly simple-minded morality play, in which children and loving but sexless eccentrics represent good, and adults represent evil. In his universe, Marilyn Monroe and Holly Golightly are good because they are children (the portrait of Monroe is even called 'A Beautiful Child'). The writer Jane Bowles is admirable because she is 'the eternal urchin, appealing as the most appealing of nonadults'. As children, his heroes and heroines are dispossessed. When Dolly, Catherine and Collin leave home to live in a tree in *The Grass Harp*, the sympathetic Judge Charlie Cool declares, 'It may be that there is no place for any of us. Except we know there is, somewhere; and if we found it, but lived there only a moment, we could count ourselves blessed.'

I should add right away that such a formulation of experience (the innocence of childhood and nature, the corruption of maturity and civilization) strikes me as no more impoverished than most of the schemes that animate literature, although it does contain little room for development or refinement. The refinement was to come in the style and in the larger strategies Capote wielded, not in his ways of conceiving character or destiny. Consequently, he is regarded in Europe, especially in France, as a major American author (although his last name is the French word for *condom*), whereas in the United States his frequent acerbic performances on television talk-shows, the great ball he hosted in New York in the 1960s, his quarrels with his rich and powerful friends, his later arrest for drunken driving, all gave him a mass celebrity and rendered him more a 'personality' than an artist. Capote once described his own writing as 'simple and clear as a country creek'. Transparent and beguiling it certainly is, with the magnificently dour exception of *In Cold Blood*, a black agate set among the other diamonds.

'In my other journalism, like *In Cold Blood*,' Capote told me, 'I kept myself scrupulously out of the picture, but in *Music for Chameleons* I've made myself visible for the first time. I realized that in most reportage, including my own, the writer is telling only half of the story. What was *really* said is missing.' The personal, even confessional note of this book certainly gives it a new electricity. Capote also comes across as a charmer, a character as winning as he is honest, as impertinent as he is down-home.

'How did Mary Sanchez react to "A Day's Work"?' I asked.

Capote threw back his head and gave his startling, mirthless laugh. 'She loved it. I read it to her out loud, because I wanted to make sure it didn't lose her any jobs, get her into trouble . . .'

A wave of anxiety suddenly overcame Capote. He stood, paced around. His hand was trembling. He excused himself and left the room. When he re-emerged in a few minutes he seemed calmer, more focused, and he came trailing a question: 'Do you ever read your own books? *I* do. Every year I re-read *In Cold Blood*. I don't mean to. I just pick it up and quickly become engrossed. I don't remember any of it – it's as though someone else wrote it. It's *enthralling*.' Loud, barking laugh.

Capote's works are as elegant and calculated as those of Prosper Merimée. Like Capote, Merimée travelled widely, worked at his best in miniature forms, despised the avant-garde, cultivated the powerful (Merimée was a friend to the Empress Eugénie, just as Capote was a companion to Empress Jackie and Princess Lee), loved a good yarn, took an anthropological interest in the violent lives of the poor (*Carmen*, *In Cold Blood*) and, though highly intelligent, wrote not for intellectuals but for that now-vanished creature, the invention of humanists and bourgeois liberals, the Common Reader.

Both Merimée and Capote justly prided themselves on being stylists, not in the Proustian sense (elaborating syntax, rhetoric and metaphor in order to assimilate the most disparate elements into a single sentence), but in the older sense in which 'style' meant fashioning the neatest, freshest, most natural classical prose in their respective traditions. Capote is a stylist who never intimidates his reader and whose poetic effects are purely local, never threatening the narrative progression. One lovely phrase follows another. Travel is a state of 'alert slumber'. Before dawn 'drooping stars drift at the bedroom window fat as owls'. A nighttime view of Tangier is 'like a birthday cake blazing in a darkened room'. One can imagine this purist cutting down Proust's usual three adjectives to the single limpid one, with a predictable loss of chiaroscuro and gain in brightness and resolution.

He told me that he thought the story closest to perfection in *Music for Chameleons* was 'Then It All Came Down', which records a visit he paid to Robert Beausoleil in prison, the mystery man in the Charles Manson cult. 'It's as linear as a fish bone,' Capote said, drawing the spine in the air with his fan. 'It *moves*, it has narrative energy and drive.' To illustrate, he snapped his fingers and sketched a little dance on the rug with his bare feet. 'No one understands anything about style, about what I'm trying to do. Now the story "Dazzle" in *Music for Chameleons* – it's taken me forty years to learn how to write that way, to make it simple. Most writers start simple, then they become more and more complex. *Then* they have to unlearn everything they've acquired. Simplicity and swiftness: that's what I value.

'Of course, the most *subtle* story, the real *subtlety* – ' he lingered on the word as though he had invented it, or as though it were some foreign expression I might not have caught – 'the most *subtle* story is "Music for Chameleons". Even sophisticated readers don't understand it. They think it's about a visit with a woman; they think it's a *travel* piece about Martinique.' Spasm of laughter that stopped on a dime. 'But it's actually a meditation on murder, about how our passions flog us.' He took off his glasses and stared at me with two perfectly clear blue eyes, the pupils tiny as gnats in the poisonous yellow light.

I asked him how he'd ever remembered the conversation he had had with Marilyn Monroe in 1955 after a funeral – one of the most touching and charming pieces in *Music for Chameleons*. 'Well, Marilyn was a *great* friend. I loved her a lot. And *never* have I read anything that has anything to do with that girl at all except the *basic* – ' his voice died away and his face sank into a grimace worthy of the Greek mask for tragedy – '. . . unpleasant . . . facts . . .' He suddenly brightened and turned to me; unfortunately the sun was glaring on his gray-tinted granny glasses and I'm staring into two silver dollars. 'But, you see, I keep these extraordinary journals. And I *suddenly* remembered I had written down everything we'd said that day. Other people who knew her tell me I've caught the most perfect likeness. She was my first choice to be in the movie *Breakfast at Tiffany's*. She and Maureen Stapleton even worked up a wonderful scene for an Actors' Studio class; *I* saw it, but Marilyn was too afraid to do it in class. Excuse me.'

Capote left the room. When he regained the couch, he spoke to me in profile. His voice was high and weak and drawling and his pronunciation slack-jawed, mushy, like a child's – or like Baby Snooks's. As he picked up confidence, volume, clarity, he turned the two silver dollars toward me. He shook the fan at me to cool me off. I stared down at his long yellow toenails, which reminded me of those four-inch thumbnails the mandarins grew to prove they were so rich they never had to pick anything up. Incapacitating nails and bound feet: emblems of regal dependence on others.

Capote is an entertainer who is never dull, who appeals to the reader's curiosity without endangering his or her values, who adds to our store of experience without undermining the categories by which we process that plenitude, whose tales of underdogs and heartbreaking failures only reinforce the political status quo.

Capote's fascinating criminals, lovable maiden aunts, precocious kids and wilted gentry, while appearing to upset the order of things, are in fact the exceptions that prove the rule. They may be rebels but Capote's presentation of them is never subversive. Take this description of a New Orleans eccentric:

> My interest in Miss Y. is rather clinical, and I am not, I embarrassedly confess, quite the friend she believes, for one cannot

feel close to Miss Y.: she is too much a fairy tale, someone real
– and improbable. She is like the piano in her parlor – elegant,
but a little out of tune. Her house, old even for N.O., is
guarded by a black broken iron fence; it is a poor neighborhood she lives in, one sprayed with room-for-rent signs,
gasoline stations, jukebox cafés. And yet in the day when her
family first lived here – that, of course, was long ago – there
was in all N.O. no finer place. The house, smothered by slant-
ing trees, has a gray exterior; but inside, the fantasy of Miss
Y.'s heritage is everywhere visible: the tapping of her cane as
she descends birdwing stairs trembles crystal: her face, a heart
of wrinkled silk, reflects fumelike on ceiling-high mirrors: she
lowers herself (notice, as this happens, how carefully she pre-
serves the comfort of her bones) into her father's father's
father's chair, a wickedly severe receptacle with lion-head
handrests.

Here we have the pairs of balanced opposites (elegant and tune-
less, shabby and rich, wraithlike and eternal, comfortable and
severe) that serve to stabilize, even freeze character – which,
moreover, is read through the house and its furnishings.

To interpret the self from its possessions is the great nineteenth-century fictional method (and a bourgeois habit of mind).
Earlier novels described actions, not belongings; later novels dramatized inner conflicts, so often at odds with the milieu. That
Capote found such a tight fit between his characters and their settings reflected his nostalgia for the traditional society of the Old
South. His first novellas – *Other Voices, Other Rooms* and *The
Grass Harp* – take place in that South of small towns and big pretensions, of genteel manners and savage prejudices.

Capote shuffled out of the room again. I, too, stood up, as
though to throw off the heat squatting on me like a nightmare in
a Fuseli painting. Art and fashion books sat in the sort of stylish
piles decorators used to distribute around rooms to give them a
studied 'casual' look. The bookshelf itself contained mostly the
various editions and translations of Capote's own titles. Puppies,
kittens and cobras seemed to be the dominant motifs everywhere.
(Now I'm interpreting Capote from his belongings!) All along

one wall were drawings, paintings and pastels of household pets, but flung across the coffee table were three snakes, one of them huge and reared up to strike. As I strolled about I spotted other puppies, kittens and snakes on desks, woven into pillows, resting on the window-sill – fitting emblems, I suppose, for a man who celebrated domestic love in 'A Christmas Memory' *and* has written the most detailed modern chronicle of murder, *In Cold Blood*. A dozen calla lilies fresh from the florist crowned the coffee table, but the geraniums along the window looked parched, neglected, a bachelor's plants.

When Capote re-emerged a minute later he'd picked up vitality. The photographer, Robert Mapplethorpe, and his assistant arrived, and Capote and I posed for our picture against a Japanese painting of fish. 'The Japanese, of course, didn't paint in oils for the longest time,' Capote explained. 'This one, which was done in the nineteenth century, is one of the first oils. The artists reached the height and then, naturally, committed suicide. All the best Japanese artists commit suicide.'

Mapplethorpe told us to look at each other, at the window, at him and we did so rather stiffly as though we were puppets gloving arthritic hands. The sweat flowed freely over our bodies. Although Capote, as he told all the world, was homosexual, he seemed not even faintly interested in either the handsome Mapplethorpe or in his friend, Marcus Leatherdale, who resembles James Dean. Not the faintest *sexual* interest, that is; he does express his admiration of Mapplethorpe's photographs. Capote let out a sigh and stood: 'I can't take it. I can't be photographed one second more,' and he hurried down the hall for the third time in twenty minutes.

Mapplethorpe and his friend left. I ambled around the living room and stopped to examine two decorative windows placed on the facing wall. The borders were painted with fruits and birds and the inner surface was studded with abstract shades of tinted glass and mirror. 'The Shah of Iran gave those to me,' Capote told me as he returned. 'They're very old and valuable – national treasures. I'm terrified the Ayatollah will send someone to recover them.'

Capote was now doing a sort of fan dance, listlessly waving his palmetto and slowly jogging in place. He dropped his fan and rubbed his stomach in long up and down strokes. 'The pain . . .' he murmured. 'Barbara Walters was here yesterday for *fourteen* hours. Their equipment broke down. But I have to admire her. She never once complained. She's a real professional.'

His tongue flickered over his lips while he complimented me on my own writing, which I was pleased to learn he'd read with such thoroughness. 'I love the piece you wrote on Texas, especially the part where you went to bed with your grandfather.' He gave me a wan smile. 'So *Southern*.' He sighed, excused himself, and ambled off into another room.

The Grass Harp is narrated by Collin, who at one point startles us by claiming he's sixteen years old and in love with Maude, though the reader finds his age and sexual tastes to be as ambiguous as Marcel's in *Within a Budding Grove*. The loving, harmonious family (which neither Proust nor Capote ever actually knew) cannot be abandoned, nor can the homosexual nature of the narrator's desires (Collin's crush on Riley, for instance) be either abandoned or acknowledged; the bizarre compromise is chronological and erotic shiftiness. Symptomatically, Capote in his early fiction becomes so fussed when he must even allude to homosexuality that his silver tongue becomes instantly tarnished. Take this line from 'A Diamond Guitar': 'Except that they did not combine their bodies or think to do so, though such things were not unknown at the farm, they were as lovers.'

Adrienne Rich once remarked that if Elizabeth Bishop had acknowledged her lesbianism she wouldn't have written better poetry but she might have written more of it. Capote was similarly gifted – and similarly blocked. His output and his range, as measured by his own ambitions, remained strangely limited. One could even say he devoted a great deal of creative energy to avoiding honesty. The relationship in 'A Diamond Guitar' is romantic but sexless. *The Grass Harp* casts dangerous longings under the sentimental glow of a fairy-tale atmosphere that, at its worst, turns into pure Disney: 'The wine-colored violin, coddled under her chin, trilled as she tuned it; a brazen butterfly, lighting on the bow, was spiralled away as the bow swept across the strings singing a music that seemed a blizzard of butterflies flying, a sky-rocket of spring sweet to hear in the gnarled fall woods.'

In 'House of Flowers' man–woman passion is presented, but among Firbankian darkies in the never-never land, a Haiti right out of Le Douanier Rousseau. Ottilie leaves Port-au-Prince and the bordello in order to live in a house of flowers with Royal, a beautiful jaguar of a husband. As in Andrew Marvell's 'The Garden', the vegetable world is active and the human inhabitants passive. By the end of 'House of Flowers', Ottilie has been bound by Royal to a tree, where she happily awaits his return from the sugar fields. She has been quite literally returned to nature. The wound of urban experience has at last healed over.

The fairy-tale aspect of Capote's talent is exquisite but a bit remote, since it seldom rehearses real feelings; the world is all too well banished. At the opposite extreme (but no less efficacious in staunching self-revelation) are his non-fiction experiments – his many portraits and travel sketches, his wickedly comic account of the American *Porgy and Bess* tour of the Soviet Union in 1955 (*The Muses Are Heard*) and his 'non-fiction' novel, *In Cold Blood*. In all these writings his own presence is either meticulously eliminated (as in *In Cold Blood*) or scarcely adumbrated.

When he returned I asked him about 'Handcarved Coffins', the 'non-fiction' novella in *Music for Chameleons*. It's the story of a rancher who methodically murders one by one the members of a committee that had diverted the major flow of a river off his property. 'Aren't you worried about libel? I mean, when that rancher reads your story?'

At the mention of the word *libel* the fan stopped. Then it began to waver tentatively. I looked at a row of three pink piggy banks, which I imagined were filled with dimes and silver dollars. As he spoke, the fan beat more and more confidently. 'I changed certain things. I'm protected. Whereas I made everything absolutely accurate in *In Cold Blood*. But in "Handcarved Coffins" I had to touch up the details. Of course there's *no* legal case against the rancher, just supposition. No one believes the rancher is guilty – not even his own cousin, who's the next in line to be murdered. He's in Hong Kong now, and I'm just waiting for his murder.' Capote strolled about and I shadowed him with my notebook like a clerk trailing a good customer through a chic shop. 'I've been following the case since 1972 and I could have made it longer than *In Cold Blood*, but I think it works better this way.'

I mention the dedication of *Music for Chameleons* to Tennessee Williams. 'Wasn't Williams irritated,' I asked, 'by your portrait of him in one of those chapters of *Answered Prayers* that *Esquire* published?' In that chapter, 'Unspoiled Monsters', Williams (or 'Mr Wallace', as he was called in the text) was portrayed as a drunk wreck inhabiting a room at the Plaza. The incoherent Wallace has been cooped up for days with his dog, which had left piles of shit all over the carpet. The narrator, a hustler, has been summoned to the room to amuse the delirious playwright. And to walk the dog. Not a very flattering portrait, all in all.

'Tennessee was *furious*!' Capote announced with the first genuine glee I'd observed. Then turning sober, adult, serious, Capote went on: 'We've had our ups and downs. We've known each other for a thousand years. I think he's a *genius*. The *abuse* he's been subjected to has been *outrageous*. Can you imagine another country that treats its major artists as terribly as America does? Those *creepy* critics torturing Tennessee, when they don't have the right to lick his *feet*. Well, I didn't ask him if I could dedicate my book to him. It's a surprise. He probably doesn't even know yet. America in general is very disrespectful of its artists,' Capote concluded tonelessly, as though this plight were too banal to merit expression.

In the extant chapters of *Answered Prayers*, he depicts some of the jumbled elements of his own life (much as Nabokov does in *Look at the Harlequins!*). The results were so scandalous, the *clefs* rattled so noisily, that Capote lacked the courage to press on. Drink and drugs dimmed his lights. The book's jet-set milieu, however, which he'd first touched on in 'Greek Paragraphs', a minor travel piece, appealed to his temperament. At last he was free from his sexless youths and corrupted adults, his fairy-tale romances and objective reportage.

The rich have the means to realize their whims and the effrontery to avow their desires. Sex, travel, gambling and intrigue are their sports, while their itineraries and adulteries provide them with conversation, just as loyalty to the clan, devotion to fashion and the display of perfect manners constitute their virtues. Above all, jet-setters love a good story. Too bad Capote didn't stay sober long enough to betray his friends more thoroughly.

To find the psychic energy to pursue a long career, it seems to me, a writer must juggle between a vigorous, recording curiosity about the world and how it works and the ongoing process of self-creation. It is the imagination, of course, that negotiates between reality and the ego, between the repetition compulsion and the pleasure principle. If the self is utterly eliminated we end up with journalism: if the ego is shamelessly gratified, we have the *longueurs* of the intimate journal. If both the self and the world are held at bay and the imagination is given free reign, then the result would be pure fantasy or tedious sci-fi. The successful novel cleverly adjudicates among these temptations and somehow combines newspaper story, confession and fairy tale.

Capote's most successful response to these various claims is *Breakfast at Tiffany's*, a sort of rewrite of Isherwood's Berlin stories. Holly Golightly plays Sally Bowles, the impoverished and sexless young Capote stands in for the similarly disabled Herr Issivoo, and in both books the various eccentrics, lovable or menacing, parade past like vaudeville performers doing their exotic 'turns'. Both Sally and Holly are at once wish-fulfilment and object-lesson, real girls and gay boys in drag, as well as innocents playing at adult vice. In both Capote's and Isherwood's tales the results make for very seductive reading.

He excused himself, but when he returned this time he didn't seem livelier but dangerously fatigued. I started to leave. 'I've been very anxious,' he said. 'It's something that's been hanging over me for two and a half years. Partly professional and partly personal. I thought it was over, but it isn't. That's why I'm so nervous. I can't tell you about it – it's a secret. But when you do eventually learn about it, then you'll understand why it's been so hard for me to finish *Answered Prayers*. Everything will come clear then.'

At the door we started talking about the hazards of the writer's career. 'I've had the phones taken out,' Capote confided. 'I get some – ' he raised his eyebrows and trippingly articulated the next words as he bounced up the scale – 'some pret-ty weird-o phone calls.'

He gave me a cheek to peck, a purely routine gesture, as though we were Gabor sisters air-kissing each other for the benefit of photographers. 'Well,' he told me, 'you'll write some wonderful books. I'm sure, but believe me . . .' He took off his glasses and stared at me. 'It's a *horrible* life.'

This is Not a Mammal: A Visit with William Burroughs

Soho News, 18 February 1981.

'Let me demonstrate,' William Burroughs said. He stuffed the dart in one end of the plastic blowgun, stood back six paces and exhaled the dart into a bull's-eye emblazoned with Chinese characters. 'I ordered it through the mail,' he said with dry satisfaction. He put the weapon aside in a graceful gesture. 'You'd be surprised what you can get through the mail. Like this.' He emptied the last bit of sugar from a box, tossed the box in the air and slashed it in half with a strange device I'd never seen before, a flexible metal rod compressed and held magnetically in a case until a flick of the wrist causes the rod to extend with murderous force and speed. 'Here, follow me. I have some literature on it you'll want to consult.'

There's a certain pale brown tinged with pink – a flesh color, really – that Burroughs likes to wear. Tonight his shirt is of that color, but only the collar shows under his argyle sweater and the plain tie and plainer gray jacket. When he sits and talks with you he has the cold immobility of a piece of sculpture. He seems imposing, carved, big. Only when he moves does he suddenly appear frail and birdlike – *discarnate*, to use his word. Very late at night, when he's stayed up past his usual bedtime of nine or ten and smoked a lot of joints and downed a few vodka and Cokes, he can become quite animated. Then he orates a bit and emphasizes each point with a preacher's raised hand or sudden lunge over an imaginary pulpit (his grandfather was in fact a circuit-riding Methodist minister); his movements then can seem perilous, as though he were slowly going out of phase. Right now, however, he is lucid and hospitable, his usual mode. Somewhat detached and formal, the Martian who's learned to be patient and cordial in his dealings with mere earthlings.

He led me into his spare room, rooted around in a filing cabinet through pornography magazines with titles like *Teen Punks* and *Jock Scene* and finally fished out a six-page pamphlet by the inventor of the weapon. In another cabinet I saw stacks and stacks of sci-fi paperbacks. 'Perhaps you'd like to look at my scrapbooks, too?'

I very much wanted to since I was avid for any clues as to what has released the imagination of one of the most puzzling and original writers America has ever produced – to say which means something in a country that has spawned such self-invented uniques as Melville *and* Henry James *and* Ezra Pound *and* Wallace Stevens, beings who emerged out of nowhere and who stand in the strongest possible contrast one to another.

I knew from conversations with other artists how inconsequential the first stimulus behind a work of genius can be. Jasper Johns, for instance, had told me that an outer wall of a Harlem store painted to resemble fieldstones, something he glimpsed from a car window once and could never find again, had provided him with a motif for some of his recent paintings. Similarly, Burroughs is alert to any source of excitement, though he is far more systematic about assembling and exploring his materials. He has kept dream journals, he's experimented with exotic hallucinogens, he's worked at thinking in images without the intrusion of words, he's devised a means of traveling through time in his imagination, as an actor he's impersonated the characters he's writing about and he has invented literary techniques contrived to produce striking and unpredictable juxtapositions.

Starting with *Nova Express*, Burroughs began to rely on the cut-up and fold-in techniques, methods of taking a text by another writer or from a newspaper and rearranging the order of the words and then introducing them into his own text. Subsequently he has played around with the tape recorder, picking up random noises and mixing them with others recorded under other circumstances. Burroughs has never been interested in random nonsense; rather, he has drawn on the aleatory as a way of presenting himself with fresh thoughts and images. He is a supremely *conscious* artist; he is also someone who believes experimental writing must be readable. Since I had just finished reading the highly readable *Cities of the Red Night*, his most ambitious book since *Naked*

Lunch, I was specially curious to know about the pendentives on which he'd floated this vast new pleasure dome.

The novel is certainly obsessed with teenage boys, with beautiful, heartless redheads covered with erotic sores, who hang one another to the point of ejaculation and whose eyes light up as they come or die – a complex network of boys who fade and cross-fade through time and inhabit other boys in other centuries. 'The subtlest assassins among them', Burroughs writes, 'are the Dream Killers or Bangutot Boys. They have the ability to invade the REM sleep of the target, fashion themselves from the victim's erection and grow from his sexual energy until they are solid enough to strangle him.' All these exotic homosexual (and hetero-sexual) couplings are quick, explosive, sometimes lethal but never romantic. As Burroughs once remarked, 'I think that what we call love is a fraud perpetrated by the female sex, and that the point of sexual relations between men is nothing that we could call love, but rather what we might call *recognition*.'

Now before me on a desk I had several large, black volumes into which pictures of naked boys had been pasted. In his sketchy, hard-to-read handwriting Burroughs had scrawled notes to himself over the photographs. 'One of the Kraut kids,' read one note. Another said, 'Possibly for Noah Blake,' a reference to a character in *Cities of the Red Night*, described as '20, a tall red-haired youth with brown eyes, his face dusted with freckles'.

I realized that for Burroughs writing is like mineral refining, many steps to extract from tons of dross an ounce of the precious substance. If so, then these scribbled-over pictures, these sleazoid sci-fi books, these files on weapons and epidemics, these *National Enquirer* stories on cancer and Commies – these were the great slag heaps of his art. So pure is that art that no matter how cruddy or *recherché* the things he assimilates may be (the orgone accumulator, Scientology, Mayan control systems), they are eventually refined and transformed into his own stamped ingots.

We returned to the main room. How appropriate it seems that Burroughs should live in the locker room of a former YMCA, for isn't he the author who celebrates ancient memories of a vanished adolescence? In the new novel someone buys a 'Firsty Pop', which we learn is compounded of 'the hyacinth smell of young hard-ons, a whiff of school toilets, locker rooms and jock straps, rectal mucus and summer feet, chigger lotion and carbolic soap – whiffs you back to your first jackoff and leaves you sitting there on the toilet – if you don't keep flying speed. Never linger over a Firsty.'

Burroughs tours me through the toilet – here are the old urinals, no longer functioning, and here the stalls with their marble walls and 1920s graffiti, a golliwog's head and a strangely bifurcated penis. The main room, which is adjacent, has been cleared of lockers, of course, though metal fittings on the ceiling attest to where they once stood. 'The locker room holds the silence of absent male voices,' Burroughs writes somewhere in the new novel. The floors are painted concrete. There is only one window, and it is small and frosted.

'I can never tell in here whether it's night or day, hot or cold outside,' Burroughs says, giving his thin-lipped smile. 'What's wonderful is the heat here. I have terrific heat. Come here. Feel this wall.'

I put my hand on the hot cement and can even sense the hot water coursing through buried pipes. In describing a friend's apartment in Paris, where he's just paid a visit, Burroughs again praises the abundant heat. Something about this insistence on heat strikes me as reptilian. Someone who's known Burroughs since the 1950s remarked, 'When you meet him you think, "This is not a mammal."' Or was I detecting the deep freeze of the ex-junky? Certainly Burroughs is the poet of decaying cities, of the cold cup of coffee nursed at the automat during the wait for a connection, the sad *froideur* of rented rooms, of 'dead fingers in smoke', of the 'Street of Missing Men', of 'loading sheds in ruins, roofs fallen in', the whole malaise of America that long ago in *Naked Lunch* was dubbed 'the US drag' ('And the US drag closes around us like no other drag in the world').

'This is really the best place I've ever lived in,' Burroughs tells me. 'There are four locked doors between me and the street.' The street is the Bowery with its streams of urine snaking out of doorways across sidewalks, its hobbling bands of beggars, its broken wine bottles, winter fires in metal drums and rag-wrapped feet – but even so, Burroughs's concern for personal security does seem idiosyncratic. He calls his place 'the Bunker' and he does sometimes give the impression of being the mad, beleaguered leader of a defeated Reich. He always carries at least three weapons on his person – a cane, a spray gun of Mace and his steel cobra, say. 'I would feel naked without my weapons,' he tells me. In a recent issue of *Heavy Metal* Burroughs published an article about civilian defense. To be sure, he is sixty-seven years old and dramatically thin but, as he puts it, 'I don't look like a mark,' nor has anyone ever mugged him. Then why this paranoia?

Burroughs defines paranoia as 'having all the facts'. Politically he takes the eschatological view; he recently delivered a talk at a Whole Earth Conference in Aix-en-Provence titled 'The Four Horsemen of the Apocalypse', in which he spoke about such coming attractions as biological warfare and 'ethnic weapons' designed to destroy one race but not the others. With me he discussed the recurrence of an epidemic like smallpox that would produce a 50 to 60 per cent mortality rate within eleven days.

'That would be a real Hollywood spectacular,' he said. When Burroughs the stylistic purist uses such an expression one looks up for the ironic twinkle, the inverted commas crinkling beside the eyes, but his delivery of even the most moth-eaten gangster slang of the 1930s is as impassive and impeccable as Cagney's. We must remember that Burroughs is the man who once announced with a straight face that it's 'time to look beyond this rundown radioactive cop-rotten planet' and who begins one chapter of the new novel with this memorable sentence: 'And here I was with a pop-happy skipper in an old leaky jinxed gallows-propelled space tramp with all the heaviest guns of the planet trained on us...' He is both the dour sower and the grim reaper, with a smile the juice of six lemons might have induced, a great misanthropic humorist in the tradition of Céline and W. C. Fields (Mary McCarthy once called Burroughs a 'soured utopian').

Not that I disagree with his politics. In fact Burroughs is a useful sort of anarchist to have around, someone who despises bureaucratic states on the Right as well as the so-called Left, who has called for the end of the nation and the family and who has written in *The Job*:

The police have a vested interest in criminality. The Narcotics

Dept has a vested interest in addiction. Politicians have a vested interest in nations. Army officers have a vested interest in war. Vested interest, whether operating through private, capital or official agencies, suppresses any discovery, product or way of thought that threatens its area of monopoly. The cold war is used as a pretext by both America and Russia to conceal and monopolize research confining knowledge to official agencies.

Paranoia is having all the facts.

Nor can I disagree with his esthetics. He is against realistic novels, which he dismisses as 'journalism'. He admires Beckett, Genet and Conrad; he was consciously writing in Graham Greene's tone in the opening pages of *Cities in the Red Night* ('Farnsworth, the District Health Officer, was a man so grudging in what he asked of life that every win was a loss'). He is against censorship of any sort. He is for the tradition of the picaresque novel. His fictions draw on pop sources – corny humor, comic strips, science fiction, the movies, newspapers, travel books, vaudeville ('May all your troubles be little ones, as one child molester said to another'). Of the writers in the generation to follow the great moderns (Joyce and Stein), Burroughs was the only one in English to remain constant to their ideal of continuing experimentation. Like them he has practiced the art of *montage* but not in a way that resembles their versions of that technique. Joyce built up a dense palimpsest from overlapping layers of talk (bar-room brogue and neural chatter) and cultural allusions (mythology and a more diffuse philology). Stein, less 'intellectual' and more temperamental, created her surprises on the local level, sometimes treating words as pure, abstract sound.

Burroughs, by contrast, devised the cut-up and fold-in technique with the painter Brion Gysin – a technique, I might add, he has rejected in *Cities* except for three or four short paragraphs. Less formally, less diligently and far more slyly, Burroughs has learned to relate narrative fragments one to another. In *Cities* three separate tales intertwine. One takes place in the present and follows a private eye as he attempts to get to the bottom of a gruesome murder. A second relates a tale (based on fact) of a pirate in the eighteenth century who sought to establish anarchist city states in the New World and thereby overturn the hegemony of Spanish colonialism and Christianity. A third narrative deals with six cities in the Gobi Desert in ancient times. At first Burroughs merely alternates his narratives, just as any Victorian novelist manipulating a plot and one or two sub-plots might have done. But soon Burroughs establishes strange links among the three tales. His characters travel through time, inhabit one another and thereby unify the work. What appeared to be far-flung and disconnected tales merge by virtue of time travel. *Montage* in *Cities* is not a Steinian juxtaposition of words nor a Joycean counterpoint of different levels of discourse but rather a *montage* of narratives. This solution seems to me wonderfully – but need I say obviously? – wonderfully suited to the genius of the novel, which prefers to verbal intricacies, no matter how splendid, such large fictional structures as suspense and mystery.

I asked Burroughs where he had come upon the notion of six cities in the red night. We were in his main room at the large dinner table. A few friends and neighbors had gathered and begun preparations for dinner (such communal meals are a nightly affair). In the background played a tape of Moroccan music recorded by Brion Gysin and Paul Bowles. 'Brion gave me the idea,' Burroughs said. 'He told me to repeat their names before going to sleep if I want the answer to a question to come to me in my dreams. The odd thing is that Brion can't remember where he learned the names – Temaghis, Ba'dan, Yass'Waddah, Waghdas, Naufana and Ghadis.'

Burroughs then took me around to look at the paintings by Gysin he owns ('He's the greatest of living painters,' Burroughs murmurs). 'Now this one I picture as the outskirts of Marrakesh,' he remarks as we stop in front of a canvas that at first glance seems entirely abstract, even calligraphic, and is painted in muted tones. 'The artist shows you the spectral street of your own past associations. For instance, when you cross a street you might half-remember that ten years ago you saw a car just here – well, see the car? The ghostly motorcycle? I try to do something of the same sort.' On to another non-figurative painting, a third and a fourth. In each painting Burroughs finds 'little scenes' of streams and meadows or of the desert that are by no means obvious. I can imagine him consulting these pictures time and again for visions of the red night. 'Now this one – photographs of Mars look just like this one, which Brion painted before those photos were transmitted. You know they found stones on Mars that had the letters B and G on them?' They did? Burroughs and Gysin?

Burroughs tells me that he is already well into the sequel of *Cities*, a book that takes off from the section in *Cities*, 'I Can Take the Hut Set Anywhere', about the Wild West in the last century. He plans yet another book after that – 'And that should about wrap it up.'

'Are you a Buddhist?' I ask, knowing how much time he's spent at the Tibetan Buddhist Naropa Institute in Boulder and recognizing the extent to which the transmigration of souls in *Cities* is a concept derived from Buddhist theology. Burroughs scoffs at the question. 'Buddhist? No. But I do believe in reincarnation, though like everything else it isn't something that comes easy. You've got to *work* at it.' Burroughs pounds the table. 'I also' – long draw on the joints, eyes become slits – 'I also think it's – I *know* it's possible to live in a' – perfect steely diction – 'a *discarnate* state. The one I prefer.'

My mind flashes on his famous remark: 'It is necessary to travel, it is not necessary to live.'

James Schuyler

Published in the journal *Little Caesar*, 1981.

Here's an admission: I sometimes wonder why people bother with poetry. After all, the best novelists (Proust and Nabokov, to name just two) offer the reader page after page of language as precise, as unpredictable and as ravishing as the language of any poet – and the novelists simultaneously make their local delights serve larger structural or thematic ambitions (the generation of suspense, the play of ideas, the revelation of character, the depiction of society, the weaving of a thick, tragic sense of duration). In great fiction the language is not only satisfying in itself, but it also fulfils larger purposes of design: it is sculptural, in the round, gestural. Fiction makes a world, dense and social. Or, to change the figure, in poetry words are like notes from a flute, the tracery of a tune, whereas in fiction words are like notes of a symphony orchestra – compositional, the integers of a giant calculus.

I say all this, at the risk of seeming philistine, in order to demonstrate that I'm no friend to poetry unless it is indispensable to me, unless it does something no prose could emulate. James Schuyler is one of the half dozen poets I need.

He is the most musical poet we have. There are others who write more sounding lines (John Ashbery) or whose diction is more resourceful and eloquent (James Merrill) or whose tone is more secure, even Olympian (Elizabeth Bishop), but no other contemporary American rivals Schuyler's music, by which I mean phrasing, breathing and the placement of patterns of sound through the stanza.

I realize 'music' is a vague word, but it is something that can be suggested by examples of predecessors – Dante in Italian, Ronsard and Verlaine in French, Heine in German and, in English, Waller, Herbert and Pound. We hear music when Herbert writes:

Grief melts away
Like snow in May,
As if there were no such cold things

Or when Pound writes:

Who has brought the army with drums and kettle-drums?
    Barbarous kings.

Or we hear it in Schuyler:

The light lies layered in the leaves.
Trees, and trees, more trees.
A cloud boy brings the evening paper:
The Evening Sun. It sets.

Such music, clearly, would not be heard as distinctly if written out as prose. Poetry sets up expectations of rhyme and rhythm that someone with an ear can fulfil or frustrate or satisfy in start-ling ways. Lineation casts peculiar emphasis on words in strong positions (the first or last in the line) and can delay or reverse meanings or confer on them an oddly formal feeling (the feeling of a compass rose), as when Schuyler ends the poem 'Spring' in this way:

It
isn't winter and it isn't spring
yes it is the sun
sets where it should and
the east
glows
rose. No.
Willow.

The minimal punctuation throughout also promotes a delicious ambiguity slow to resolve itself.

Music in poetry is often a matter of the strange, vivid repetition of a word, as when Schuyler opens 'Evening Wind' in this way:

October hangs in grape
bunch lights among the leaves
of a giant tree whose leaves
are not unlike grape leaves:
a plane tree, or a sycamore?

Sometimes the music resonates off a single sound (the short *a*
in the following example) drawn down through the lines:

Brassy tarnished leaves of lilacs
holding on half-heartedly and long
after most turned and fell to make
a scatter rug, warmly, brightly brown
Odd, that the tattered heart-shapes, etc.

A musical poet is never committed to filling out a set, umptydum
measure in predictable beats; he keeps the reader off balance by
dilating a phrase here and contracting the next – the literary
equivalent to rubato, as when Schuyler writes:

. . . you are moonrise
you are pain,
you're mine
and I am yours, streaming
out silk ties, they bind.

Deceptively simple as these words may at first appear, mine is an
off-rhyme with pain and bind (a sort of aural compromise between them) and it is also a contradiction of the initial consonant
and final vowel of moonrise. The first three lines cited here
contract only in order to release the relaxed fourth line, with its
feminine ending that tumbles over by way of enjambment into
the monosyllabic last line with its very strong caesura, queer
grammar and grave closing words.

None of these distinctions would be seen or heard in prose; it
is the formal power of poetry to enforce upon us such observations.

These technical refinements, of course, can interest us only if
we are simultaneously drawn toward the poet's temperament and

intelligence. The very titles of Schuyler's books – *Freely Espousing*, *The Crystal Lithium*, *Hymn to Life* and *The Morning of the Poem* – suggest his calm, concentrated acceptance of the world around him, especially the world of nature and the round of daily life. Characteristically, Schuyler writes in 'Hymn to Life', the long title poem in the book of the same name:

> Time brings us into bloom and we wait, busy, but wait
> For the unforced flow of words and intercourse and sleep and
>   dreams
> In which the past seems to portend a future which is just
>   more
> Daily life . . .

The fierce hum of tranquility, the ability to 'wait, busy,' informs all his activities, whether making art or making beds or supper – activities that are equated to one another. For Schuyler, the goal of his art is not to create 'masterpieces', those willed monuments to one's own singularity that awe us by excluding us. As he writes in 'Hymn to Life':

> Coasting among the masterpieces, of what use are they? *Angel*
>   *with*
> *Hurdy-Gurdy* or this young man in dun clothes who holds
>   his hat so that
> The red lining shows and glows

The question is not rhetorical, and later the poet answers:

> This twilight Degas a woman sits and holds a fan, it's
> The just rightness that counts. And how have you come to
>   know just
> Rightness when you see it and what is the deep stirring that it
> Brings? Art is as mysterious as nature, as life, of which it is
> A flower.

Schuyler's is the Taoist view of art, then, the belief that the true poet is part of nature, immersed in it, even coincident with it. For this reason Schuyler strenuously rejects the notion of art as emblematic ('All things are real / no one a symbol'). He is an esthete of the particular, a gourmet of the real, and it is this out-look (along with some of his jokey, gee-whizzy mannerisms) that he shares with other members of the New York School, notably Frank O'Hara. The approach to nature, however, is all his own. Whereas the landscape for most Westerners has usually been treated as a heightening of human moods or as a coded message from God to humanity, for Schuyler nature is the great breath that blows through the world, the rhythm to which one must tune one's own breathing.

No wonder he has written short poems that seem more genuinely, more intrinsically Chinese than all other American imitations. One poem in *The Morning of the Poem* begins:

The grass shakes.
Smoke streaks, no,
cloud strokes.
The dogs are fed.
Their licenses
clank on pottery.

Landscape, pets, dishes are all equivalent elements in the con-figuration of the moment; the human ('smoke streaks') and the natural ('cloud strokes') are separated only by a vowel. The ether-eal and the mundane are re-ordered into a sort of democracy of sensation. This profound grasp of the Taoist feeling for nature eschews the chinoiserie of poetic props (huts on cliffs, boats in the mist) in favor of whatever is at hand (the very next lines in this poem are: 'The phone rings. / And is answered'). Schuyler avoids the neutral or pretentiously gnomic utterances of most big-nosed, red-haired 'sages' in their borrowed mandarin robes. As Schuyler writes:

'Your poems',
a clunkhead said, 'have grown
more open.' I don't want to be open,
merely to say, to see and say, things
as they are.

This is a poetry of transparent renderings of the world, not of self-expression nor of appropriation. Although Schuyler admires Whitman, he does not share Whitman's urge to assimilate everything and everyone to himself. Schuyler is worn away by the world until he lapses into it; Whitman seizes the world and gathers it into himself. Schuyler forgets; Whitman remembers. Schuyler becomes the world, whereas Whitman remade the world in his own image.

Whatever can be achieved in the short 'Chinese' poem written in American, Schuyler has certainly done. He brings together – without apparent system but with perfect pitch for detail – those observations and events that will strike a single (if unusual) chord in the reader's mind. The best of the short poems are in the present tense and give a relaxed account of the setting in which they are being written:

> I sit scribbling in a little
> notebook at a garden table,
> too hot in a heavy shirt
> in the mid-October sun
> into which the Korean mums
> all face.

Slowly, like a chill off the night, a sense of evanescence floats up from the casual debris:

>   . . . what
> is there I have not forgot?
> Or one day will forget:
> this garden, the breeze
> in stillness, even
> the words, Korean mums.

Satisfying as these short poems are, they're still very chancy, depending as they do on whether the reader's private associations correspond to those of the poet. It strikes me that a poet today can amplify a short poem either by linking it to other poems he has written earlier or by situating it within a large public tradition. Schuyler is too much a phenomenologist, too antagonistic to symbols, to build up his own private set of invariable associations (in the way Yeats or Stevens, say, were able to do). The second possibility – to lock into a widely shared set of conventions – Schuyler also rejects; he is too much of the New York School to invoke mythological names, for instance, or religious symbols. But it occurs to me that the short lyrics of earlier centuries were usually written and read within such a set of conventions – the tradition of the Petrarchan sonnet, for instance, or the tradition of the Chinese lyric. The Chinese epithet, 'mountain man', for example, immediately reminded the initiated reader of that long line of poets who left the world, became hermits and took as their sobriquet some variation on these words. Not a single word in the Chinese poetic vocabulary is innocent, no more so than the phrase, 'A lady asked me', or the epithet 'gray-eyed' is innocent in the West. The poet working within such a tradition can assume on the part of the reader years of studying just such poems (Milton's 'Lycidas', therefore, uses a vocabulary that extends back to Theocritus); the slightest formal or thematic variation will figure as an abrupt rupture, a striking act of originality. For the modern poet, however, the lack of a living poetic tradition (not to mention the lack of shared social and ethical values) introduces too much indeterminacy into the system. The contemporary short poem, I'm suggesting, can no longer manipulate in a few words long chains of bound associations, can no longer count on fixed interpretations. More importantly, Schuyler would reject such a tradition even if it existed, since he seeks only unmediated truth ('the truth, the absolute / Of feeling, of knowing what you know, that is the poem . . .').

For this reason, I suspect, Schuyler has moved in recent years toward the long poem, a form in which he has the room necessary for fixing and accumulating all those responses he needs – for teaching his reader how to read this kind of poem. The growing predilection for the long poem Schuyler shares with many of his contemporaries, including Ashbery, Merrill and Howard Moss, and for the same or similar reasons.

Certainly Schuyler's long poems are his most convincing performances. His first attempt at the form, 'The Crystal Lithium', is a vertiginous Baroque phantasmagoria in which elements metamorphose into one another, the senses fuse through synesthesia, the seasons commingle, levels of diction rise and fall, scraps of unassigned dialogue invade the narrative, and even the syntax becomes snarled and collapses under the conflations of multiple antecedents and tenses. In this poem, for instance, eyes taste, wintry exhalations invoke a broiling day, the sky shows blue as flames, electricity is damp and lightning sluggish and we learn

> that's temperature enough and the temperature
> Drops to rise to snowability of a softness even in its scent of
> roses
> Made of untinted butter frosting . . .

Those roses, yellow as butter and extruded from the decorative pastry bag, materialize where he had expected real roses – surprise enough in a winter snow!

This poem is still under the influence of the French surrealists ('In its parking lot vast as the kiss to which is made the most complete surrender . . .') and lacks the conversational ease, the unassumingness, of the later poems. One feels as though Schuyler, intimidated by the form itself, were displaying his ingenuity and contriving a machine to dazzle the dubious reader.

By the time Schuyler writes 'Hymn to Life', he has found a broad calm; the architectonics of 'The Crystal Lithium' have been replaced by the natural sport of the ruminating mind. Oddly enough, he is still building his lines around pairs of opposites and the tension between contrasting places, moods and seasons, but now this is a strategy less apparent, more motivated, better disguised as an account of thoughts flickering from the country to Washington, DC, from life to death, from memory to forgetting. Tenses still shift, but now in imitation of a psychological process – the dropping of a scrim that distances an event and makes it shimmer. Bits of dialogue still crop up to lighten the page, but now they are assigned to plausible speakers. Transitions now seamless, lead us from one universe of discourse into another quite different, then back to the first:

> And now the yardwork is over (it is never over), today's
> Stint anyway. Odd jobs, that stretch ahead, wide and mindless
> as

Pennsylvania Avenue or the bridge to Arlington, crossed and
   recrossed
And there the Lincoln Memorial crumbles. It looks so solid:
   it won't
Last. The impermanence of permanence, is that all there is?
   To look
And see the plane tree, its crooked branches brush the
   ground, rear
In its age, older than any of us, destined, if all goes well with
   it,
To outlast us all . . .

In just a few words we are drawn on silent coasters from yard-
work in the garden to Washington to thoughts of evanescence
and back again to the garden. Sometimes the transitions are
abrupt – Pound's 'radical juxtaposition without copula'. Often
the shift relies on taking the literal sense of figurative words
('wide and mindless'). At other times a comparison is developed
to the point of acquiring a life of its own:

Day, suddenly sunny and warming up for more, I would like
   to stroke
                           you
As one strokes a cat and feels the ridgy skull beneath
   the fur and
                            tickles
It behind its ears. The cat twists its head . . .

In the long poems Schuyler achieves an intimate grasp of the
healing rhythm of nature, a rhythm that can encompass wild
shifts of scale, place and level of meaning and seriousness. Rocked
to this rhythm, we become passive ('The day lives us', or days
'stamp us' and we think of 'these years of living and being lived').
Experience is no longer a matter of the will nor of the assembling
of knowledge but of surrender and forgetting ('Have you learned
nothing in all these / Years? "Take it as it comes." Sit still and
listen: each so alone' and elsewhere: 'Each day forgetting: / What
is there so striking to remember?'). We hollow ourselves out so
much that the breath of life, the Chinese *ch'i*, can whistle through
us.

Such a reality is more powerful when experienced than cited, and the triumph of 'Hymn to Life' and 'The Morning of the Poem' is the recreation of the novelistic sense of duration, of life being lived through slow accretion, change, repetition. The lyric poem may be able to *invoke* duration, a philosophical poem can *meditate* upon it, but only the long poem by Schuyler can *re-create* the experience of time living through us. Because he has submitted to the simplications of suffering and endurance and forgetting, this poet has emerged as our version of the Chinese sage, a chortling demented patriarch on a stormy cliff tearing the Sutras into tatters as he casts aside conventional knowledge for the wisdom of the bone.

Thoughts on White on Black on White*: Coleman Dowell*

This essay combines an article in the *Journal of Contemporary Fiction*, 1982, and a 1992 introduction to the posthumously published novel *A Star-Bright Lie*. (Dowell committed suicide in 1985, aged sixty, despondent about his future as a writer.)

1

White on Black on White is a transcript of America's unconscious, a translation out of the mumbling or shrieking patois of our collective nightmare about race. Structuralists have suggested that the unconscious conforms to paradigms, that it arranges experience into patterns, which in social terms would be male and female or old and young – and in the United States would also be Northern and Southern, straight and gay, rich and poor and, most particularly, Black and white.

(Even orthography reveals a reality by disguising it: Blacks, having no power, receive the empty honor of a capital letter whereas whites, owning and controlling everything, hide behind their lower-case façade, the not-so-charming discretion of the bourgeoisie.)

2

Good fiction, like all art, is useless, a realm so fully bodied forth that it cannot stand for another but must lead a separate existence, which parallels but never transects life. A named meaning is a dead meaning. Or so we say. Of course there's something too airtight about such a definition, too philosophically absolute to be adequate to an art that is at least half journalism and whose very medium is language, the code that has no function save symbolic. Coleman Dowell's book reminds us of the difficulties of any definition of the novel that's not piebald, for *White on Black on White* shows that good fiction must be half fairy tale and half newspaper story.

The newspaper half deals with Blacks in prison, the early civil rights movement, the Vietnam War, the echoes of race riots. The fairy-tale aspect of the book is frightening and progressive, in the sense that an illness progresses. The narrator, a white man of independent means, a writer, conceives a hungry physical passion for a Black man, Calvin, who's heterosexual, an ex-convict, now a hit man. The two spend a few weeks together off-season in a rented summer house on Long Island. Calvin alternately hates and befriends his companion and alternately cherishes the white man's old, blind dog Xan and threatens to beat in her brains. The white man alternately lusts after Calvin (his lust is never fully satisfied) and despises him. The mood is tense and grows tenser. Two men and a feeble dog circulate through Partridge House, a luxurious glass structure waiting to be broken. Both of them drink constantly and too much (Calvin gin, the narrator brandy) – and since we see things only through the narrator's eyes, the ellipses and distortions of his drunkenness occlude our vision.

This opening section is subtitled 'The Snake's House', a name explained by this passage:

> But I lay awake remembering a time on the farm when I had found a snake and a toad in primitive congress. The toad was partially swallowed, the snake too far gone in passion to try to move. I took a stick and forced their separation. The snake, hissing, went into its hole but the toad sat there covered with narcotic slime. With the stick I prodded it until it moved, but too sluggish for me and I picked it up in disgust and put it far from the hole. Sometime later, propelled by certainty, I went back to the spot and found the toad, recognizable by the undried slime, once again beside the snake's house waiting.

In the same way the narrator is terrified by the menacing Calvin and cannot leave him.

The section begins ritualistically with each of the two men shaving the other's head, as though imposing baldness on themselves were a way of achieving fraternity and defeating the distinctions of race. But race is everywhere around them. Serena Westlake, a post-deb neighbor, can't help drooling over Calvin and uttering jive talk to suggest how soulful she can be. The coolly scathing narrator paraphrases in satiric indirect discourse Serena's childhood recollections: 'She thought that her constant

state of feeling pissed off was because in those days she was surrounded by funky exciting Blacks with whom she was forbidden
to get down.'

The language of this single sentence comically captures the two
cultures, oscillating between the white 'constant state' and the
Black 'pissed off' or, more rapidly, the dialect 'funky' and the
bland 'exciting', the Victorian 'forbidden' and the contemporary
'get down'.

In this honky resort, Calvin begins to wonder 'where the niggers live'. As the two men drive through the attractive and only
slightly faded 'slums' of Greenport, they see another interracial
couple, a Black policeman and a red-haired white woman. (These
two people later turn out to be principal characters, Ivy and
Cayce.) Calvin reacts by muttering obscenely about the 'sickness'
of whites obsessed by Blacks, while the white narrator thinks
about queers fixated on 'normal' men. In each case the forbidden
heightens desire – *doubles* the narrator's desire for Calvin, who is
both Black and heterosexual.

3

I met Dowell in the mid-1970s after I wrote a mostly favorable
review of his gnarled post-modernist novel *Island People*. I call it
'post-modernist' because it plays tricks with point of view, the
level of reality and fantasy and the wavering reliability of its
various narrators, some of whom were masks of yet other narrators. Reviewing it cold on a two-week deadline was a bit like
working out the literary references after a first reading of the
newly published *Ulysses*, but I now see that all those shifting perspectives beautifully deployed Dowell's own inner contradictions.
When in fiction he could impersonate many different people, he
could dramatize and slow down his alarmingly busy thoughts. In
real life, however, when he was obliged to express everything he
felt with just one voice and in conversational order, he would
become tongue-tied. He spoke in a deep baritone, which alternated vanishing sentences, embarrassed stuttering and startling
cries of disapproval, outrage or just frustration, as though if he
could only shout his tongue might come unfettered. He would
stutter and finish sentences with a helpless hand gesture or almost
inaudible suspension points . . .

Similarly in his novel *A Star-Bright Lie*, when he is forced to

speak in his own right (that most baffling of all acts of ventriloquism), he has a hard time keeping pace with and notating his
fragmented thoughts and shifting moods. I've seldom known
someone so victimized by his own complexities. Some of them
come through on the page – his paranoia, his bedevilled fascination with glamor, his lyric response to nature, his nostalgia for
a Kentucky he fled and then re-invented, his bawdiness, his
Gothic sense of humor, his touchy pride, his passion for Black
men, his alienation from both heterosexual society and the two
forms of gay life he'd known – first, the martini-swilling campi-
ness of the 1950s, and then the triumphant machismo of the 1970s.

Early on in *White on Black on White* the narrator grumbles
about Calvin playing the radio constantly and too loud. Almost
parenthetically he recalls, 'When I had visited Jamaica, Long
Island, the Sunday before we left for the country, to meet Calvin's wife and daughters, I had heard to my amazement that
WBLS was kept on full blast and that they somehow were able to
talk around it . . .' This passage reveals in its casual everyday manner that Calvin is not just an instrument of the narrator's
passionate ambitions, not just a stray integer in the calculus of
race but . . . a family man, that is, someone whom others have
liens on. And this connectedness, this social integration, is characteristic of Dowell's entire novel, which presents a reality of
imperious great-aunts and sassy nieces, of tenderly devoted
brothers and sisters, of stern, disapproving mothers and their out-
law children, of neighbors, childhood friends, couples of long
standing. These are the people who have a social existence, who
are implicated into the thick stuff of humanity. They cannot be
pornographic actors. Lust demands isolation (Partridge House) to
work out its diabolic (because single-minded) designs; life
avenges itself on lust by creeping back in, washing in like junk
floating up on the tide and stranded high on the beach. The tension between the lonely exaltations of the pornographic
imagination and the banal to-and-froing of daily life provides a
subliminal dialectic to Dowell's novel. It's a book about people
looking at each other: a public novel.

4

Proust in one of his more despairing (that is, accurate) remarks
argues that friendship is useless in the development of the artist.

Only love (that is, jealousy) can train the writer's mind, since constant suspicious questioning of every motive, every movement, and the conversion of each innocent story into a guilty alibi – only this restless and piercing scrutiny can teach the writer to observe. Despite his own sovereign intelligence, Proust is deeply anti-intellectual. He neither trusts nor respects the fruits of disinterested inquiry. He honors only that wisdom we acquire out of necessity, to survive, since only a lover's anguish can compel the tireless vigilance required of the great artist.

It is, then, no accident that Dowell's narrator is both a writer and a jealous lover, those two terms we now see are synonymous. Calvin's fascination with Serena, hers with him, their attempts to be alone with each other, Calvin's sudden disappearances, his mysterious long-distance phone calls and unexplained trips into New York – these are the tin soldiers the narrator draws into the ranks of his ruminations. Jealousy and fear, the two emotions that find meaning everywhere, that marshal stray events into phalanxes of intention – these are the drillmasters that organize the first section of Dowell's book.

In the second section Calvin has vanished and the narrator is back in New York, remembering him, longing for him, repeatedly 'telling' (as one tells beads) the things Calvin has left behind – toiletries, a bit of marijuana. In this section, which might be called *Calvin disparu*, the beloved is 'spiritualized', in that his essence is freed from the opaque materiality of his presence; his spirit, liberated from resistant actuality, can now be more fully assimilated to the thoughts of the lover, that is, the beloved can now become the perfect hero of the lover's story (one recalls Mallarmé's line, 'M'introduire dans ton histoire en héros'). Absence permits readerly art to triumph over the illegibility of reality. The narrator constructs a tantalizing tale of Calvin's life on the basis of a single document: a telephone bill. While Calvin had been living with the narrator, he had secretly placed many long-distance calls. Now, by calling those numbers as listed on the bill, the narrator is able to speak to Calvin's young, illegitimate daughter, to an unidentified (and very surprised) woman, to Calvin's severe, disapproving mother, to an angry, cast-off Black gay man, then to a man who is still enamored ('You lookin' for him too? I sure wish he was here now, that sweet devil'), finally to a desperate Spanish woman.

5

When I knew Coleman he seldom emerged at night from his big apartment that looked down on Central Park. There he'd receive people for dinner and give them simply the best food I've ever eaten – better than the food at Lucas Carton or L'Archestrate or L'Ami Louis or the Tour d'Argent and far more varied, for one night it would be *rifstofel*, another a *feojada*, a third Kentucky fried chicken made according to the elaborate dehydration and deep-lard frying method of yesteryear. Once guilty about the effort and expense he went to in his preparations, I told him I'd come to dinner only if he would serve hamburgers and potato chips. He observed the letter but not the spirit of the law: he *baked* the buns, *purée'd* the ketchup, *sliced* and *fried* the potato chips, and probably *pickled* the cucumbers.

Evenings at Coleman's were long, even very long. They started with cocktails and his handmade patés, moved on to the narrow refectory table and its anything but monastic fare, and ended up with Coleman playing his own tunes on the piano. He sang in a deep baritone. Like many composers he splashed notes around more than he played them, but his voice and piano were adequate to rendering ballads as sweet and conventional as his novels were frightening, disabused and permanently new.

After the concert Coleman's lover would walk the dog one more time and go off to bed. It was then, after midnight, that Cole could turn into an ugly drunk, bellow his rage and denounce everyone, or become coolly sure of his visitor's iniquity. In my case he'd remember the few mild qualifications with which I'd seasoned that *New York Times* review I'd written before I'd known him ('You don't like my books, do you?' was a typical question), and he'd bring up each criticism, memorized and believed, whereas the praise had been dismissed and forgotten. The next day he'd ring up to apologize for anything he might have said that was *beastly* (he punched the one word *forte* in his otherwise *piano* sentence).

Whereas in Gothic novels the dire events usually happen at night, in Cole's life they happened during the day when his lover was away and his next dinner was still only in the *macerating* stage. It was during the day he'd descend from his sparkling eyrie

and stage raids on the homeless or unemployed black male population wasting time in Central Park. Or he'd concoct love letters
to prisoners who'd advertised for penpals. Or he'd pamper and
scold his dachshund Tammy, or after her death, his terrier Daisy.

Once I read that the greatest love of Emily Brontë's life was
her dog, which she beat then nursed back to health and on which
she apparently based the character of Heathcliff. Cole's feelings
for Tammy reached similar dimensions. He bought her a fur coat
and diamond jewelry, but thrashed her when he thought she was
dying on him. He once told me most of his female characters –
the human ones – were derived from his tormented feelings over
her. It was by day that Coleman conducted his violent affairs,
canine and human. When evening fell, his lover would come
home from work, the apartment would be impeccable, the guests
would be arriving and Cole would be unsealing the venison
daube that had been bubbling for twenty-four hours.

6

In *White on Black on White* the narrator's obsession with Calvin
leads him to what we can only call racist thoughts. Were these
thoughts expressed as the author's own or presented in an essay
as the truth, we'd slam the book shut. But, given the dramatic
context, these thoughts (for instance, 'The "cool" stance is essential to febrile Blacks, otherwise they would incinerate
themselves') are valuable data about how race is perceived. The
narrator, after all, is a middle-aged upper-class Southerner who
freely if not always clearly recognizes how charged, how corrupt,
how over-determined his feelings toward Blacks are. We might
even be tempted to say that his sexual obsession with Blacks is
nothing more than a condensation of those feelings, desire itself
nothing but a simplification of emotional contradictions. The narrator's companion Berthold, a German immigrant, has none of
these responses to Blacks – no anger, no guilt, no lust, little
curiosity. For Berthold, Blacks are not the Other, simply others,
unimportant people beyond his social horizon. The politics of
White on Black on White are irreproachable because they are
documentary not propagandistic, because the book renders rather
than recommends.

7

Obsessives search out companions in anguish, just as the characters in any extended piece of narrative must be matched with doubles – the psychological principle of life paralleled by the constructive principle of fiction. The narrator finds Ivy, a chance acquaintance at a dinner party but one recognized quickly enough as a fellow traveler, if a 'traveler' is a peripatetic salesman of small goods. The goods in this case are brief encounters with Blacks. The narrator is a Southern gay man drawn to a single Black, whereas Ivy is a Yankee heterosexual woman attracted to a whole host of Blacks. She first discovers this taste while participating down South in the early civil rights movement. One of the unwritten chapters of our history has been the true account of the sexual aspect of the civil rights movement; Dowell writes it now. He moves from the rhetoric of fraternity to the plain talk of sexual curiosity, the false ideal of universal humanity giving way to the spontaneous recognition of deep (and exciting) racial differences.

Nabokov once remarked that Freud got it all wrong. It's not that we come to love a woman's lustrous hair and smooth skin because we associate them with sexual pleasure. Rather the reverse: we want to sleep with a woman because we hope, somehow, to possess that hair and skin we've admired since childhood. The so-called secondary sexual characteristics are the primary focus of desire. Childhood is an absence because children cannot possess what they love; adulthood is a frustration because sexual possession is only momentary. What Ivy demonstrates is that the most extreme form of adult love focuses on what is purely Opposite, what is Black to one's white; for her, making love to countless Black men condenses more and more moments of possession until, charged with these bursts of energy, she performs a miracle: she becomes Black herself and kills a white man. In this scared frenzy (insanity) she becomes Black *by* killing a white, so steeped in hatred and love are the two races, so totally do they depend on one another for both their identity and annihilation.

This destructive reciprocity is usually buried. Who knows how much psychic energy American whites invest in *not* thinking about Blacks? One could say that the function of Black films, Black books and Black television programs is to ensure an apartheid of information, to isolate ghettos of consciousness. What Dowell has done is to integrate the races by focusing on those hedonistic freebooters who long for the forbidden.

When Ivy holds back information about her sexual encounters, the narrator hungers for the details: 'It was not just prurience; I insist upon that. It was also a hunger for knowledge, knowledge of the way Blacks see us whites, see us differently as women and men, as we see them, male and female, differently, an historical weight pressing upon and distorting that vision as variously as cataracts and belladonna.' A few pages later, Ivy visits a Black prisoner with whom she has been exchanging pornographic letters: 'Ivy felt sure that he had specialized in white women and could imagine that such a man wore a special sign for the seekers or the initiate, just as women like herself must be marked in some way for Black men to see.'

Coleman had no normal or offhand way of treating people. He had only one mode – passionate. He wrote his nervous, muscular prose with passion. He gave dinners with haggard devotion more appropriate to serving a jealous god than fickle friends. He loved his dogs and prisoners with passion and hated literary enemies (most of whom were unaware of his existence) with poisonous rapture. His 'marriage' was also a consuming, year-round, long-run passion play. Since his lover was Jewish, Coleman chose to be anti-Semitic. Since his lover lived for Cole alone, Cole took up with one demon lover after another. In an era when middle-class people aspire to well-regulated relationships that are sexually, morally, and emotionally expressive to just the right degree, Cole and his lover ignored such utopian precepts and contented themselves with a love worthy of Wagner and King Ludwig or Bacchus and Pentheus, namely, one as destructive as it was deep and transfiguring.

8

Anthropologists tell us that interstitial figures (hermaphrodites, for instance, or incestuous siblings) must be encoded by the tribe as either sacred or profane, as gods or pariahs. In a mythology there can be no gaps, no remainder; everything must be accounted for, even the extraordinary. Crustaceans are taboo because they are fish but with legs: interstitial. Ivy, as a white who loves Blacks, is an outcast deity. Her descent into degradation (physical dirtiness, poverty, drug addiction, venereal disease, prostitution) is a simultaneous ascent toward the ideal of fraternity she had once glibly espoused as a young civil rights worker. She earns with suffering and ecstasy what she had once so lightly professed. The saint must endure, not merely proclaim. Although all the action is clearly etched, there clings to these pages an atmosphere of fantasy or, better, mythology, as though a photo-realist had added unnatural, excruciating highlights to his literal renderings.

Ivy goes into Central Park and fraternizes with bums under a culvert all night long, passing the bottle and drunkenly submitting to sex some twenty times with five men. In her mind they are all 'mer-creatures in the grotto'. This episode of transformation, a regression in the service of enchantment, this intimacy-in-anonymity and life-in-death – this rich, disturbing metamorphosis bears all the marks of myth, not as recollected in tranquility but as improvised through experience. If the cave is the womb of rebirth, it is one fertilized by five nocturnal fathers – as though to compensate for the one father Ivy never had. (Freudians call Blacks 'nocturnal fathers', tracing racism back to the primal scene.)

This mythic crisis releases a flood of other archetypal scenes and situations. The second half of the book takes place on an island that is poor, rural, and completely isolated from the mainstream of American culture. In this redneck outpost Ivy grew up in brother–sister intimacy with Cayce Scott, a Black boy (one of the few Blacks on the entire island). Now Ivy returns, worn, ill, disgraced, a tramp, to discover Cayce, who's become quite literally the 'soul of respectability', i.e. a policeman. These two characters point the way to a Black and white utopia for if the title *White on Black on White* sometimes means the superimposition of Black and white bodies in sexual congress, here it simply locates a vision of sexless love, the only pure (that is, static) emotion in Dowell's fiction:

She lay her head for a moment backward onto his white-linen clad shoulder, and one of his big hands with the preposterously phallic thumb lay upon her black-silk clad shoulder, and it was marvelously intricate, like looking inside them: white on black on white on black on white. But, lovers? And again there was the brother–sister impression, devoid of eroticism, full of some old sweetness like mutual memories of a playroom on a rainy day, and innocence of everything.

So suggestive is this vision that the narrator is inspired to write Cayce's memoirs for him. The impersonation of a Black by a white (a Black, moreover, who is meditating on whites) provides the final meaning of the title, the *on* signifying 'about' as we would say *On Love*.

9

The final section of the novel, as I hinted, is a set of Chinese boxes. The containing box is the narrator, by nature a voyeur, by trade a writer. The document we're reading is his work, so long as we accept Dowell's fiction (Dowell's own consciousness, of course, is the shadowy outermost envelope, once we break through the fictive membrane). The next box in is Cayce, whose memoirs we're presumably reading, though in fact these pages are the narrator's attempt to become Cayce (an instance not only of a white becoming Black but also of a gay becoming straight). Cayce finally interrupts this narrative to give corrections and to provide his own version. Cayce, in turn, is trying to understand Ivy and to reconstruct her lost time in Harlem. Such a reconstruction, of course, we the readers have already read, based on the narrator's talks with Ivy (but with his distortions – and hers, since she displays both candor and canniness).

All of these boxes might seem to constitute only one more dull post-modernist 'experiment'. But since Dowell's entire effort is to define each race in terms of the other, to uncover their interdependence, to build up a palimpsest of white on black on white, the Chinese-box construction is syntactically parallel to the semantic content – indeed the form *is* the message, which turns out (surprisingly in such an angry book) to be optimistic: the races *can* understand each other, approximately if not perfectly. As Cayce himself says of the narrator's impersonation, 'There's not a lot I'd object to or change . . .' Indeed, so convincing is Dowell's own performance that we keep wondering whether *he* is Black or white. Our speculations about him amount to a secret dialectic that accompanies any reading. I suggest the publisher might preserve this dimension by suppressing the author's portrait. To be sure, in this masterful novel we already have his true likeness, the portrait of his perverse and wise sensibility.

The Emperor of Signs: Roland Barthes

Review of *The Empire of Signs*, translated by Richard Howard, and *A Barthes Reader*, edited by Susan Sontag, *New York Times Book Review*, 12 September 1982.

Since his death in 1980, Roland Barthes's reputation as a writer has continued to grow. To be sure, he has long been recognized as a thinker: he was, after all, the father of semiology, the study of signs (which the linguist Ferdinand de Saussure, who first proposed such a study, defined as 'a science that studies the life of signs within society'). What is new about Barthes's posthumous reputation is the view of him as a writer whose books of criticism and personal musings must be admired as serious and beautiful works of the imagination.

In her introductory essay to *A Barthes Reader*, and indeed in her very selection of readings from Barthes, Susan Sontag makes a convincing argument for Barthes the Great Writer. She sees him as the true heir to André Gide, since both are 'supple, multiple' as well as 'elusive, willing to be minor'. She contrasts Barthes with Jean-Paul Sartre, whose 'evangelical contempt for literature' and insistence on the writer's need to be politically committed led him finally to make a mockery of his own great talents. In this context Barthes emerges as the Artful Dodger of French letters – canny, evasive, a modest, subtle commentator, someone who disowned or revised his earlier work with each new book.

This complexity was something Gérard Genette observed in a 1964 essay on Barthes. 'The Obverse of Signs' (included in his volume of essays called *Figures of Literary Discourse*). Genette remarked that in the ten years after the publication of his first book, *Writing Degree Zero*, Barthes passed from a Sartrean blend of existentialism and Marxism, through the 'substantial psychoanalysis' of Gaston Bachelard, on to a feisty, sarcastic Marxist 'critique of everyday life' in *Mythologies*. From there Barthes proceeded to a more Freudian form of psychoanalysis in his study of Racine. Genette concluded that the 'texts collected in *Critical Essays* (1964) seem to express a decisive conversion to structuralism, understood in its strictest form, and the abandonment of any responsibility towards meaning; literature and social life are now merely languages, which should be studied as pure formal systems, not for their content, but for their structure'.

Barthes underwent at least one more conversion, evident in three of his last books: *Roland Barthes, A Lover's Discourse* and *Camera Lucida*. With this trilogy Barthes in a sense returned to his Gidean beginnings (his first published essay was on Gide), to the self-examining if not confessing Gide of the *Journals*, for Barthes in these books (to use the lovely phrase of his expert translator, Richard Howard) is 'intimate but not personal'.

Despite these changes in method (all of them well represented in *A Barthes Reader*), a remarkable consistency characterized Barthes's temperament, his style and his eye. One might say of him what he wrote about his model: 'Gide is a simultaneous being. To a greater or lesser degree, Nature has posited him as complete, from the very first. He has merely taken the time to reveal the various aspects of himself in succession . . .' One of the unifying, 'simultaneous' aspects of Barthes's literary personality is his fastidiousness. As Genette said, 'Barthesian semiology is, both in its origin and in its active principle, that of a man fascinated by the sign, a fascination that no doubt involves, as it does for Flaubert or Baudelaire, an element of repulsion, and which has the essentially ambiguous character of a passion.'

This repulsion for the 'overfed' meanings of the 'diseased' signs of our petit-bourgeois culture with its advertising, glossy theatrical spectacles, agony columns and child prodigies is one of Barthes's reasons for writing his book about Japan, *The Empire of Signs*. In two volumes of *Mythologies* he rubbed his hands with gruesome relish over the hidden meanings latent in nearly every artifact of Western pop culture. In *The Empire of Signs* (which might more properly be called 'The Empire of Empty Signs') Barthes writes with admiration of the place Susan Sontag calls an 'esthete's utopia', where nothing lurks behind the beguiling surface.

Barthes more than once said, 'A named meaning is a dead meaning,' and one of his favorite images was of Orpheus (the signifier) condemning Eurydice (the signified) to eternal death by looking back at her. One might say that Barthes, contradicting Aristotelian Nature, abhorred everything that wasn't a vacuum. He was far too elegant and tentative, too much the dandy, to feel entirely at home in the West with its looming, unmistakable pregnancies of meaning. To me Barthes has always been unexpectedly funny, never more so than in the superficially sober and meticulous *S/Z*, his line-by-line analysis of a short story by Balzac. Barthes decodes and deflates the pretensions to meaning present everywhere in Balzac's 'realistic' text, which he ends up by treating as a sort of grand computer stocked with clichés and chattering away to itself. Behind this chatter, this cultural yammering, Barthes detects a terrible anxiety in Western society, an unarticulated fear that language itself means nothing, that it is merely an automaton's gesture flagging down the void.

If Japan did not exist, Barthes would have had to invent it – not that Japan *does* exist in *The Empire of Signs*, for Barthes is careful to point out that he is not analyzing the real Japan but rather one of his own devising. In this fictive Japan, there is no terrible *innerness* as in the West, no soul, no God, no fate, no ego, no grandeur, no metaphysics, no 'promotional fever' and finally no meaning.

In Barthes's Japan, Zen is all important, especially for 'that *loss of meaning* Zen calls a satori'. If *S/Z* is an examination of the stink of personality and the baneful yearning for transcendence that has corrupted the West, *The Empire of Signs* is its antidote, a study of a hypothetical society where things possess an innocence. For instance, in Japan, Barthes declares that 'sexuality is in sex, not elsewhere; in the United States, it is the contrary; sex is everywhere, except in sexuality'. Similarly, the famous flower arranging of Japan is an art not concerned with symbolism but with gesture; there the point of a gift is not what it contains but the exquisite package that encloses it, and the Bunraku puppet theater is superb because of its reserve, its avoidance of the hysteria of Western theater, its delegation of 'the whole cuisine of emotion' to the speaker who sits to one side of the stage. Barthes contrasts the attitudes of the Western theater and the Japanese: 'The voice: real stake of our modernity, special substance of language, which we try to make triumph everywhere. Quite the contrary, Bunraku has a *limited* notion of the voice; it does not suppress the voice, but assigns it a very clearly defined, essentially trivial function.'

Barthes once called Voltaire 'the last happy writer', by which he meant, among other things, that Voltaire was the last writer who could cheerfully assume that the whole planet, both the known and the unknown parts, reflected principles that were perfectly grasped, so that, for Voltaire, the world was an exotic projection of familiar arguments. In a paradox that is characteristic of Barthes, he said that the purpose of Voltairean travel is 'to manifest an immobility'. But for Barthes travel is quite a different project. To be sure, much like Voltaire, he uses the Orient as a pretext for a lesson, but the lesson is not one he already knows. For Barthes Japan is a test, a challenge to think the unthinkable, a place where meaning is finally banished. Paradise, indeed, for the great student of signs.

Movies and Poems: Pier Paolo Pasolini

Review of *Pasolini* by Enzo Siciliano, and Pasolini's *Poems*, translated by Norman McAffee and Luciano Martinengo, *New York Times Book Review*, 27 July 1982.

Pier Paolo Pasolini was violently murdered near Rome on 2 November 1975. He was only fifty-four years old, but he had managed to produce a lifetime of work in several genres. The publication in English of both Enzo Siciliano's biography – the first biography of Pasolini – and Norman McAffee's translation of the best poems remind us what an extraordinary man he was.

Pasolini had gained fame first as a poet in the dialect of his native region, Friuli – the area north of Venice that extends into Yugoslavia. Soon he switched to Italian, in which he went on to publish more than forty volumes of poetry, fiction, travel notes and cultural and political criticism.

But it was as a film maker that he won international fame. His first feature, *Accattone*, was released in 1961. Three years later he made his spare, smoldering *The Gospel According to Saint Matthew*. His biggest successes at the box office (at least in Europe) comprised *The Trilogy of Life*, of which the best was the innocent, spontaneous and delectable *Arabian Nights*. His last film, *Salo or the 120 Days of Sodom*, was surely his masterpiece, an appalling study of sadism in the last days of Italian Fascist rule. No film has come closer to genuine Satanism; *Salo* seems as much a transgression against decency as a condemnation of evil.

The man behind this work was an enigma. Pasolini led an exemplary life in the sense that he embodied most of the contradictions troubling modern Italy. He was a sort of Marxist and, off and on, a Communist, but his politics were too personal, too shifting and too adversarial to fit into any orthodoxy. He was an atheist, but two of his films (*The Gospel According to Saint Matthew* and *Teorema*) received awards from Catholic organizations. Moreover, he had a devout respect for what he considered 'divine' in human beings (youth, the body, spontaneity). He was a big-city sophisticate and moved easily in international film circles but, like his exact contemporary, the Japanese novelist Yukio Mishima (also a globe-trotting cosmopolitan), Pasolini rejected the glossy consumer culture that had made him famous in favor of the standards of an earlier, more rigid and more traditional society.

The greatest social change in the industrial world since the Second World War has been a shift away from conservation to consumption and, in the consumers themselves, a corresponding movement away from an ethic of self-sacrifice to a hedonistic code of self-fulfilment. Both Pasolini and Mishima opposed this fitful, always painful and disruptive process. Both of them had a utopian vision of an earlier, more honorable, more disciplined time. Thus Pasolini argued against the liberalization of the abortion law on the grounds that sacrificing procreation to pleasure is a way of 'Americanizing' sex, making it into a diversion. More broadly, Pasolini bitterly ridiculed the 'economic miracle' that quadrupled Italian income in the 1960s but also polluted the nation's shores and countryside, led to wholesale migrations of workers out of southern Italy and created a tacky mass culture. Similarly, Mishima scorned the industrialization (Westernization) of Japan.

To be sure, most political theorists would say that Pasolini was on the Left and Mishima on the Right. Pasolini felt that the Italian Communist Party was the only decent, uncorrupted, long-sighted and humane political organization in the country. Indeed, he was from a poor family, and his own early years of deprivation made him champion the poor everywhere, not only in Italy but also throughout the Third World (he wrote a book about India and another about Africa). By contrast, Mishima was from an upper-class family, and he committed *seppuku* (ritual suicide by disembowelment) in the name of emperor worship and a return to a feudal code (he even had a private army).

In short, Mishima was a Fascist and Pasolini a Communist. But underneath that ambiguous distinction one can detect strong affinities between them. Both were powerhouses who almost hysterically produced works in many genres: Mishima wrote plays, novels and poems and practiced body building and martial arts.

Pasolini was tireless throughout his adulthood, typically tossing off a novel while shooting a film. Both men were homosexuals who were remarkably well integrated into heterosexual social circles and who worked overtime in order to transcend the isolation imposed on them by their sexual identity. Mishima was married, though he was quite public about his homosexuality; Pasolini's great friendships were with the actress Laura Betti, the singer Maria Callas, and the novelists Elsa Morante and Alberto Moravia, all of them heterosexual.

Given the cult of machismo in Italy, Pasolini's candor was a tribute to his feistiness. He had been hounded out of Friuli (and out of the Communist Party) on charges of corrupting the morals of three teenage boys. He and his mother fled to Rome, where over the years he was subjected to other legal actions. But none of these efforts to repress him silenced Pasolini: he referred quite openly to his homosexuality in his regular newspaper columns and employed it as a theme in many of his films. But my point is that though both Pasolini and Mishima were frankly, even scandalously, homosexual (Mishima's first book is the semi-autobiographical *Confessions of a Mask*), neither man withdrew from the world into the gay subculture of Tokyo or Rome. Both were determined to be dominant figures of their national artistic and intellectual life, and both succeeded publicly, although neither could ever overcome private feelings of alienation.

Finally, both men died violent deaths – Mishima by his own hand, Pasolini in a ghastly encounter with a young Roman hustler who apparently beat him and then ran over his body with an automobile. The facts of Pasolini's murder remain cloudy. At the time, Communists insisted that several Fascists had killed him for political motives and then covered up the crime (and discredited Pasolini) by staging the event as a sordid encounter with a prostitute. Those who didn't interpret his death politically interpreted it morally, as though the excesses of *Salo* had invited just such violence. Surrendering to paranoia or blaming the victim seem to be the only possible responses to what probably (and more horribly) was merely random violence.

Was Pasolini a great artist? His *Gospel According to Saint Matthew* is a radical and original re-imagining of the Christ story in the terms of peasant culture, filmed in a corresponding visual style of poverty. *Salo* is great for its unforgettable assault on the sense and sensibilities of the viewer. Of his copious writings, his poems seem the most likely to endure. In the United States we have become used to a poetry that is subjective, dreamlike, mysterious, obvious only in its agitated or exalted state of emotion. Pasolini wrote poems of a very different sort. His poems, which Norman McAffee and Luciano Martinengo have translated faithfully, clearly, and ingeniously, are chatty letters to the world, by turns confessional and polemical.

Of the confessional poems, the most convincing is 'The Tears of the Excavator', in which Pasolini recalls his years as a poor schoolteacher when he lived in a shanty town outside Rome. Of the polemical poems, 'A Desperate Vitality' will shock Americans with its explicit references to names and political jargon:

> as in a film by Godard – rediscovery
> of romanticism in the seat of
> neocapitalistic cynicism and cruelty.

This is not the vatic tone of American lyricism. Indeed, an American who reads Enzo Siciliano's biography of Pasolini is struck by how much Pasolini was immersed in ideology. To us, a writer is political only peripherally, when he or she makes political pronouncements. But Pasolini worked in a milieu where an artist was supposed to situate each of his works in an ideological context and to have a ready opinion on every occasion about Freud, Marx and Lévi-Strauss.

Mr Siciliano himself is the same sort of intellectual. At times the American reader feels daunted when encountering such a sentence as 'The conflict, in essence, was between a residue of traditional humanism to be revitalized through Marxist historicism and neopositivist sociological thinking imbued with existential inhibitions.' No matter, Mr Siciliano tells the fascinating facts clearly enough and with sympathy (he was a friend of Pasolini's); the story is steadily absorbing.

Paradise Found

First published in the journal *Mother Jones*, June 1983.

My mother, after years now of getting used to the idea of a 'liberated gay' who happens to be her son, nevertheless will say from time to time, 'Why don't you get married? To a nice career girl, someone not too interested in sex. A good companion who will take care of you when you're old and feeble. A nice, sexless marriage, the sort we used to call a *marriage blanc* but that now, I suppose, you call a "New York Marriage".'

Her sophisticated nomenclature and equally up-to-date way of thinking about marriage scarcely conceal the conservatism of being a parent: we expect for our children the ideal bourgeois lives of the past (lives no one perhaps ever led). Similarly, we fear our children will be crushed by fates we've already embraced. My mother, for example, divorced my father thirty-five years ago, has lived on her own ever since, runs a clinic for mentally retarded children, had one long love affair and is now about to turn eighty as unmarried as the day she was born and a good deal happier. Although she has never been conventional, she has found her freedom privately exhilarating but theoretically regretable; the regret is applied to the next generation, as though it were a debt that had to be paid.

The truth is that American gay men today (I won't presume to speak for lesbians) are like banyan trees, which with their elaborate root systems can draw sustenance from an acre of ground, as opposed to the simple taproots of marriage, deep but narrow. Of the two kinds of arrangement, the marital seems to be the more easily uprooted, the less tenacious. In the past, before people moved around so much, the married couple naturally ramified into the extended family, the neighborhood and the whole tangled undergrowth of friendships that had lasted since childhood. But now the mobile home is a sadly self-contained unit, shunted from Boston to Kalamazoo to Denver (where one popular service does nothing but instantly integrate the arriving corporate wife into the community before she's whisked off somewhere else). In traditional China, literary training was a prerequisite to entering the bureaucracy and officials were not permitted to serve in their native district; that is why so much Chinese poetry is about parting – a theme that would surely dominate our verse as well if execs were bards.

Gay men, of course, move around quite a bit, too; but since there are relatively few gays in corporate life, they are seldom moved anywhere against their will, and the places they migrate to are usually predictable. For instance, it's almost a rite of passage for a gay New Yorker in his early thirties to feel he must enjoy the twilight of his youth in San Francisco or Los Angeles. But this transplantation seldom sticks, and even during the three or four years he's out west, he's scarcely out of touch with his old friends (many of whom have also made the move). Bicoastals are far more frequently encountered these days than bisexuals, and city-hopping for holidays – even for one great party – is common among affluent gays. A week after the Hawaiian Shirt Party on Fire Island, gays in Laguna Beach are conspicuously displaying their snapshots of the event – the bronzed bodies in the pool or on the deck and there, in their midst, like the ghost of Banquo, a pale Andy Warhol in black with his shock of white hair and his camera poised for attack. It's a bit like a Noël Coward play, in which the same four or five faces keep regrouping all over the world.

In Andrew Holleran's novel about the smart gay set, *Dancer from the Dance*, there are many references to 'circuit queens', those men who not only live in a milieu of bars, baths and discos in their own town, but also relentlessly fly from one gay watering place to another – New York to Atlanta to Key West to New Orleans to Los Angeles to San Francisco to Denver and home again. In each of these cities, despite local differences, a uniform gay culture is being created: a standard look, with its emphasis on macho work clothes and the heavily muscled body; and a uniform set of values, cheerfully hedonistic though recently being imbued with a sense of responsibility to less fortunate members of the gay community. This new social consciousness is evidenced by such organizations as the Gay Men's Health Crisis, which raises money to underwrite research into such diseases as AIDS (Acquired Immune Deficiency Syndrome), the mysterious and usually fatal affliction that has been spreading at an alarming rate throughout the gay community. No one knows for sure how AIDS is transmitted, but most medical experts are warning against anonymous sex. As a result, attendance at baths and back-room bars is dropping. And more and more gays are either entering monogamous affairs or forging circles of partners.

Camaraderie has always been a feature of American gay life. When I was a gay teenager in the 1950s I first discovered the democracy of the bars, the instant intimacy of the one-night stand; but in those good/bad old days before gay pride, there was always a trace of contempt in the air ('You're sick, Miss Thing, and you're an evil bitch') or of bathetic self-pity ('Oh, God, why can't I push a button and just be *normal*?'). That was the era of outcasts clustering for comfort, pariahs seeking a sullen consolation in one another. But don't let me paint too bleak a picture – there really was a speakeasy excitement about those gay bars of the past, where not only gays congregated but also every other misfit in town: the drunk old lady who belted out show tunes as she accompanied herself on a rinky-tink piano; the unshaved little guy who was some sort of a preacher and would start sermonizing late at night; and the quiet, middle-aged black insurance salesman and his fat white lady friend, the waitress, the two of them contentedly holding hands in the obscurity of a back booth and murmuring words of love.

Today, fourteen years after the Stonewall uprising and the beginning of gay liberation, there is a great deal more self-acceptance among gays, even a welcome show of arrogance. Moreover, in the 1970s the Clone emerged, that over-exercised, monosyllabic, aggressively masculine monument to machismo, and he had a good deal less tolerance for weirdos than did the old-fashioned Queen of the past. But in truth, the Clone look is more a look than an essence: it's a convenient, easily acquired and highly efficient set of appearances rather than an indelible identity.

The Clone may not be a troubling phenomenon, but conformism in gay life certainly is. Gay liberation grew out of the progressive spirit of the 1960s – a strange and exhilarating blend of socialism, feminism and the human potential movement. Accordingly, what gay leaders in the late 1960s were anticipating was the emergence of the androgyne, but what they got was the superbutch stud; what they expected was a communal hippie freedom from possessions, but what has developed is the acme of capitalist consumerism. Gays not only consume expensive vacations, memberships in gyms and discos, cars, elegant furnishings, clothes, haircuts, theater tickets and records, they also consume each other. From the perspective of the present, we can now look back at the beginning of gay liberation and observe that it flowered exactly at the moment when gays became identified, by themselves and by the market, as a distinct group of affluent and avid consumers. There had been earlier gay uprisings against straight oppression long before Stonewall, but none of them commanded the attention of the media nor had the far-ranging consequences of Stonewall. The success of gay liberation in the 1970s, of course, was largely political, but it was also, I'd contend, strongly related to the rise of the gay market. Unfortunately, today this rampant and ubiquitous consumerism not only characterizes gay spending habits but also infects attitudes toward sexuality: gays rate each other quantitatively according to age, physical dimensions and income: and all too many gays consume and dispose of each other, as though the very act of possession brought about instant obsolescence.

I don't want to overstate this point or suggest that to the degree it exists it's exclusively a gay problem. Moreover, if anonymous sex in the gay world can be consumerist, friendship is warm, wry, sustaining. The women's movement is permitting a whole new generation of women to enjoy each other's company, whereas in the past they were all too often ashamed to be seen together in public 'unescorted', as though belonging to a 'hen party' were the ultimate admission of failure in the mating sweepstakes; in the same way, gay liberation has enfranchised gay society, making it sufficient unto itself. Militancy has led to a sense of authenticity, surely the prerequisite of any genuine society. Gay men no longer look longingly over their shoulders at straight life, and they take each other seriously as mentors, buddies, sidekicks, brothers, lovers. When I was a boy, gay men were always mooning over straight GIs; now we lust after each other. Perhaps that's the origin of the Clone: we've become what we always wanted.

The singles scene among straights is quickly taking on the fluidity of the gay mainstream; but even so, the flow of straight society is always impeded or diverted by the pull of its institutions: Marriage, Childbirth, Divorce, Property Settlements. What I'm suggesting is that the economic, social and religious *consequences* of straight life – the subliminal historic sense that the second date can lead to holy matrimony and a station wagon full of toys and groceries – lend a certain gravity, even stiffness, to straight courtship. What's more, there is a mathematical difference as well, since during any country weekend spent together by four strictly heterosexual couples, there are only sixteen possibilities for coupling whereas four gay couples can link up into twenty-eight possible pairs. As suggested before, Feydeau and Labiche should have made gay life their subject, since the two gay rivals who duck under the bed can easily emerge as the newest pair of lovers. I remember that in my own case, when I was in my early twenties, I tricked out with a famous playwright – my first infidelity to my lover of two years. After I had sex with the playwright, he told me that I made love exactly like this kid he'd met a week before – and he named my lover, whom I promptly telephoned from the playwright's apartment. We all dissolved into peals of laughter.

Because gay life is not institutionalized and because, at least potentially, anyone can become anyone else's partner, romantic arrangements are a good deal more casual than they are among straights. This casualness is still further enhanced by the fact that one is dealing with members of the same sex, i.e. people programmed with the same expectations and values. In this easygoing fraternity of sex and sociability, which is presided over by the male spirit of the hunt, dramatic break-ups have a way of quickly settling down into cozy friendships. Again and again I've seen two men who have stopped being lovers continue to live together; as for myself, I can count on several ex-lovers as close friends. Movies and pop songs are, after all, about heterosexual love, and parents and priests weep over straight marriages and straight divorces. Gays have been largely ignored by the shamans

– a silence that may sometimes make us feel strangely invisible, though the mercy of obscurity is that our unions and severings are less public, less mythic, altogether less resonant. As marginal beings we are able to invent ourselves.

For instance, my next-door neighbor is a six-foot-four blond muscleman with a love of books and a flair for business, a cultivated and soon-to-be-rich thirty-three-year-old who can get himself up on Saturday nights to look like a Hell's Angel, but whose heart is truly angelic, scholarly and wise. Five years ago I dated 'Tom' for six months. At the time the affair was intense. We were together constantly and he stayed over with me almost every night. From time to time I'd see Tom's roommate, 'Bill', a Southern man who's close to forty but looks twenty-five and who's a bit of a loner, a whiz at every kind of computer game and electronic folly, but who never speaks at a party, though he follows the conversation avidly with eyes so big and glossy they seem to have been buttoned on. Bill was always wonderfully cordial to me. Not until a year after Tom and I drifted out of our affair did I learn that Bill was not just Tom's roommate but also his lover – that in fact they've been together almost a decade in nearly perfect tranquility. Bill stays home with his gadgets or goes to dance class, counsels Tom in his extramarital sprees, keeps books for Tom's expanding empire, while Tom has affairs that are much more short-lived than his adventures in business.

But this kind of attachment is more common than rare in contemporary big-city gay life. I know many gay couples, and in every case the marriage is open; the only question is how that given is to be legislated. Most couples discuss their 'contract' frankly and set their own rules for their 'infidelities'. Pointless to go into all these arrangements here; suffice to say that open marriages can turn into disasters or into complex networks of friends and lovers. Even the word *lover* is too rude for all the gradations of commitment and intimacy; one friend uses an ascending scale of Trick, Number, Fuck Buddy, Lover and Husband. My point is gays, in their efforts to invent themselves, have become equally ingenious in devising complex erotic molecules.

Of course promiscuity, no matter how institutionalized and hedged round by rules it might be, can threaten and even end a relationship. If one permits one's lover to sleep around or, especially, to date other men, he may well fall in love with someone

else. That's the danger of giving too long a leash, though the resentment that crops up from keeping someone on too short a
leash is likely to doom a relationship even more rapidly. This
double-edged problem is very similar in straight and gay life, with
a few differences. It seems that gays are more capable than
straights of distinguishing between sex and love. I know two gay
guys who have met for lunch once a week for several years,
though each man has a lover whom he's not about to give up. The
luncheons (or 'nooners', as we used to call them) are strictly for
pleasure, a joy that is completely self-contained, that leads nowhere.

The other odd feature about gay promiscuity is that the
jealousy (I don't want you to sleep with that guy) can actually be
a disguised form of lust or envy (I wish I were sleeping with that
guy). Many years ago I was hopelessly in love with someone who
didn't want to sleep with me but who was wildly infatuated with
a third guy. I never did seduce my love, but at least I had the
rather wan and philosophical consolation of sleeping with my
rival. In fact, that rival came to prefer me to the man I loved; I
became my own love's rival – surely a peculiar twist possible only
in gay life.

A year ago I was without a lover but I felt elated in a wonderful square dance of partners and friends, an allemande-left of
amorous intrigue in which no one got hurt and everyone was
amused, stimulated, appreciated. For the past five years I have
been friends with 'Hank', a tall, dark hunk from Colorado with a
mixture of Spanish and Irish blood, a boxer's body and the soul
of a saint. He's someone who will go to bed with anyone; as he
says he practices the 'generosity of the body'. His way of dealing
with the clawing, scratching and conniving that others resort to in
order to trick him into bed is to surrender at once. For that
reason I call him 'the Bodhisattva of Sex', in honor of those
Buddhas who forestall personal salvation out of compassion for
needy humanity.

Despite his philosophy, I had somehow assumed his beauty put
him out of my league – until, after four years of knowing him we
stumbled into each other's arms. Since he was a writer as well, we
always had plenty to talk about, and sex merely confirmed a
longstanding intimacy. Hank's generosity inspired me to emulate

him by introducing him to all my friends. One of these friends was 'Kevin', a slender blond Norwegian and at that time my roommate. Kevin was someone I had fallen for so hard that I had tried to dissuade him from moving in with me, since I realized he reciprocated my love but not my passion. But Kevin had convinced me everything would work out – and two months later I knew it was working out splendidly. We seldom had sex but we slept with our arms around each other every night he was in town (he was often away on business). When he was around he had a way of making me calm down – he seemed to generate alpha waves. On the night of his twenty-eighth birthday, I invited Hank over to help us celebrate. After a lot of champagne and a few joints, the three of us went to bed – but it wasn't five feverish minutes in the dark; rather an emotional and sensual ceremony, that frankly physical and physically frank kind of love-making men like.

Hank and Kevin went out with each other for a while. I wasn't jealous, but I don't know whether to ascribe my equanimity to age, wisdom, indifference or, simply, self-discipline. Had I at last learned not to expect devotion from much younger and more attractive men about town (and in Kevin's case, an especially hot man new to town)? Or were we trading in romance for something less exclusive, more nourishing, less futile and feudal?

Perhaps we were all just finding safety in numbers, for soon a young student of French politics had joined the circle, someone who read two books a day (the book read before noon had to have been written before 1900; the afternoon book, after), who worked out two hours a day at the gymnasium yet still found time for us. He slept with Hank, he slept with Kevin, he slept with me – and we all still laugh about that delirious month, that ecologically sound recycling of affection and (as the mad general in *Dr Strangelove* put it) 'precious bodily fluids'.

I'm certainly not denying that gays are as capable as anyone else of turning their romances into soap operas. The ways people behave in love are determined probably not so much by sexual orientation as by experience, ethnic background and one's momentary expectations. If Kevin, Hank, the French scholar and I were all civilized as we danced *la ronde*, we could afford to be: no one was in love, and now, a year later, though we're still all very close, we sleep with each other rarely. Yet I'm proud to have been a member of that erotic society, to have heard Hank's novel and to have watched Kevin take New York by storm (in his low-key, alpha-wave assault), to have witnessed the French scholar's adventures in reading – and to have experienced them and myself bodily as well as socially. In his late books, the French critic Roland Barthes speaks again and again about a utopian entity, 'the body', something sacred and separate from the corruptions of social codes; for that brief moment I felt our bodies expressed both our public sense of forming a society as well as our more private emotions. In conventional, straight America, people honor only the permanent and dismiss, even forget (or at least forget to mention) the transitory. Only what lasts is good. This prejudice in favor of what endures is unfortunate, I'd say, a concession to social institutions rather than a recognition of human experiences – of *lived beauty* in particular

Friendship need not be transitory, of course: my point is precisely that friendships outlast passion. Nor need friendships originate in or pass through a sexual stage. It's a luxurious pleasure to be able to sleep with our friends – a privilege and a resource – yet sex is by no means a prerequisite for intimacy (sex can, of course, be a way of avoiding intimacy). Rather than rehearse that truism, however, I would like to dwell a moment longer on the unexpected consequences of the primacy of sexuality in gay life. Whereas a straight man may even nowadays choose his wife not mainly for sexual compatibility but for her social connections, her religious affiliation, the likelihood that she will be a good mother, her maturity and constancy, her chances of helping him rise in the world, her aura or glamor, a gay man by contrast has nothing concrete to gain from the status of his partner. His choice, uncensored by society and based solely on desire, can be rather eccentric; when a whole social set is pieced together out of one's friends and the men they've made into lovers the result is richly improbable. The forty-year-old professor of German and his lover, the twenty-year-old windsurfer, sit down to dinner with the exiled Argentine rancher and his lover, the Harvard University MBA. It's no wonder that gays always seem to know such funds of recherché information; they've listened to the most heterogeneous table talk imaginable.

The only society of the past that approximated to the conditions of the current gay world was ancient Japanese court life as pictured in Sei Shonagon's tenth-century diary *The Pillow Book.* As a wit celebrated for her tart tongue and dandiacal whims, Sei Shonagon gives us in her fascinating jottings a cleanly etched representation of the values of her world, that of imperial court functionaries and ladies in waiting. The women are free to bestow their favors on whomever they please, and the rule is the one-night stand conducted with a measure of decorum and a nod toward sentiment (the gentleman sends the lady a morning-after poem comparing the dawn dew on his sleeve to his tears at parting). But despite the decorum, sexual interest flares up suddenly, even ferociously; sex seems incompletely assimilated into society, not quite housebroken. Friendship – and Sei Shonagon has several long-lasting friendships with men who admire her taste and her knowledge of the classics – intertwines with sexual adventure and almost always outlasts it; a casual encounter can lead to a lifelong romantic but sexless friendship. (Marriage arranged by older relatives strictly for dynastic purposes is never confused with love or sexual attraction.)

I cite Heian court life simply as a precedent for a society in which sex, love and friendship may overlap but are by no means wholly congruent. In this society, moreover it is friendship that provides the emotional and social continuity, whereas sexuality is no more and no less than an occasion for gallantry (the game, the thrill, the poetic pretext). Love in the Proustian sense – a grand, consuming, one-sided passion based on jealousy and thwarted possessiveness that evaporates the instant it is reciprocated – this sort of love is unknown, just as is the domestic bliss of bourgeois marriage.

To be sure, Sei Shonagon belonged to a tiny, privileged elite whose functions were almost entirely ceremonial – a special case if there ever was one. But her book can be read at least as a hypothesis about a world in which sex is not required to bear the emotional and mythic burden it carries for many. I'm suggesting that among gay men today, as among the Japanese of *The Pillow Book*, sex serves many purposes – as a form of curiosity of symbolic conquest and submission, as an exercise in the serious business of fantasy – but the one purpose it does not serve is the promotion of continuity and fidelity. I have no doubt many gays are reading me now and mumbling indignantly, 'How dare he speak for us?' but I'm not attempting to describe those homosexuals whose lives follow straight conventions. Indeed by saying *gay* instead of *homosexual* I'm attempting to describe a lifestyle rather than a sexual orientation.

The one part of straight life I may seem to be describing is adolescence. That's always the insult tossed ever so casually at gays by modern moralists, those artful dodgers who have learned they dare not tell us we're bad but who don't hesitate to tell us we're 'immature'. I should mention right away that the charge may or may not be accurate, but it never sounds to me as condescending as intended; I have no contempt for that time of life when our friendships are most passionate and our passions incorrigible and none of our sentiments yet compromised by greed or cowardice or disappointment. The volatility and intensity of adolescence are qualities we should aspire to preserve: interestingly, those societies in which the participants can afford to behave as they please (Versailles under Louis XIV or Hollywood now) always choose to preserve their 'adolescent' character – the rapid succession of affairs, the scheming and intrigue, the scrambling after popularity, the dismissal of the solid future in favor of the shimmering present.

If gay men seem attractively adolescent (steamy with emotion available to romantic imaginative discovery), they should not be credited with superior wisdom or staying power. It occurs to me throughout this essay that I might seem to be ascribing unusual virtues to gay men, but in fact I know that no group is innately superior to another. Nevertheless, the conditions of one's existence – even the seemingly unfortunate conditions – can promote new understandings and new modes of behavior. In the case of gays our childlessness, our minimal responsibilities, the fact that our unions are not consecrated, even our very retreat into gay ghettos for protection and freedom: all of these objective conditions have fostered a style in which we may be exploring even in spite of our conscious intentions, things as they will some day be for the heterosexual majority. In that world (as in the gay world already), love will be built on esteem rather than passion or convention, sex will be more playful or fantastic or artistic than marital – and friendship will be elevated into the supreme consolation for this continuing tragedy, human existence.

Sexual Culture

First published in *Vanity Fair*, 1983.

'Do gay men have friends – I mean', she said, 'are they friends with each other?' Since the woman asking was a New Yorker, the owner of one of the city's simplest and priciest restaurants, someone who's known gays all her life, I found the question honest, shocking, and revealing of a narrow but bottomless abyss between us.

Of course New York is a city of total, even absolute strangers rubbing shoulders: the Hasidim in their yellow school bus being conveyed back to Brooklyn from the jewelry district, beards and black hats glimpsed through mud-splattered windows in a sun-dimmed daguerreotype; the junkie pushing the baby carriage and telling his wife, the prostitute, as he points to his tattooed biceps, 'I haven't partied in this vein for years'; Moonies doing callisthenics at midnight in their Eighth Avenue center high above empty Thirty-fourth Street . . . But this alienation wasn't religious or ethnic. The woman and I spoke the same language, knew the same people; we both considered Marcella Hazan fun but no substitute for Simone Beck. How odd that she, as lower-upper-middle-class as I, shouldn't know whether gay men befriended one another.

It was then that I saw how mysterious gay culture is – not homosexuality, which is merely an erotic tropism, but modern American gay culture, which is a special way of laughing, spending money, ordering priorities, encoding everything from song lyrics to mirror-shiny military shoes. None of the usual modes for a subculture will do, for gay men are brought up by heterosexuals to be straight, they seek other men through what feels very much like a compulsion though they enter the ghetto by choice, yet once they make that choice it reshapes their lives, even their bodies, certainly their wardrobes. Many gay men live among straights as Marranos, those Spanish Jews who pretended during the Inquisition to convert to Christianity but continued to observe the old rites in cellars, when alone, in the greatest secrecy. Gays aren't like blacks or Jews since they often are black or Jewish, and their affectional preference isn't a color or a religion though it has spawned a culture not unlike an ethnic minority's. Few Jews have Christian siblings, but most gays have straight brothers and sisters or at least straight parents. Many American Jews have been raised to feel they belong to the Chosen People, at once superior and inferior to gentiles, but every gay discovers his sexual nature with a combination of pain and relief, regret at being excluded from the tribe but elation at discovering the solution to the puzzle.

Gays aren't a nationality. They aren't Chicanos or Italo-Americans or Irish-Americans, but they do constitute one of the most potent political forces in big cities such as New York, Philadelphia, Washington (where gays and blacks elected Marion Barry mayor), Houston, Los Angeles, and San Francisco (where gays are so numerous they've splintered into countless factions, including the lesbian S and M group Samois and the Sisters of Perpetual Indulgence, a group of drag nuns, one of whose members ran in a cowl and wimple as a candidate in the last city-wide election). Not ethnic but a minority, not a polis but political, not a nationality but possessed of a costume, customs, and a patois, not a class but an economic force (not only as a market for records, films, vacations, and clothes but also as an army of worker ants who, for better or worse, have gentrified the city centers, thereby creating a better tomorrow for single young white heterosexual professionals).

Imagine a religion one enters against one's parents will – and against one's own. Imagine a race one joins at sixteen or sixty without changing one's hue or hair texture (unless at the tanning or beauty salon). Imagine a sterile nation without descendants but with a long, misty regress of ancestors, without an articulated self-definition but with a venerable history. Imagine an exclusive club that includes a PR (Puerto Rican) boy of sixteen wearing ankle-high black-and-white Converse basketball shoes and a petrol green shirt sawn off to reveal a Praxitelean stomach – and also includes a PR (Public Relations) WASP executive of forty in his Prince of Wales plaids and Cole-Haan tasseled loafers.

If one is gay, one is always in a crucial relationship to gayness as such, a defining category that is so full it is nearly empty (Renaud Camus writes: 'Homosexuality is always elsewhere because it is everywhere'). No straight man stands in rapt contemplation of his straightness unless he's an ass. To be sure, heterosexuals may wonder over the significance of their homosexual fantasies, though even that morbid excuse is less popular now than formerly; as Barbara Ehrenreich acutely observes in her new study of the heterosexual male revolt, *The Hearts of Men*, the emergence of gay liberation ended the period in which everyone suspected everyone else of being 'latently' homosexual. Now there are open homosexuals, and heterosexual men are exempt from the automatic suspicion of deviance.

No homosexual can take his homosexuality for granted. He must sound it, palpate it, auscultate it as though it were the dead limb of a tree or the living but tricky limb of a body; for that reason all homosexuals are 'gay philosophers' in that they must invent themselves. At a certain point one undergoes a violent conversion into a new state, the unknown, which one then sets about knowing as one will. Surely everyone experiences his or her life as an artifact, as molten glass being twirled and pinched into a shape to cool, or as a novel at once capacious and suspenseful, but no one is more a *Homo faber* (in the sense of both 'fabricator' and 'fabulist') than a homo. It would be vain, of course, to suggest that this creativity is praiseworthy, an ambition rather than a response.

Sometimes I try to imagine how straights – not fundamentalist know-nothings, not rural innocents, not Freudian bigots, but educated urban heterosexuals – look at gay men (do they even see lesbians?). When they see gay men, what do they see? A mustache, a pumped-up body in black jeans and a tank top, an eye-catching tattoo (braided rope around the biceps)? And what do they think ('they', in this case, *hypocrite lecteur*, being you)? Do you see something at once ludicrous and mildly enviable in the still youthful but over-exercised body of this forty-year-old clone with the aggressive stare and soft voice? If you're a woman, do you find so much preening over appearance in a grown man

... well, if not offensive, at least unappetizing; energy better spent on a career, on a family – on you? If you're a man, does it incense you that this jerk is out of harness, too loose, too free, has so lightly made a mockery of manhood? Once, on a radio call-in show a cop called in to tell me he had to admire the old-style queens back when it was rough being queer but that now, jeez, these guys swapping spit wit' a goil one week, wit' a guy the next, they're too lazy, they just don't know the fine art of being a man, it's all just too easy.

Your sentiments, perhaps?

Do you see gays as menacing satyrs, sex fiends around whom it's dangerous to drop your soap, and as feeble sissies, frail wood nymphs locked within massive trunks and limbs? Or, more positively if just as narrowly, are you a sybaritic het who greets the sight of gays with cries of glee, convinced you've stumbled on liberty hall, where sexual license of every sort – including your sort – is bound to reign? In fact, such sybarites often do regard gay men as comrades in arms, fellow libertines, and fellow victims in a country phobic to pleasure.

Or do gays just irk you? Do you regard them as tinsely distraction in your peripheral vision? As errant, obstinate atoms that can't be drawn into any of the usual social molecules, men who if they insist on their gayness won't really do at any of the solemnities, from dinner parties to débutante balls, all of which depend on strict gender dimorphism for a rational seating plan? Since any proper gathering requires the threat of adultery for excitement and the prospect of marriage as a justification, of what earthly use are gays? Even the few fearless straight guys who've invaded my gay gym drift toward one another, not out of soap-dropping panic but because otherwise their dirty jokes fall on deaf or prettily blushing ears and their taunting, butt-slapping mix of rivalry and camaraderie provokes a weird hostility or a still weirder thrill.

And how do gays look at straights? In Andrew Holleran's superb novel, *Nights in Aruba*, the narrator wonders 'what it would be like to be head of a family, as if with that all my problems would drop away, when in fact they would have merely been replaced by another set. I would not have worried about the size of my penis, the restrictions of age, the difficulty of finding love; I would have worried about mortgages, tuition, my young-est daughter's asthma, my competition at Shearson Loeb Rhoades.' What makes this speculation so characteristically gay is that it is so focused on the family man, for if the nineteenth-century tart required, even invented the convent-bred virgin to contemplate, in the same way the homosexual man today must insult and revere, mock and envy this purely imaginary bourgeois paterfamilias, a creature extinct except in gay fantasies. Mean-while, of course, the family man devotes his time to scream therapy and tai-chi, ticking off Personals in the *Village Voice* and wriggling out of visits from his kids, two punked-out teens who live in a feminist compound with his divorced wife, now a lesbian potter of great sensitivity and verve if low energy.

So much for how the two sexes (straight and gay) regard each other. If the camera were to pull back and frame both worlds in the lens, how would the two systems compare?

The most obvious difference is that whereas heterosexuality does include two sexes, since homosexuality does not, it must im-provise a new polarity moment by moment. Such a polarity seems necessary to sexual desire, at least as it is constructed in our culture. No wonder that some gay men search out the most ex-treme opposites (someone of a distant race, a remote language, another class or age); no wonder that even that convinced hetero-sexual Flaubert was finally able to unbend with a boy prostitute in Egypt, an exotic who provided him with all the difference desire might demand. Other gay men seek out their twins – so that the beloved, I suppose, can stand in for oneself as one bows down to this false god and plays in turn his father, teacher, son, godfather, or god. Still others institutionalize the polarity in that next-best thing to heterosexuality: sado-masochism, the only vice that anthologizes all family and romantic relationships.

Because every gay man loves men, he comes to learn at first hand how to soothe the savage breast of the male ego. No matter how passive or girlish or shy the new beau might be in the bou-doir, he will become the autocrat of the dinner table. Women's magazines are always planning articles on gay men and straight women; I'd say what they have most in common, aside from a few shared sexual techniques, is a body of folk wisdom about that hardhead, that bully, that maddeningly self-involved creature, the human male. As studies have surprisingly shown, men talk more than women, interrupt them more often, and determine the topics of conversation and object to women's assertions with more authority and frequency. When two gay men get together, especially after the first romantic urge to oblige the other wanes, a struggle for conversational dominance ensues, a conflict only symptomatic of larger arguments over every issue from where to live to how and whom to entertain.

To be sure, in this way the gay couple resembles the straight duo that includes an assertive, liberated woman. But while most of the young straight liberated women I know, at least, may protect their real long-range interests (career, mode of life, emotional needs) with vigilance, they're still willing to accommodate him in little social ways essential to harmony.

One benign side of straight life is that women conceive of men as 'characters', as full-bodied, multi-faceted beings who are first social, second familial, third amorous or amicable, and only finally physical. I'm trying politely to say that women are lousy judges of male beauty; they're easily taken in by such superficial traits as loyalty, dependability, charm, a sense of humor. Women don't, or at least didn't, judge men as so much beefcake. But men, both straight and gay, start with looks, the most obvious currency of value, worth, price. Let's say that women see men as characters in a long family novel in which the men are introduced complete with phrenology, genealogy, and one annoying and two endearing traits, whereas men see their partners (whether male or female) as cars, makes to be instantly spotted, appraised, envied, made. A woman wants to be envied for her husband's goodness, his character, whereas a man wants to be envied for his wife's beauty, rarity, status – her drivability. Straight life combines the warmth and *Gemütlichkeit* of the nineteenth-century bourgeois (the woman) with the steely corporate ethos of the twentieth-century functionary (the man). If gay male life, freed of this dialectic, has become supremely efficient (the trapdoor beside the bed) and only momentarily intimate (a whole life-cycle compressed into the one-night stand), then the gain is dubious, albeit an extreme expression of one trend in our cultural economy.

But of course most morality, that is, popular morality – not real morals, which are unaffected by consensus, but mores, which are a form of fashion – is nothing but a species of nostalgia, a cover up for pleasurable and profitable but not yet admissible innovations. If so many people condemn promiscuity, they do so at least partly because there is no available rhetoric that could condone, much less glamorize, impermanence in love. Nevertheless, it strikes me that homosexuals, masters of improvisation, fully at home with the arbitrary, and equipped with an internal compass that orients them instantly to any social novelty, are perhaps the most sensitive indicators of the future.

The birthrate declines, the divorce rate climbs and popular culture (movies, television, song lyrics, advertising, fashions, journalism) is so completely and irrevocably secularized that the so-called religious revival is of no more lasting importance than the fad for Kabuki in a transistorized Japan – a temporary throwback, a slight brake on the wheel. In such a world the rate of change is so rapid that children, once they are in school, can learn little from their parents but must assimilate new forms of behavior from their peers and new information from specialized instructors. As a result, parental authority declines, and the demarcations between the generations become ever more formidable. Nor do the parents regret their loss of control, since they're devoting all their energy to cultivating the inner self in the wholesale transition of our society from an ethic of self-sacrifice to one of self-indulgence, the so-called aristocraticization of middle-class life that has dominated the peaceful parts of this century in the industrialized West.

In the contemporary world the nineteenth-century experiment of companionate marriage, never very workable, has collapsed utterly. The exact nature of the collapse isn't very clear yet because of our distracting, probably irrelevant habit of psychologizing every crisis (thus the endless speculations in the lowbrow press on the Irresponsible Male and the Defeminized Female or the paradoxical and cruelly impracticable advice to women readers to 'go for it all – family, career, marriage, romance, and the reveries of solitude'). We treat the failure of marriage as though it were the failure of individuals to achieve it – a decline in grit or maturity or commitment or stamina rather than the unraveling of a poorly tied knot. Bourgeois marriage was meant to concentrate friendship, romance, and sex into an institution at once familial and economic. Only the most intense surveillance could keep such a bulky, ill-assorted load from bursting at the seams. Once the hedonism of the 1960s relaxed that tension, people began to admit that friendship tranquilizes sexual desires (when mates become siblings, the incest taboo sets in) and that romance is by its very nature evanescent though indefinitely renewable given an endless supply of fresh partners. Neither sexual nor romantic attraction, so capricious, so passionate, so unstable, could ever serve as the basis for an enduring relationship, which can be balanced only on the plinth of esteem, that easy, undramatic, intimate kind of love one would say resembled family love if families were more loving.

It is this love that so many gay couples know about, aim for, and sometimes even express. If it all goes well, two gay men will meet through sex, become lovers, weather the storms of jealousy and the diminution of lust, develop shared interests (a hobby, a business, a house, a circle), and end up with a long-term, probably sexless camaraderie that is not as disinterested as friendship or as seismic as passion or as charged with contradiction as fraternity. Younger couples feel that this sort of relationship, when it happens to them, is incomplete, a compromise, and they break up in order to find total fulfilment (i.e. tireless passion) elsewhere. But older gay couples stay together, cultivate their mild, reasonable love, and defend it against the ever-present danger of the sexual allure exercised by a newcomer. For the weak point of such marriages is the eternally recurring fantasy, first in one partner and then the other, of 'total fulfilment'. Needless to say, such couples can wreak havoc on the newcomer who fails to grasp that Bob and Fred are not just roommates. They may have separate bedrooms and regular extra-curricular sex partners or even beaux, but Bob monitors Fred's infatuations with an eye attuned to nuance, and at a certain point will intervene to banish a potential rival.

I think most straight people would find these arrangements more scandalous than the infamous sexual high jinks of gays. Because these arrangements have no name, no mythology, no public or private acknowledgment, they're almost invisible even to the participants. Thus if you asked Bob in a survey what he wanted, he might say he wanted a 'real' lover. He might also say

Fred was 'just a roommate, my best friend, we used to be lovers'. So much for explicit analysis, but over the years Bob has cannily steered his affair with Fred between the Scylla of excessive fidelity (which is finally so dull no two imaginative gay men could endure it) and the Charybdis of excessive tolerance (which could leave both men feeling so neglected they'd seek love elsewhere for sure).

There are, of course, countless variants to this pattern. The men live together or they don't. If they don't, they can maintain the civilized fiction of romance for years. They plan dates, honeymoons, take turns sleeping over at each other's house, and avoid conflicts about domestic details. They keep their extra-curricular sex lives separate, they agree not to snoop – or they have three-ways. Or one of the pair has an active sex life and the other has abandoned the erotic arena.

Are gay men friends with each other? the woman asked me.

The question may assume that gays are only sexual, and that a man eternally on the prowl can never pause for mere affection – that a gay Don Juan is lonely. Or perhaps the question reveals a confusion about a society of one gender. Since a straight woman has other women for friends and men for lovers, my questioner might have wondered how the same sex could serve in both capacities.

The first supposition – that gay men are only sexual – is an ancient prejudice, and like all prejudices mostly untrue but in one sense occasionally accurate. If politically conscious homosexuals prefer the word *gay* to *homosexual*, they do so because they want to make the world regard attraction to members of the same gender as an affectional preference as well as a sexual orientation.

For instance, there are some gay men who prefer the feel of women's bodies to men's, who are even more comfortable sexually with women, but whose emotions crave contact with other men. Gay men have unfinished emotional business with other men – scary, promising, troubling, absorbing business – whereas their sentiments toward women (at least women not in their family) are much simpler, more stable, less fraught. Affection, passionate affection, is never simple; it is built out of equal parts of yearning, fear, and appetite. For that reason the friendship of one gay man fiercely drawn to another is as tense as any heterosexual passion, whereas a sexless, more disinterested gay friendship is as relaxed, as good tempered as a friendship, say, between two straight men.

Gay men, then, do divide other gays into two camps – those who are potential partners (lovers) and those who are not (friends). But where gay life is more ambiguous than the world at large (and possibly for that reason more baffling to outsiders) is that the members of the two camps, lovers and friends, are always switching places or hovering somewhere in the margin between. It is these unconfessed feelings that have always intrigued me the most as a novelist – the unspoken love between two gay men, say, who pretend they are just friends, cruising buddies, merely filling in until Mr Right comes along (mercifully, he never does).

In one sense, the public's prejudice about a gay obsession with sex is valid. The right to have sex, even to look for it, has been so stringently denied to gays for so many centuries that the drive toward sexual freedom remains a bright, throbbing banner in the fierce winds whipping over the ghetto. Laws against sex have always created the biggest problems for homosexuals; they helped to define the very category of homosexuality. For that reason, the gay community, despite its invention of a culture no more eroticized than any other still cannot give up its origin in sexual desire and its suppression.

But what about the 'excessive' promiscuity of gay men, the infamous quickies, a phenomenon only temporarily held in check by the AIDS crisis? Don't the quickies prove that gay men are essentially bizarre, fundamentally lacking in judgment – *oversexed*? Of course, gay men behave as all men would were they free of the strictures of female tastes, needs, prohibitions, and expectations. There is nothing in gay male life that cannot be attributed either to its minority status or to its all-male population. All men want quick, uncomplicated sexual adventure (as well as sustained romantic passion); in a world of all men, that desire is granted.

The very universality of sexual opportunity within the modern gay ghetto has, paradoxically, increased the importance of friendship. In a society not based on the measured denial or canalization of sexual desire, there is more energy left over for friendship. Relationships are less loaded in gay life (hence the celebrated gay irony, a levity equivalent to seeing through conventions). In so many ways gays are still prisoners of the dominant society, but in this one regard gays are freer than their jailers: because gay relationships are not disciplined by religious, legal, economic, and political ceremonies but only by the dictates of conscience and the impulses of the heart, they don't stand for anything larger. They aren't symbols but realities, not laws but entities sufficient unto themselves, not consequential but ecstatic.

Nabokov: Beyond Parody

This essay appeared in shortened form in the *New York Review of Books*, 29 March 1984. The present version was included in *The Achievement of Nabokov*, edited by George Gibian and Stephen Jen Parker, 1984.

Nabokov is the most passionate novelist of the twentieth century, the high priest of sensuality and desire, the magus who knows everything about what is at once the most solemn and elusive of all our painful joys – the stab of erotic pleasure, that emblem of transitory happiness on earth. As Proust observed, ardor is the only form of possession in which the possessor possesses nothing.

But if passion is the treasure (that is, the absence) that lies at the heart of the great pyramid of Nabokov's art, he has been careful to protect it from the vulgar, the prying, the coarse, the smug – against whoever might seek to despoil him of his fragile hoard; he has surrounded his secret riches with a maze of false corridors, of precariously balanced, easily triggered and quite lethal megaliths. These are the notorious traps, the crushing menhirs of Nabokov's wit, his scorn, his savage satire. None the less I'd insist that passion, not brilliance or cruelty or erudition or the arrogant perfection of his craft – that passion is his master motif. All of his intelligence is at the service of the emotions.

In a superb story, perhaps his best, 'Spring in Fialta', first written in Russian and published in 1938, the love between the narrator and the heroine, Nina, is considered with – I'm tempted to say safeguarded by – the contempt directed at her husband, Ferdinand. Nina is an impulsive, generous but negligent woman who has often given herself to the narrator (and to many other men along the way); just as suddenly and often she has forgotten the gift she's conferred on them. The narrator first meets Nina in Russia 'around 1917', as he says with an eerie casualness, and they exchange their first embrace outdoors in winter:

Windows light up and stretch their luminous lengths upon the

dark billowy snow, making room for the reflection of the fan-
shaped light above the front door between them. Each of the
two sidepillars is fluffily fringed with white, which rather
spoils the lines of what might have been a perfect *ex libris* for
the book of our two lives. I cannot recall why we had all
wandered out of the sonorous hall into the still darkness,
peopled only with firs, snow-swollen to twice their size; did
the watchmen invite us to look at a sullen red glow in the sky,
portent of nearing arson? Possibly. Did we go to admire an
equestrian statue of ice sculptured near the pond by the Swiss
tutor of my cousins? Quite as likely. My memory revives only
on the way back to the brightly symmetrical mansion towards
which we tramped in single file along a narrow furrow between snowbanks, with that crunch-crunch-crunch which is
the only comment that a taciturn winter night makes upon
humans. I walked last; three singing steps ahead of me walked
a small bent shape; the firs gravely showed their burdened
paws. I slipped and dropped the dead flashlight someone had
forced upon me; it was devilishly hard to retrieve; and instantly attracted by my curses, with an eager, low laugh in
anticipation of fun, Nina dimly veered toward me. I call her
Nina, but I could hardly have known her name yet, hardly
could we have had time, she and I, for any preliminary;
'Who's that?' she asked with interest – and I was already kissing her neck, smooth and quite fiery hot from the long fox fur
of her coat collar, which kept getting into my way until she
clasped my shoulder, and with the candor so peculiar to her
gently fitted her generous, dutiful lips to mine.

When the narrator sees Nina indoors a minute later, he is
astonished 'not so much by her inattention to me after that
warmth in the snow as by the innocent naturalness of that inattention . . .'

This passage is a microcosm of Nabokov's art. His perfect
visual memory turns instantly into perfect visual invention when
the lit doorway nearly becomes an *ex libris*. The seemingly innocent description soon enough resolves itself into an emblem –
'out of books', indeed, since the scene that follows is reminiscent
of Chekhov's 'The Kiss' – the same mansion, a similar party, the

same passionate kiss between strangers. Moreover, the quality of the narrator's and Nina's intermittent affair is always novelistic and the language used to recount it is invariably the language of literature: 'Again and again she hurriedly appeared in the margins of my life, without influencing in the least its basic text.'

If this marginal romance – lusty, a bit sentimental, not quite honest, genuinely moving but also tinged with *poshlust* – is related by a narrator who is a writer *manqué*, then the ghastly Ferdinand, Nina's husband, is nothing but a writer – cold, diabolic, coldly technical. In fact, he is one of those many grotesque versions of himself Nabokov planted throughout his fiction, a sort of signature not unlike Hitchcock's fleeting appearances in his own films. This particular double is particularly unappetizing, driven as he is with a 'fierce relish' for ugly things and woebegotten people: 'Like some autocrat who surrounds himself with hunchbacks and dwarfs, he would become attached to this or that hideous object; this infatuation might last from five minutes to several days or even longer if the thing happened to be animate.'

In 'Spring in Fialta', which is just twenty-one pages long, Nabokov manages to generate as dense a sense of duration, of lived-through time, as can be found in most novels. He achieves this narrative density by two means: a complex but rigorous time scheme; and the juxtaposition of highly contrasting moods. The story progresses on two planes: connected episodes at Fialta in the present that alternate with memories of past trysts with Nina in many cities over the years. Both the present and the past are told sequentially and the last flashback to be presented is the narrator's most recent memory of Nina. In other words these two systems of time converge to produce the final scene, in which Nina is killed when her car crashes into a traveling circus company, whose arrival has been heralded throughout the tale by dozens of tiny details, as at sea the approach of land is promised by a quickening flux of grass, twigs and land birds. The convergence of the two time schemes and the disclosure of the promise extended by the hints of the approaching circus conspire to produce a strong effect of closure.

The satisfying *thickness* of this story, its feeling of duration, derives not only from the time scheme but also from the juxtaposition of highly contrasted scenes, a technique of tessellation perfected by Tolstoy. These scenes fall into two groups – the satirical and the romantic. Some of the romantic scenes are not scenes at all but instead beautifully rendered telescopings of time:

> Once I was shown her photograph in a fashion magazine full of autumn leaves and gloves and windswept golf links. On a certain Christmas she sent me a picture post card with snow and stars. On a Riviera beach she almost escaped my notice behind her dark glasses and terra cotta tan. Another day, having dropped in on an ill-timed errand at the house of some strangers where a party was in progress, I saw her scarf and fur coat among alien scarecrows on a coat rack. In a bookshop she nodded to me from a page of one of her husband's stories . . .

The tone of these passages is elegiac, tender and sensual: it is Nabokov's genius (as one might speak of the genius of a place or of a language) to have kept alive almost singlehandedly in our century a tradition of tender sensuality. In most contemporary fiction tenderness is a sexless family feeling and sensuality either violent or impersonal or both. By contrast, Nabokov is a Pascin of romantic carnality. He writes in 'Spring in Fialta': 'Occasionally in the middle of a conversation her name would be mentioned, and she would run down the steps of a chance sentence, without turning her head.' Only a man who loved women as much as he desired them could write such a passage.

What makes the narrator of this tale a writer *manqué* is his uncritical – one might say his uninjured – ease in the world of the sentiments. There is no bite, no obliqueness, no discomfort in his responses and, though he is in no danger of becoming vulgar, he is close to that other Nabokovian sin, philistinism. No wonder he is repelled by the real writer, Ferdinand, the focus of the satirical scenes, passages that send up the culture industry, the whole fatiguing milieu of art groupies. Ferdinand sounds a bit like a combination of the sardonic Nabokov and, improbably, a naïve Western European devotee of Russian Communism. But let's not focus on Ferdinand's bad politics. Let's concentrate instead on his peculiarities as a writer:

> Having mastered the art of verbal invention to perfection, he

particularly prided himself on being a weaver of words, a title
he valued higher than that of a writer; personally, I never
could understand what was the good of thinking up books, of
penning things that had not really happened in some way or
another; and I remember once saying to him as I braved the
mockery of his encouraging nods that, were I a writer, I
should allow only my heart to have imagination, and for the
rest rely upon memory, that long drawn sunset shadow of
one's personal truth. I had known his books before I knew
him; a faint disgust was already replacing the aesthetic pleasure which I had suffered his first novel to give me. At the
beginning of his career, it had been possible perhaps to distinguish some human landscape, some old garden, some
dream familiar disposition of trees through the stained glass of
his prodigious prose ... but with every new book the tints
grew still more dense, the gules and purpure still more
ominous; and today one can no longer see anything at all
through that blazoned, ghastly rich glass, and it seems that
were one to break it, nothing but a perfectly black void would
face one's shivering soul.

In this remarkable – and remarkably sly – passage, the narrator's relationship to the reader (and to the writer Nabokov)
becomes intricate. We know that Nabokov's own great art is
decidedly not autobiographical in the simple photographic sense,
and we resist the narrator's bland assumptions about the suffi-
ciency of memory to art. The narrator sounds too sincere, too
Slavic, to our ears, although his objections to Ferdinand are
phrased with all the suavity and eloquent conviction at Nabokov's command. Since we, the readers, know that a figure much
like the diabolical Ferdinand has written even this argument for
sincerity, our relationship to the text is deliciously slippery. The
irony, the hard brilliance of such passages contrasts with the
tenderness of the alternating sections to give a high relief, an
almost *topographical* sense of traveling through time.

Many writers proceed by creating characters who are parodies
of themselves or near misses or fun-house distortions, or they
distribute their own characteristics across a cast of characters and
they especially like to dramatize their conflicts and indecisions by

assigning them to different personages. One thinks of Proust, who gave his dilettantism to Swann, his homosexuality to Charlus, his love of his family to the narrator and his hatred of his family to Mlle Vinteuil, his hypochondria to Aunt Leonie, his genius to Elstir and Bergotte, his snobbism to the Guermantes, his Frenchness to Françoise. In this sense (but this strict sense only) every novel, including Nabokov's, is autobiographical. Indeed the notion of a parallel life that does, impossibly, converge with one's own may have suggested the concept of two worlds and two histories slightly out of sync – the moiré pattern of Terra and anti-Terra woven by *Ada*.

But it was Nabokov's particular delight to invent sinister or insane or talentless versions of himself, characters who are at least in part mocking anticipations of naïve readers' suspicions about the real Nabokov. For all those innocents who imagined that the author of *Lolita* was himself a nympholept, Nabokov prepared a hilarious response in *Look at the Harlequins!*, in which the narrator's biography is composed from nothing but such crude suppositions: 'As late as the start of the 1954–55 school year, with Bel nearing her thirteenth birthday, I was still deliriously happy, still seeing nothing wrong or dangerous, or absurd or downright cretinous, in the relationship between my daughter and me. Save for a few insignificant lapses – a few hot drops of overflowing tenderness, a gasp masked by a cough and that sort of stuff – my relations with her remained essentially innocent...' Essentially innocent – that's the kind of essence that lubricates our villainous society.

Nabokov's model for inventing such characters, the author's disabled twin or feebler cousin, mad brother or vulgar uncle, was surely Pushkin, among others, for it was Pushkin, following Byron's lead in *Don Juan*, who fashioned a distorted portrait of himself in Eugene Onegin, the young man of fashion whose attitudes and deeds sometimes draw a crude outline of the poet's own silhouette and just as often diverge completely. Of course Pushkin scrupulously disowns the resemblance (I use Nabokov's translation):

I'm always glad to mark the difference
between Onegin and myself,

lest an ironic reader
or else some publisher
of complicated calumny,
collating here my traits,
repeat thereafter shamelessly
that I have scrawled my portrait
like Byron, the poet of pride . . .

Before Pushkin establishes their differences he points out the similarities. He tells us that he likes Onegin's 'sharp, chilled mind' and explains their friendship by saying, 'I was embittered, he was sullen . . .'

Wit, scorn, and the parody of romance can be a way of rescuing romance. Just as Schönberg remarked that only the extreme recourse of his twelve-tone system was able to provide German romantic music with another fifty years of life, so Nabokov might have asserted that only by casting *Lolita* into the extreme terms of a Krafft-Ebing case study, the tale of a European nympholept and his gum-snapping, wisecracking, gray-eyed teenage enchantress – that only by making such a radical modulation could he endow the romantic novel with a glorious new vitality.

That vitality is attributable to obsession, the virtue that is shared by vice and art. As Adorno observes in the *Minima Moralia*: 'The universality of beauty can communicate itself to the subject in no other way than in an obsession with the particular.' The lover, like the artist, loathes the general, the vague, the wise and lives only for the luminous singularity of the beloved or the glowing page. Everything else is insipid.

Lolita, as all the world knows, is full of parodies – parodies of literary essays, of scholarly lists of sources, of scientific treatises, of psychiatric reports and especially of the confession and the legal defense. It is also a compendium of sometimes serious, but usually jocular allusions to key works of nineteenth-century romanticism, especially French fiction and verse (Humbert's first language is French, of course, and *Lolita* is more Gallic than American or Russian, at least in its explicit references and models). But the function of this brilliant panoply of literary allusions is not to disown romanticism but to recapture it. As

Thomas R. Frosch remarks in 'Parody and Authenticity in *Lolita*', as essay published in the recent collection *Nabokov's Fifth Arc*:

> In relation to romance, parody acts in Lolita in a defensive and proleptic way. It doesn't criticize the romance mode, although it criticizes Humbert; it renders romance acceptable by anticipating our mockery and beating us to the draw. It is what Empson calls 'pseudo-parody to disarm criticism'. I am suggesting, then, that *Lolita* can only be a love story through being a parody of love stories.

To be sure, the entire history of romantic verse and fiction has been self-consciously literary. One could go further and insist that romantic passion itself is literary; as La Rochefoucauld said, no one would ever have fallen in love unless he had first read about it. Humbert and Lolita's mother, Charlotte Haze, represent two quite distinct romantic traditions, the courtly versus the bourgeois. For the courtly lover, love is useless, painful, unfulfilled, obsessive, destructive and his very allegiance to this peculiar, seemingly unnatural ideal is proof of his superiority to ordinary mortals. As Frederick Goldin has remarked about the origins of courtly love in the Middle Ages:

> Ordinary men cannot love unless they get something in return – something they can get hold of, not just a smile. If they do not get it, they soon stop loving, or, if the girl is from one of the lower orders, they take it by force. But usually, since ordinary men love ordinary women, they get what they want; and then, their mutual lust expended, they go their separate ways, or else, if they are restrained by some vulgar decency, they mate and settle down. In this wilderness of carnality and domesticity, nobility declines; there is no reason, and no change, for the longing, exaltation and selfdiscipline of true courtliness. This is one of the basic creeds of courtly love.

One of the most amusing paradoxes of *Lolita* is that the satyr Humbert Humbert becomes the *minnesinger* of courtly love for the twentieth century. To be sure, before he can fully exemplify the 'longing, exaltation and self-discipline of true courtliness', Humbert must lose Lolita and kill his double, Quilty. If Humbert and Quilty have mirrored one another in the first half of the book, in the second half they turn into opposites, as Humbert become leaner, older, more fragile, more Quixotic and Quilty grows grosser, drunker, fatter and more corrupt; the murder of Quilty expiates Humbert of everything base.

If Humbert embodies courtly love, Charlotte comes out of a different, more recent tradition – the ideal of bourgeois companionate marriage. A tribute to Nabokov's compassion is his gentle treatment of the ridiculous Charlotte, who in spite of her constant smoking, her bad French, her humorlessness, her middle-brow cultural aspirations and her actual cruelty to her daughter is none the less shown as a lonely, touching, decent women: 'To break Charlotte's will I would have to break her heart. If I broke her heart, her image of me would break too. If I said: "Either I have my way with Lolita, and you help me to keep the matter quiet, or we part at once," she would have turned as pale as a woman of clouded glass and slowly replied: "All right, whatever you add or subtract, this is the end."' Even the grudging Humbert must testify to Charlotte's perfect moral pitch and characterize her, poetically, as a creature of 'clouded glass', a description that denotes nothing but connotes beauty.

Charlotte has been shaped by her reading – the reading of women's magazines and home-decoration manuals and popular novels. Her pious expectations of the monogamous and 'totally fulfilling' marriage in which sex, sentiment and even religious faith coincide is at odds with Humbert's stronger emotions and more desperate aspirations. The best Humbert can do by way of a domestic fantasy is to imagine marrying Lolita, fathering a daughter and living long enough to indulge in incest not only with that child but *her* daughter as well: 'bizarre, tender, salivating Dr Humbert, practicing on supremely lovely Lolita the Third the art of being a granddad'. Even when he attempts for a moment to abandon his own brand of romantic literature, the script of his courtly and obsessive passion, for Charlotte's kind of pulp, the attempt fails: 'I did my best; I read and reread a book with the unintentionally biblical title *Know Your Own Daughter* . . .'

Nabokov wrote in *The Gift* that 'the spirit of parody always goes along with genuine poetry'. If 'genuine poetry' is taken to mean romantic literature about passion, one can only concur, since passion is parody. Critics keep trying to find some Ur-text that all later romantic fiction is commenting on, but that search has turned into an infinite regress. *Don Quixote* is a parody of tales of knightly adventure; in Dante the lovers Francesca and Paolo discover their mutual passion when they read 'of Lancelot, how love constrained him'. The pump of Emma Bovary's ardor has been primed by her reading of cheap romantic magazine stories. In *Eugene Onegin*, Tatiana is besotted by romantic fiction:

> With what attention she now
> reads a delicious novel,
> with what vivid enchantment
> drinks the seductive fiction!

But her reading, alas, is different from Onegin's, for Tatiana reads Rousseau's fiction and Goethe's *Sorrows of the Young Werther* (as Nabokov comments in his notes, 'Werther weeps on every occasion, likes to romp with small children, and is passionately in love with Charlotte. They read *Ossian* together in a storm of tears.') Immersed in her own brand of Lachrymose Lit, Tatiana

> sighs, and having made her own
> another's ecstasy, another's melancholy,
> she whispers in a trance, by heart, a letter
> to the amiable hero.

That letter sounds weirdly like Charlotte Haze's avowal. Charlotte writes:

> I am nothing to you. Right? Right. Nothing to you whatever. *But* if, after reading my 'confession' you decided, in your dark roman-European way, that I am attractive enough for you to take advantage of my letter and make a pass at me, then you would be a criminal – worse than a kidnapper who rapes a child. You see, cheri. *If* you decided to stay, *if* I found you at home . . .

and so on. Surely this letter is a parody of Tatiana's infinitely more touching but no less fervent appeal:

> My fate
> henceforth I place into your hands,
> before you I shed tears,
> for your defense I plead . . .
> I'm waiting for you: with a single look
> revive my heart's hopes;
> or interrupt the heavy dream,
> alas, with a deserved rebuke.

Humbert may fake an acceptance of Charlotte's avowal, but Onegin rejects Tatiana in rolling Byronic phrases:

> But I'm not made for bliss;
> my soul is strange to it;
> in vain are your perfections:
> I'm not worthy of them.

This misunderstanding, fatal to the future happiness of both characters, is not so much due to intrinsic character differences as to different reading lists. Whereas Tatiana has read of lovers given to sacrifice, duty and devotion, Onegin has been coached by Byron's egotistical and disabused *Don Juan*:

> My days of love are over; me no more
>   The charms of maid, wife . . .
> Can make the fool . . .
> The credulous hope of mutual minds is o'er.

Years go by, Tatiana suffers, becomes stoic, and then one day is drawn to Onegin's deserted country house. She enters his library, reads the books he once read, and in a stunning passage she wonders whether Onegin might not be 'a glossary of other people's megrims, / a complete lexicon of words in vogue? . . . Might he not be, in fact, a parody?' Just as Charlotte recognizes Humbert's criminal passions for Lolita once she reads his diary, so Tatiana understands Onegin is a fraud once she peruses his books.

The Byronic hero could, in his most degraded form, become coldly indifferent to women and with men murderously touchy on points of honor. If the calculating seduction is the way the Byronic monster approaches women, his characteristic exchange with other men is the duel. Here again Humbert executes a grotesque parody of the duel in his stalking down of Quilty; this is the final sorry end to the already shoddy, senseless business of the Lenski–Onegin duel.

My point, then, seems to be that we should not be surprised if *Lolita* is a parody of earlier works of romantic literature, including not only Onegin but much more obviously a whole succession of French novels devoted to the anatomy of the passions – that line that runs from the *Princesse de Clèves* through *Les Liaisons dangereuses, Adolphe, Atala* and *René* and on to *Mademoiselle Maupin, Carmen* and *Madame Bovary* – a tradition, moreover, that Humbert specifically alludes to again and again. His mind is also well-stocked with French poetry from Ronsard to Rimbaud. Whereas some Russian Formalists (I'm thinking of Tynyanov's *Dostoevski and Gogol: Remarks on the Theory of Parody*) argued that parody is a way of disowning the past in an act of literary warfare, in Nabokov's case we see that parody can be the fondest tribute, the deepest embrace, the invention of a tradition against which one's own originality can be discerned, a payment of past debts in order to accrue future capital.

I may also seem to be saying that if *Lolita*, the supreme novel of love in the twentieth century, is a parody of earlier love novels, we should not be surprised, since love itself – the very love you and I experience in real life – is also a parody of earlier love novels. I have even intimated that conflicts in love, whether they are those between Onegin and Tatiana or Humbert and Charlotte or you and me, are attributable to different reading lists – that amorous dispute is really always a battle of books.

If I made such an assertion, or if I attributed it to Nabokov, I would be subscribing to the approach to literature and art advanced by Roland Barthes in *S/Z*, though later disowned by him in *A Lover's Discourse*. In *S/Z*, that detailed, elusive, dense, patient analysis of a story by Balzac, Barthes proposes that the literature of the bourgeoisie is nothing but an interweaving of cultural codes. Various strategies are employed by the writer (one might say via the writer, since he is scarcely conscious of what he is doing) to provide the illusion of reality, to hoodwink the reader into believing that 'love' and all its rituals (the declaration, the tryst, the impediments to happiness, the vow, the discovery, the catastrophe) – that 'love' is something natural and not cultural. In exploding the convention of realism, the illusion of the naturalness of love, Barthes destroys every term in the literary equation. In this extreme view, there is no reader, no text and no writer. No reader, because as Barthes puts it: 'This "I" which approaches the text is already itself a plurality of other texts.' No text, because the text is merely a mathematical point traversed by the codes, a braid in the interweaving of voices. And finally no writer because he is merely a stenographer taking down dictation from the culture around him. In this absence we have, alas, 'literature', that is, the ceaseless read-out of the well-stocked computer as it jabbers to itself. It would be foolish to attribute such views to Nabokov. Everything in his proud and lonely nature would have been opposed to such an automatism. As a critic, after all, he is the great spokesman for the genius and the masterpiece; he had no tolerance for schools, movements, minor works, influences. As an artist he was a convinced believer in inspiration; if he was taking dictation, it was not from the culture around him but from the angels.

For Nabokov true literature – the literature of genius – is not self-enclosed but transcendent, not reductive but inductive. Although he was exuberantly, even boisterously alert to the conventional, parody was his method of quarantining it and even curing it. If he acknowledged the nauseating repetitiveness of all past love stories, he did so in order to write one that was utterly new, just-born, perfect. As he said in the postscript to *Lolita*: 'For me a work of fiction exists only in so far as it affords me what I shall bluntly call aesthetic bliss, that is a sense of being somehow, somewhere, connected with other states of being where art (curiosity, tenderness, kindness, ecstasy) is the norm.'

This curiosity includes a close scrutiny of nature. Nabokov is our freshest landscape painter in words, and not surprisingly he was an admirer of other gifted writers of description. In his book on Gogol he argues that Gogol was the first Russian writer to free himself from the rigid conventional color schemes of the eighteenth-century French school of literature. As Nabokov writes:

> the development of the art of description throughout the centuries may be profitably treated in terms of vision, the faceted eye becoming a unified and prodigiously complex organ and the dead dim 'accepted colors' (in the sense of *'idées reçues'*) yielding gradually their subtle shades and allowing new wonders of application. I doubt whether any writer, and certainly not in Russia, had ever noted before [Gogol], to give the most striking instance, the moving pattern of light and shade on the ground under trees or the tricks of color played by sunlight with leaves.

For Nabokov, such observations constitute news; one might even say they figure as scientific discovery. One sometimes feels that Nabokov the lepidopterist is not unlike Chekhov the doctor, and that like Chekhov Nabokov might have declared: 'My familiarity with the natural sciences and the scientific method has always kept me on my guard; I have tried wherever possible to take scientific data into account, and where it has not been possible I have preferred not writing at all.' To be sure, Nabokov once remarked that fiction began with fairy tales, but again one is reminded that, as Howard Moss has observed, 'Chekhov's stories tread the finest line between a newspaper account and a fairy tale.'

With Chekhov and Nabokov, observation constitutes an importation of something brand new, something unprecedented into the realm of discourse. To all those critics who consider literature to be an entirely self-referential system, a grand tautology, I would submit that if their assertion is being made on an epistemological plane about the possibility of communication of any sort, then literature is certainly no *more* disabled than any other form of language (including criticism). But if the assertion is being made about literature in particular as distinct from language in general, then the assertion seems to me, quite simply, wrong, for surely literature, at least as practiced by Nabokov, is both descriptive and expressive, a new compilation of exact statements about the natural world and the self arranged into large fictional structures (mystery, suspense, plot) that recreate in the reader the very emotions that are being felt by the characters. In fact, the very old claim that fiction is a privileged form of communication because it falls between the disembodied or at least undramatized abstractions of philosophy and the random circumstantiality of history seems to me still true, not because fiction is a mirror to reality, a flawless reflection of it, but because the same convergence of pattern-making and sensation that creates perception functions in the writing and reading of fiction in much the same way as it functions in our experiencing of the real world. To be less vague about it, one could argue that in *Pale Fire* Kinbote's paranoid glimpses of meaning everywhere fascinate us not because we identify with his character but with his process of gathering data and constructing and revising theories about what's happening.

Love, like paranoia, is also an organizing obsession, an imposition of pattern on the atoms of experience. But Nabokov the realist, the scientific observer, is not content to treat the sentiments as either personal or cooperative delusions, nor does he view love as merely a literary exercise. In his treatment of love in particular, Nabokov points the way beyond parody and convention. At their best his characters act out of character, transcend their roles. The most sublime moment in *Lolita*, of course, occurs when Humbert sees the 'hugely pregnant' Lolita after searching for her for several years.

> There she was with her ruined looks and her adult, rope-veined narrow hands and her goose-flesh white arms, and her shallow ears, and her unkempt armpits, there she was (my Lolita!) hopelessly worn at seventeen, with that baby, dreaming already in her of becoming a big shot and retiring around 2020 AD – and I looked and looked at her, and knew as clearly as I know I am to die, that I loved her more than anything I had ever seen or imagined on earth, or hoped for anywhere else . . .

Here the pervert breaks through the narrow confines of his perversion, the connoisseur of *le fruit vert* looks longingly at the no-longer-ripe apple in a now vanished Eden. Passion – fastidious, tyrannical, hostile – has given way to compassionate love, a grand obsession in the mode of Racine has been supplanted by tender esteem à la Corneille. Correspondingly, Lolita shrugs off her own grudges and forgives Humbert for having taken away her youth; when Humbert asks her to leave with him, she says, 'No, honey, no.' In the most heartbreaking line I know, Humbert writes: 'She had never called me honey before.'

A similar moment when love transcends passion, when sentiment exceeds sexuality, occurs in *Pale Fire*. The exclusively homosexual Kinbote, who had always treated his wife with 'friendly indifference and bleak respect' while drooling after 'Eton-collared, sweet-voiced minions' – Kinbote begins to *dream* of Disa, his Queen, with throbbing tenderness:

> He dreamed of her more often, and with incomparably more poignancy, than his surface-like feelings for her warranted; these dreams occurred when he least thought of her, and worries in no way connected with her assumed her image in the subliminal world as a battle or a reform becomes a bird of wonder in a tale for children. These heartrending dreams transformed the drab prose of his feelings for her into strong and strange poetry.

The transcendent virtue of love is seen again in *Ada* when aged rake Van Veen is reunited after many years with his now plump and no longer appealing Ada: 'He loved her much too tenderly, much too irrevocably, to be unduly depressed by sexual misgivings.' This from the great sensual purist! Of course this very passage, in which love goes beyond its conventional limits, is, paradoxically, itself a parody of the end of *War and Peace* and the marriage of Natasha and Pierre.

Andrew Field writes, 'All of his novels, Nabokov told me once, have an air – *not quite of this world, don't you think?*' Field didn't take the remark seriously; he thought it was just more leg-pulling. But I think the hint that his novels are 'not quite of this world' should be taken seriously. After boyhood Nabokov was not conventionally religious, although the poetry of his early twenties continued to rely occasionally on religious imagery. Nevertheless, he retained within his pages a quick, visceral sense of disturbing spiritual presences. His is a haunted world, and to prove it W. W. Rowe has just published an entire volume to that effect: *Nabokov's Spectral Dimension*. Inspiration itself is such a specter of course; in *The Gift* when Fyodor begins to write, he is conscious of 'a pulsating mist that suddenly began to speak with a human voice'. Vera Nabokov, the writer's wife, editor, mentor and the dedicatee of virtually every book from his pen, has said that a main theme in all of Nabokov's writing is 'the hereafter'. Of Fyodor's father, the boy thinks: 'It was as if this genuine, very genuine man possessed an aura of something still unknown but which was perhaps the most genuine of all.'

The luminous unknown, this aura of the ghostly genuine, is always bordering the picture Nabokov presents to his reader. The narrator of his last novel, *Look at the Harlequins!*, is afflicted with recurrent bouts of madness. His perception of space is so personal and so harrowing that at one point he becomes paralyzed. 'Yet I have known madness not only in the guise of an evil shadow,' he tells us. 'I have seen it also as a flash of delight so rich and shattering that the very absence of an immediate object on which it might settle was to me a form of escape.'

It is in those flashes of delight, which illuminate almost every passage, that Nabokov's glimpses of another world can be detected. Lolita's smile, for instance, 'was never directed at the stranger in the room but hung in its own remote flowered void, so to speak, or wandered with myopic softness over chance objects'. In *The Gift*, the hero imagines returning to his ancestral home in Russia: 'One after another the telegraph poles will hum at my approach. A crow will settle on a boulder – settle and straighten a wing that has folded wrong.' That straightened wing – the precision of an *imagined imaginary* detail – is worthy of a Zen master. In 'Spring in Fialta', we encounter 'that life-quickening atmosphere of a big railway station where everything is something trembling on the brink of something else – a phrase that might well serve as Nabokov's artistic credo (and that recalls Quine's notion that a verbal investigation of language is akin to building a boat while sailing in it).

In Nabokov's fiction the strong, even melodramatic lines of the plot are subverted by the fluent language, phrases so joyful and highly colored that they transform tales of dimwits, freaks and madmen into ecstatic tributes to youth, glamor and the exhilaration of genius. When Humbert is about to seduce Lolita for the first time (as it turns out, she seduces him), he pulls his car into the parking lot of a country hotel called The Enchanted Hunters. Everything in this passage is cast in mythic terms, the language of the Circe episode of *The Odyssey*. The car approaches by 'falling under the smooth spell of a nicely graded curve', the 'pale palace' materialized under 'spectral trees'. 'A row of parked cars, like pigs at a trough, seemed at first sight to forbid access; but then, by magic,' a space is provided. 'A hunchbacked and hoary Negro in a uniform of sorts took our bags.' At the desk they are registered by a 'porcine old man'. And so on. Again, when Humbert shoots Quilty, the scene is set as in a fairy tale with echoes of Browning's 'Childe Roland to the Dark Tower Came'.

The function of mythology in Nabokov is not (as it is in Joyce's *Ulysses*) to limit the neural *sprawl* of a stream of consciousness. Nor is it to provide a ready-made plot (as in the neoclassical drama of Anouilh and Giraudoux). Nor is it to lend false dignity to an otherwise dreary tale, as in the plays of Archibald MacLeish or Eugene O'Neill. In Nabokov the vocabulary of religion, fairy tales, and myths is the only one adequate to his sense of the beauty and mystery of the sensual, of love, of childhood, of nature, of art, of people when they are noble. It is this language that metamorphoses the comic bedroom scene in *Lolita* into a glimpse of paradise. Once they're in the hotel room, Lolita

> walked up to the open suitcase as if stalking it from afar, in a kind of slowmotion walk, peering at that distant treasure box on the luggage support. (Was there something wrong, I wondered, with those great gray eyes of hers, or were we both plunged in the same enchanted mist?) She stepped up to it, lifting her rather high-heeled feet rather high, and bending her beautiful boyknees while she walked through dilating space with the lentor of one walking under water or in a flight dream.

Nabokov's novels are not of this world, but of a better one. He has kept the romantic novel alive by introducing into it a new tension – the struggle between obsessive or demented characters and a-seraphic rhetoric. Given his inspired style, no wonder Nabokov chose to write about not the species nor the variety but the mutant individual. Only such a subject gives his radiant language something to do, to overcome – a job to perform. In fact, there is only one story, 'Lance', in which Nabokov relaxed this tension and indulged in his verbal splendors with chilling abandon. In that story the young hero, Lance Boke, ascends into the heavens as his old parents watch through field glasses: 'The brave old Bokes think they can distinguish Lance scaling, on crampons, the verglassed rock of the sky or silently breaking trail through the soft snows of nebulae.' I like to think of Nabokov himself, the supreme alpinist of the art, ascending those new heights.

He must be ranked, finally, not with other writers but with a composer and a choreographer, Stravinsky and Balanchine. All three men were of the same generation, all three were Russians who were clarified by passing through the sieve – should I say the *chinois*? – of French culture but were brought to the boiling point only by the breezy short-order cook of American informality. All three experimented boldly with form, but none produced 'avant-garde trash', as Nabokov called it, for all three were too keen on recuperating tradition. In a work such as the *Pulcinella* ballet score, the Baroque mannerisms of Pergolesi are aped, even insisted upon, but Baroque squares are turned into modernist rhomboids and scalenes and mechanical Baroque transitions, the yard goods of that style, are eliminated in favor of a crisp collage built up out of radical juxtapositions. Everything is fresh, new, heartless – and paradoxically all the more moving for the renovation. Similarly, Balanchine eliminated mime, a fussy *port de bras*, story and decor to make plotless ballets that distil the essence of the Petipa tradition. As parodists, all three artists loved the art they parodied and made it modern by placing old gems in new settings.

Most important, all three men had a vision of art as entertainment, not, to be sure, as a vulgar courting of debased popular taste but as a wooing of shrewder, more restless though always robust sensibilities. Sartre once attacked Nabokov for his lack of political content, but one could reply to that charge without hesitation that the paradise Balanchine, Stravinsky and Nabokov have made visible to us is one of the few images of happiness we have, that very happiness politics is working to secure, the promise of harmony, beauty, rapture.

In 'Fame', a poem he wrote in Russian in 1942, Nabokov bitterly echoed the 1836 poem *Exegi monumentum* of Pushkin, which in turn echoed the poem by Horace and many another earlier poet. Whereas Horace and Pushkin could well consider their verse a monument they had raised to their own eternal glory, Nabokov, writing in exile for a tiny Russian-speaking audience that would soon be dying out, could only imagine a fantastic, garrulous visitor:

'Your poor books,' he breezily said, 'will finish
by hopelessly fading in exile. Alas,
those two thousand leaves of frivolous fiction
will be scattered . . .'

As we know now, and know with gratitude, the prophecy was not fulfilled. More glorious and surprising in his metamorphosis than any butterfly he ever stalked, Nabokov, the Russian master, turned himself into a writer in English, the best of the century. He raised a monument to himself after all.

Writer on a Hot Tin Roof: Tennessee Williams

Review of *The Kindness of Strangers: The Wife of Tennessee Williams*, by Donald Spoto, *New Republic*, 13 May 1985.

There are no second acts in the lives of American writers because everyone gets drunk during the intermission. At least that's the conclusion to be drawn from the biographies of one generation: Carson McCullers, Jane Bowles, William Inge, Truman Capote, and Tennessee Williams. Of that group, I can think of only Paul Bowles, Gore Vidal, and Ned Rorem who survive and still work. They also seem to be the three with the widest culture and interests.

But I don't want to fall into the very mistake most of their biographers make, who regard alcoholism as psychologically caused rather than as a physiological result. Again and again boozing is presented as passionate, life-affirming paganism gone awry, or as the insulation of a sensitive soul against a brutal milieu. Williams himself subscribed to the metaphysical theory of drink, as in this passage from *The Night of the Iguana*, when a New England spinster addresses an Irish drunk who's having the DTs:

HANNAH: Liquor isn't your problem, Mr Shannon.
SHANNON: What is my problem, Miss Jelkes?
HANNAH: The oldest one in the world – the need to believe in
    something or in someone – almost anyone – almost anything
    . . . something.

Never is alcoholism or drug addiction seen in writers' biographies as a self-perpetuating habit and a chemical dependency that leads to growing isolation, confusion, and depression. The artist-as-martyr continues to be a potent romantic myth; the writer is punished by alcoholism for having dared to steal heavenly fire. No wonder it's Prometheus's liver that bird keeps pecking at. Alcoholism-as-retribution, say, makes a better literary theme than alcoholism-as-disease, unless, of course, the reader finds the perspective false. Dare I suggest that many biographies (and even some novels, such as *Under the Volcano*) that take the romantic approach to drink are beginning to seem dated – writable perhaps, but no longer readable?

Donald Spoto comments extensively on Williams's vast œuvre – his twenty-five full length plays, more than forty short plays, his volume of memoirs, two novels, sixty-odd short stories, some hundred poems, published letters, and occasional pieces. Although Williams was immensely noticed during most of his writing career (there are thirty-three volumes of collected reviews of his work), *The Kindness of Strangers* is the first biography. I tired of the show-bizzy 'philosophy' of Spoto's text, the 'she-was-a-warm-wonderful-wise-human-being' kind of prose, but I do admire the book's thoroughness and its obvious affection for its subject. Williams is a man any lesser spirit would have quickly come to detest. But Spoto never loses sight of Williams's genius, and never lets his excessive knowledge of the playwright's failures as an artist or man lead to condescension.

Tom Williams was the child of a mismatch – and instantly we're plunged into his most autobiographical play, *The Glass Menagerie*. His mother, Edwina Davis, was the daughter of a refined Episcopalian clergyman, and in her girlhood she was besieged by 'gentlemen callers' until she married a coarse, hard-drinking, womanizing salesman. Their first child was Rose. Two years later, in 1911, Tom was born in Columbus, Mississippi, followed eight years later by a younger brother, Walter. The family settled in St Louis, an industrial city quite alien to their previous life in genteel small towns.

Growing up gay in the classic American way, Tom was a sissy who hated sports and whom his father dubbed 'Miss Nancy'. He never showed much talent as a student; he preferred daydreaming or playing with his sister to everything else. Nor did he discover sex of any sort until he was twenty-six. Williams and Kerouac are among the few writers I know of who didn't read much. Despite this lack of curiosity, Williams did manage early on to discover both Strindberg and Chekhov, who influenced his major plays.

The violent confrontations of Strindberg's unhappy couples in his realistic plays and the symbolic fantasias of his dream plays surface in Williams's work. So does the poetic realism of Chekhov's lovable incompetents in minutely observed, tightly structured but apparently disorganized dramas, so unstable in their shifts of tone from comedy to tragedy, from wisdom to banality.

Tom's low grades and the family's strained budget during the Depression caused his father to withdraw him from college in 1932 (before graduation) and set him to work in a shoe factory. By this point, however, Tom had begun his rigorous, lifelong habit of writing daily and prolifically. He first received recognition as a poet, although today his poems read like a blend of A. E. Housman and Sara Teasdale, a fusion that isn't admirable but is certainly likeable. While living at home, he looked on as his mother encouraged 'gentlemen callers' to visit her terrified, fragile daughter Rose. Both of the older children, exposed to their parents' quarrels and the gibes of working-class neighbor kids, showed signs of strain. Tom had a shocking anxiety attack and Rose began her decline into insanity. By 1936, Rose was under psychiatric treatment – to no avail. The next year, she witnessed her drunk father beat her mother and became hysterical for days when her father then made a pass at her. As in *A Streetcar Named Desire*, or like Mrs Venable in *Suddenly Last Summer*, Mrs Williams was unable to accept Rose's allegation against her father and gave permission for Rose to be lobotomized. For the rest of her long life, Rose was to be institutionalized, except for brief stays with Tom.

After going back to school, this time to the University of Iowa, Tom finally received a degree in English at the age of twenty-seven. He drifted to New Orleans, lived in boarding rooms, slept with men for the first time, and, with his sharp instinct for his 'image', changed his name to Tennessee (his maternal grandparents, whom he adored, lived in Memphis). He started drinking, carousing, raising hell – and writing the plays and stories that would provide him with his literary capital for years to come. Indeed, one of his very last plays was *Vieux Carré*, based on those New Orleans days.

A consolation prize in a literary contest led Williams to his agent, Audrey Wood, and she, after a long struggle, managed to launch her client into stardom. By the time he was in his thirties, Williams was an international celebrity with *The Glass Menagerie* (1944), soon followed by *A Streetcar Named Desire* (1947). More than any other American playwright, Williams wrote plays that were not only hits but also enduring works of the repertory. They include *Summer and Smoke* (1948), *The Rose Tattoo* (1951), *Cat on a Hot Tin Roof* (1955), *Baby Doll* (1957), *Suddenly Last Summer* (1958), *Sweet Bird of Youth* (1959), and *Night of the Iguana* (1961).

Williams was an early master of publicity. In the 1960s when his talent was drying up, he turned himself – his excesses and reverses – into an eye-catching product. Only Andy Warhol and Norman Mailer understood as well as he how to give a good interview. On the Sunday before a new play was to open, Williams would write in the *New York Times* about his disputes with his psychoanalyst – confessions that were fatally readable. Or he'd announce his conversion to Catholicism – and then, a year later, his disillusion with the church. Or he'd tell an interviewer, 'I'm a built-in definition of hysteria. I hate myself. I feel I bore people – and that I'm too physically repulsive.' Of course the slipping in of the word 'too' suggests comic perspectives, and indeed in his later writings Williams was often comically grotesque, obscenely Gothic.

A persistent sentimentality haunts even the most successful of Tennessee Williams's plays. If sentimentality means unearned and unrendered emotion, then we must find sentimental his habitual recourse to such an automatic bid for sympathy as madness (an undefined, 'pure' state of madness), just as his invariable linking of madness to sexual frustration (or, conversely, to sexual violation) seems blandly and routinely Freudian. Sympathy for the crazed sex victim is the expected audience response in *The Glass Menagerie*, *A Streetcar Named Desire*, and *Summer and Smoke*.

But if such expectations give these plays their lurid appeal, as irresistible as a Sousa march, their enduring value lies elsewhere – in their ventriloquism. Williams recognized that great theater begins with great talkers, and that great talkers obey two rules: they never sound like anyone else and they never say anything directly. In *Streetcar* Blanche confesses to having only 'sixty-five measly cents in coin of the realm', just as earlier she announces, 'I can't stand a naked light bulb, any more than I can a rude remark or a vulgar action.' This is a line of varying poetic stress – 'light bulb' an emphatic spondee, 'rude remark' an elegant, old-fashioned anapest, and 'vulgar action' a pair of irritable but helpless trochees. Or the mother in *The Glass Menagerie* veers hysterically from faded coquetry ('All of a sudden – heavens! Already summer! – I ran to the trunk an' pulled out this light dress – Terribly old! Historical almost! But feels so good – so good an' cool, y'know . . .') to biblical cadences of reproach ('You are the only young man that I know of who ignores the fact that the future becomes the present, the present the past, and the past turns into everlasting regret if you don't plan for it!').

Amanda, Blanche, Serafina (in *The Rose Tattoo*), Big Daddy (in *Cat on a Hot Tin Roof*) – these are only some of the great talkers Williams invented and recorded. Here's Big Daddy: 'I haven't been able to stand the sight, sound, or smell of that woman for forty years now! – even when I *laid* her! – regular as a piston.' Like a line in W. S. Merwin, 'even when I laid her!' modifies the phrase that precedes and follows it.

Sometimes, like Shakespeare's Richard II, Williams's characters aren't given actions adequate to their verbal splendors, but even their undramatized soliloquies outshine the hard-working dialogue of lesser characters by lesser writers. For lesser characters are lesser poets. As it turns out, quite contrary to what we learned in school, the most memorable people in plays are not representative figures. They are not condensations of the normal. No, they are unique, and if they fascinate us on stage they do so because they'd also fascinate us at a cocktail party. We can't stop listening to them and looking at them, not because the intellectual content of their speech is so gripping but because their timing, their dilations and contractions, their periphrases, their musical instinct for rubato are spellbinding.

Many of Williams's intimates (as well as his biographer) ascribe his decline to the death of his lover Frank Merlo in the early 1960s. Merlo, a New Jersey-born Navy veteran and a second-generation Sicilian, had been Williams's long-suffering companion for fifteen years, someone who had never flattered the master but rather evaluated his work with acuity and lent his chaotic, peripatetic life some dignity and stability. And Merlo was the one with the charm. People took up with the couple because they were attracted by Williams's fame, but if they stuck around they did so because they were seduced by Merlo's easygoing amiability.

I met Tennessee Williams once toward the end of his life, at a party given in Key West by the poet James Merrill and David Jackson. The afternoon before the cocktail party, David called to say Tennessee would be bringing his sister Rose, who'd gotten it into her head she was the true queen of England. We were instructed to bow to her and call her 'Your Majesty'.

I passed these protocol instructions along to my houseguest, the crusty octogenarian composer Virgil Thomson. Virgil said, 'I'm too old to jump through Tennessee's hoop. I'll call Rose "ma'am", which is a good Southern expression – *and* a perfectly good way to address a queen.'

Looking tanned, sober, and fit, Tennessee made a late entrance with his companions, the actor John Uecker (who resembles the young Marlon Brando) and Rose. I noticed right away that all three of them had a wad of yellowed cotton in their right ears and that when separated they still kept communicating with each other through little eerie grins. Rose, with short styled hair, clear skin and huge sapphire eyes, behaved with composure, even when she stole all the soap and matches in the house. If she said incoherent things, John Uecker slapped his thigh with amusement as though she were concocting delightful Dada nonsense to entertain us. When we left, Virgil insisted that Rose-as-queen was Tennessee's delusion, not his sister's.

Spoto includes a touching anecdote about Rose. In the autumn of 1949, when Rose was already forty, Tennessee visited her at her hospital in Ossining, New York. When he came back to the car, the multimillionaire was clutching a ten-dollar bill. Rose had given him the money as he was leaving.

'Tom,' she had whispered, 'I know how hard you are working at the shoe warehouse. I know you want to be a poet, and I believe in you. I have been saving some change for you, and I hope this will help things to be a little easier. If you will just be patient, I know good things will be ahead. Always remember I believe in you.'

The Woman Who Loved Memory:
Christina Stead

Review of *Ocean of Story: The Uncollected Stories of Christina Stead*, edited by R. G. Geering, *New York Times Book Review*, May 1986.

Christina Stead, the Australian-born author of thirteen novels and, if we include this new volume, two collections of short stories, lived from 1902 to 1983. With some stretching she could be seen as a female counterpart to D. H. Lawrence. Like him, she grew up amid great hardship, fought free of her binding family, wrote copiously with the natural ease of a born novelist, recycled her own childhood and adult experiences into radically transposed fictions, traveled widely, won renown but lived outside the literary establishment – and shocked her contemporaries with the unsmutty high seriousness with which she treated the sexual relations between men and women.

Like Lawrence, she saw sex as, at its best, a means of exaltation, transcendence and intimate accord and, at its worst, a degrading enslavement. Unlike Lawrence, she recognized that women are as complex and varied as men: she once wrote in a note to a correspondent, 'I often felt that quite well known writings lacked truth, and this was particularly so of the pictures of women, I felt, not only because women took their complete part in society but were not represented as doing so, but because the long literary tradition ... had enabled men completely to express themselves, while women feared to do so.'

And unlike Lawrence, Stead carried very little theoretical baggage, felt no attraction to Fascism or psychoanalysis and had no program for reforming humanity. She had leftist sympathies but no doctrines. She accepted people as they are. Stead troubles many readers who keep struggling to uncover what she 'really' believes or stands for. Having just reread five of her books I'd be hard pressed to give a précis of her philosophy, partly no doubt because she herself thought in the concrete particulars of dailiness rather than in abstract universals. Her characters might discuss the Spanish Civil War, the profit motive, the need for premarital chastity, the law of the jungle as applied to Wall Street, but the author's own views of these questions remain shadowy. Just as a Chekhov character might belabor everyone on the need to work and then stagger off for another vodka and a nap, leaving the audience uncertain as to what to think about either work or the character, so, too, in Stead's fiction, ideas are used to render fine shading in portraits, not to ring up an ideological total.

I wish I had read Stead when I was growing up in the 1950s; she might have taught me to view the world with her own brand of refinement and independence. In that harshly intolerant period she might have coaxed me to smile at a whole array of possibly regrettable but indisputably human failings. And in that Hollywood-haunted era she might have enabled me to find pleasure in people less than picture-perfect. In Stead's world people over sixty make love and even the tired and overweight live in a nimbus of desirability.

Ocean of Story, a hefty volume of her previously uncollected stories, edited by R. G. Geering, brims over with her curiosity about other people's lives and her compulsion to recount what happened to them. For Stead a story is not a shapely fable but a thickly detailed rendering of an individual. In a story titled 'The Old School', she remembers another child back in Australia, a girl too poor to bring lunch or supplies with her from home, who 'never volunteered word or action. There she is though, the little girl in white, with her bowed heavy shoulders and black eyes, in my mind; and with her, the horror of money'. (That last bit is all of Stead's politics we're likely to get – oblique, terse, effective.)

Or there's the old lady in Alsace ('A Household') who keeps stuffing her ailing husband with dangerous sweets and drink in order to polish him off as soon as possible, so she can move upstairs with her more appealing landlady. Or there's the beautiful young heiress drunk on a luxury ship ('A Night in the Indian Ocean') who keeps a nurse awake all night as she rambles through accounts of her tormented life.

In 'About the House', a married woman tells her husband's mistress:

If I could have got a divorce after my first child, I would have ... but I couldn't. I didn't know what to do and they had got rid of me at home, they didn't want me back. I am sure a good many women stay married because they have nowhere to go. Women usually only get married because they have nowhere to go.

Or there's the old man in 'The Azhdanov Tailors' who was a celebrated labor organizer back in Poland. Decades later he finds in exile in New York a Jewish tailor who remembers his glorious past. The discovery cheers both men and the tailor says, 'Now I know you are here, I have something to live for and I promise you that every year I'll come down to see you; and there is a friend of mind who knew you in Azhdanov who will come down, too, perhaps at Easter.' End of story.

Several stories in this collection prefigure or rework themes that appear in Stead's novels. 'A Harmless Affair', for instance, expands the odd triangle that comes at the conclusion of the 1944 novel, *For Love Alone*, based on Stead's escape from her family and Sydney toward London and love (her counterpart to Lawrence's *Sons and Lovers*). And *Ocean of Story* contains two abandoned false starts to Stead's masterpiece, *The Man Who Loved Children* (1940).

Randall Jarrell considered this novel to be as great as *Moby Dick* and thought Stead as unfairly neglected in our century as Melville was in his. In an essay about her titled 'An Unread Book', Jarrell said he prized the portrait of the father, Sam Pollit, whom he considered a buffoon as extraordinary as anything in Dostoevsky. He went on to say:

A style like Christina Stead's, so remarkable for its structural variety, its rhythmical spontaneity, forces you to remember that a style can be a whole way of existing, so that you exist, for the moment, in perfect sympathy with it: you don't read it so much as listen to it as it sweeps you along – fast enough, often, to make you feel a blurred pleasure in your own speed.

Although Jarrell touts Stead's realism (all critics consider their preferred brand of beauty to be the truth), she's a queer kind of realist. She does not serve up a stale slice of life on a greasy plate. Nor is she a notebook writer (as Chekhov and Marianne Moore were), a collector of facts and turns of phrase later tilted and tessellated into a shimmering mosaic. Memory, not observation, is Stead's mode – and memory causes her vision to be heightened, mythic, often operatic. As in Proust, her characters speak at great length, all parentheses and subclauses rigorously observed, in what can only be taken as a summary of many different scraps of utterance rendered here in a 'representative' pose (as one might combine details from ten of Napoleon's battles in a single portrait of the victor). The tirades of Henny, the vixen-mother in *The Man Who Loved Children*, are too full of ornamentation to be anything but a transcribed aria. The big set-pieces, such as the pungent cookout of mackerel just before Henny's suicide, are precursors of such bravura magic realist scenes as the fishing up the horsehead squirming with eels in *The Tin Drum*, or the dirt-eating episode in *One Hundred Years of Solitude*.

During her long and varied professional life, Christina Stead worked for a grain merchant in London and became a secretary in a Paris bank in the early 1930s. For two years she and her American husband, William Blake (a novelist and a political economist), lived in Spain. In 1937 they settled in New York, but returned to Europe after the war. They hopped about from country to country; *Ocean of Story* contains tales set in shabby Swiss hotels, a tumbledown stately home outside Paris and a middle-class London suburb.

Her characters are often businessmen with hearty manners, good intentions and crude jokes and restless women with strong bodies, sudden enthusiasms and wavering loyalties. When I read Stead I picture a Hopperesque man and woman on a stoop staring into the sunset, their bodies sculpted, their air detached. Unlike most writers who have treated businessmen and their secretaries, Stead is never satirical. She once wrote: 'I know the literary life is just what some people need, it helps many; but my life has been spent in different places, in touch with businessmen and people interested in economics – and even medicine.' She discovered that businessmen will tell a writer anything, even business secrets.

Stead's language strikes me as delightfully rearguard in its succulent vocabulary, unpredictable syntax, handcrafted turns of phrase. But her approach to larger fictional structures is fresher than tomorrow. She freely mixes dialogue, narration and analysis without subordinating motivation (the spirit) to description (matter); rather, she maintains both on an equal, anarchic footing. She flows easily from one character's mind to another's without ever worrying over 'problems' of point of view. Similarly, as a psychologist she refuses to make all the traits in a character cohere. She resists the evil reductionism of our culture and never 'totalizes' the self (an ugly but useful word).

She seems so perversely alive because as soon as she's summed up a character, that person starts to elude the definition, to drift like a radio signal; before long we're listening to a fascinating overlap of voices and music. Stead crowds so many stories into her glowing, mythic pages because, like Rilke, she seems to believe 'we possess of our past only what we love, and we want to possess everything we've lived through'.

Keeping Up With Jones

Review of *Into Eternity: The Life of James Jones, American Writer*, by Frank MacShane, *New Republic*, 9 December 1985.

The people on the Île St Louis still remember James Jones as a man who looked like a commando, but who revealed upon acquaintance an extraordinary sweetness. His appearance suited the French preconception of an American writer – an inspired savage, usually drunk – but his real gentleness disarmed them utterly. When I mentioned to the people who run the Brasserie St Louis that I brought them greetings from Jones's daughter Kaylie, my former writing student, they went into raptures over the great man who'd used their restaurant as his living room; they even had to summon their daughter and her new baby from some inner recess to meet the man who'd know *les Jones*.

In fact I'd never known James Jones, although his daughter did once bring her mother, Gloria, to an end-of-the-semester party I gave my Columbia fiction workshop. When I politely asked Mrs Jones (who once worked as a stand-in for Marilyn Monroe) what she was doing for Doubleday, she replied, 'I fuck writers.' She then asked me why I was gay and wanted to know if I was afraid of women, had I ever tried one, did I think there were teeth down there . . . I suddenly felt terribly prissy and *dépassé*, not at all the sort of writer James Jones, in his frank, searching way, would have liked.

Gloria was the great love of Jones's life – she and his writing. Once, when he thought he might die, Jones left a note for Gloria: 'I've always loved you an awful lot. More than I've ever loved anything or anybody. Maybe my own work I've loved as much.' The letter is pure Jones in its sincerity, its sacrifice of eloquence to the graceless truth, its egotism, and its generosity.

Despite his macho exterior, Jones had none of Hemingway's alternating sadism and self-hatred. He liked to help other writers and was extremely friendly with, among others, Irwin Shaw, Peter Matthiessen, Norman Mailer, James Baldwin, Willie Morris, William Styron, and Mary McCarthy. Jones would have been incapable of displaying the malice Hemingway evinced when Scribner's asked him for a comment on *From Here to Eternity*. Hemingway said of Jones:

> Things will probably catch up with him and he will probably commit suicide . . . To me he is an enormously skilful fuck-up and his book will do great damage to our country . . . I hope he kills himself as soon as it does not damage your or his sales. If you give him a literary tea you might ask him to drain a bucket of snot and then suck the pus out of a dead nigger's ear.

So much for the literary life.

Unlike Hemingway, Jones was concerned with analyzing the relations between men and women. His later books, so often misunderstood, can best be read in this light, especially *Go to the Window-Maker* and *Whistle*. As Frank MacShane writes in his analysis of *Go to the Window-Maker*, Jones researched that book by examining

> the lumpen world of male America as he found it in the West Indies. Consisting mainly of self-made men, it is a world of sports, drinking, and crude language. The men have no interior lives and spend most of their time together. Their sexual lives are unsatisfactory and most of them are maladjusted. Either they cannot perform at all or dissociate feeling from sex and settle for sensation.

Jones equated Hemingway's 'big masculine bullshit' with people's need for dangerous but consoling myths – the same need that had engendered 'heroes, great generals, and war'. Despite this rejection of Hemingway's influence, however, Jones recognized his talent as a writer and made his Florida workshop read *The Sun Also Rises*.

Like Hemingway, Jones was born in an Illinois town. Both writers were sons of professional men (a doctor in Hemingway's case, a dentist in Jones's) and both had Christian Scientist mothers they despised. And in both cases their fathers committed suicide by shooting themselves. It occurs to me that one could build a case that the best American writers of this century have been the children of that endangered species, the small entrepreneur or self-employed professional – precisely the class to which the most had been promised by free-enterprise rhetoric and less and less delivered. Thomas Pynchon, that foe of corporate internationalism, seems to belong to this class.

Like Hemingway, Jones left the States for Paris, but Jones's Paris was less artistic than his predecessor's, and far more luxurious and worldly. Jones's large *art nouveau* house on the Île St Louis, with its view of Notre-Dame and the Left Bank, became a sort of canteen for visiting American writers. But after Jones had to stop drinking, he and Gloria cultivated an ultra-chic set of the established rich, a group typified by Ethel de Croisset, a New York heiress who married a Frenchman and still lives in the 16th *arrondissement* surrounded by Matisses and Giacomettis. She was born a Woodward; her brother was shot by his wife, the subject of Capote's chapter at the Côte Basque in *Answered Prayers* and of a popular novel, *The Second Mrs Grenville*. Of all rich crowds in the world, this is the one most responsive to artists; frequenting artists (and supporting them when necessary) is as obligatory for the Paris *gratin* as charity work is for their New York counterparts.

Such a milieu could not have stood in greater contrast to Jones's background. Jones had grown up in Robinson, Illinois. As a boy he failed to distinguish himself in sports or academic work and frequently picked fights. He entered high school in 1935, during the heart of the Depression. His father was a drunk who lost all his money and spent most of his time away from home, indulging in self-pity at the local bar. His mother once warned her son that if he masturbated his hand would turn black – and she went so far as to paint his hand while he slept in order to prove her theory.

The Army freed Jones from his dismal home life. He'd enlisted first in the air corps, but he later transferred to the famously tough 27th Infantry Regiment. He participated in the Battle of Gaudalcanal. While in the Army he also discovered the novels of

Thomas Wolfe, which served as his main inspiration to write –
and as a model for many passages in his first published novel,
From Here to Eternity. That Maxwell Perkins, Wolfe's editor at
Scribner's, took an early interest in Jones only confirmed this
association.

From Here to Eternity took four years to write; in the process
Jones tore up three-quarters of everything he put on paper.
During this long period of composition, just after his Army discharge, Jones lived back in his native Robinson with an older
woman, Lowney Handy, who fed him, occasionally slept with
him, and submitted him to her bizarre and thoroughly American
philosophy drawn from bits of Zen, Emerson, xenophobia, and
anti-intellectualism. She detested other women, and felt certain
women always kill the artist in a man. (It never occurred to her
that a woman herself might be an artist.)

Lowney believed in cold showers, early to bed and early to
rise, a long morning's work on an empty stomach, and other
spartan deprivations. She encouraged her disciples (for she
eventually founded a writers' colony) to use double negatives and
coarse language, and to copy out long passages from such manly
native writers as Hemingway and Dos Passos. She forbade her
boys to read the 'effete' authors she referred to as 'Walter
Stevens', 'Kafkia', and 'Dieland Thompson'.

Jones, an intensely loyal person, put up with Lowney's eccentricities – until his marriage to Gloria precipitated a crisis. Gloria
tried to live at the Handy Colony, and at first Lowney was cool
and correct with her, and with Gloria's niece Kate, who was visiting. But as MacShane recounts:

> One afternoon, while sitting in the living room with Kate,
> Gloria heard a loud crash. Lowney had just smashed through
> the screen door and was standing in the living room, beside
> herself with rage. 'The only reason Jim married you,' she
> shouted, 'is that you're the best cocksucker in New York!'
> Gloria sent Kate out of the room and then Lowney lunged at
> her with a bowie knife. Gloria and Lowney rolled around on
> the floor, scratching and punching, until Jones came in and
> separated them.

After the violence and deprivations and philistinism of the Handy Colony, Paris must have seemed a refreshing change.

Despite his years in France, Jones remained the quintessential American writer. If he often recalls Wolfe, he is just as apparently a descendant of Whitman, as can be seen in page after page of *From Here to Eternity*:

> The music came to him across the now bright, now dull, slowly burning cigaret of each man's life, telling him its ancient secret of all men, intangible, unfathomable, defying longwinded descriptions, belying intricate cataloguings, simple, complete, asking no more, giving no less, words that said nothing yet said all there was to say. The song of the one-eyed man who had driven the ox sled through the summer hills in the Kentucky mountains, the song of the Chogaw on his reservation, the song of the man who had laid the rollers for the stones heavy as death to build the glorious monument to the King.

His sympathy for the average guy, his impeccable ear for the American dialect ('Draft or no draft, they'll never get me back'), even his patient piecing together of the autodidact's 'philosophy of life', make Jones the most representative spokesman of his generation. Even his omnivorous and pressing drive to narrate suits his subject – and his readers.

In his stories he reached back to his childhood, to its humiliations and bleak joys. With a sure sense of which details would 'tell', he composed this passage in 'The Valentine', for instance, about a paperboy awakening before dawn:

> Outside it was steely cold and the handlebars and sprocket of his bike creaked with frost when he moved them. The air burned his nose like dry ice, and as he tucked the scarf up over it and put on his goggles, his eyes were already watering. The freezing cold air flushing the last threads of sleepiness and of reluctance out of his mind, he took off on his bike, giving himself joyously up to, and embracing happily, the discomfort which always made him feel important and as though he were accomplishing something, riding the bike downtown

along deserted streets of darkened houses where nothing moved or shone and people slept except for a few boys like himself, scattered across town, converging on the Newsstand where the city papers would already have been picked up by the owner of the train.

In his *Viet Journal*, written during the closing days of the war, Jones speaks with lucid objectivity of the farce being played out around him – yet without ever losing sympathy for the American soldiers involved. His self-created Illinois childhood and his own military service gave him that sympathy; his years as a famous writer in Paris provided the objectivity, as did his profound skepticism about politics. He summarized his view of the war by remarking, 'They're shits and we're shits so we might as well be for us as for them.'

Frank MacShane's biography never forces Jones into a Procrustean bed of preconceptions (one of the biographer's chief temptations), nor does it condescend to its subject (the other temptation). Jones's virtues (his intense loyalty, his burrowing intelligence, his fortitude under hostile criticism, his genuine curiosity about other people) are as graphically presented as are his shortcomings (his clumsy style, his alcoholic rages, his often unrealized artistic intentions). Best of all, the book gives a sense of the animal reality of the man with 'his thick neck, broad shoulders, Western clothes and turquoise bracelets', and his peculiarly penetrating independence of mind. After all, it was Jones who made this complex observation: 'The middle class rejects anything that is dishonest. Thus they miss the whole language of all common man – the rich texture of it.' Only an uncommon man could have grasped that slippery truth about the elegance of falsehood.

Their Masks, Their Lives – Harry Mathews's Cigarettes

First published in *Review of Contemporary Literature*, 1986: Harry Mathews is another expatriate American writer living in Paris.

In a famous letter to her niece, an aspiring novelist, Jane Austen armed her against letting her characters stray off to London, where the story would be subject to too many possibilities, its scope too large. Much better to confine things to a few country families.

The most obvious precedent for Harry Mathews's *Cigarettes* is Austen's own prose. Austen's involving circumstantiality and her elaborate structuring of plot are both here in Mathews's work, as is a ready appreciation of the social consequences of wealth and power. Mathews, following Austen's example, scarcely describes even the main characters or principal settings. Like her, he alternates between scenes of direct dialogue and narratives covering longer periods and employing indirect discourse – that most novelistic of all tones, the flying narrative ('They were happy for two years until . . .'). More important, Austen's peculiar tone of grave seriousness towards morals and satirical benevolence towards manners finds an echo in Mathews's approach.

Of course the differences are as marked as the similarities. Unlike the race of recent or contemporary English women novelists, from Barbara Pym to Anita Brookner, who are routinely compared to Austen, Mathews is more psychological than sociological, more fascinated by the genteel rich than the genteel poor, by artists or would-be artists than by retired civil servants or teachers, and he is far more bizarre and violent than Austen or any of her progeny would ever dare to be.

More concretely, Mathews is not afraid to exchange Austen's 'inch of ivory' for a whole tusk. He roams over several decades and many locales, manipulates a large cast and assimilates the point of view of many characters, old and young, male and female. This range and flexibility relates his sophisticated fictional world to our own largest sense of experience; we are never able to smile at the charming foibles and self-deceptions of his people, as we might smilingly condescend towards Austen's.

But Mathews's expansive ambitions, of course, threaten his design. Social comedy cannot sustain a lack of rigor and compression; *le jeu de l'amour et du hasard* does not properly admit of too much *hasard*. Austen's narrow preoccupation with finding suitable husbands for her eligible and not-so eligible girls, Mathews has replaced with a quite broad interest in such subjects as sexual conquest; the fostering of reputation; the love and hate between mother and son, father and daughter, brother and sister; the links (and abysses) between affection and imagination; the parallels between homosexuality and heterosexuality; and the nature of the amorous friendships linking quite old people.

No one would deny the intrinsic fascination inherent in Mathews's topoi nor the wisdom and compassion he brings to his human situations, but he has not been content merely to catalog them. He's sought to impose on them a necessary form, one that would lend his book the concision Austen achieves through unities of place, cast and problem. Mathews's former rigor is precisely what makes him modern. His structures are not imposed on pre-existent contents; rather the exigencies of form generate incidents and even descriptions. The analogy is with poetry (verses suggested by rhymes) and music (variations hatched out of themes, themes out of motives). Future studies will reveal the almost maniacal regularity of his form, an aspect I will not dwell on lest it overshadow the even more marked sense of lived life, of spontaneous event in this breathing text. Suffice it to say that *Cigarettes*, which at first (and last) glance seems his most realistic book, is also the one most manipulated by combinatorial devices, such as those Mathews has described in an essay in Oulipo's *Atlas de littérature potentielle*. After all, Mathews has long been a member – along with such writers as Italo Calvino, Raymond Queneau and Georges Perec (to whom *Cigarettes* is dedicated) – of this Parisian literary group, so fancifully serious, devoted to fictional research. In *Cigarettes* the 'time signature' varies in every chapter as does the 'key' (i.e. 'Louisa and Lewis: 1938–1963' or 'Priscilla and Walter: Summer 1962–

Winter 1963'). Moreover, certain themes (the portrait of Elizabeth, shady business deals, the problems of inheritance, horses) repeat and evolve in 'free' (i.e. undetermined) fashion. In short, several elements follow a program, whereas others are introduced *ad libitum*.

Another thoroughly contemporary aspect of the text is its language. The syntax is intricate but nimble, the sentences short but never falsely naïve or monotonous, the mode nominative rather than adjectival, verbal rather than adverbial. The comic tone depends on shifting neatly from one register to a quite different one, as in this exchange of dialogue:

> '*On pourra déballer tout notre linge sale.*'
> 'If it's French, it must be exciting.'

The first speaker (Maud) is so cosmopolitan (and timid) that she naturally expresses her dismay in French, whereas the second speaker – one of those breezy hard-drinking American hellraisers – greets the unfamiliar words with mindless gusto. Later, when the two middle-aged women, already in love with each other, decide to stay home and not go out carousing, the narrator remarks: '"Men" hardly seemed worth the trouble.' The quotation marks around 'men' speak volumes, since they invoke the exasperated American female cry, 'Oh, *men*,' and tell us that for these women, at least, men are a separate species, a vexation, a hobby and a quaintly 'period' topic to be spoofed. In another passage the harsh power of clichés is invoked ('money in the bank', 'paying our dues'). Elsewhere birds are described as 'yammulkaed chickadees', at once an accurate observation (hence amusing), an odd cultural reference in such a Gentile novel, and a linguistic frisson.

The quirkiness of Mathews's style enables its humor, just as the leanness makes for efficiency in getting tales told. Throughout his career, and in his four major novels, Mathews has always loved telling stories: indeed adventure and mystery have been his preferred genres, just as religion and science have been his preoccupations. The prose in the first two books, *The Conversions* (1962) and *Tlooth* (1966), was objective, whereas in the epistolary *The Sinking of the Odradek Stadium* (1975) he brilliantly mimed the lyrical if half-insane effusions of the American

Zachary as well as the grotesque pidgin English of his Oriental mistress, the fortune-hunting Twang. Unlikely as was the choice of two such correspondents, their letters provoked Nabokovian mirth and pathos and treated the reader to a deft notation of passion.

In *Cigarettes* Mathews has forged his most expressive style, although never does he allow the language to exhort or persuade – he's always a bit cool. As in the earlier books, suspense is ubiquitous (will Maud find out that Allan is cheating on her? Will the true nature of Phoebe's illness be diagnosed in time to save her? Are Irene and Morris plotting against Walter?) Science in the form of probability theories of betting and medical definitions of Phoebe's illness are invoked, as is religion in the form of art and love.

But the book is mainly funny, though the humor no longer depends on freaks such as Zachary and Twang. Now it is enacted by well-heeled ex-urbanites as glamorous as Fitzgerald's characters and as silkily hedonistic as Henry Green's. The omniscient narrator (who, at the last minute, we discover is one of the characters – though we should have suspected it sooner) shows us Louisa from the point of view of her son Lewis, then after we're convinced she's a meddling neurotic, plunges us into her thoughts only to reveal her loving solicitude for her difficult children. In the same way we see Maud from Pauline's viewpoint and Pauline from Maud's.

In *The Conversions* and *Tlooth* Mathews amuses us by rendering the tragicomedy of insisting upon interpreting the facts of experience even when they are senseless. In *Tlooth*, for instance, Robin Marr comes across a sheet of paper slipped into Frost's *Lives of Eminent Christians*. The paper is covered with three handwritten letters in a vertical column, a riddle in English and a phrase in German. How do these elements relate to one another and what do they mean? Marr publishes his speculations, but he is refuted by a reader whose theory is still more brilliant. Unfortunately the theories concocted by both Marr and the reader are wrong; the enigmatic jottings, which have prompted the most arcane exegeses, turn out to be nothing more than quite uninteresting notes a student has taken in a first-year German class.

In *Cigarettes* the characters interpret each other's motives and are frequently wrong because they fail to attribute to friends and enemies such traits as timidity, generosity, love and wounded pride. The narrator also interprets the characters, usually by paraphrasing their thoughts: 'With her, he insisted, he "was not himself." He meant only that he had lost his script – he had nothing to hide behind, she could see him plain, and she felt tenderness for what she saw.'

The plot of *Cigarettes* is as dense and sensationalistic as that of any good melodrama. Maud and Pauline are sisters, though Maud inherits and Pauline doesn't. Pauline pretends she's rich and tricks Oliver into marrying her, though the marriage of course is unhappy. Maud marries Allan, who's a successful insurance man but who feels so outclassed by his wife's wealth that he indulges in shady business deals. Their daughter Priscilla becomes the mistress of the painter Walter Thrale and the friend and business partner of Morris. Morris's sister Irene is Walter's dealer. Morris's lover is Lewis, brother of Phoebe, Walter's studio assistant. Phoebe's parents are Louisa and Owen Lewison; Owen decides to investigate Allan's shady deals with the help of Pauline, who's always been eager to sleep with Allan, partly to get revenge on her sister Maud, who 'cheated' her out of her inheritance. Allan is gratified by Pauline's apparent interest in him, since he has just lost his last girlfriend Elizabeth to his wife Maud.

Elizabeth was the subject of an early portrait by Walter Thrale, his 'breakthrough' painting. The portrait has been scrupulously copied by Phoebe. The painting (or copy) is sold, destroyed, stolen. One of the dealers involved, Morris, dies of a heart attack while Lewis, his masochistic lover, immobilized inside a plaster cast, watches helplessly. This résumé, no matter how cursory, should suggest opera buffa twists and turns. *Così Fan Tutte*, of course, has a plot no less absurd, although the music for many burlesque moments (such as the terzettino '*Soave sia il vento*') is inappropriately sublime.

Similarly, just after a passage of high farce (a naked man, face covered in mud, races through a sauna for women in search of his tempestuous love), the same lovers lounge in a boat: 'He let the boat drift. He had no place to go. He did not think this – what he thought also became a part of the dreaming. Everything that had ever happened was a seeming, a seeming of having been dreamed

– it did not matter, it was no matter.' The sublime is unexpected – and ravishing.

The soap-opera plot also turns up implausible occasions, which Mathews knows how to write with exquisite veracity. For instance, Owen settles a fortune on Phoebe but then tries to coerce her into conforming to the sort of bourgeois rules he himself observes. He worries about her, wants in on her life and aches to control her. She, however, is in happy thrall to Walter Thrale. Owen arrives in town unexpectedly, sees his daughter posing naked for Thrale, recovers from the shock, admires Phoebe's own paintings, goes on the town with her (jazz club, marijuana party, race track at dawn) – and all these high jinks are articulated with wisdom and tenderness. The stoned Owen after his day at the races muses on the train: 'He shyly glanced at others near him: Veterans of one summer afternoon, each encased in his rind, each of us accumulating incongruities, pains, shames, even signs of happiness, to conceal that unceasing light – their masks, their lives.'

There are two things that make this book remarkable. First, it is as involving as a nineteenth-century saga and as original as any modernist invention – a rare combination of readability and ingenuity. Second, it shows compassion towards characters usually slighted or ridiculed in contemporary fiction – the middle-aged and old, the successful, mothers, homosexuals, even sadists. Nor does it treat these characters with a governessy solicitude; rather it judges them on the basis of the good they do and the happiness they feel and give.

Esthetics and Loss

Originally published in *Artforum*, January 1987, and reprinted several times, this essay was written while White was working on the stories collected in *The Darker Proof*.

I had a friend, a painter named Kris Johnson, who died two years ago of AIDS. He was in his early thirties. He'd shown here and there, in bookstores, arty coffee shops, that kind of thing, first in Minnesota, then in Los Angeles. He painted over color photos he'd color-Xeroxed – images of shopping carts in parking lots, of giant palms, their small heads black as warts against the smoggy sun: California images.

He read *Artforum* religiously; he would have been happy to see his name in its pages. The magazine represented for him a lien on his future, a promise of the serious work he was about to embrace as soon as he could get out of the fast lane. Like many people who are both beautiful and gifted, he had to explore his beauty before his gift. It dictated his way of living until two years ago, before his death. His health had already begun to deteriorate, when he moved to Santa Fe, where he painted seriously his last few months.

By now there have been many articles about how the AIDS virus is contracted and how it manifests itself. The purely medical horrors of the disease have received the attention of the world press. What interests me here is how artists of all sorts – writers, painters, sculptors, people in video and performance art, actors, models – are responding to AIDS in their work and their lives. If I narrow the focus, I do so because of the impact the epidemic has had on esthetics and on the life of the art community, an impact that has not been studied.

The most visible artistic expressions of AIDS have been movies, television dramas, and melodramas on the stage, almost all of which have emphasized that AIDS is a terribly moving human experience (for the lover, the nurse, the family, the patient), which may precipitate the coming out of the doctor (the play *Anti Body*, 1983, by Louise Parker Kelley) or overcome the homophobia of the straight male nurse (*Compromised Immunity*, 1986, by Andy Kirby and the Gay Sweatshop Theatre Company, from England) or resolve long-standing tensions between lovers (William M. Hoffman's play *As Is*, 1985, and Bill Sherwood's beautifully rendered movie *Parting Glances*, 1985). Although Larry Kramer's play *The Normal Heart* (1985) is almost alone in taking up the political aspects of the disease, it still ends in true melodramatic fashion with a deathbed wedding scene. John Erman's *An Early Frost* (1985), a made-for-television movie on NBC, is the *Love Story* of the 1980s; the best documentary is perhaps *Coming of Age* (1986), by Marc Huestis, who filmed scenes from the life of a friend of his diagnosed with the virus.

But even on artists working away from the limelight, AIDS has had an effect. Naturally the prospect of ill health and death or its actuality inspires a sense of urgency. What was it I wanted to do in my work after all? Should I make my work simpler, clearer, more accessible? Should I record my fears obliquely or directly, or should I defy them? Is it more heroic to drop whatever I was doing and look disease in the eye or should I continue going in the same direction as before, though with a new consecration? Is it a hateful concession to the disease even to acknowledge its existence? Should I pretend Olympian indifference to it? Or should I admit to myself, 'Look, kid, you're scared shitless and that's your material'? If sex and death are the only two topics worthy of adult consideration, then AIDS wins hands down as subject matter. It seems to me that AIDS is tilting energies away from the popular arts (including disco dancing, the sculpturing of the living body through working out, the design of pleasure machines – bars, clubs, baths, resort houses) and redirecting them toward the solitary 'high' arts. Of course I may simply be confusing the effects of aging with the effects of the disease; after all, the Stonewall generation is now middle-aged, and older people naturally seek out different pursuits. But we know how frightened everyone is becoming, even well beyond the 'high risk' group that is my paradigm and my subject here.

What seems unquestionable is that ten years ago sex was for gay men a main reason for being. Not simple, humdrum coupling, but a new principle of adhesiveness. Sex provided a daily brush with the ecstatic, a rehearsal of forgotten pain under the sign of the miraculous – sex was a force binding familiar atoms into new polymers of affinity.

To be sure, as some wit once remarked, life would be supportable without its pleasures, and certainly a sensual career had its melancholy side. Even so, sex was, if not fulfilling, then at least engrossing enough at times to make the pursuit of the toughest artistic goals seem too hard, too much work given the mild returns. 'Beauty is difficult,' as Pound liked to remind us, and the difficulties held little allure for people who could take satisfaction in an everyday life that had, literally, become ... sensational. Popular expressions of the art of life, or rather those pleasures that intensified the already heady exchange within a newly liberated culture, thrived: the fortune that was lavished on flowers, drugs, sound systems, food, clothes, hair. People who were oppressed by the brutality of the big city or by their own poverty or a humiliating job could create for at least a night, or a weekend, a magical dreamlike environment.

Now all that has changed. I, for one, at least feel repatriated to my lonely adolescence, the time when I was alone with my writing and I felt weird about being queer. Art was a consolation then – a consolation for a life not much worth living, a site for the staging of fantasies reality couldn't fulfill, a peopling of solitude – and art has become a consolation again. People aren't on the prowl any more, and a seductive environment is read not as an enticement but as a death trap. Fat is in, it means you're not dying, at least not yet.

And of course we do feel weird again, despised, alien. There's talk of tattooing us or quarantining us. Both the medical and moralistic models for homosexuality have been dusted off only fifteen years after they were shelved; the smell of the madhouse and the punitive vision of the Rake Chastised have been trotted out once more. In such a social climate, the popular arts, the public arts, are standing still, frozen in time. There's no market, no confidence, no money. The brassy hedonism of a few years back has given way to a protective gay invisibility, which struck me forcibly when I returned to New York recently after being away for several months. As Joe Orton in his diary quotes a friend remarking, 'all we see are all those dull norms, all norming about'.

But if the conditions for a popular culture are deteriorating, those promoting a renewed high culture have returned. Certainly the disease is encouraging homosexuals to question whether they want to go on defining themselves at all by their sexuality. Maybe the French philosopher Michel Foucault was right in saying there are homosexual acts but not homosexual people. More concretely, when a society based on sex and expression is de-eroticized, its very reason for being can vanish. Yet the disease is a stigma; even the horde of asymptomatic carriers of the antibody is stigmatized. Whether imposed or chosen, gay identity is still very much with us. How does it express itself these days?

The main feeling is one of evanescence. It's just like the Middle Ages; every time you say goodbye to a friend, you fear it may be for the last time. You search your own body for signs of the malady. Every time someone begins a sentence with 'Do you remember Bob . . .' you seize up in anticipation of the sequel. A writer or visual artist responds to this fragility as both a theme and as a practical limitation – no more projects that require five years to finish.

The body becomes central, the body that until recently was at once so natural (athletic, young, casually dressed) and so artificial (pumped up, pierced, ornamented). Now it is feeble, yellowing, infected – or boisterously healthy as a denial of precisely this possibility. When I saw a famous gay film-maker recently, he was radiant, with a hired tan; 'I have to look healthy or no one will bankroll me.' Most of all the body is unloved. Masturbation – singular or in groups – has replaced intercourse. This solitude is precisely a recollection of adolescence. Unloved, the body releases its old sad song, but it also builds fantasies, rerunning idealized movies of past realities, fashioning new images out of thin air. People think about the machinery of the body: the wheezing bellows of the lungs, the mulcher of the gut – and of the enemy it may be harboring. 'In the midst of life we are in death,' in the words of the Book of Common Prayer. Death – in its submicroscopic, viral, paranoid aspect, the side worthy of William Burroughs – shadows every pleasure.

The New York painter Frank Moore told me last fall that in developing possible sets and costumes for a new Lar Lubovitch ballet, he worked out an imagery of blood cells and invading organisms, of cells consuming themselves – a vision of cellular holocaust. In his view, the fact of death and the ever-present threat of mortality have added a bite to the sometimes empty rhetoric of East Village expressionism. 'Until now anger has been a look, a pose,' he told me. Now it has teeth.

The list of people in the art world who have died of AIDS is long and growing longer. I won't mention names for fear of omitting one – or including one that discretion should conceal (it's not always possible to verify how much a patient told his family).

Maybe it's tactless or irrelevant to critical evaluation to consider an artist, writer, dealer or curator in the light of his death. Yet the urge to memorialize the dead, to honor their lives, is a pressing instinct. Ross Bleckner's paintings with titles such as *Hospital Room, Memoriam,* and *8,122 + As of January, 1986* commemorate those who have died of AIDS and incorporate trophies, banners, flowers and gates – public images.

There is an equally strong urge to record one's own past – one's own life – before it vanishes. I suppose everyone both believes and chooses to ignore that each detail of our behavior is inscribed in the arbitrariness of history. Which culture, which moment we live in determines how we have sex, go mad, marry, die, and worship, even how we say Ai! instead of Ouch! when we're pinched. Not even the soul that we reform or express is God-given or eternal; as Foucault writes in *Discipline and Punish* (1978), 'The soul is the effect and instrument of a political anatomy; the soul is the prison of the body.' For gay men this force of history has been made to come clean; it's been stripped of its natural look. The very rapidity of change has laid bare the clanking machinery of history. To have been oppressed in the 1950s, freed in the 1960s, exalted in the 1970s, and wiped out in the 1980s is a quick itinerary for a whole culture to follow. For we are witnessing not just the death of individuals but a menace to an entire culture. All the more reason to bear witness to the cultural moment.

Art must compete with (rectify, purge) the media, which have thoroughly politicized AIDS as Simon Watney tells us in *Policing Desire: Pornography, AIDS and the Media.* (Watney, Jeffrey Weeks, Richard Goldstein, and Dennis Altman rank as the leading English-language intellectuals to think about AIDS and homosexuality.)

This winter William Olander at the New Museum in New York has organized 'Homo Video – Where We Are Now', an international gay and lesbian program that focuses in part on AIDS and the media. For instance, Gregg Bordowitz's '. . . *some aspects of a shared lifestyle*', deals with the contrast between the actual diseases and the 'gay plague' image promoted by the media. John Greyson's *Moscow Does not Believe in Queers* (1986), inserts lurid Rock Hudson headlines into a taped diary of ten days at a 1985 Moscow youth festival where Greyson functioned as an 'out' homosexual in a country that does not acknowledge the rights – or even the legitimate existence – of homosexuals. And Stuart Marshall's *Bright Eyes* (1986), tracks, among other things, the presentation of AIDS in the English media.

If art is to confront AIDS more honestly than the media have done, it must begin in tact, avoid humor, and end in anger. Begin in tact, I say, because we must not reduce individuals to their deaths; we must not fall into the trap of replacing the afterlife with the moment of dying. How someone dies says nothing about how he lived. And tact because we must not let the disease stand for other things. AIDS generates complex and harrowing reflections, but it is not caused by moral or intellectual choices. We are witnessing at long last the end of illness as metaphor and metonym.

Avoid humor, because humor seems grotesquely inappropriate to the occasion. A sniggering or wisecracking humor puts the public (indifferent when not uneasy) on cozy terms with what is an unspeakable scandal: death. Humor domesticates terror, lays to rest misgivings that should be intensified. Humor suggests that AIDS is just another calamity to befall Mother Camp, whereas in truth AIDS is not one more item in a sequence, but a rupture in meaning itself. Humor, like melodrama, is an assertion of bourgeois values; it falsely suggests that AIDS is all in the family. Baudelaire reminded us that the wise man laughs only with fear and trembling. Only a dire gallows humor is acceptable.

End in anger, I say, because it is only sane to rage against the dying of the light, because strategically anger is a political response, because psychologically anger replaces despondency, and because existentially anger lightens the solitude of frightened individuals.

I feel very alone with the disease. My friends are dying. One of them asked me to say a prayer for us all in Venice, 'in that church they built when the city was spared from the ravages of the plague'. Atheist that I am, I murmured my invocation – to Longhena's Baroque octagon if not to any spirit dwelling in Santa Maria della Salute. The other day I saw stenciled on a Paris wall an erect penis, its dimensions included in centimeters, and the words *Faux Pas Rêver* (You mustn't dream). When people's dreams are withdrawn, they get real angry, real fast.

Danilo Kiš: The Obligations of Form

Originally published in *Southwest Review*, 1987.

Danilo Kiš, the Yugoslav novelist, lives in Paris but he's certainly not part of Paris literary life, although he's published by the nearly mythic Gallimard and a whole number of *SUD*, the prestigious literary review, is being devoted to essays about his work. Nevertheless Kiš jokes that for most Americans and Western Europeans, a Yugoslav writer sounds more or less 'African' – as remote and as exotic.

Kiš lives alone in one room in a working-class district (his metro stop, significantly, is Goncourt, the name of the most prestigious establishment literary prize he has yet to win and that may never be conferred on his iconoclastic work). In his room there are a desk, a chair and a bed, nothing more – the Platonic room. Or, better, the room of a writer who has embraced simplicity to ensure his freedom. A big, rumpled man with a surprisingly penetrating, resonant voice, ungovernable spikes of hair, strong features some peasant whittled out of a white radish, Kiš seems to be irresistible to women. His solitary days are followed by riotous evenings.

There are good reasons to admire him. Kiš is not an American-style macho author, beautiful but dumb. He is profoundly cultured. For one thing he's read and translated into Serbo-Croatian many Russian and French classics, and he is thoroughly versed in English and American literature (in translation – his English is rather impressionistic).

Politically sophisticated and disabused, he has a comically black view of totalitarianism. His book *A Tomb for Boris Davidovich* is a mordant and hilarious distillation of all the tragic tales to emerge out of the Soviet Union – a miniaturized and strangely sparkling *Hope Against Hope* (it in fact relies heavily on Karlo

218

Stajner's *7000 jours en Siberie*). If Kiš had been given a chance to speak at the PEN conference in New York early in 1986, he would have had things to say not only about the state and the imagination (the official topic) but also about the absurdity of marginal writers maundering on about political topics beyond their grasp.

The first volume of the Kiš trilogy, called *Rani Jadi* in Serbo-Croatian and *Chagrins précoces* in the beautiful French translation by Pascale Delpech, is a book ostensibly for adolescent readers – or, as the French subtitle puts it after a line from Max Jacob, *'pour les enfants et les raffinés'*.

The essential narrative, which will emerge more clearly in the later two volumes, is splintered here, refracted, reflected. The horror of the situation (war-torn Yugoslavia in 1942 under Fascist rule) and the anguish of the child's parents (the mother a Christian, the father a Jew already enlisted in crushing forced labor and soon to be sent off to Auschwitz) are glimpsed from a boy's point of view. For instance, on the very first page, we read a lyrical description of chestnuts in autumn. We learn: 'Certain chestnuts contained twins; but it's still possible to tell them apart, for one wears a mark on its forehead, like a horse. So its mother will always be able to pick it out – by the star on his forehead.'

This innocent-appearing 'star' becomes more ominous when we learn in the later *Hourglass* that Edouard Sam, the father, was forced to wear the yellow Star of David. And in an interview Kiš has remarked that although he was the baptized son of an Orthodox Christian mother, she had been obliged to sew a yellow star for him, a stigma that was held in readiness should the racial laws in Yugoslavia change.

Similarly, the boy's Jewish heritage, which the mother understandably attempts to conceal, emerges in another tale, 'The Game'. The Jewish father spies on his son through a keyhole as the child plays. Although the Gentile mother has felt her 'Little Blond Boy' will be above suspicion, the boy, unprompted and unconscious, amuses himself by impersonating his Jewish grandfather, 'Max the Wanderer', Max Ahasverus, the feather merchant. The child bows before a reproduction of the Mona Lisa and addresses her, 'Madame, wouldn't you like some pure white swan's down?' His gestures and carriage, even his wheedling voice, reproduce those of the old man – whom he's never seen or even heard of. The anxiety this mimicry awakens in his mother (and the perverse pride in the father) are mostly left to the reader to infer. It's a cruel story, made harsher by the title.

If these short tales (some no longer than a page) are subtle, their subtlety is that of phenomenology – the presentation of sensuous experiences with a minimum of interpretation and a maximum of incomprehension, the celebrated 'defamiliarization' of the Russian Formalists, that strategy whereby the quotidian is observed as though it were miraculous, and whereby the dross of habit is transformed into the gold of the first encounter. Kiš is never at home in the world, and his uneasy purchase makes him alert to metaphor and detail – the metaphor that hears unexpected chords struck off disparate objects, like one of those Jamaican bands that sounds a steel drum with a half-filled milk bottle; and the keen, bizarre detail that dips dusty things into lucent liquid.

Both metaphor and detail are, on the level of rhetoric, two methods of interrupting an easy flow of eloquence, of rupturing and impeding the automatic unreeling of line into line. On the level of experience, metaphor and detail shed a queer, unfamiliar light on used objects. For instance, when Kiš renders a pogrom in *Chagrins précoces*, he merely describes a raid by Gentiles on a Jewish grocery storehouse: 'Some flour was floating in the air like rice powder, drifting down on eyebrows and lending people a solemn note, but one that was also a bit farcical – a festive note.'

Fifty years ago in *The Psychology of Art* Lev Vygotsky analyzed Ivan Bunin's story 'Gentle Breath' and discovered that the details of the descriptions, far from conforming to the depressing, downward slant of the anecdote, actually leave us with a feeling of lightness and airiness. Vygotsky noticed that there is a kind of antic, buoyant energy in the descriptions and in the figurative language, at variance with the depressing tale of thwarted love in a provincial town. Far from lessening the beauty of the story, this treatment that goes against the grain of the plot actually enhances its power and mystery. From this story, and an analysis of many works of art, from fairy tales to *Hamlet*, Vygotsky concludes that the traditional notion that form must echo content is in fact wrong; what we see in the highest art is form that subverts content, treatment that undermines theme, so that the story or novel or play becomes a field of dynamic tension, of opposition between text and message. This principle of respiration in the rhetorical figures, Vygotsky implies, is what provokes our para-doxical pleasure, not the celebrated purging or *catharsis* Aristotle had posited. In the same Kiš tale, 'Pogrom', one sentence ('By the gleam of a match lighting up his face for an instant, I saw his teeth turned bright red by the reflection off the silk') quite literal-ly sheds a calm if unsettling luminosity on the surrounding violence.

In the foreground of these stories are animals – a dog Dingo, the cow Mandarine which Andi, our hero, loses, the cavalrymen's mounts which founder from hunger. Psychologists tell us that children often identify with pets since children see that they and animals occupy the lowest status in the household, and that parental attitudes toward animals parallel their true attitudes toward children. In one three-paragraph story, 'Pears', a woman neighbor makes a quite explicit connection between the child and the dog: '"Just look," said Mrs Molnar, the child's new employer, "the Sam boy is sorting the pears, God forgive me, like a dog, by smell. We should take him out hunting. That's just what we're missing, good dogs."'

If animals are in the foreground, what hovers in the back-ground – retained only as a faint after-image – is the boy's father. 'Autumn Meadow' starts out like Joyce's 'Araby' about the con-frontation of a child with the magical world of the circus and adult sexuality, but the direction suddenly veers off with the father's entrance: 'Suddenly in the west out of the tall grass loomed my father, his cane raised high.' The father discovers, trampled into the mud, a leaf torn from a German cookbook and left behind by someone in the circus – a recipe for sorrel sauce. The father has a sorrel recipe of his own that calls for nothing but water, salt, and 'some spices anyone could find but whose names he jealously conceals'. With the ferrule of his cane he stabs at the offending German recipe and its vile call for *crème fraîche* – a petty act of vengeance reminiscent of his use elsewhere of Hitler's newspaper photos for toilet paper.

The very next tale, 'The Fiancés', is a story of first love written in the third person (since 'after so many years Andreas Sam is perhaps no longer me'). It ends with a vision of the father in the distance, a force of nature or a change in the weather: 'When he opened his eyes he saw his father, immense, cane in hand, wearing his black hat with the sturdy brim, lingering behind the cart, standing out distinct against the purple horizon.'

The father ('the man who came from far away') is seen full-face only in the story 'Pages from a Velvet Photograph Album', from which paradoxically he has already vanished. In this text the young writer fully discovers the duty of literature to serve as necrology. When his aunt announces that the father 'no longer exists' (i.e. has been arrested), the boy persists in believing in his father's immortality. The boy is certain that when the soldiers separate the fit men from the women, the children, and the ill, his father will be cast into the group rejects ('for at the same time he was a major invalid and a hysterical woman eternally swollen with a false pregnancy like an enormous tumor, and he was also a child, the big baby of his period and tribe').

As the boy, his mother and sister board a train, they take with them a suitcase that, like a funeral urn, contains 'the ashes and sad remains of my father: his photographs and papers', especially two of his letters, to which the boy gives the Villon-like names 'Le Grand et le Petit Testament'. The so-called 'Grand Testament', a litany of woes and a jeremiad of accusations, will supply the artistic center and the last pages of *Hourglass*.

For the child, his sole heritage consists of these papers, the family's eiderdown quilts and a few books, among them his father's unpublished travel guide, *l'Indicateur yougoslave et international des lignes d'autobus, de train, de bateau et d'avion* – a volume, the narrator avows, 'which would undergo its reaffirmation and astonishing metamorphosis, its Assumption, in one of my books'.

In this very first volume of the trilogy *Chagrins précoces*, Kiš already established his themes (loss, memory and fear) and began to cast a mythic glow over the figure of the father with his bowler hat, his cane, his peripatetic habits – this combination of the Little Tramp, the Wandering Jew, and Don Quixote. *Garden, Ashes* will magnify this radiance and turn the father into a classical deity, all stormy petulance and fabulous gab. *Hourglass*, in turn, will dismantle the legend, discovering the suffering, fragile, historic man under the myth. In the first of the three books, the father appears as a sliver of the moon glimpsed by day; in the second as a fully bloody harvest moon; in the last as a pale, leprous moon consumed by clouds.

From one volume to the next, there is an alternation and several kinds of progression. First the books address readers of different ages – adolescence, early adulthood, and maturity. The three texts are geared to those different audiences in content and style, since *Chagrins précoces*, as the title suggests, is about early losses (of love, home, innocence, a father), whereas *Garden, Ashes* (a title that is also made up of a pair of opposites) concerns both the noon of life and the evening of regret. Finally, *Hourglass* is a reckoning, the clear-eyed measure of things an old man makes, a demystification. If *Chagrins précoces* is composed of short lyrical fragments, *Garden, Ashes* is a continuous myth, carried along by the tone of romantic elegy. By contrast, *Hourglass* is a dry *procès-verbal*, an inquest; poetic license has been traded in for a prosaic order for arrest. One could even say that the three books trace a sentimental education, or rather graph out the stages passed through before one can contemplate horror. These stages move from childish incomprehension to a self-protecting exaggeration and end with a painfully concrete, objective catalog.

In *Garden, Ashes* the father is shown as having courted his misfortunes. If he is a victim, he has wilfully, perversely elected to play that role; we are told 'he is artfully hiding behind one of his numerous masks'. The conventions of theater and religion, Christian and pagan, are elicited precisely because the reader is assumed not to believe in them. The father is a lyrical clown and a pharoah. If the father is the master of make-believe, he can undo his doom as easily as he originally conjured it into being. The adjectives applied to the father and his stage properties (even his cigarettes are 'ubiquitous and immortal') as well as the nouns that describe his essence ('his absence, his somnambulism, his messianism') emphasize his mysterious invulnerability. Even before he is shipped off to the concentration camp, he is invulnerable, since he is already an invincible legend, a Christ before the crucifixion: 'All the stories stamped with earthly signs and framed within a specific historical context take on secondary significance, like historical facts bound up in a destiny that no longer concerns us: we shall record them without haste, when we can.'

His suffering, like Christ's, is something he has chosen, and like Christ he can predict his own Passion: 'My role as a victim, which I have been plotting with greater or lesser success all my life – we all act out our lives, our own destinies, after all – that role, as I said, is coming to an end.' His attitude is *defensive voluntarism*, we might say, a sort of prophylaxis against catastrophe. Psychoanalysis *is* familiar with the phenomenon – indeed, psychoanalysis is the phenomenon, since the patient is encouraged to attribute his misfortunes to an affliction of the will rather than to the slings and arrows of outrageous fortune.

Similarly, the helplessness of the son, although dramatized by his twin fears of sleep and death, is disguised by the tone of the entire book, which alludes to both Proust and Nabokov, those chroniclers of the sheltered bourgeois childhood. In an echo of Nabokov's 'First Love', Kiš writes: 'I had become intoxicated by the music of travel, sounded by the train wheels and inscribed by swallows and migrating fowl in closely bunched trios on the tele- phone-wire notation system, in ad-lib performances and improvisations in between three-quarter pauses interrupted – sud- denly and noisily – by the great organs of bridges.' The Proustian fear of sleep is re-enacted, as is the Proustian education of the youthful narrator through sensual exploration and amorous dis- appointment.

The function of these borrowings and assimilations (for Kiš is as quick as T. S. Eliot to expose his influences and sources) is in the service of wish-fulfilment. The narrator develops problems (the neurotic fear of sleep as an emblem of death) in order to ward off real fears (the father's inevitable death in a concentration camp). These imaginary problems are both proleptic and apotro- paic, for they delay or avert more painful recognitions.

Of all Kiš's books, *Garden, Ashes* is the favorite of most readers. Everyone feels affection for (sometimes affectionate ex- asperation over) the father, that combination of Meistersinger, mage, god, bum, and Old Testament prophet. He is the seer in- toxicated with glory and alcohol, the epic wanderer, the man who is a 'bankrupt in love and stockholder in sentiment'. It is the father who 'would have been able to befuddle death with his elo- quence, with his philosophy, with his theories'. He is the Wandering Jew, the Ahasuerus after whom his father was named.

He is a pantheistic hermit and a wandering philosopher, a Zoroastrian – whatever is a mythic embodiment of the forces of nature.

The book, moreover, is filled with a tender, magical regard for detail that most writers would envy. Everything glistens under the 'golden dust of time'. The diction takes pleasure in its own versatility; we read about a dog and 'these trembling paws that open and close like a thorny blossom'. At points the style swells and resonates with the *vox humana* of a great organ. As the boy works his way through his small school Bible, he re-experiences all the epochs of man and imagines Noah's ark as

> that great laboratory of life . . . sailing away, full of human and animal sperm, of specimens of all species classified and labeled with Latin inscriptions as in a pharmacy, with a fresh crop of onions and potatoes, with apples sorted in wooded crates as in a fruit market, with oranges and lemons that conceal within themselves a grain of light and eternity, with birds in cages that will soon enrich the air with the tiny seedlings of their chirping and will ennoble the wasted emptiness of the sky with their skilful flights.

This, surely, is a passage that in its religious intensity surpasses anything in modern literature with the possible exception of some pages written by Bruno Schulz, whose fiction is the most evident model for *Garden, Ashes*.

F. W. Dupee once observed that in *Pale Fire* Nabokov made a 'team' of the poet and novelist in himself. Similarly, Kiš in *Garden, Ashes* captures in prose all the poetry of wish-fulfilment. He wishes his father had been a free agent who had chosen his destiny rather than [a victim who had] passively suffered his fate. The mythic mode itself aspires toward a world in which character defines action, in which deeds are decisive and in which everything can be read as a portent or as a consequence (the mythology of causation). Even when the actions themselves are gloomy (the boy's fears, the father's death), the overall *stimmung* enjoys the freedom of a dream, since here intentions produce results and the only tragedies are self-inflicted.

Myths move from the specific to the general. In a classical

Greek myth the fable ends in the explanation of the origin of plants (the reed, the narcissus) or of a phenomenon (the echo) or of various customs or rites. In each case a metamorphosis transforms the individual into a whole species. This proliferation in *Garden, Ashes* is comforting, since it makes private suffering into universal pain.

Hourglass is an entirely different enterprise. Nothing, in fact, could be a better demonstration than a comparison of the two books of the power of presentation to change subject matter – of physiology to modify anatomy. The fable, the setting, and even many of the incidents remain the same, but the spirit of *Hourglass* is as dry and accurate and pitiless as a legal investigation. The experimental technique that *Hourglass* invents is realism.

The title itself refers partly to the sense of time running out and partly to that familiar perceptual trick in which the figure–ground relationship reverses, first to produce a white hourglass against a black background, then to resolve into identical black profiles facing one another across a white background.

Who are the facing twins? Psychologically they are the son who writes the trilogy and the father who is the principal character, two interchangeable faces contemplating one another across a void of time (that white 'noise of time' Kiš so often mentions). At the end of *Garden, Ashes* doesn't the narrator declare that his first ideas at age eleven of love and of the future were merely a 'supplement to my father's book'?

Esthetically the facing profiles represent the principle of symmetry that governs this elegantly structured book. In particular, the symmetry is one of a miniature but repeating figure *en abîme*. For example, in the opening pages a man in a dark room lights a flame that animates the wallpaper design, a pattern repeated every ten centimeters: 'Because of this symmetry and repetition to infinity of the gray design, all the sleighs were reduced to a single image, as were all the little characters, but the picture scene, far from seeming static, came alive despite this exact reproduction, or rather precisely because of it.' The man lowers the lamp and in the darkness the sleigh and the woman descending from it take on a new reality ('the coachman has whipped the horses, the sleigh has glided off into the darkness'). Transparently the focus shifts back to the real world – and the woman in the wallpaper has become a real person who has arrived in the snow and is now in the next room, glimpsed through slats as she wears a nightgown and carries a lamp. Later there will be several scenes of Edouard himself in a hired horse-drawn wagon that is transporting his belongings through the snow.

Even in these opening pages Edouard walks past a window and looks in to see his smug relatives gathered around a lavish Easter (or Passover) feast to which he and his wife and children have not been invited: 'On each side of the table, of nearly the same height, symmetrically, two people are seated sideways, in profile: two women in black dresses . . .'

While Edouard Sam and his dependents have nothing to eat except cold milk, his relatives laugh merrily over a roast suckling pig, a kosher defilement. Here the symmetry is sinister complicity.

Equally well ordered are the divisions of the book into repeating units of several sorts: 'travel pictures', which recount actions objectively observed in the third person; 'instruction', a series of questions and answers in which someone is reporting on Edouard Sam; 'hearing of the witness', questions and answers in which the responses are given by Edouard Sam; and 'notes from a madman', which are selected jottings from Sam's own notebooks. Finally, the book ends with a letter from Edouard to his sister Olga, a long reproachful document written after that disagreeable Easter of 1942. This letter is also the table of contents, in the sense that everything that precedes it, the bulk of the book, is nothing but Danilo Kiš's imagined recreation of the circumstances that led up to that letter (the letter is a real document).

What is important to notice is that every word in *Hourglass* is something that has been *written* by one person or another. In *Garden, Ashes* the narrator speaks as a voice through a cloud from the timeless, placeless vantage of memory. This unspecified situation of the narrator is a common but always potent mystification that contributes to the illusion of narrative freedom. In *Hourglass*, by contrast, the text is a series of discontinuous documents. Why they are cited and by whom is at first no easier to determine than what they refer to, but at least the factuality, the written, impartial nature of these documents, is incontrovertible, and they are all written by people (Fascist interrogators or Sam himself) whom we can easily locate in a time and place virtually coterminous with the actions they describe. Indeed, the rhetorical device of the document, the miniaturization *en abîme*, the compression of narrative time, the tone of cold objectivity – these are all *nouveau roman* strategies Kiš has adopted as one might take up any device of advanced fiction.

Incidentally, as one reads on one begins to structure a hypothesis that the behind-the-scenes narrator of the entire novel may be the son of Edouard Sam, a boy who has now become an adult and is reading his father's letter. While Edouard's son muses over the letter during the course of one long night, he rehearses imaginatively the scenes the letter conjures up. At first such fictions are vague, jumbled, inexpert, but as dawn approaches the occasions become sharper, clearer. This transition from partial vision to fearful clarity is the same trajectory the entire trilogy describes.

Victor Schlovsky once observed that the character of Don Quixote, far from having inspired the book Cervantes wrote, is in fact almost a technical afterthought, a solution to the purely formal problems of juxtaposing literary genres. This argument used to strike me as more fanciful and suggestive than true, but my skepticism was due to a lack of counter example. What other character could Cervantes (or Pierre Menard) have invented?

Now I take the theory more seriously, since Kiš has provided an answer to the question. Whereas the father in *Garden, Ashes* must be a demigod – elemental, free, eccentric (he must be eccentric in order to explain how a free being can become a victim), the father in *Hourglass* is quite simply the victim, a more or less ordinary man crushed by tyranny. A demigod is consonant with a mythic novel, a victim with an objective novel composed largely of documents.

But to consider *Hourglass* as a mere piece of virtuoso writing would be impertinent, absurd. Ravishing and ingratiating as *Garden, Ashes* is, *Hourglass* is a greater work of art because it is truer. Whereas the Freudian notion of wish-fulfilment might explain our heady pleasure in *Garden, Ashes*, our more sober but lasting satisfaction in *Hourglass* derives from a set of feelings Freud explained with the later theory of the repetition complex: we recreate traumas in all their painful detail – through art, dreams, or play – in order to feel a retrospective mastery over events that originally crushed us. A Yugoslav Jew forced to wear a yellow star and to perform chain-gang labor (though he is past fifty and in bad health) is not a deity but a victim. He does not choose the role of victim; other people have imposed it on him.

Readers are wily in ducking out from encounters with pain. Holocaust literature (embracing Holocaust documents, films, television programs) is by now, alas, so familiar that the reader or viewer has become expert in substituting solemnity for suffering. To give this ax a new cutting edge, it must be ground on a new stone. Kiš has found the artistically (and politically) potent approach – that of the oppressor. For page after page an interrogator asks precise, exhaustive questions about the subject's slightest activities and affiliations. When the subject faints from weariness, he is forced to go on. The questions are circular. They betray ulterior motives – but which ones? We already know where these questions will lead, so we listen to the investigation with drawn breath. Again and again, as though we are attached to a satanic Möbius strip, we hear replayed details about Edouard's bleeding hands wrapped in rags, about his smashed teeth and glasses, about the humiliating time when he was ousted from a first-class train compartment because he was a Jew. When he is exhausted, the dialogue reads like a passage from Beckett:

Go on.
I'm tired.
Go on. Go on.

Again and again we relive the moment when Edouard Sam watches his rat-infested house founder, fall, collapse until it is utterly destroyed.

I think a rat made it collapse.
When did you see the rat?
I've seen it twice . . .

In *Garden, Ashes* the father is given to Lear-like rages against his relatives. These rages now have become the victim's effort to find someone, something he can oppose, combat, force to submit to his will, if even for a second. His love of litigation is no longer Jovian ire but rather a half-mad, wholly human vaccine against the legal processes about to destroy him.

The mythic style of *Garden, Ashes* suppresses the specificity of locale and time in order to emphasize the universal applicability of the tale. The only details that are lingered over are those luminous with fond memory, Proustian keys to recollection. In *Hourglass*, however, we learn everything, absolutely everything, and in the most painful specificity. We learn in photographic detail exactly which train tracks can be seen from a certain window. We find out that on 5 April 1942 the sidereal daybreak was at 3.33 a.m. for an observer at 46.5 minutes north of the equator and one hour ten minutes west of Greenwich. We learn that the father's nephew George sold bakelite telephone boxes for the firm of Slonski & Strauss. We learn what the main character was carrying in his briefcase on a certain day:

> Three dry herring sandwiches wrapped first in graph paper then in a greasy newspaper; four hard-boiled eggs, also wrapped in newspaper; an empty bottle of beer; two shirts, one white and one ochre, with the Kaiser label . . .

The list goes on. In the midst of this profusion, we learn almost incidentally of the deaths of Jews. We learn that while Zsigmond Lukacs was being beaten to death, his mouth was 'stuffed with dirty rags. Grossinger told me'.

> Who is Grossinger?
> Also a druggist. First locked up for a while in Petervarad, then shot as a hostage . . .

And what about Rosenberg's son? He worked as an anesthesiologist, swallowed a fatal dose of morphine, was 'rescued', later committed suicide. In the third-person account of a 'travel picture', we read that when one prisoner helps another, he is struck by the guards: 'Then a blow to the nape makes a hard lump shoot out of his mouth, mixed with saliva and blood, which he spits out with shocking ease. Horrified, he realized he's just spat out his false teeth.'

In the third section of 'instruction', a question is asked about the novel Edouard might have written. We learn that the action would have taken place one night from the last hours of day to the first of the following dawn. In this interval the hero would have relived the major episodes of his life. In fact the hero's conflict is his conflict with death, a struggle against the death he knows is approaching.

In this discussion I've touched on only one aspect of this complex novel, which embraces so many other themes and techniques, a whole panoply of feelings (sensuality, familial *schadenfreude*, love and primarily fear) and literary devices (including gargantuan inventories, as when the effects of drink are listed, and dazzling syncopes, as when the sound of a moving train is imitated in a passage about travel). All that I've wanted to underscore here, however, is the way in which the movement in the trilogy from sketch to myth to document parallels an intensification in authorial vision and reader response. No wonder *Hourglass* is the most convincing account we have of the Jewish experience in the Second World War.

In Kiš's collection of stories, *The Encyclopedia of the Dead*, the title tale is about a Borgesian library that houses volumes recounting the lives of every dead person who was *not* celebrated, the person who 'doesn't figure in any other encyclopedia'. Moreover, each volume on each person speaks of him or her in the very terms that would have mattered most to that individual. The book gives the names of the subject's favorite authors, of the circus shows he saw; it lists the day when he smoked his first cigarette, and it cites the pointed shoes he bought with the money his father gave him upon graduation. Everything is here, and the essential message of the encyclopedia is: 'nothing ever repeats itself in stories about people, everything that at first glance seems identical is scarcely similar; each man is a star apart, everything happens always and never, everything happens once and repeats itself indefinitely'. The encyclopedia is a monument to difference, human difference. I would venture to say that *Hourglass*, though paradoxically told from the enemy's point of view, renders up, in the terms that would have most mattered to Edouard Sam, the saving difference of his life.

The Critic, the Mirror and the Vamp:
A. W. Symons

Review of *Arthur Symons: A Life* by Karl Beckson, *Times Literary Supplement*, 13 November 1987.

In the preface to *The Renaissance*, Walter Pater writes, summing up: 'What is important, then, is not that the critic should possess a correct abstract definition of beauty for the intellect but a certain kind of temperament, the power of being deeply moved by the presence of beautiful objects.' By this standard Pater's disciple Arthur Symons was the most prescient critic of the turn of the century, for he was instinctively drawn to every writer in the England and France of his day who is still read. Although he often laid claims to being systematic in his approach, to the end his writing on art and artists remained somewhat disjointed, as though he could do nothing but alternate admiration with intuition, Pater's biographical and impressionistic methods. He lived well before the era of 'close reading', a practice that would have enabled him to demonstrate in detail his enthusiasms. Nor did he know how to look at literature in a mythic light, although Jung's approach to art seems to have been tailor-made to Symons's sensibilities. Symons seldom put his contemporaries into a political, economic or even broadly cultural context, although he could analyze such forces in a distant forbear, as he did in his excellent book on Blake, published in 1907.

Symons knew almost everyone worth knowing. Among his English-speaking friends he included Yeats, Havelock Ellis, Ford Madox Ford, Edmund Gosse, Ernest Dowson, William Michael Rossetti, Joseph Conrad (whose first story he published) and James Joyce (whose early poems and stories he helped to place). By the time Symons was twenty-one he had received the praise of Browning and Pater and the friendly acknowledgment of Meredith. Among his French friends he numbered Renan, Leconte de Lisle, Taine, Rémy de Gourmont and Dumas *fils*, but his particular intimates and idols were Verlaine and Mallarmé. In his later years Gide and Larbaud visited him in England (he'd met Gide earlier in France).

Symons's strength – his many ways of rehearsing his enthusiasms, his curiosity and sympathy – come through in his masterful essay on Aubrey Beardsley, first published in 1898 in the *Fortnightly Review* shortly after Beardsley's death. Symons starts off at full tilt, remembering Beardsley at Dieppe haunting the gambling rooms ('He liked the large, deserted rooms, at hours when no one was there; the sense of frivolous things caught at a moment of suspended life, *en déshabillé*'). He recalls that at concerts Beardsley was always adding a bejeweled sentence to his never-finished Tannhäuser story, 'Under the Hill'. ('It could never have been finished, for it had never really been begun.')

The tumbling accumulation of insights grows phrase by phrase: 'He seemed to have read everything, and had his preferences as adroitly in order, as wittily in evidence, as any man of letters; indeed, he seemed to know more, and was a sounder critic, of books than of pictures; with perhaps a deeper feeling for music than for either.' Symons pinpoints Beardsley's exact shade of dandyism when he assures us that he 'hated the outward and visible signs of an inward yeastiness and incoherency'.

Symons had a remarkable knack for affirming the seriousness of what other people dismissed as frivolous, and this gift proceeded more through earnest affirmation than skilled argument, more through revelatory paradox than sustained analysis. He finds Beardsley an artist who 'expressed evil with an intensity which lifted it into a region almost of asceticism, though attempting, not seldom, little more than a joke or caprice in line'. Similarly, he regards Beardsley as 'a satirist who has seen the ideal'. Or he proposes that Beardsley is an abstract artist who meditated on real things, someone for whom puff-box, toilet-table and ostrich-feather hat 'were the minims and crotchets by which he wrote down his music; they made the music, but they were not the music'.

This engaging critic stood in an equally benign relationship to his subject and to his reader. He assumed that both were friendly and that the reader was discriminating but not dismissive, more eager to find something to like than impatient to shrug something off. Symons believes his reader is an esthete not an intellectual, a hedonist not a student, an amateur of art not a historian of ideas. His amiable assumptions – the same as those animating Virginia Woolf's *The Common Reader* – have now pretty well vanished.

Symons's gusto is his great virtue as a prospector for talent. Like the much earlier French romantics whom he admired, Symons enjoyed confounding genres and elevating the so-called minor arts to the status of the major. Of the café singer Yvette Guilbert he could declare, 'She is simply a great, impersonal, dramatic artist, who sings realism as others write it.' He could also discuss pianists with the sort of seriousness most critics reserve for composers.

Curiously, the very vagueness of his writing about performers throws into relief Symons's own inner conflicts, as though the release from a strict account of his subject allowed him to rave in revealing ways. Thus in discussing the pianist Pachmann, he at first expresses his desire to be objective and non-programmatic about art: 'Pachmann gives you pure music, not states of soul or of temperament, not interpretations but echoes.' But a few sentences later, discussing Pachmann's sound, he writes: 'You see his fingers feeling after it, his face calling to it, his whole body imploring it. Sometimes it comes upon him in such a burst of light that he has to cry aloud, in order that he may endure the ecstasy.' Repressed moralizing returns as ecstatic utterance.

His biographical approach to writers made him particularly good at quick sketches of those he'd known. His favorite, Paul Verlaine, he renders in a few strokes: 'He lies back in his corner at the Café François Premier, with his eyes half shut; he drags on my arm as we go up the boulevard together; he shows me his Bible in the little room up the back stairs; he nods his nightcap over a great picture book as he sits up in bed at the hospital.' And his travel writing is some of the most vivid I've ever read, for he simply records what he sees. That his eye was characteristically urban – the eye of Baudelaire and Walter Benjamin – is suggested by a few of his titles: *Cities*; *Cities of Italy*; *Cities and Sea-Coasts and Islands*; *Colour Studies in Paris*; *Parisian Nights*.

These titles also indicate another preoccupation. In Symons's day the cultural influence of France on England was far more vital than it had been at any time since the eighteenth century.

Symons's own poems, which retained traditional forms and kept in all the logical and discursive links of Victorian verse, nevertheless took up the lurid themes of the decadents (self-absorption and the *femme fatale* – the mirror and the vamp). Typically, in the poem 'Satiety', Symons writes: 'I cannot sin, it wearies me. Alas!' Such posing (so at odds with Symons's real puritanism) awakened the full grumbling thunder of Mrs Grundy – one critic denounced his 'inexpensive amours', although his friend Yeats told him with more sympathy, 'You are a perfectly moral man, but they are the morals of Thessaly.' (Behind Symons's back Yeats took a different line. He told Joyce, 'Symons has always had a longing to commit great sin, but he has never been able to get beyond ballet girls.')

In response to English moralizing, Symons quite sensibly wrote: 'Art may be served by morality: it can never be its servant. For the principles of art are eternal, while the principles of morality fluctuate with the spiritual ebb and flow of the ages.' This formulation reveals the quasi-religious role that Symons assigned to art. France served Symons as a counter-example to England in many useful ways. In 1900, for instance, he was able to write, 'at least literature in France is not a mere professional business, as so much of what passes for literature is in England, it is not written for money, and it is not written mechanically, for the mere sake of producing a book of verse or prose'. Oddly enough, today the descriptions could be reversed, since France has become the country where, between serious works, writers feel obliged to turn out a *livre de présence*.

The French influence on Aubrey Beardsley and Oscar Wilde is well known, but one sometimes forgets that Yeats patterned his notion of the priest-like vocation after the example of Mallarmé. And Karl Beckson quotes T. S. Eliot, who called Symons's best-known book, *The Symbolist Movement in Literature*, 'an introduction to wholly new feelings' and who wrote in 1930:

> I myself owe Mr Symons a great debt: but for having read his book, I should not, in the year 1908, have heard of Laforgue or Rimbaud; I should probably not have begun to read Verlaine; and but for reading Verlaine, I should not have heard of Corbière. So the Symons book is one of those which have affected the course of my life.

In spite of his stated devotion to form, style and technique and his scorn for uplift, Symons was, nevertheless, haunted by some sort of moral force in literature, if we define 'moral' as Henry James might have conceived of it – a dramatic confrontation of personalities, a brilliantly lit staging of choices, a sense of personal destiny lived out under the prestige of religion (despite a deliberate rejection of most of the Christian credo). Or perhaps as John M. Munro (quoted by Beckson) has suggested, Symons 'merely sought intimations of spirituality, early manifestations of a world which lay beyond the senses'. Perhaps Symons might have agreed with Yeats who called the imagination 'the philosophical name of the Saviour'.

In his introduction to Pater's *The Renaissance*, Adam Phillips contends, 'It is part of Pater's subtlety to have exploited the invitation of inexact words. His indefinite words, "sweet", "peculiar", "strange", "delicate", are resonant as blanks that can evoke powerful personal associations in the reader.' Certainly this same poetic glow, inviting but unspecified, radiates from much of Symons's criticism. In Symons the words are often 'strangeness', 'exquisite', 'strange beauty', and a whole set of paradoxes ('visionary of reality', 'tender economy'). Like Ezra Pound, who could find very few reasons beyond the stern, stuttering dictates of his tautly attuned if cranky taste for liking what he liked, Symons, although vastly less hieratic, championed the artists he was attracted to with an ardent, energetic vagueness. As he wrote in the 'Editorial Note' to the first issue of the *Savoy*, 'For us, all art is good which is good art.'

Karl Beckson's biography, enriched by several newly unearthed caches of letters, is a vivid picture of the man, his era and his contribution to it. Symons was born in Wales to Cornish parents. At an early age, like a true decadent, he professed his indifference to nature and his preference for the urban and the artificial and a corresponding urge 'to write books for the sake of writing books'. He early on evidenced an extraordinary faculty for picking up language and for assimilating English literature.

By the time he was nineteen, despite his lack of a university education, he'd written an introduction to Shakespeare's *Venus and Adonis*. Two years later he published his *Introduction to the Study of Browning*. Representative of the acuity of this book is his comparison of a lyric poem by Tennyson with one by Browning: 'The perfection of the former consists in the exquisite way in which it expresses feelings common to all. The perfection of the latter consists in the intensity of its expression of a single moment of passion or emotion, one peculiar to a single personality, and to that personality only at such a moment.' Beckson astutely remarks that in such a passage Symons anticipated Virginia Woolf's 'moments of being' and Joyce's 'epiphany'. The line Symons takes also has its antecedents in Pater's notion of the 'significant moment' and Arnold's of 'a great action'.

Whereas most admirers of Browning at the time praised his moral profundity, Symons stressed the method rather than the message and viewed Browning as primarily a dramatic poet. After he met Browning the younger Symons stated that 'in greatest poets the genius is seen in the man'. Too often such a remark is regarded as a simple equation of the life and the work, but Proust, for instance, who devoted so much energy to attacking biographical criticism in his *Contre Sáinte-Beuve*, nevertheless recognized no contradiction when he asserted the largest spirits are the greatest writers and that nothing compares to the friendship of a great writer.

Beckson's central thesis is that Symons's life falls into two contrasting halves. In 1908, when he was forty-three, Symons suffered a mental breakdown while travelling in Italy with his wife. He spent the next two years in mental institutions, incoherent, grandiose and paranoid ('General Paralysis' was the diagnosis of the period). His doctor predicted his imminent death. But Symons recovered, went on to publish some thirty more books (mostly collections of earlier work) and to live until 1945, when he died at the age of eighty. According to Beckson, before 1908 Symons was alert to all the trends of his day and an exemplary critic of them all, whereas after his breakdown 'his capacity for critical discernment was damaged permanently by chronic incoherence'.

Yeats blamed Symons's breakdown on his marriage, especially on his wife's extravagance – Yeats claimed she was always dressed up like a 'dragonfly'. When Symons was thirty-three, he met the twenty-four-year-old Rhoda Bowser, an aspiring actress from a rich family and married her in 1901. That very year, in order to pay for the upkeep of their new flat, Symons wrote more than 100 theater reviews, for which he earned £5 a week from the *Star*. Money and the scramble to earn it were constant themes in his letters (and in his discussions with Rhoda). When the couple bought a seventeenth-century cottage in Kent, the repairs quickly mounted to £400. As Beckson tells it,

> Symons sought to meet the unexpected burden by undertaking new literary projects: in addition to some thirty-six articles and reviews that he published in 1906, he prepared a new edition of *An Introduction to the Study of Browning* for Dent ('for the sake of £50 on account,' he told Hutton), promised to do a history of English criticism 'for solid cash' (a project never undertaken), worked on his Blake book, and completed *Studies in Seven Arts* for autumn publication. All these projects, he told Hutton, would not bring in the £300 or so that he had to pay out in May to cover repairs thus far.

He often rose at 4 a.m. to begin his writing day.

Given these mounting worries and continuing pressures, no wonder Symons collapsed in Venice in 1908 – madness earned him some rest. And it forced Rhoda to start dipping into her own capital (at the time of her death, despite the declining value of her inherited investments, she was still worth more than £43,000).

Beckson's interpretation of Symons's madness is more ingenious. He argues that Symons was haunted by his obsession with sin and damnation. His father was a Wesleyan minister. Although Arthur broke away from the faith, the bohemian excesses of his bachelor years in London and Paris tormented him – at least unconsciously. Late in 1893, Symons became the lover of a ballet dancer named Lydia, half English, part gypsy. In his passionate affair with Lydia, Symons, like Tannhäuser, discovered transcendent bliss through sin. As Symons put it:

> Sin was with us in my room; the Flesh was with us always; the Arch-demon arose from Hell whenever I evoked him and certainly my Venus and I came near night after night, afternoon after noon, hell's mouth. There, after much mad dancing of my senses, I sought and found the Cloven Hill. Alas and alas,

for the sweet and eternal hell; wherein to spend my Eternity in the arms of Venus!

As Beckson concludes: 'Lydia's breaking off of the affair in 1896 "against her will" and his mother's death several months later undoubtedly reinforced Symons's experience of transgression, rejection, devastating loss, and corrosive guilt.' Exactly why this guilt took fourteen years to surface isn't exactly clear. Of course there's always the possibility that he was suffering from a strictly organic deterioration.

Symons's character was at once racy and remote. He bragged of his conquests of actresses, of his affair with a snake charmer, and prided himself on being 'a scholar in music halls'. When he was only twenty-six he was described by George Moore with allegorical facetiousness. Moore saw Symons as 'a man of somewhat yellowish temperament, whom a wicked fairy had cast for a parson', although a good fairy had bent over his cradle and bestowed on him extraordinary literary gifts in compensation. Virginia Woolf admired his poetry and said of his criticism, 'He had so fine an instance for the aim and quality of each writer that the result seems effortless and brimming with truth.'

Symons's exalted notions of art and the artist led him to like Maeterlinck but not Shaw or Ibsen, to prize Debussy but not Ravel, to love Hawthorne and to dismiss the Wordsworth of *The Excursion*, to prefer the Symbolist shadowiness of Gordon Craig's set to the realism of Sir Henry Irving's. In his essays Symons frequently quotes Bacon, who wrote: 'There is no excellent beauty that hath not some strangeness in the proportion.' Symons even found an echo of his judgment in Baudelaire's '*l'étrangeté, qui est comme le condiment indispensable de toute beauté*'. Strangeness certainly makes this biography wonderfully delicious.

The Paris Review *Interview*

The interview with Jordan Elgrably appeared in the *Paris Review* in 1988 at the time of publication of *Caracole*.

I first met Edmund White following his move from New York to Paris in 1983. His novel *A Boy's Own Story* (1977) had been recommended to my by Odile Hellier, in whose American bookshop, The Village Voice, White was scheduled to read. On the evening of the reading the upstairs wing of Hellier's store was packed with curious newcomers. White's generous and genial personality as well as his effective reading of his autobiographical novel – the first in a tetralogy dealing with gay experience in America – won White many new readers and inspired me to ask him to sit for an interview for the *International Herald Tribune* in April 1984.

Over the next four years White and I ran into each other often at various Paris gatherings, or at Village Voice literary evenings, and I meanwhile followed his essays and reviews in the *New York Review of Books*, the *New York Times Book Review*, and *American Vogue*, where he is a contributing editor. White's previous books, *Forgetting Elena*, *Nocturnes for the King of Naples*, and *States of Desire: Travels in Gay America*, had already identified him as a fresh original voice in American fiction as well as one of the country's most eloquent representatives of the gay community, but it was with *A Boy's Own Story* that he acquired a wide international readership. French critics praised his Proustian sensibility and compared his prose to that of Henry James; in Britain the novel sold well over one hundred thousand copies and began White's regular contributions to *The Times Literary Supplement* and the *Sunday Times*, among others. His fourth novel, *Caracole*, was described by the British magazine *Time Out* as 'something to revel in: elegant fabulous, almost sublime'. Earlier this year White's second autobiographical novel in the tetralogy,

The Beautiful Room is Empty, appeared. At present White is at work on a biography of Jean Genet.

Our interview took place on a Sunday afternoon in mid-April 1988. We met in White's apartment, a three-room walk-up in a seventeenth-century building that looks directly out on to the church of St Louis en L'Île. Edmund White's persona is very much that of his nameless autobiographical narrator in *A Boy's Own Story* and *The Beautiful Room is Empty* – a man who yearns for beauty and love yet who often lives at the edge of the society he so painstakingly observes, his highest good the truth of the imagination.

You've been variously congratulated by your peers as one of America's outstanding prose writers today, as a master of language and imagination. How does the kind of encouragement you need now differ from when you were just starting out?

I feel I'm getting all the encouragement I need. I almost feel spoiled. I wish I were more disciplined and taking better advantage of the time I have now.

Are literature grants such as the Guggenheim, which enabled you to settle and write in Paris, healthy for an author's sense of independence? Does the writer remain nonpartisan to the politics of the supporting institution?

Oh yes, there are no strings attached. You don't have to do anything but write and you don't feel compromised in any way. And often one may have no idea what those politics are.

Do you think there are enough grants available to writers who are just starting out?

There ought to be more grants that go to people in their late twenties and early thirties. That's a crucial age, although it's very hard to judge who is worth supporting and who is not. Looking back on my own life, I see that was the period when I was closest to giving up as a novelist and when I most needed some encouragement. I didn't get anything published until I was thirty-three and yet I'd written five novels and six or seven plays. The plays, I should point out, were dreadful.

How were you making a living?

I was working for Time–Life Books from 1962 to 1970, as a staff-writer, and after that I was a journalist. Eventually I became an editor at the *Saturday Review* and *Horizon*.

These positions didn't allow you to think for yourself as a writer?

No, because a journalist and novelist are not quite the same thing. I was writing all the time and I was considered a good journalist but I had no idea if I could write a novel. Part of my problem as a young writer was that I was too much a New Yorker, always second-guessing the 'market'. I became so discouraged that I decided to write something that would please me alone – that became my sole criterion. And that was when I wrote *Forgetting Elena*, the first novel I got published. In my courses later I always forbade my writing students to discuss in class the commercial side of publishing. I wanted to save them the time I'd lost; I wanted them to be serious artists free of all constraints. I believe it was Schiller who said that the only time a human being is free is when he or she makes a work of art; if that's true, then art is sacred and shouldn't be compromised by mere ambition.

You taught writing at Yale, Columbia and Johns Hopkins University. What do you, as a confirmed novelist, acquire from teaching experience?

These are positions which are offered to you once you've already published a few books. I began teaching in 1977. In the beginning it served to clarify my thinking about my own methods. Then I used teaching to improve my work. For instance, I saw I was a weak plotter and so I would talk a lot in class about how to write strong plots, and how to analyze other people's novels and stories from that angle. That helped me to some degree; I was teaching myself. After a point, however, you become too immersed in other people's work to be able to think about your own, and it seems almost vulgar to write. You're surrounded by all of these struggling egos and it seems sort of impertinent. And yet being able to work out some of my own ideas about fiction was admittedly a useful process. I estimate there is a period of seven or eight years when you can do it, but then you burn out, and I think you should stop for a few years before starting again.

Could you elaborate?

When I was teaching, some of my students were much better educated than I, and so I felt I really had to struggle to keep up with them and be worthy of their level of seriousness. I was also aware of just how much money they were spending in tuition and felt I had to give them their money's worth at every moment. I tended to over-prepare, or let's say to prepare very, very carefully, for which I think they were grateful. But it's true that at the same time I was pursuing my own interests. Certain writers interested me, for instance Proust, whom I'd read many times in my life though never with enough care. I taught a course in Proust, which was a way of making myself read him with great attention. In the same way, I taught a course in Pynchon. Though I had admired *Gravity's Rainbow*, I'd never been able to get through it. I think it is a great but boring book.

In terms of lack of action?

Of suspense.

Is this inability to write fiction while teaching similar to the unwillingness to read novels while you're writing one?

Not in my case. I enjoy reading novels while I write. First, to steal ideas from other writers, particularly the classic ones – they remind you of just how good you have to be to be any good at all. It's very easy for one's standards to slip. I mean that I'm not an especially anguished writer; I tend to like what I write and am possibly satisfied too readily. When you finish reading a book like *Lolita* you feel that there's nothing more wonderful in the whole world than writing a novel; you feel challenged and awake and alive, and you have a desire to write with the same keen response to the sensuous world. Nadine Gordimer once said to me she felt that one of the things that goes out of writing as you become more mature is an attention to sensuous detail. I thought that was probably true, but a terrible thing if it is true, and I've always tried to guard against what may be an inevitable process by reading some of my touchstone writers who never lost that love of sensuous detail, such as Colette, Nabokov and Knut Hamsun.

There isn't a fear that a spark of originality might be taken away from you by reading earlier novels?

No, no, I find, for instance, that when Cocteau wrote what I think is one of his best novels, *The Impostor*, he thought he was copying *The Charterhouse of Parma*; or when Raymond Radiguet wrote *Le Bal du Comte d'Orgel*, he thought he was copying *La Princesse de Clèves* by the Comtesse de Lafayette – but you could read those two novels and never suspect their antecedents. There are many writers who enjoy seeing their books as a kind of *homage* to an earlier book. And yet very few readers would suspect such a link unless it was explicitly pointed out.

There may also be some truth in the notion that a good novel should have the ingredients to spawn a hundred other good novels, so that a succeeding novelist ought to be able to seize upon a predecessor and somehow further them in his own work.

I think there is a balance between the literary and the human interest in a book, if we can make that distinction. For instance, a novel like *Caracole* maybe errs in the direction of being too literary without being sufficiently human. I think that *Lolita* is the greatest of all novels because it is both simultaneously. I mean that for those people who are interested in literature, it makes reference to a whole library of French poetry – everything from *Carmen* to Arthur Rimbaud. But for those who don't care about literature, they can read the book and be swept up by the strictly human interest of it. I think that probably a novel like the one I just finished, *The Beautiful Room is Empty*, is very human in its orientation and may be the kind of book that pleases most readers – it holds a mirror to life; whereas *Caracole*, which is literary and fantastical and not obviously mimetic, has a much smaller readership.

From reading the French reviews of your work, one learns that they consider you very much an author in the European tradition. To what do you attribute this?

I believe they are struck by the echoes of Proust, in both *Nocturnes for the King of Naples* and *A Boy's Own Story*, and I think by that they mean a neo-Freudian, psychological analysis written in a nuanced flowing style. Americans don't necessarily associate that style with Proust; I think we usually attribute it to James, who is much more our figure.

Would you say the European literary tradition differs from its American counterpart more in style and form rather than in content or concerns?

It very much depends on which period you're talking about. I think that the nineteenth century in America is extraordinarily different from the twentieth century. There may be certain preoccupations which are similar, such as the individual versus nature, or the dynamics of male companionship, or the loss of innocence – you could track those as three concerns that unite the nineteenth with the twentieth century, but those are moral preoccupations. In terms of style, nothing could be more different than the prose of Emerson and, say, Richard Ford, or that of Raymond Carver and Hawthorne.

Isn't this more a question of evolutionary progress in terms of writing technique?

Yes, but style has evolved more rapidly in the States. I would say that there's more uniformity between the styles of Angelo Rinaldi and Proust or even Flaubert than there is between Carver and Hawthorne. Even though Europe witnessed a tremendous upheaval in experimental techniques in the 1920s and 1930s, namely with the surrealists (and with Joyce in English), that innovative moment has left a rather small effect, and now most French novelists, and English novelists, are writing rather like their nineteenth-century antecedents. Barbara Pym, for instance, writes like Jane Austen, and Jonathan Raban or Alan Hollinghurst like E. M. Forster – just to name some of the writers I admire. Obviously there are some changes; for instance there is a great deal more interiority in contemporary fiction than in nineteenth-century fiction, and a lot less incident, or plot. And there is far more sexuality now than then, and so on. But English novelists continue to be primarily concerned with analyzing character in terms of social class. American novelists are not at all interested in that.

Aren't American novelists quite often less political in a worldly sense than Europeans?

Yes. I think a novelist like Milan Kundera, for instance, could not exist in America. A person with the stature of Kundera, let's say somebody like William Gass, doesn't have a political analysis of society so much as a mythic one. A novel like *Omstetter's Luck* by Gass, which I consider a masterpiece, is a big, mythic, Faulknerian, highly poetic view of an almost Jungian archetype, and this is the American tendency, one which starts with the greatest of all American novels *Moby Dick*. It's a quasi-religious view of society, where as in Europe a novelist such as Kundera is extremely interested in questions of individual authenticity versus political 'kitsch', as he would put it.

Not to stray too far from the question of American and European literary counterparts, it does seem odd that American novelists rarely work within a vast political framework, particularly when you evaluate US interests and involvements abroad, which have of course escalated since 1945.

I think you have to look at the social conditions under which writers live in the various countries. For instance, in France writers have often been involved in politics and as diplomats or ministers – Paul Claudel was the ambassador to Japan and André

Malraux was de Gaulle's minister of culture. Carlos Fuentes and Octavio Paz were diplomats and García Márquez was a journalist who knew Castro as a friend. Alejo Carpentier was stationed for years in Paris. Most Russian or Middle European writers have *suffered* for their political views – they cannot afford to be indifferent to politics. Now, if you glance at the social situation of most American novelists, you'll see they are professors on small isolated provincial campuses and the larger world of politics is not part of their experience. If you take someone like Raymond Carver, for instance, he is from a working-class family, he is a man who had a serious drinking problem. Now that he has stopped drinking and is writing very brilliantly, what he writes about is a different kind of social problem; that is, the disenfranchisement of people in America itself. This is a perfectly legitimate concern and one which I think falls within his experience. I can't imagine him writing about the American oppression of people in Vietnam or Nicaragua; it's just not in his bailiwick. Of course there are American novelists who fought in Vietnam and who have written about that. I think the truth is that novelists are not universal legislators of morality, they don't set out to write about the most important issues; they write about the ones that have actually touched their lives. I agree with you, however, that there's something very insular about American fiction. So many books are first-person novels that deal with questions of adultery, personal poverty or misunderstanding between generations – suburban problems.

There is a paradox at work here, I think, because America has become more and more dependent on the outside world. If you took the inkwell of US interests and involvements and spilled it on a map of the world, you would see how it sinks in nearly everywhere. And yet it seems that so many Americans don't want to know that they are no longer protected from the larger scale of things.

Americans do not keep up with world events. It may be partly that people don't travel very much, or it may be a kind of arrogance. Or maybe we should blame the press, which highlights personalities, not issues.

Occasionally one finds foreign words and phrases in your novels, and sometimes the odd word coined by yourself. How do you decide when to employ foreign words or coin new ones and when to remain within 'the riches' of the English language?

Actually, the odd thing is that since I moved to France I've probably used fewer foreign words in my fiction. While I was living in America I always had a kind of longing to live in Europe, which expressed itself in such linguistic borrowings. But now that I actually live here I'm so worried about my English becoming too Gallicized that I tend to eliminate French words. Although you think I've made up a lot of words, it's not quite true. I once knew a woman who read books for dictionaries, and she would circle unusual or sub-standard or odd variant uses of words; she told me it had been a waste of her time to read my books because the uses were utterly conventional. I think that writers, like Joyce, who invent new words are admirable.

In The Beautiful Room is Empty, *however, you chose to use the words* malade imaginaire *in reference to a character, instead of* hypochondriac.

If you say 'hypochondriac' it suggests a mild psychiatric problem that should be cured; if you say *malade imaginaire*, it suggests a character in a Molière play – a comic figure whom experience will chide.

Can you talk a bit about the writers who most helped to form you as a novelist?

Valdimir Nabokov is my favorite writer, and I like Colette a great deal – I've learned a lot from the way she uses herself as a character in her own books and tantalizes the reader with the question: 'Is this autobiography or is it fiction?' I also love her descriptions of nature and her handling of love. She is greatly underrated in France. I read Knut Hamsun all the time for inspiration, though he's so entirely different from me. Of course, I don't like his later work, when he came under the influence of Fascism. But those early novels – *Mysteries, Victoria, Pan* and *Hunger* – are beautiful books. I'm drawn to the simply lyricism that runs through his writing. There is not much plot, but intense outbursts of feeling.

And what is it about Nabokov that so moves you?

It wouldn't be his intellectual high jinks, but his passion, his sensuous detail, the wonderful rendering of the physical, visual, material world around us. It's almost a spiritual way he has of describing the world; he makes it so glowing, so mouth-watering and so precise that you feel it has been irradiated. Writers can use literature as a mirror held up to the world, or they can use it as a consolation for life (in the sense that literature is preferable to reality). I prefer the second approach, although clearly there has to be a blend of both. If the writing is pure fantasy it doesn't connect to any of our real feelings. But if it's grim realism, that doesn't seem like much of a gift. I think that literature should be a gift to the reader, and that gift is an idealization. I don't mean that it should be a whitewashing of the problems, but something ideally energetic. Ordinary life is *blah*, whereas literature at its best is bristling with energy. Someone once said Balzac's only fault is that he makes all of his characters into geniuses, like himself. What a wonderful fault!

Which of your American contemporaries do you admire?

I like Robert Coover, John Hawkes, Richard Ford, Carver, Pynchon, Gass, William Gaddis, Robert Ferro and especially Cynthia Ozick. W. M. Spackman is someone I admire as well, James Merrill is, I think, my favorite living writer at the moment. I feel that his trilogy *The Changing Light at Sandover* is a masterpiece. I've been very involved with that book, following it as each episode appeared. His entire *œuvre* seems to me enormously impressive and again, imbued with the same kind of lyric quality that Nabokov has. Both of them constantly change register. They go from slang to the most serious or elevated speech, from the medieval language of courtly sentiment to the most recent street talk – a constant movement from the hieratic to the demotic, from the historic to the contemporary. This shift in register seems to be the genius of English, going back to Shakespeare, but it is not at all the genius of French, which is more concentrated and uniform in diction.

What have you read in French since you moved to Paris?

Chateaubriand's *Les Mémoires d'outre-tombe*, Stendhal's *La Chartreuse de Parme* and, in more recent literature, Nathalie Sarraute's *Enfance*, which I admire tremendously. I think her style is ideally suited for early childhood memories because it is so spare and fragmentary. Most people writing about childhood tend to inflate what are actually very small memories into a continuous and rapturous narrative. She doesn't do that. Her refusal to part from the facts, the actual phenomenological memories of experience is careful and honest . . . I've been reading both Richard Ford and Raymond Carver, whom I admire immensely – Ford, I think, may be one of the most important new American fiction writers to emerge in the last five or six years. And of course, I've been reading a lot of Jean Genet for the biography I'm writing of him, and then other writers who he read and liked, such as Racine and Jouhandeau. And I do quite a bit of book reviewing as well. So I do read a good amount of fiction.

Do you find yourself reading more slowly now than, say, twenty or thirty years ago, when you just began to write? Are you reading from a craftsman's point of view, or are you still able to appreciate reading fiction as a kind of nostalgic literary enterprise?

I get quite caught up in books, but rarely in French because I'm always too aware of reading another language. But I do often get caught up in English-language novels. I don't find that technical awareness stands in the way of pleasure; it can even make that pleasure more piercing if you're constantly excited by the writer's technique.

In A Boy's Own Story, *your nameless narrator 'awakened to the idea that a great world existed in which things happen and people changed, took risks . . .' What kind of risks do you feel you take as a writer?*

Writers are always taking risks economically. You don't have a retirement plan, you don't have health insurance necessarily, and little in the way of personal savings. In other words, if you were to become ill tomorrow, or if you were to write two or three bad or unpopular books, you'd be very, very poor. Nevertheless I have always made it a point of honor to write as though I had a million dollars; that is, I try to write in the most original way I know how, and that feels like a risk each time you do it. André Gide said that with each book you write you should lose the admirers you gained with the previous one.

One takes the risk of changing audiences or styles?

Yes, I think so. In the nineteenth century people wrote rapidly and they wrote a great deal; books were almost like chapters in people's writing today. Then there wasn't any question of changing the basic style, or basic premises. In the twentieth century the serious writer strives to evolve. Someone once said that each good novel should also advance a theory of the novel.

There seems to be two distinct voices in your fiction, with Nocturnes *and* Forgetting Elena *falling into a kind of Baroque, rather dreamlike reality, while* A Boy's Own Story *and* The Beautiful Room Is Empty *are in that register of possible autobiography you admire in the novels of Nabokov and Colette. (*Caracole, *however, is somewhere between them and in a genre of its own.) How many convincing voices or styles can a novelist hope to master, and might they reflect the nature of his or her worldly concerns?*

Caracole was consciously about society and the individual's place in it. In *The Beautiful Room* I was interested in showing the puritanical oppression of sexual freedom. In any event, those two books have a special political concern. If a writer keeps changing his style, he could be accused of dilettantism – or he could be defended as someone who resists the sort of packaging designed for quick product recognition and smooth consumption. Is a stylistically unpredictable writer a luxury product – or is he refusing to be a product? More subjectively, my mercurial literary personality reflects a general feeling of unreality. Like the narrator in *Forgetting Elena*, I'm an amnesiac – a guilty, not an innocent amnesiac. I keep feeling I've accomplished nothing, never written a 'real' novel. Today, when so many of my friends are dead or dying of AIDS, that feeling of unreality has been heightened. People say we should seize the day, but just *one* day turns out to be too cold (or slippery) to hold.

Until Caracole *you wrote principally of gay experience. Why did you make the departure into 'straight' fiction?*

The writing of *Caracole* coincided with my coming to Europe. In New York, without even really noticing it, I had come to live an almost exclusively gay life (except for my teaching). I had gay friends, I dealt with gay shopkeepers, I lived in a gay community in Greenwich Village, and I was interested mainly in gay politics and read a lot of gay literature. My reference group, as a sociologist would say, was gay. But, when I came to Europe, partly because there isn't such a strong gay ghetto in Paris, I began to lead a more ordinary life. *Caracole* represents that renewed participation in society. I suppose that the idea for the novel came from reading, many years ago, eighteenth-century French pornographic fiction – the novels of Crébillon *fils* – which struck me as very odd. The heterosexual characters seemed so gay in that they were interested only in promiscuity and conquest. War was constantly a metaphor for love, and there was a highly structured and artificial nature to courtship. Sex was seen as sport, time-killer, self-expression, pleasure and war – whereas in nineteenth-century conventional heterosexual fiction it's seen as an urge toward companionship, affection, familial values or lust. Crébillon showed me how one could write about heterosexual sex in a very different way.

Did you receive any reaction from heterosexual readers either confirming or disavowing some of the experiences they read about?

A number of heterosexual men told me they found it arousing. An English novelist said that he'd gotten very embarrassed reading *Caracole* in a train. A reviewer from *L'Express* was reportedly confused and disappointed to learn I was gay.

Let's go back to your early years as a novelist. You mentioned you'd written several novels but couldn't get any of them published until you were thirty-three. What difficulties were you experiencing?

I was writing gay books well before gay liberation and before there was a recognized gay reading public. One actually existed, although no publisher was aware of it. There was also a tremendous amount of self-repression among gay editors. A gay editor would turn down a gay book because if he admitted to liking it he would have to defend it in an editorial meeting, and that might lead other people to suspect he was gay.

What became of all those unpublished novels?

They are gathering dust. But I quarry them for other books I write. They are a source for a lot of information, particularly about the 1950s and 1960s. For instance, *A Boy's Own Story* and *The Beautiful Room* contain material from previous novels. I could not employ much of the actual language because I've come along as a stylist, but the material serves to refresh my memory of the years I was dealing with, when I was in my twenties and early thirties. It's very easy to rewrite the past in your mind and to assume that in the 1960s you had the same sophistication – let's say politically – that you might have had in the 1970s. In the 1960s we harbored utopian notions which were extremely naïve. I feel that it's hard to recreate that naïveté unless you're faced with documents of the period.

Why does one write a book like A Boy's Own Story *– as a coming to grips with the ghosts of childhood once and for all, a sort of final self-analysis of one's rudiments?*

I think you're making it sound a little more pragmatic than it is, but there is something crucial about the relationship in that book, for me, between the narrator and the younger self. I call it the pederasty of autobiography; the older self actually loves the younger self in a way the younger self never could have felt or accepted at the time. There is a kind of lapse in time in self-approval. One is filled with self-loathing at sixteen, but when one

is forty one can look back with this kind of retrospective affection at the younger self – which is very curative.

From Nocturnes: *'We label the feelings of our childhood with the
names we learn as adults and brightly, confidently refer to that old
"anguish" or "despair" or "elation". The confidence of liars. For
those words meant nothing to us then; what we lacked as children
was precisely the power to designate and dismiss, and when we
describe the emotions of one age with the language of another, we
are merely applying stickers to locked trunks, calling "fragile" or
"perishable" contents that even were we to view them again,
would be unrecognizable.' Is this representative of the writer's responsibility to 'tell the truth'? What precisely does that mean?*

Piaget makes a very good case for the fact that the language – and
even the concepts and the thoughts we have as adults – really
don't fit with childhood experience. There is a radical disconti-
nuity between childhood experience and adult experience. We
complain of a kind of amnesia, that we don't recall much of our
early childhood, and Freud of course said that this was because
we were repressing painful or guilty desires. But Piaget argues
this couldn't be true, because otherwise we would forget only
those things that were painful but remember everything else –
which is clearly not the case. We have an almost blanket amnesia,
and Piaget argues that the terms in which we experienced our
childhood are incommensurable with the terms in which we now
think as adults. It's as though it's an entirely different language
we knew and lost. Therefore I feel that any writer who is writing
about childhood as an adult is bound to falsify experience. But
one of the things you try to do is to find poetic approximation;
an elusive and impossible task. It is like trying to pick up blobs of
mercury with tweezers – you can't do it. You nevertheless
attempt to find various metaphorical ways of surprising that experience. I think you often times feel it is there, but you can't get
at it and that's the archeology of writing about childhood.

In Caracole *you write, 'children never question what happens
around them' although in* A Boy's Own Story *your narrator is
quite inquisitive. Thus one's childhood becomes a kind of myth so*

that as an adult one is more dependent on imagination than memory.

Yes, I think that our notion of what we experienced as children is highly infected by whatever is the prevailing philosophy of childhood. In other words, if you'd asked somebody in the seventeenth century to write a story of his childhood, he would have perceived it as a rough draft, an inferior version, of maturity – or as comical, deformed. Then in the nineteenth century the child becomes an angel, innocent and pure, who must be protected. And then in the twentieth century, with Freud, the child becomes a monster seething with vice and lust.

Might we say that a true novel, when it is the truth of the creative subconscious, is a kind of rendering of one's past as a mythology?

It's curious that if you take certain facts from your childhood and perceive them in a kind of glow, and arrange them in a certain sequence, it will not only move you and your mother and sister, but also people who don't know you. It's very odd how that works and I'm not quite sure why it works. I'm always struck by it because I've invented childhoods for imaginary characters which seem to have a lot less impact on readers than my actual childhood has when I recount it.

You underwent psychoanalysis for a time. Can you talk about that experience, and how it did or didn't help you to write?

I started psychoanalysis very much as the narrator does in *A Boy's Own Story*, at the early age of fifteen, and I would say my early experiences with it were almost entirely destructive. However, towards the end of the twelve years I spent in therapy over a period of some twenty years, I did finally find a therapist who I felt approved of me in some fundamental way, and who was himself a writer. He was quite helpful to me as a writer, yet in ways that would make you smile. For instance, when I had a writer's block and I went to him, he said to me, 'Well, it is very hard to write and you're feeling very frightened of it. It's simply a question of courage. You must find some courage within you and go home and write.' I found that very useful advice coming from him, though I don't think I would've accepted it from anyone else. This kind of primitive advice that you could get from your grandmother turns out to be the most useful 'insight' the analyst offers. And perhaps self-acceptance leads to tolerance, just as self-knowledge leads to insights into other people. I've had people say to me, not so much after reading my fiction as a book like *States of Desire* that they felt I was a compassionate writer – I don't really know what they mean by that, as I can be pretty arrogant as a commentator on other people. But I suspect what they mean is that I'm able to put myself in other people's shoes and see things from their point of view without being too judgmental early on in the process.

I was wondering if the analysis might not be destructive in the sense that you begin to feel too much guilt, and find yourself in a kind of endless process or exorcism when that guilt may be merely a minor aspect of your personality.

I would say that writing, in its own way, is a rival to therapy. You should recognize that literature is a separate province. It has its own rules. It cannot be simply an embodiment of Freud's notions on human nature, for otherwise it will soon seem hopelessly dated and hollow.

In A Boy's Own Story *your character reflects: 'I see that what I wanted was to be loved by men and to love them back but not to be a homosexual ... It was men, not women, who struck me as foreign and desirable.' When did you eventually conceive of your sexuality as healthy and acceptable?*

Well, I was actually in the Stonewall riot, the harbinger of gay liberation in New York in 1969. The riot itself I considered a rather silly event at the time; it seemed more Dada than Bastille, a kind of romp. But I participated in that and then was active from the very beginning in gay liberation. We had these gatherings which were patterned after women's and ultimately, I think, Maoist consciousness-raising sessions. Whether or not our sessions accomplished anything for society, they were certainly useful to all of us as a tool for changing ourselves.

But what did you have to change? The fact that there was nothing to deny or repress?

You see, many of us began by thinking that we were basically heterosexual except for this funny little thing, this sexual habit we had somehow picked up carelessly – but we weren't homosexuals as people. Even the notion of a homosexual culture would have seemed comical or ridiculous to us, certainly horrifying. We would have wanted to confine our disease to the smallest possible part of our life, to our sexual behavior and nothing else.

You've said previously that you're writing for gays and straights. But do you think of yourself as a gay spokesman?

It was a political act for me to sign *The Joy of Gay Sex* at the time. The publisher could not have cared less, but for me it was a big act of coming out. Charles Silverstein, my co-author, and I were both aware that we would be addressing a lot of people and so in that sense we were spokesmen. We always pictured our ideal reader as someone who thought he was the only homosexual in the world. *States of Desire* was an attempt to see the varieties of gay experience and also to suggest the enormous range of gay life to straight and gay people – to show that gays aren't just hair-dressers, they're also petroleum engineers and ranchers and short-order cooks. Once I'd written *States of Desire* I felt it was important to show one gay life in particular depth, rather than all of these lives in a shorthand version. *A Boy's Own Story* and its sequel, *The Beautiful Room is Empty*, grew out of that.

'The world is governed by a minority, the sexually active' is one of the boy's rationales. What do you mean by designating the sexually active as a minority?

If you look at most people in the subway or on the street they're either sick or old or ugly or crippled or crazy. That's 'most' people, and they can't get sex and sex is hard to buy. It's ex-pensive. There are a lot of Arab men in Paris, for instance, who would do anything to get a sex partner. There are a lot of black men from the Antilles, you know, who are too poor to afford sex, except occasionally, with a prostitute.

Do you see the range, the reactions, the emotions in heterosexual love and homosexual love to be approximately similar?

I think there is an equally complex gamut, but the two experiences are not coincident. You can't say all the things a straight woman goes through in her courtship, marriage and divorce are the same as a gay man experiences in meeting another man, living with him and breaking up with him. They're not the same emotions, they don't occur in the same sequence nor do they have the same social repercussions. But there are enough similarities to permit us to speak to each other. When a straight man breaks up with his girlfriend, the break is often decisive; it's very hard for them to move from the end of their affair into an ongoing friendship. However, I would say that many – if not most – gay men who break up continue to be best friends. And they may even continue to live together. They may enter into a period of rivalry during which each of them tries to meet somebody new first. When that phase wears out their friendship gets mellower and better. This is something which seems unthinkable to most straight people; they don't know how we can do it, but there is a great deal of comradeship that lies under the discourse of homosexual. There is a discourse of gay friendships and then there is a kind of male/male friendship which straight men know about, and there is also a discourse of love which straight men have with women. The idea that those discourses can come together in one relationship, and that when the love ends the friendship can continue, astonishes many outsiders.

Can you discuss your work process? When do you sit down to write, and what do you do to warm up?

Oh, it's very tormented. I try to write in the morning, and I write in longhand, and I write in very beautiful notebooks [*White displays a couple of hardbound notebooks filled with thick hand-laid paper*] and with very beautiful pens. I just write now and then . . . This is a first go at it, and then I start crossing out, and it gets crazier and crazier, with inserts and so on. Finally, two or three years of this go by and then one day I call in a typist. I dictate the entire book to her or him. The typist is a sort of editor in that he or she will tell me what is really terrible and what's good, or what's inconsistent and doesn't make sense. I get together a whole version this way and then I stew over it some more. Eventually my editor reads it, and then he tells me to change things, and it goes on like that. If I write a page a day, I'm lucky. But I write less. And months go by without my writing at all, and I get very crazy when I write! Sick, physically.

You are more neurotic when you write than when you don't?

It's a very uncomfortable process; I don't like it at all.

In everyday life, what sort of things spark off your imagination?

Other works of art, as I've said, challenge me. Then, when I'm writing, I find that my brain begins to store information in a different way than it usually does. That is, I'm out looking for things that I need, and I will grab them anywhere. And there's a magic which any writer can tell you about: the world provides you with just the information you need, it seems, just when you need it.

Has it happened that you've been blocked and you go to sleep and upon waking the following morning you've been given what you needed?

Yes, but my plots are rather primitive, so that is not a worry. I'm more concerned with controlling the mood. I find that when I'm writing well, I have a real zest for detail, for description. When I'm not writing well, I can't think of anything to say, and there is a lackluster, mechanical quality to the writing. But, basically, when the sentences get longer and more ornate, and there's more and more sensuous detail, that's when I'm writing happily or well. When the sentences get shorter, clearer, more pure or classical, then I'm not enjoying the book and neither is the reader.

You seem to be more a creature of inspiration than habit, which counters the dictum many writers have about getting up every morning and writing for several hours a day, come what may.

Writers say two things that strike me as nonsense. One is that you must follow an absolute schedule every day. If you're not writing well, why continue it? I just don't think this grinding away is useful. The other thing they say: I write because I must. Well, I have never felt that, and I doubt most of them do either. I think they are mouthing a cliché. I don't think most people write because they must; perhaps economically they must, but spiritually? I wonder, I think many writers would be perfectly happy to lay down their pens and never write again if they could maintain their prestige, professorship and PEN membership.

In A Boy's Own Story *you describe the character as having imaginary playmates, but he thinks, 'And yet I didn't really like my imaginary playmates precisely because they were so irritatingly vague and unreal.' Does it ever seem to you while writing or reading that fiction is vague and unreal?*

Yes, and the stewing I'm talking about, getting ready to write, the thinking about writing and trying to find your way, all of that is meant to find a way of doing a scene that is full of energy, so that it has conviction, a sharp outline, progression and intensity. You should find that your writing overcomes the besetting feeling of vagueness and ennui which is characteristic of everyday life.

In your New York Review of Books *essay on Nabokov you wrote, 'Many writers proceed by creating characters who are parodies of themselves or near misses or fun-house distortions or they distribute their own characteristics across a cast of characters, and some especially like to dramatize their conflicts and indecisions by assigning them to different personages.' How do you find yourself adapting to your characters, or do they perhaps adapt themselves to you?*

Well, I do two things. One is that I pattern a lot of my characters on people I know, but there is a strictly imaginary element which creeps in after I start writing. I begin by writing a fairly close portrait of somebody I know, but then the character begins to seem real to me in his own right. If I'm stuck at some point I try to find something in my own experience that I can use, even if the character is going through something I never experienced. I have had my writing students read Stanislavsky, and of course his whole method requires the actor to find real-life experiences to draw on for even the most improbable and wild scenes that he must portray. I think the writer must do something like that, and most writers go through that process without thinking about it. What Stanislavsky says is that you cannot hope to recuperate an emotion by going for it directly. What you can do is to reconstruct the original sensuous details of the room in which you were sitting, what you were eating, what you were wearing, whether it was hot or cold; and if you get all those things right, then the emotion will come flooding back, of its own. I think that is an important exercise for writers. People always ask what do you teach in creative writing? People insist: there's nothing to teach. Well, of course, there is something you can teach; you teach people to find ways of tapping their own emotions.

When you're writing, do you look more towards innovation or towards tradition?

Originality is important, and one of the dangers of creative writing classes, for instance, or any critical approach to literature, is that it underemphasizes originality. After all, a professor of literature is trying to find a tradition, and influences, which can be traced. People would rather talk about Poe as the typically American genius than as the total kind of lunar nut that he really is. There is nothing typical about Poe: he's from the moon.

How do you go about being original?

Well, of course, if you ask this question of somebody in a *Paris Review* interview, he will say, 'You do it by being yourself, by being true to your own vision.' I think that is somewhat true. As you gain confidence as a writer, you learn to spot your own funny ways of looking at things, and you learn how to notate them – because at first, of course, it's very elusive. You've never seen your vision before, so you wouldn't know how to put it down on paper, and it might not occur to you that the vision is something suitable for writing about. After you have acquired a

certain amount of technique and confidence, you learn how to
notate these rather passing, elusive thoughts. A young woman
came up to me once after a reading and said, 'I love what you do,'
and I said, 'What do I do?' and she said, 'You completely jump
over the important plot points, and then develop the minor things
that nobody else would think to develop.' I decided to profit
from her intelligence.

In A Boy's Own Story *you evaluated your readers as 'eccentric'
as they were 'willing to make so much out of so little'. Is it not the
writer, ostensibly, who must make so much out of so little?*

In *Nocturnes*, I thought I had been almost perverse in how few
clues I gave to the reader, and I was amazed by how much was
made of so little. That is, if you go back to the text, there are only
the strangest little traces of slime that indicate where the snails
once crawled, just a few phosphorescent, glimmering paths, and I
was astonished by just how much intelligent readers were able to
get out of this, and to reconstruct more or less the same picture
I'd intended. It is a rather eccentric enterprise on both the part of
the reader and the writer, but technically it is the reader who
must be willing to take all these faint clues and reconstruct them
into a novel. This is very different from the process of reading a
nineteenth-century novel, where all the work has been done for
you.

The non-dit, *the art of ellipsis, is certainly within the European
tradition, and more noticeably so, I think, in post-war fiction.
Isn't this not only a result of an increasing sophistication in
readers, but also a reflection of the mass media, which tends to
condense everything for quick consumption?*

It is precisely film that has promoted the use and understanding
of ellipsis. In the nineteenth-century novel, the reader was
oriented for a full chapter before the action began. A film, however, will begin with one man chasing another and they're
desperately racing over rooftops, and then suddenly they're
speeding away in cars and – who are these people, and what are
they doing? You don't care; you're suddenly seized by the action.
Poetry also proceeds in an elliptical way. Anyone who's studied

English in America, for example, has read T. S. Eliot, Ezra Pound, and Wallace Stevens, not to mention John Ashbery, and such a reader is used to suspending a demand for instant intelligibility. They're willing to fall into line after line of language without quite knowing where they are or what's happening or what it all means.

I was wondering how your life has significantly changed in the move from New York to Paris. Has it been good for your writing?

French people are extremely formal and they don't call you up all the time, whereas in America total strangers look you up in the phone book and want you to read their nine-hundred-page manuscript.

What sorts of notions do you have of what a writer's life should be like?

I wish I were more at home with writing. I can go a year or two or three without picking up my pen and I'm perfectly content. The minute I have to write I become neurotic and grouchy and ill. I become like a little wet, drenched bird, and I put a blanket over my shoulders and I try to write and I hate myself and I hate what I'm writing. Writing depends upon a fairly quiet life, whereas I am a sociable person. I think every writer goes back and forth on this question; it's a constant struggle to find the right balance between solitude and society and I don't think anyone ever does. I find it reassuring to read the complaints of Chekhov: 'My country house is full of people, they never leave me alone; if only they would go away I could be a good writer.' He's writing this close to the end of his life.

Originally you moved to Paris to be in Europe for a year or two, but five years have passed. What keeps you here in Paris?

I think mainly the quality of life is so attractive, and there is still a certain degree of exoticism for me here. And just from a practical point of view, I can make my living here as an American journalist writing for American magazines about Europe. In New York everything is done for a motive, and people are even quite frank about it, whereas here people get together simply to have fun with each other. In a way it's more like small-town America, which I like, and not like big-city life. I think New York is a city for ambition. In Paris people cultivate social life as an art form; in New York people cultivate it as a form of self-advancement.

Do you find journalism as pleasingly painful as writing fiction? What inspired you to turn to biography and to work on Genet?

In both journalism and biography the *assignment* is fairly clear, which is never true of fiction. Moreover, in journalism and biography one is obliged to study, observe, record, whereas in fiction one is left to one's own melancholic devices.

Social life has been very important in your fiction, especially in Caracole. *Aren't people too often victims of what is fashionable, whether it be a social theory or a political ideology, and isn't that moment as subject to change as the kinds of clothing they wear?*

I would say a novelist's proper job is to be sensitive to the way things look; I agree with Conrad that fiction is primarily a visual medium, and that there is something very concrete and valuable and eternal in any accurate description of the way things look. No one would ever require fiction to be totally divorced from its period, in fact, most people believe, and I believe, that the more it's anchored in a specific locale, period and milieu, the more universal it is. This is quite different from, for instance, espousing a Freudian view of sexuality and imposing that in a rigid way on your characters, and then ten years later a Foucaultian view – because then you get a *roman à thèse*. After all, fiction writers are not professional thinkers.

Caracole *treats fashion and* la société mondaine *in a context of political upheaval. Does fashion, for you, influence politics in any perceivable way? Why was the leitmotif of fashionable society so important to you in that novel?*

I was trying to show a society in which the conquerors were less evolved than their subjects and in which they were even intimidated by their victims. This is a situation that can be observed in life. Oscar Wilde unnerved his jailers. Wit, style and intelligence can outweigh, or at least hold at bay brute power and wealth. The Chinese intimidated their Manchurian conquerors, just as the Nazis, upon conquering Paris, became respectful of French culture and were eager to win the approval of the subjugated. Of course, Cesare Borgia respected Urbino so much he destroyed it.

In terms of the kinds of ideas which are a writer's staple, there is something in Forgetting Elena *I'd like to take issue with. You write, 'We all know that human emotions are banal...' Is this meant to provoke the reader or, for you, is it axiomatic?*

When I say human emotions are banal I mean that they are familiar, we all have them; if we didn't we wouldn't be able to write novels that each of us could read and understand. Originality in writing is in the presentation of those emotions or even in their occlusion – the way in which feelings are stopped or diverted or disguised.

Writing, then, with originality should prevent the banal from creeping into the tone of the novel.

There is a tendency to talk about the Platonic novel as though there were but one novel we're all striving to write, an Ideal, perfect novel which is outside time, outside history, outside any particular cultural tradition – an eternal, floating and perfect book. An opposed point of view, which is the one I hold, is that each person has it within him to write a novel unlike everybody else's. If you're a teacher this is very important, because you either have a normative notion of the novel and you struggle to make all writers ascribe to your notion of what the great novel should be, or you have a pluralistic notion, whereby each person should write a novel unlike all others.

Is writing a way of rendering the banal beautiful?

Or making the banal strange. There is a term that comes up in

Russian Formalist criticism called *defamiliarization*. It's a way of talking about the events of everyday life (in Tolstoy, Natasha's first ball or her first opera, for example) and making them utterly weird because they are described by an innocent or inexperienced person. Good fiction often takes the banal around us and defamiliarizes it.

Writing from an unfamiliar point of view must be one of the great challenges of a novelist. In The Beautiful Room is Empty, *your character at one point during his university days says he thinks the Buddhists were right in their belief that the self is an illusion, although as a writer he reacts to the individuality of everyone he meets. 'I was potentially everything or nothing. I could wake up one morning gay or straight...' I thought this seemed like a desire to convince yourself that Edmund White, writer, transcends Edmund White, self; transcends his class, race and sexuality.*

You're right.

Yet there are two contradictory points of view at work here.

I'm convinced that *the self* is an illusion, and that actually all we are consists of several piles, or, as the Buddhists call them, *skand-has*, of associations and memories and so on, that the way to enlightenment is to dissolve the illusion of unity and return all these elements to their original constituents, thereby ridding one-self of the notion of identity. Although all that appeals to me philosophically, as a novelist I don't believe it. As a novelist I believe there is a kind of smell that's very distinctive about each living creature, and I enjoy being a sort of sketch artist, like a sidewalk artist, who tries to catch a likeness – and I somehow manage to believe that there are likenesses, and that they do tell you something about people.

In A Boy's Own Story *you write, 'It seemed to me then that beauty is the highest good, the one thing we all want to be or to have or, failing that, destroy.' One is immediately reminded of Yukio Mishima, who made youth and beauty into a cult and ulti-mately committed* hara-kiri *at the age of forty-five, already an old man by his standards. You are in the vicinity of that age now. What do you see as the 'highest good'?*

Are you suggesting I make the supreme sacrifice? Artists should be honest about the tremendous glamor and impact of physical beauty. It is not fair that it should be so important, since so few people possess it, but, in fact, beauty *is* a glimpse of the beautiful. A beautiful person embodies in her or his flesh what an artist is struggling to represent in his work. But a writer shouldn't have too many answers. Barthes has a phrase in which he suggests that the artist is like Orpheus leading Eurydice out of the underworld. Everything is fine, the novel follows along behind the novelist, until he looks back . . .

III

The Nineties –

The Angel in the House: Tennessee Williams's Letters

Review of *Five O'Clock Angel: Letters of Tennessee Williams to Maria St Just, 1948–1982* in the *New York Times Book Review*, 27 May 1990.

These letters provide us with the most cheerful, most tender, most civilized picture of Tennessee Williams we're likely to get. After so many lurid accounts of his drugging and drinking, his hustlers and hangers on, his boorish ranting and egotistical sulks, at last we're provided with a thirty-year-long record of a friendship that enables us to see the source of everything in his work that was lyrical, innocent, loving and filled with laughter.

To be sure, Maria St Just brought out the best in Tennessee Williams. Charles Bowden, the producer of *The Night of the Iguana*, and his wife, Paula, remarked in a 1987 interview cited in *Five O'Clock Angel* that 'Maria would arrive, and suddenly Tennessee would start to entertain, and be with those friends who were deeply his friends – not the fly-by-nights who, when Maria wasn't around, he was apt to be with. She brought a family feeling, a continuity.'

Perhaps the best proof of the richness and intimacy of their relationship is that it provoked jealousy in both her husband and Williams's companions, one of whom once sent a bill for $500 to the playwright because he'd had to endure several dinners with Lady St Just.

Maria Britneva was born in Russia shortly after the Revolution. After her father's death she was brought to London where her grandparents already lived. She was raised in sometimes grand, sometimes precarious circumstances. She began her career as a ballet dancer as a young child, but a foot injury made her switch to acting. Though never a big star, she did act with the most important performers of the day. As a young woman in post-war

London, attending a party at the home of John Gielgud, she spontaneously befriended an ill-at-ease American whose name she hadn't caught. They chatted, and soon admitted to each other that they had each been brought up by a grandmother.

The young man turned out to be Tennessee Williams; his first Broadway hit, *The Glass Menagerie*, was in rehearsal for a British production. The play didn't do so well in London, but Maria Britneva soon became the confidante Williams wrote to in the evening after his day's work – his 'Five O'Clock Angel', as he called her in a typically genteel, poetic periphrasis.

Although Williams preserved few of her letters ('Ah, dear child! Tennessee was so sentimental . . .' Gore Vidal said), she kept all of his, so we hear much more about his triumphs and sufferings than about hers. We can, of course, infer her side of the correspondence from his remarks, and fortunately she kept rough drafts of a few of her letters, which are so sprightly and gossipy it's hard to imagine she actually worked them up.

Such fastidiousness as drafting letters, however, typifies the attention they lavished on every aspect of what they labeled their *amitié amoureuse* – their loving friendship. As Williams wrote in 1976 in a note intended to be added to the English edition of his autobiography,

> It is a delicate feeling, of course, and of course it is frangible and most certainly of all it must not be neglected. And yet it is long-suffering. It survives many unavoidable separations without disrepair, since it does not depend on physical presence as much as carnal attachment. Extended absences of one from the other do not affect it, probably because these absences are a material element and this feeling that I call *l'amitié* has so little concern with material things.

Those fools who've argued that Williams's female characters were based on men will be surprised to learn that Williams based Maggie in *Cat on a Hot Tin Roof* on Maria and that he could write, 'I have had many close friendships with men which were without any sexual connotations, God knows. But I have found them less deeply satisfying than those I have had with a few women.'

Neither Williams nor Maria St Just had an easy time of it, if these letters are taken as evidence. Williams hoped that she would marry one of his best friends, his publisher James Laughlin, to whom this book is dedicated, but Mr Laughlin couldn't make up his mind to take the plunge, abandoned his fiancée in the Mediterranean and left for India and Japan. The two correspondents speculate that the wealthy American might have been afraid the impoverished and impetuous young woman wanted to marry him for his considerable fortune. Maria Britneva subsequently married a despondent Englishman, Peter Grenfell, who became Lord St Just and inherited Wilbury Park, the first Palladian house in England. He died in 1985.

On his side, the great love of Tennessee Williams's life was Frank Merlo, a prickly but intelligent and loyal man who advised Williams on his art and career and somehow acted as a keel to steady this otherwise out-of-control ship. When Merlo died in 1963, Williams fell apart – he later referred to the 1960s as his 'stoned age'. A decade later he pulled himself together (there are very few extant letters from the 1960s). When he did recover, he discovered that his new plays pleased the critics less and less often. He suffered from the terrible paradox of being acknowledged as America's greatest living playwright – whose new work was universally ridiculed.

Maria St Just gave Williams what Gertrude Stein said every genius needs: praise. She became an informal agent for him in England, informal because she never accepted a fee, and she is now the co-trustee of his estate. She steadfastly defended a brilliant but neglected play, *Out Cry*, which was dedicated to her.

The only text she criticized outright was his autobiography – and that, possibly, because he unaccountably left her out of it, or nearly so. *Five O'Clock Angel* fills in that missing chapter with a detailed, living, breathing account of their laughter and gaiety. They give pet names to all their friends. John Gielgud becomes 'the Old One', Frank Merlo 'Little Horse' (because of his big teeth) and Robert Carroll, one of Williams's hopped-up psycho boyfriends, 'the Twerp' (his earlier sobriquet was 'the Enfant Terrible').

As sentimental and amused as characters in a Noël Coward play, but without the brittleness, in their letters Maria St Just and

Tennessee Williams provide us with a stylish, brave version of friendship and its rugged staying power.

Out of the Closet, on to the Bookshelf

Originally published in the *New York Times Magazine*, 16 June 1991 as part of the celebration of Gay Book Month.

For me the revolution of the gay male novel has seemed breathlessly rapid and strangely personal. As a young teenager I looked desperately for things to read that might excite me or assure me I wasn't the only one, that might confirm an identity I was unhappily piecing together. In the early 1950s the only books I could find in the Evanston, Illinois, Public Library were Thomas Mann's *Death in Venice* (which suggested that homosexuality was fetid, platonic and death-dealing) and the biography of Nijinsky by his wife (in which she obliquely deplored the demonic influence of the impresario Diaghilev on her saintly husband, the great dancer – an influence that in this instance had produced not death but madness).

In the 1960s I was lucky enough to discover *A Single Man* by Christopher Isherwood, a sane, unapologetic picture of George, a British professor living in Los Angeles whose lover has recently died. George muddles through a long, eventful day and confides his feelings to his straight friends, but these feelings are shown to be the same ones everyone knows – the suffering that arises from the death of loved ones, the numbing of routine, the fear of loneliness. The protagonist, neither more nor less witty or wise or courageous than his friends, is not presented as damned in ways supposedly peculiar to homosexuals.

I also came across André Gide's journals and his memoir *If It Die,* which showed a civilized adult mind given over to far-ranging interests (classical piano music, Greek theater, Russian politics, travel in Africa) as well as to a veiled attraction to boys. William Burroughs's *Naked Lunch,* John Rechy's *City of Night* and Jean Genet's *Our Lady of the Flowers* moved in the opposite direction; they rendered gay life as exotic, marginal, even monstrous. Not incidentally, all of these books were original and genuine works of art. Burroughs's collage techniques, Rechy's ear for gay speech and sympathy for the gay underdog, Genet's way of turning ordinary values upside down – these were shock tactics for transforming our received notions of reality.

The beginning of gay liberation in 1969 did not produce a new crop of fiction right away, but by 1978 the new gay novel was beginning to emerge. That was the year Larry Kramer's controversial *Faggots* and Andrew Holleran's romantic *Dancer from the Dance* were published. Both books documented the new gay culture that had been spawned by liberation prosperity and societal tolerance.

By 1979 seven New York gay writers, myself included, had formed a casual club named the Violet Quill. We'd meet once a month in one another's apartments. Four of us each time would read our latest pages, then settle down to high tea. The members were Felice Picano (who had written a gay psychological thriller, *The Lure*, and later on an elegiac love story, *Late in the Season*); Andrew Holleran (writing his second novel, *Nights in Aruba*); Robert Ferro (*The Family of Max Desir*); George Whitmore (*The Confessions of Danny Slocum* and *Nebraska*); Christopher Cox (*A Key West Companion*); Michael Grumley (then at work on *Life Drawing*, a lyrical autobiographical novel soon to be published posthumously). I was in the midst of my autobiographical novel *A Boy's Own Story*. Our occasional visitor was Vito Russo, who was writing the authoritative book about homosexuals in Hollywood, *The Celluloid Closet*.

I left the group in 1983, when I moved to Paris. When I came back to the States in 1990 this literary map had been erased. George Whitmore, Michael Grumley, Robert Ferro and Chris Cox were dead; Vito Russo was soon to die. Of our original group only Felice Picano, Andrew Holleran and I were still alive; better than anyone else, Holleran has captured the survivors' sense of living posthumously in his personal essays, *Ground Zero*. Many younger writers had also died; of those I knew I could count Tim Dlugos, Richard Umans, Gregory Kolovakos, the translator Matthew Ward and the novelist John Fox (who'd been my student at Columbia). My two closest friends, the literary critic David Kalstone and my editor, Bill Whitehead, had also died.

For me these losses were definitive. The witnesses to my life, the people who had shared the references and sense of humor, were gone. The loss of all the books they might have written remains incalculable.

The paradox is that AIDS, which destroyed so many of these distinguished writers, has also, as a phenomenon, made homosexuality a much more familiar part of the American landscape. The grotesque irony is that at the very moment so many writers are threatened with extinction gay literature is healthy and flourishing as never before. Perhaps the two contradictory things are connected, since the tragedy of AIDS has made gay men more reflective on the great questions of love, death, morality and identity, the very preoccupations that have always animated serious fiction and poetry. Or perhaps AIDS has simply made gay life more visible. As a result even straight readers are curious to read books about this emerging, troubled world that throws into relief so many of the tensions of American culture.

Skeptics object that gay fiction is, after all, rather ... specialized, ghettoized, limited. But those of us who write it are convinced that the potential audience for our work is no more circumscribed than it is for any other constituency. 'It's no less universal than the writing of urban male Jews or black women,' argues Michael Denneny of St Martin's Press. 'It's particularized – but so is all great fiction, as a second's consideration of Dostoevsky, Synge or Flaubert should make clear. When reviewers say they're tired of reading about gay life, they're in the same position as Bill Moyer when he asked August Wilson if he ever got tired of talking about black life.'

George Stambolian – the editor of three anthologies of gay fiction called *Men on Men* – is also convinced that gay lit has entered the mainstream. 'We have to remember that America is a pluralistic society, and the pluralism also governs evolution of its literature,' he says. 'In the past, our literature has been changed by writers from different ethnic and racial minorities, and that change has always involved struggle, a turf war for power. Now the time has come for gay fiction to renew American literature in the only way it can be renewed – by contesting its social and literary assumptions.'

Not everyone, of course, looks at the matter in the same way. I

recently attended the Out/Write writers' conference in San
Francisco, along with 1,800 lesbians and gay men; one of the key
speakers, Edward Albee, was booed when he deplored the literary ghetto and suggested that writers who happened to be
homosexual accomplished more when they were forced to disguise feelings or infiltrate society from within – Proust, Mann,
Forster ...

It seems to me I've heard aspects of this question explored in
the last decade. When the first European gay literary conference
was held in London a few years back, not a single male writer
from France accepted the invitation to attend; they all felt the
sobriquet 'gay writer' was insulting. I remember that when the
French gay literary magazine *Masques* asked me if I was a gay
writer, the editors told me I was the first writer they'd ever interviewed who answered yes.

The other extreme was expressed at the San Francisco Out/
Write conference by a young short-story writer named Bo
Huston, who said he thought the term 'ghetto' was inappropriate;
no one was forcing us to wear this label. Still, he was personally
delighted to have an all-gay readership, he said, and wouldn't
mind if in fifty years he was listed as a minor gay writer of the
1990s.

What seems undeniable is that there is a gay literary movement
in America, even if no one can exactly define it. Gay short stories
are appearing in such quality reviews as *Outlook*, *The James
White Review*, *Christopher Street* and *Tribe*. Lesbian and gay
studies are being introduced on many American campuses, and
people who follow such things claim that these gender-related
pursuits will soon enjoy the cachet that once belonged to semiot-
ics and structuralism. Certainly an academic critic like Eve
Kosofsky Sedgwick, whose *Epistemology of the Closet* was recently published (a study of Melville, Wilde, Nietzsche, James
and Proust), is as highly esteemed as Yale's gay medieval historian
John Boswell (*The Kindness of Strangers*) and the French feminist
critic Luce Irigaray (*This Sex Which Is Not One*). Harvard recently sponsored a huge lesbian and gay conference, and Yale
now has an extracurricular Center for Lesbian and Gay Studies.
At Brown, where I teach, I'm currently offering a course in lesbian and gay literature that examines such classic authors as
Virginia Woolf, Willa Cather, Djuna Barnes, Forster and Proust.

Arnold Dolin is a bit guarded about this renaissance. As the editor of the Plume imprint that includes gay paperback fiction at NAL/Dutton, whose thirty titles constitute perhaps the most successful gay male list in the States, he's well placed to express an opinion. 'Even though there's a lot of talk about crossover books and the whole phenomenon of gay publishing,' he told me, 'my own impression is that the audience isn't growing. David Leavitt and Michael Cunningham – two of the younger stars of gay fiction – may be the only writers who've actually "crossed over".'

But enthusiasm within the publishing world itself belies this skepticism. The Publishing Triangle, a group of lesbian and gay editors and book people, now counts more than 250 members. Among other activities, it gives the annual Bill Whitehead Award to a gay writer for a lifetime of distinguished achievement. There are some twenty prosperous bookstores in the United States that specialize in lesbian and gay literature. While ordinary shops return unsold books after the shelf-life of a mayfly, gay bookstores maintain year after year a strong backlist of gay titles – a durability that gives gay writers time to find their public. In addition, all of these stores have a large mail-order business. Glad Day in Boston, Giovanni's Room in Philadelphia, A Different Light in New York, San Francisco and Los Angeles are among the leading stores, as is Lambda Rising, with outlets in Washington, Baltimore, and Rehobeth Beach, Delaware.

Nor does Arnold Doblin's skepticism take into account Armistead Maupin, perhaps the biggest money-maker in gay publishing. His beloved *Tales of the City* has sold more than 600,000 copies in the States alone. These vignettes about eccentric straight and gay San Franciscans began as a regular column in the *San Francisco Chronicle*. Speculating about his success, Mauphin says: 'My innovation was simply to incorporate gay characters naturally into a larger world which is what David Leavitt does and Michael Cunningham does. I've never made any bones about being gay and I don't mind being called a gay writer, but I know I reach a large heterosexual audience as well. I see myself as a bit like Bette Midler, who had a gay following who told their straight friends about her.'

Has the 'mainstream' accepted this literature? Many lesbian and gay critics argue that judgments of quality are inevitably politically motivated. Certain negative epithets – adjectives like 'overstated', 'uncontrolled', 'precious', 'trivial', 'sentimental', 'tendentious', 'preachy', 'underdramatized' – reveal as much about hostile heterosexual critics, in their view, as about the gay books they're supposed to be evaluating. Such acknowledged literary virtues as understatement and control may suit writers with conventional values and conventional lives: they can afford to 'show not tell' since they can be sure their equally conventional reader will make the same safe assumptions that are axiomatic for the writer.

But it could be argued with equal plausibility that gay writers have been liberated by the extremity of their situation. What interests them is the exploration of their own most intimate feelings, the struggle to orient themselves in a world – the gay world – they're just beginning to map. The reticence that you find in, say, a Raymond Carver story about a troubled marriage just isn't meaningful to a gay writer, who finds himself faced with a whole constellation of relationships – between men and men, men and women, women and women – that have almost never been described before. I'm slightly nervous about discussing the 'gay sensibility', since I think any discussion of a group's sensibility (the 'black sensibility'?, the 'Jewish sensibility'?) is too general to be useful. But if such a sensibility does exist in gay fiction being written now, it's more lyric than dramatic, more psychological than oriented to action, more conscious than unconscious.

Perhaps unexpectedly, gay fiction is often open to the problems of other minorities. At the Out/Write conference I met gay Japanese-American writers, gay Pueblo Indians, gay black writers, and heard a whole panel devoted to gay Jews. There were panels conducted by writers recovering from addiction, by authors with disabilities, by Latin American authors, by Chicanos and Chicanas, and of course by those with AIDS. Few of these writers are interested in how mainstream America evaluates them, though quite a few would like to change public opinion. For most of them questions of artistic excellence cannot be separated from questions of political persuasion. One heard many heated references to 'canon formation', the process by which powerful critics select a few books to become classics, to be taught in college curricula and earmarked as the essential books of our civilization.

Certainly as our society becomes more and more pluralistic and its minorities more vocal, the canon will be stretched wider and wider – perhaps to bursting point.

I, for one, find much to admire in contemporary gay authors. One of my favorites is Robert Glück, who in his novel, *Jack the Modernist*, explores nuances of love never annotated before:

> How did he see me? I experimented. 'I know I'm being a pest.' My sentence fell like a pebble down a well. After waiting in vain for a splash, 'I must be boring you.' I asked this in a higher voice – my fear annoyed me. Jack maintained that the opposite was true. 'I really can't believe this, Jack, do you think I'm a fool?' Jack put a finger to his temple and deliberated a moment. 'No, you're not a fool.' I was startled. He took the question seriously, had to consider the answer. Finally, still smiling, I was humiliated. I couldn't have felt more suddenly chilled and excluded if I'd learned Jack was a ghost.

One of the best new novelists to emerge in recent years, straight or gay, is Allan Gurganus, whose *Oldest Living Confederate Widow Tells All* was a spectacular début. In 1974, however, long before his novel appeared, Gurganus had published 'Minor Heroism' in the *New Yorker* – the first story in the magazine to deal with homosexuality as a central theme. In his new collection of short stories, *White People* (which includes 'Minor Heroism'), he has included several gay short stories, although what seems to intrigue him most is homoerotic excitement between ostensibly heterosexual men – D. H. Lawrence's turf:

> He'd turn up at Little League games, sitting off to one side. Sensing my gratitude at having him high in the bleachers, he'd understand we couldn't speak. But whenever one of my sons did something at bat or out in center field (a pop-up, a body block of a line drive), I could feel Barker nodding approval as he perched there alone; I'd turn just long enough to see a young bachelor mumbling to himself, shaking his head Yes, glad for my boys.

While such gay writers as Michael Cunningham, David Leavitt and Armistead Maupin show gay men living in the larger context of straight friends and relatives, another group of writers insists on gay singularity. The strongest (and sometimes the most repellent) of these writers is Dennis Cooper, the author of *Closer, Safe* and the just published *Frisk*. As obsessive as Sade and as far from ordinary morality as Georges Bataille, Cooper meditates ceaselessly on violence and perversion. This is the very stuff of Jesse Helms's worst nightmares. Cooper is the spokesman for the bored, sensitive, nearly inarticulate Blank Generation, dedicated to drugs, kink and a fragile sense of beauty fashioned out of the detritus of American suburbs. He also has a terrifying gift for finding a death's head under every pretty face:

> The man grapples forward and locates a skull in Mark's haircut. He picks out the rims of caves for his eyeballs and ears. The lantern jaw fastens below them, studded with teeth. He comes to the long shapely bones of Mark's shoulders, toying with them until two blades resembling manta rays swim to the surface. He clutches his way to both elbows. Ribs ride short breaths to the touch. He grasps Mark's hips and their structure floats up to him.

Perhaps no other body of literature is as subject to political pressures from within the community as gay fiction. Few writers in history have ever been 'politically correct' (a notion that rapidly changes in any case), and there's no reason to imagine that gay writers will ever suit their readers, especially since that readership is splintered into ghettos within ghettos. ('What about the plight of the Jewish lesbian in Mexico?' one participant at the Out/Write conference called out.)

Even the question of whether to write about AIDS or not is strife-torn. Some gay writers think that it's unconscionable to deal with anything else; others believe that since gay culture is in imminent danger of being reduced to a single issue, one that once again equates homosexuality with a dire medical condition, the true duty of gay writers is to remind readers of the wealth of gay accomplishments. Only in that way, they argue, will a gay heritage be passed down to a post-plague generation.

This generation is imperiled. Every other writer at the Out/ Write conference appeared to be ill. People who were HIV positive (like me) exchanged T-cell counts as though they were the latest Wall Street figures. Many who were robust a year ago were now dramatically thin or blind or covered with lesions. During the last session of the last day of the conference a member of the audience seized the microphone, ostensibly to denounce Edward Albee once again. But in an instant the pale, emotional man had segued into a cry from the heart: 'I wanted everything to be perfect since obviously I won't be at the conference next year.'

Gay fiction, written by anguished writers for readers in disarray, is under extraordinary pressures. Holocaust literature, exiles' literature, convicts' literature – these are the only possible parallels that spring to mind. Seldom has such an elusive and indirect artistic form as fiction been required to serve so many urgent needs at once. Some of our best imaginative writers, like Larry Kramer and Andrew Holleran, have turned away from fiction to essays, as though only direct address is adequate to the crisis. But many have remained true to their art. Will the world recognize those writers who have had the courage and energy and honesty and sympathy to raise a cenotaph to this era of blasted lives?

The Wanderer: Juan Goytisolo's Border Crossings

First published in the *Voice Literary Supplement*, June 1991.

Juan Goytisolo is perhaps the quintessential example of the writer who lives internationally, a group that includes Borges, Calvino, Cortazar. I'm not thinking of gad-abouts in search of cheaper drinks or more exotic women, but rather those writers (including stay-at-homes) who turn their stories and novels into layered, multicultural tests, sites transected by lines of force extending out of entirely different traditions.

Goytisolo is a Spaniard of Catalan and Basque heritage, born in Barcelona, who thirty-five years ago, in opposition to Franco, left for Paris. Now he lives part of every year in Marrakesh, and he's just completed a series of programs for Spanish television on the Muslim world. Belatedly, his novels and memoirs are making their way into English. Serpent's Tail has brought out his great trilogy, *Marks of Identity*, *Count Julian* and *Juan the Landless*. North Point has published *Forbidden Territory: The Memoirs of Juan Goytisolo, 1931–56* and *Realms of Strife: The Memoirs of Juan Goytisolo, 1957–82*.

In the second volume of his memoirs, Goytisolo describes a visit he made to the Soviet Union in the 1960s. Everyone, Russians and tourists alike, was sighing over a natural wonder: 'The difference between my tastes and theirs is as sharp as it is extreme,' he writes:

> When I tell them I'm an urban animal, made to run dozens of miles in the streets of a city that excites me but incapable of even budging a few steps in a serene setting that bores me, they're surprised and incredulous. Aren't silence and calm ideal for work and inspiration? Without the least desire to sound paradoxical I tell them that for me work and inspiration

are linked to the hustle and bustle of a city: if its buzzing and raging scarcely disturb me, the crackling of the leaves or the trilling of birds distract me and keep me from concentrating.

He repeats the idea in a television portrait *Goytisolo: Geographies of Exile*, which Pierre Aubry and Stephen Javour filmed last year in France and Morocco (it just won a prize at the Montreal Film Festival). In the film Goytisolo quotes Walter Benjamin, who said that 'to become lost in a city as one gets lost in the woods requires an entire education'.

Soon after he arrived in Paris in 1955 Goytisolo met the writer Monique Lange, whom he still lives with in a 1930s brick apartment building that belongs to her family. It's in the garment district of Paris, called the Sentier, an area that is alas ripe for gentrification but that until now has preserved its complex ethnic character. Before the war it was settled by Polish Jews and Armenians, but since 1958 it's been buffeted by successive waves of immigrants from Spain, Yugoslavia, Greece, Portugal, Turkey, North Africa, and Pakistan.

Some have left, others have stayed and the neighborhood has been gradually enriched. It's never become a ghetto, rather a place you might say of encounters, of osmosis, of cultural exchange.

That's what's admirable, in my opinion. For me that is the very definition of the city, the definition of the modern city.

After the modern Turks came into the neighborhood, one day while I was walking I discovered that I didn't understand what was written on most of the walls.

I decided, since I feel completely integrated into this neighborhood, to do what was necessary, that is learn Turkish.

I started going to a club and for the last four or five years whenever I have the time I go there in the afternoon, I spend half an hour or an hour with guys I know and I practice Turkish in Paris.

(from *Geographies of Exile*)

Goytisolo began life in a very different milieu. His family was upper middle class and pro-Franco. His great-grandfather had made a fortune as a sugar planter in Cuba, and Juan's discovery of his letters back in Spain (and of the exploitation of slaves and other brutal realities on which this fortune was based) awakened his social conscience, already sensitized by his first readings of Marx. This family adventure in Cuba influenced much of *Juan the Landless*. In one passage, slaves gather before the mansion to see the master demonstrate the new flush toilet just arrived from England. A Spanish priest meditates on such questions as how the Virgin defecated and what sort of music is played in heaven, then fulminates against the irrepressible sexuality of the slaves.

> ... we have taken the females away from you in order to guard you against the opportunity to commit sin and incidentally to increase productivity, and with stubborn perversity you have persisted in your vice: your wickedness is too deeply rooted and doubtless is irremediable: nonetheless, how beautiful a spectacle it would have been to see the innocent lily-white soul beneath the modest disguise of a dark and unworthy skin!

When he was seven years old, Goytisolo's mother was killed in the streets of Barcelona during the Civil War. The exact details of her death remain obscure, but he and his brother Luis (who is also a novelist now) reacted violently. They took an ax to all the family furniture in storage behind the house.

> One piece of furniture after another one, without sparing a single one, you destroying, cutting off feet, arms, backs, demolishing tables, gutting seats, scratching veneers, stretching the springs, breaking chairs, seized by a joyful, absorbing inspiration which you were never able to find again, as you now know, except in the establishing act, the airy vandalism of adult writing ...
>
> (from *Forbidden Territory*)

Goytisolo's maternal grandparents lived in the Barcelona house long after the death of their daughter. They slept in a room just next to Goytisolo's, and one night the grandfather played with the little boy – sexually embracing him and masturbating him.

Troubled, Juan told his brother, who repeated the story to their father. The father had always loathed his father-in-law, whose promising career had been destroyed by a homosexual scandal. Now he forced the father-in-law and mother-in-law out of the house into a rented apartment, but he still received them every day for lunch and dinner because the family was dependent on the father-in-law's modest investments. Within the intimacy of the family circle, however, the father tortured the grandfather, mocking him for his homosexual 'crime'. The father even confided to his sons his admiration for Mussolini, who simply put to death these 'sickening perverts'. Years later Goytisolo would discover that he belonged to this damned race.

In school he came under the influence of French and American writers, especially Faulkner, and he began to write. The rancor between his father and grandfather alienated him from his family and soon drove him towards radical politics, a betrayal of everything his Catholic, bourgeois family stood for. In the late 1950s he moved to Paris, where he took political refuge from Franco's regime, which soon banned the sale of his books. As a fellow traveler of the Communist party, he found himself very divided on esthetic questions. In France he was discovering the work of such difficult, original, and imaginative writers as Jean Genet, Céline, Artaud, and Beckett, and felt drawn to this artistic fraternity. But as a socially conscious political exile, he wondered if a progressive Spanish writer could afford the luxury of writing anything except straightforwardly realistic *engagé* novels.

Mary McCarthy once said that the difference between an expatriate and an exile is that expatriates have freely chosen to change countries in order to improve their standard of living (moving as a hedonistic choice), whereas exiles have been forced by their principles or their enemies to move to new countries where they instantly set up a magazine or press in their native language and remain focused on the homeland (moving as a political necessity). By this definition Goytisolo is the classic exile since he never stopped writing in Spanish, continually encouraged revolt in Spain and, with his friends, established a magazine open to Spanish-speaking intellectuals of every country.

Early in his exile Goytisolo met Monique Lange and, thanks to her, Genet. They were to become the two most important people in his life – Monique because she would be his life-companion, Genet because he would come to represent a standard of artistic integrity, personal simplicity, political activism, and sexual freedom that Goytisolo would ever after strive to emulate. When Genet first met Goytisolo, the older writer asked him right off if he was a fag. Frightened, nearly speechless at this casual probing of his deepest fears, Goytisolo stammered that he'd had homosexual fantasies – but Genet impatiently interrupted, dismissing him by saying that everyone had fantasies, they were of no interest whatsoever.

Despite the relatively permissive world of Saint-Germain intellectuals and artists in which he was moving, Goytisolo was incapable of expressing his sexuality. He was living with Monique Lange and her daughter, but felt wounded by Monique's affairs with other men. Monique Lange was herself intrigued by Genet's homosexual world, which she obliquely mirrored in her first novel, *Les Poissons-chats*, translated by Richard Howard as *The Kissing Fish*. Confused and oppressed, Goytisolo took refuge in drink, constant trips abroad and activist politics. In the 1960s he visited revolutionary Cuba.

One Sunday in November 1962, Franqui leads you to a farming concern near Havana where Fidel often goes. You wander in the orchards, then a parade of official automobiles alerts you to his arrival: the Commandante is there surrounded by other *commandantes* who smoke cigars like him and approve his least suggestion. Franqui greets you and introduces you to each other: here's the Spaniard, he says, smiling, who instead of running away, like certain writers whom you know, thought he'd come visit us.

Fidel jokes with you and, while he presents his plans for cheese and milk products with a passion that would have enchanted your father, you observe him with curiosity. He has a lively, ever-changing face: from the corner of his eye he observes the effect his words produce, and sometimes he surprises you with an expression that is crafty or skittish, instinctively suspicious.

Unfortunately for you, he suddenly decides to make you visit the superb vinegar storehouses: you go in gallantly, determined to listen to his speeches to the end, but your allergy to acetic acid gets the better of you; just before you're asphyxiated you're forced to rush out of the cellars. The violence of your reaction seems to disturb him, after a lordly tour of the property, he leaves without saying goodbye.

(from *En Los Reinos de Taifa*)

Goytisolo, this uptight young man whom Genet called *l'hidalgo*, found the release he had so long been seeking in a chance encounter with an Arab worker. Goytisolo had just come back from his second, exultant visit to Cuba, where he'd thrown himself into the revolutionary spirit, partly as a way of disguising from himself his real worries. In the spring of 1962, alone in Paris, he was drawn to the Arab district known as Barbes. In a café where he was the only European, Goytisolo began to talk with a stranger: 'Thin, nervous, of average height, with black eyes, a black mustache, he emanated a lively impression of strength and friendliness.' Soon the two men were checking into a hotel. After a night of passion, Goytisolo accompanied Mohammed at dawn to a place where he was working as a miner hollowing out the underground route of a new highway.

This brief erotic encounter not only provided Goytisolo with a personal release, but also proved decisive to him as a writer. This effect would not be felt until the late 1960s, when he'd already published seven books. But at that time he would bring out *Marks of Identity*, the first volume of his breakthrough trilogy. Significantly, in the trilogy he would celebrate (and impersonate) Count Julian.

Count Julian Ulyan, Ulynao or Urbano is both a historical and legendary character. All we know is that he was the Visigoth governor of Tingis, that is, present-day Tangier and Ceuta, and that at the moment the Arabs arrived in North Africa he betrayed the king of the Visigoths and helped the Arabs to invade Spain. After that he became in Spanish history synonymous with treachery . . .

(from *Geographies of Exile*)

Goytisolo's fascination with Arabs and Arab culture gave him a new take on Spain and *its* culture. He launched a full-scale attack on literary language.

> We Spaniards speak in a highly codified and traditional manner. The quantity of set phrases, proverbs and clichés is enormous. These become transcribed into the excessively Castilian rhetorical prose that so pleases the readers of ABC. What hyperbole! What metaphors! What adjectives! And subject matter: Seneca, bulls, Castile, the Cid, the Generation of '98, Soria the pure, the pains of Spain. The Andalusians with their flowers and jasmine and the Castilians with their poplar trees. It's repugnant. The writer who wishes to break with this tradition cannot rely on a current of popular language, he must engage in an individual act of treason which is far more difficult. That is why I must commit a personal treason, an individual violation.
>
> (from *Marks of Identity*)

Goytisolo now came to see the expulsion of the Muslims from Spain as that country's downfall; accordingly he identified himself with the 'traitor', Julian.

In order to renew Spanish literary language, Goytisolo forged a new literary tradition for himself. He put fresh emphasis on some previously neglected works of the past and emphasized odd aspects of established masters. His new hero was Juan Ruiz, the Archpriest of Hita (1290?–1350?), whose long lyric poem *Libro de Buen Amor* was inspired by both Islam and Neoplatonism, and incorporated bits of Latin, Hebrew, Arabic, and Spanish. Goytisolo has written about Ruiz in the aptly named *Saracen Chronicles* as well as in more recent collections of essays, *Disidencias* and *Contracorrientes*. What he loves in the Archpriest is his refusal to resist literary temptations and distractions, his taste for polyphony.

> If, after more than six centuries, the work of the Archpriest remains intact and exemplary, it owes its endurance to its atypical and informal structure, an amalgam of different and opposed genres, a brilliant confusion of vocabularies and dialects, to its mixed, multicolored, heterogenous nature,

resistant to all norms and classifications; to this miraculous
mix of experiences typical of a scholar with the tastes and
leanings of a goliard fascinated at one and the same time by
Latin literature – that of the *joca monachorum* and farces that
mix the sacred and profane – and by Arab culture – erotic
tales, minstrels' poetry – that is, to an ensemble of traits that
gives him a unique, absolutely irreplaceable position in our
literature . . .

(from *Saracen Chronicles*)

Similarly, Goytisolo read the bawdy play *La Celestina*, by Fer-
nando de Rojas, as the bitter, coded work of a Jew in hiding
during the Inquisition inaugurated by Ferdinand and Isabella
after the reconquest of Spain – 'an unprecedented cataclysm that
generation after generation must suffer from'.

Even in considering the sacrosanct Spanish classic *Don Quixote*, Goytisolo cannot stop his urge to revisionism, to 'treachery'.

Spain, Cervantes and Islam – an experience at once literary
and human, which constitutes the founding act of my adult
writing, binds me tightly to these three terms. In 1967 I paid
several rather long visits to Tangier which profoundly marked
me and led me to identify myself mentally with the mythic
Don Julian whose treason opened to the Arab armies the path
to the Peninsula. My goal is to imitate his exploit: to demolish
the structure of a dusty oppressive culture, to profane its fos-
silized values, to save the texts and works that nourish my
frantic destructive obsession.

(from *Disidencias*)

In his 'destructive' revisionism Goytisolo reads Saint John of
the Cross as a Sufi poet, extols the Baroque over-the-top poet
Gongora and links him to another idol, Lezama Lima, the
modern Cuban author of *Paradiso*, a sprawling masterpiece that
took a lifetime to write and that records, through allusions to and
parodies of virtually all of world literature, the gay adventures of
a young man in Havana.

If in his criticism Goytisolo elevates older writers for uncon-
ventional reasons, in his fiction he often demolishes the sacred

figures of the Spanish literary pantheon. In *Trilogy of Treason: An Intertextual Study of Juan Goytisolo*, Michael Ugarte writes, 'One of the most common ways in which Goytisolo integrates other texts with his own is by turning the famous men of Spanish letters into characters and placing them in situations that undermine their greatness.' Goytisolo, for instance, makes Seneca into a character. Seneca, whose *Idearium español* is one of Spain's most revered texts, admits in *Don Julian* that he wrote his epistle on intemperate desires while sitting on the toilet. He praises censorship (the 'quintessentially Spanish theory of information'), bullfighting, and the negation of the body and its desires, although finally he degenerates into a dirty old man advertising the attractions of a French whore he happens to know ('a real tigress in bed').

In his trilogy Goytisolo quotes from classic authors (with and without identifying his sources). He parodies everything from *Don Quixote* to current advertising. In *Juan the Landless* there are references (unidentified) on the same page to both Pasolini and Cavafy. Here's his mini-portrait of Cavafy:

(no, you are spouting delirious nonsense,
and the Alexandrian poet knows it
the town where you have wasted your days
continues to exist and you are condemned to living in it
you will wander endlessly down its back streets
old age will overtake you in its suburbs
your hair will turn white beneath its rooftops
you will await the barbarians in vain.)

(from *Juan the Landless*)

Since finishing his trilogy, Goytisolo has published the short, polyphonic *Landscapes after the Battle*, in which he apostrophizes the Paris he likes and lives in – not the *grande dame* of pearl-gray mists, of the French Academy and the Louvre, but rather the black and tan Paris of African women in bright robes, of the Chinatown near the Porte d'Italie, of the Arab merchants selling *djellabas* on the rue de la Goutte d'Or, of the turbaned old men sipping mint tea in Belleville. He invents a *flâneur* right out of Baudelaire or Benjamin to dawdle in these teeming, non-European streets; in this promiscuity he finds health and the future.

Goytisolo's latest book, not yet translated, *Las Virtudes del pájaro solitario* ('The Virtues of the Solitary Bird'), pushes the novel towards something resembling Pound's *Cantos*. The chapters are short, paragraphing is frequent, lineation almost poetic or at least strophic. Plot and characters are replaced by a palimpsest of recurring figures – monastic orders, Turkish baths – and references to nuclear weapons, AIDS, Saint John of the Cross, and psychiatric treatment. Like such poets as Pound and Rilke, Goytisolo has taken his personal tastes (for Turkish wrestling, for a Paris sauna) and elevated them to the level of mythology, infusing them with mysticism. He joins the capaciousness of prose to poetry's ability to pattern attention through the *mise en page*, and to signal telepathically changes in diction, high to low, European to Islamic, slangy to medieval.

Like Genet and Pasolini, Goytisolo is a gay European drawn to the Third World through his erotic tastes but who has, as they did, developed that impulse both through political activism and artistic innovation. Politically, Goytisolo was first a declared, eloquent enemy of Franco; he has become a voice for the multitudes of North Africans in France, a population despised on all sides and the object of organized right-wing hostility. Artistically he has taken the post-modernist technique of intertextuality but given it an Arabic flavor not only through quotations from Arabic and Persian writers but also through the imitation of the esthetic rules behind Muslim music and architecture – repetition, abstraction, fluid variations on fixed themes, improvisation. Whereas Western art subordinates the parts to the whole, demotes decoration and promotes functional or structural clarity, Muslim art dissolves or rejects these hierarchies and prizes ornamentation and spontaneity. In that sense Goytisolo is writing 'Muslim fiction'.

Like Genet and Pasolini, Goytisolo is an apostle of the revolutionary, anarchic power of sexuality, of the desiring body, to break through the sterile confines of class and societal institutions. Just as Pasolini declared, while defending *The Decameron* against left-wing critics, that 'a body is always revolutionary because it represents what cannot be codified', just as Genet turned to Algerian revolutionaries, Black Panthers, and Palestinian soldiers and pitted their sensuality against European white

American puritanism, in the same way Goytisolo juxtaposes the promiscuity of Tangier against the aridity of white Paris or Barcelona.

Today, of course, in America we've moved into a different left-wing rhetoric. An artist such as Pasolini or Genet who could speak for homosexuals *and* workers, for white progressives *and* Black revolutionaries, for political activism *and* art experimentation is unimaginable. In America gays have been ghettoized or so thoroughly identified with AIDS that their opinions on all other topics seem irrelevant to the public at large. Nor does such a public exist, since we're parceled out into so many special-interest, single-issue factions.

The idea that 'the body is always revolutionary' is outmoded in a society where feminist puritans join hands with Christians to ban pornography, where authorities (even certain gay authorities) urge gays to practice abstinence or monogamy, where inter-racial coupling is branded 'sleeping with the enemy', where 'political correctness' of the most banal but rigid sort is used to paralyze sexual spontaneity, artistic and intellectual expression, compress individual differences into a few 'acceptable' scenarios. It's a good thing Goytisolo is finally being published in America; we need his pages, open as they are to the flute-song of sex and the polyphony of diverse culture.

Genet's Prisoner of Love

Introduction to the 1981 English translation by Barbara Bray of Genet's last book.

When Jean Genet died in 1986, many people, especially outside France, were surprised to discover he hadn't died years before. Even in France the astonishment mounted when a few months after his death a long posthumous work, *Prisoner of Love*, was published. It was unlike anything Genet had written before and few people had even suspected he remained capable in his seventies of such a sustained effort. It was his first major work to be published in nearly twenty-five years. *The Screens*, his last play, had been published in 1961 but it hadn't been staged in Paris until 21 April, 1966.

Since then Genet had published only a few articles and introductions: among them the preface to the prison letters of George Jackson, a Black Panther; a notorious defence of the German Red Army faction; and a meditation on the slaughter of Palestinian refugees in Lebanon. He had also written two or three short essays about art, including one on Dostoevsky's *The Brothers Karamazov*.

In the English-speaking world almost nothing had been published by or about Genet in years except for the translation of a long interview that had been conducted by the German novelist Hubert Fichte. Little was known of Genet beyond the legend of the orphan and welfare child who had become a petty thief, jailbird, homosexual prostitute and vagabond and who in the 1940s had turned himself seemingly overnight into the author of five novels: *Our Lady of the Flowers*, *Miracle of the Rose*, *Funeral Rites*, *Querelle* and the semi-autobiographical *Thief's Journal*.

This was the man Jean-Paul Sartre had made the subject of a massive 'existential psychoanalysis', *Saint Genet: Actor and Martyr*, a tome (some people said 'tomb') that appeared as the first

295

volume of Genet's 'complete works' when Genet was still only in his forties.

After a silence of several years in the late 1940s or early 1950s, Genet re-emerged as a playwright. To be sure, the theater and cinema had been the art forms that had first intrigued him, and even during his novel-writing years he'd finished two one-acts, *Deathwatch* and *The Maids*. Now he added to his theatrical *œuvre* three masterpieces – *The Blacks*, *The Balcony* and *The Screens* – which were played all over the world and which remain, along with the plays of Bertolt Brecht and Joe Orton, the most substantial theatrical legacy of the post-war epoch.

Following that second burst of creativity Genet sank back into an obscurity he eagerly courted. He resolutely refused to give interviews (with only a few exceptions), to chat on television, to attend opening nights (even of his own plays) or in any other way to lead the life of a professional man of letters, an existence which is busier and more decorous in France than in any other country.

As rigorously as the other three great writers living in France during those years – Samuel Beckett, Claude Simon and Julien Gracq – Genet cultivated silence and anonymity. A new portrait emerged in bits and pieces of a writer who was depressed (a suicide attempt was reported in the press), of someone who lived in cheap hotel rooms near train stations, of a man who seldom changed his clothes or bathed, who frequented street kids and fell out with such old literary friends as Cocteau (who'd discovered him) and Sartre (who'd made him famous).

The truth was that Genet was depressed in the 1960s, especially after the death in 1964 of his lover, Abdallah, a high-wire artist, and Genet subsequently attempted suicide at least once. But in the late 1960s and early 1970s he took up an entirely new activity that engaged all his energies – backing the political aspirations of marginal groups. *Prisoner of Love* is a record of his years spent with the Black Panthers in the United States and Palestinian soldiers in Jordan and Lebanon. His involvement with the Panthers was substantially over by 1972, but his commitment to the Palestinians continued until his death.

In explaining the title of his book, Genet writes:

When I arrived to an enthusiastic welcome from the fedayeen,

I probably wasn't clear headed enough to evaluate the opposing forces or make out the divisions within the Arab world. I ought to have seen sooner that aid to the Palestinians was an illusion. Whether it came from the PLO or North Africa it was ostentatious and declamatory, but flimsy.

Gradually my feelings changed, especially after the 1973 war. I was still charmed, but I wasn't convinced; I was attracted but not blinded. I behaved like a prisoner of love . . .

In this passage Genet makes clear that his commitment was based on ties of affection, not ideology, and that not even disillusionment could weaken those ties.

As early as 1974 Genet had said in the Paris newspaper *Le Monde*: 'It was completely natural for me to be attracted to the people who are not only the most unfortunate but also crystallize to the highest degree the hatred of the West.' Almost ten years later Genet was interviewed by the Austrian journalist Rudiger Wischenbart, who asked: 'What was it that led you to become so deeply involved with the PLO? Previously, with the exception of the Black Panthers in the US and the Red Army factions in West Germany, wasn't it relatively unusual for you to take such a concrete stand for a political group or movement?'
To which Genet replied:

What led me to it first of all is my personal history, which I don't care to go into, which is of no interest to anyone. If you want to know more about it, you can read my books. It's not all that important. But what I will say to you is that the books I wrote previously – I have stopped writing for over thirty years now – were all part of a dream or a day-dream. And since I outlived this dream, this day-dream, I had to take action in order to achieve a sort of fullness of life. You mentioned the Black Panthers, the German Army Faction, and the Palestinians. To be brief about it, I will say that I have immediately gone towards those who asked me to intercede. The Black Panthers came to Paris and asked me to go to the United States, which I did at once.

For the Red Army Faction, it was Klaus Croissant who came to ask me to intervene in favor of Baader. And ten years ago, it was Leila Shahid [a member of the editorial board of the *Revue d'études palestiniennes*] who asked me to go to Beirut. Obviously, I am drawn to peoples in revolt. And this is very natural for me, because I myself have the need to call the whole of society into question.

This response reveals Genet's deliberateness about setting the record straight. He admits that political action filled the void left in his life when he was awakened from his reverie as an artist – a frank acknowledgment of his creative and personal despair, despite a reluctance to discuss it. He then points out that he was invited by each group to come to their aid, a point important to clarify lest he be blamed for embracing causes that were not his own. The radical rhetoric of the post-1968 era often rejected the sympathy of outsiders; Genet emphasizes that in each case his help was coherent with his own revolt against established forms of society. As he told Hubert Fichte, he was a black who might look white or pink, but he was still a black.

Genet's many imprisonments for 'crimes' that never amounted to anything more serious than running away from school, boarding a train without a ticket or stealing a book had made him detest France. When he was only eighteen he'd served in the French army in Damascus, where he'd fallen in love with a younger hairdresser and where he played cards all night with Syrians – and where he first came to despise French colonialism. He'd joined the army in order to cut short the sentence he was serving at Mettray, a reform school near Tours. It didn't require a great leap of the imagination for him to see the link between the oppression he was suffering under French authority and the oppression of colonial peoples (Syria was under French control between the two World Wars).

Nevertheless, to regard *Prisoner of Love* as a political act would be a mistake. As Genet remarked in 1970 in the French periodical *Le Nouvel Observateur*: 'I believe that Brecht did nothing for Communism, that the revolution was not provoked by Beaumarchais's *The Marriage of Figaro*. The closer a work of art is to perfection, the more it turns in on itself. Still worse, it awakens a taste for the past.'

In the same way, one could say that almost any statement

about this dense, ambiguous book demands an instant retraction. Just before Genet started to write *Prisoner of Love* he published a short essay on *The Brothers Karamazov*, which he reads as a giant joke, rife with contradictions – a serious joke. As Genet puts it, 'It seems to me, according to this reading, that every novel, poem, painting, piece of music that doesn't destroy itself, I mean that doesn't set itself up as an Aunt Sally, in which it is one of the heads, is a fake.'

What about the contradictions in his own book? One could say that it is a paean to two virile, male-dominated societies, which for Genet recreate the feudal, all-male worlds of his youth at Mettray, in the army and later in prison, and which gibe well with his persistent fantasies (related in his novels) about pirates, prison colonies, slave galleys, and the German military. It's important, however, to point out right away that *Prisoner of Love* is not an explicitly erotic work, even if nearly every page is warmed by Genet's admiration for these young men's courage, beauty and gaiety and intellectual and verbal inventiveness. His description of a singing contest among the Palestinian soldiers, for instance, in which their voices weave into an intricate, improvised polyphony, is full of love, but a love as chaste as Muslim puritanism might demand. As he writes, he recognizes the erotic waves of 'smiling serenity' emanating from the fedayeen without being troubled by them. Perhaps, as he suggests, he is suddenly living amongst teen-age men toting weapons and 'adorned' with red berets tipped over one eye and leopard uniforms – their fulfilment makes those very fantasies weaken, dissolve: 'The sudden appearance of a flock of living, laughing, independent infantrymen left me on the brink of purity. They were like a cloud, a barricade of angels come down to keep me from the edge of an abyss: for I realized at once, with joy, that I was going to be living in a vast barracks.'

One night Genet stays awake until dawn debating the existence of God with a squadron of Palestinians. Another evening he has his hair cut in a camp, which serves as the occasion to bring together a group of weary, laughing fedayeen, who tease their elderly French friend in a mixture of literary Arabic, French and English. Genet records the scattered, feeble jokes, then adds in a tone that typifies the simple lyricism of his prose in this book:

They all laughed. And not only my shoulders but my knees as

well were covered with snippets of white hair. The first stars came out, timidly in the beginning, then in armfuls all over the still purple sky and everything was more beautiful than I can say. And Jordan is only the Middle East! By now locks of my hair were falling down to my slippers.

But if Genet glorifies such all-male societies (they're the same desert desperadoes William Burroughs conjures up in *The Wild Boys*), he less predictably evidences a new interest in women, especially the noble, warlike, self-effacing but devious Palestinian peasant women. His affection, to be sure, is directed to mothers, not daughters, but despite such limitations it's a lively enough curiosity, genuine and observant.

The contradictions proliferate. The book was commissioned in a casual way by Yasser Arafat, the head of the Palestinian Liberation Organization, but the text does everything but follow the party line. Genet even compares Arafat to Hitler at one point (only in the sense that every charismatic leader has a symbol, as Hitler his mustache, Churchill his cigar and Arafat his checked headcloth). Genet is also highly critical of the old Palestinian elite.

And then in an interview he once went so far as to say: 'The day the Palestinians become institutionalized, I will no longer be on their side. The day the Palestinians become a nation like other nations, I will no longer be there.' Such anarchic impulses originate in Genet's own past.

He felt himself to be profoundly disinherited and his hatred of France was unrelenting, just as his sympathy for criminals and the outcast was unwavering. In the last incarnation of this Manichaeanism, Genet placed on one side Israel, the United States, France and the conservative Arab states and on the other he put himself, the Panthers and the Palestinians.

This dichotomy is not based on anti-Semitism. Genet is clearly anti-Zionist and he sometimes claims that the Israelis are master manipulators of the media as well as of brainwashing techniques, but his objections are political, not racist. He attacks Israeli policies, not 'Jewish traits' (the very phrase is racist). Of course many Jews think that no distinction can be made between Jews and Israelis, and such readers will doubtless consider *Prisoner of Love* a monstrous concoction.

Yet for a book about one of the most ideologically heated conflicts of modern times, *Prisoner of Love* is curiously cool and unpolemical. As always, Genet knows how to sink a probe into a politically sensitive area without proposing a cure or a procedure or even an opinion. In his play *The Blacks*, as Jeanette L. Savona points out in her book *Jean Genet*, the interest shifts between the 'dreamlike world of the stage' and the 'naturalistic backstage world of political action'. It's a play that was *perceived* by black theatrical troupes in the United States as a political statement, although it would be hard to extrapolate a clear directive from the action and dialogue. Similarly, *The Screens* created a violent reaction in the audience when it was first performed in France, since it was perceived as an insult to the French military in Algeria, which it clearly is, but there is no way the play can be fairly read as an endorsement of the Algerian Revolution. Genet was able to have it both ways – he appeared to be politically committed in his writing, but actually he maintained complete artistic independence.

Oddly, this very independence has a source that feminists and gay activists, say, would consider 'political' (in the sense of heightened individual consciousness, not group enterprise). When Wischenbart asked Genet if he'd come to the Middle East as a spectator, he replied:

> You said to me – and you were right – that very probably I had come as a spectator. When I was very young, I quickly understood that everything in life was blocked for me. I went to school until I was thirteen, to the local primary school. The most I could hope for was to become an accountant or a petty official. So I put myself in a position not to become an accountant, not to become a writer – I didn't know that yet – but to observe the world.

Genet's writerly neutrality and acuity, in other words, represent a rejection of *petit bourgeois* values and an affirmation of independence and a passive resistance against the forces of order.

There is also a strictly esthetic aspect. Genet has a strong sense of where his talent lies, and he knows it is a talent that begins with a rejection of slogans and heroics. In part his caution is due to a fear of unintentionally injuring the Panthers or the Palestinians. He recognizes how susceptible both groups are to misrepresentation in the press. But even deeper is his adherence to his personal skepticism and his original state as a loner and outsider.

Throughout his long career Genet maintained a purported admiration for *treachery* that I've never comprehended. I recognize that a prisoner might be *forced* to betray his friends, but how can one be *proud* of such a failing? Philosophically, Genet was no doubt being systematic in affirming everything that is negative, in reversing all values. But humanly what could such a claim mean?

When Genet in his novels insists he admires stool-pigeons and spies or traitors, could he simply be erecting a giant alibi for a strictly personal (and humiliating) lapse of his own? And yet I've never heard of a single charge of betrayal lodged against Genet. He may have broken cruelly with faithful friends, even stolen from them, but no one ever accused him of being an informer or traitor. In *The Thief's Journal* he admits to being an informer, but the confession may be bravado.

Finally I've decided that 'treachery' is Genet's code word for the incorrigible subjective voice that can never be factored into the consensus. In *Prisoner of Love* he catches himself using words like 'hero' and 'martyr' and he admits that the Palestinians are responsible for a debasement of his vocabulary.

A page later Genet finds that the temptation to betray arises when people ignore the 'collective emergency' and attend only to private desires. More than in any of his earlier books, Genet seeks in this one to honor the collective emergency, but in the end he remains true to his equally radical (and politically rooted) need for independence. Fidelity to oneself is treachery to the group; artistic quirkiness pokes holes in any political rhetoric.

A recurring theme in *Prisoner of Love* is an old man's longing for a home somewhere on a hill, say, in Cyprus where he can watch in perfect security a distant maritime battle, remote and toylike. At one point Genet daydreams about living in another house he sees in Jordan; when someone tells him he could rent it, the house instantly loses all its appeal. Elsewhere he mentions the house he built in his last years for his Moroccan friend Muhammad el Katrani in Morocco, but he regards it as a gift to the devil.

Of course neither the Panthers nor the Palestinians possess a home, a country. They are people without land, perennial exiles, who set up phantom bureaucracies and shadow administrations but who live in a permanent diaspora. As Genet told Tahar ben Jelloun, the Moroccan novelist: 'As you know, I'm on the side of those who seek to have a territory, although I refuse to have one.'

One of the repeated images of this book is a card game played without cards. Fearing a breakdown in company discipline, a Palestinian officer forbids card-playing. The men, to while away the time, go through the motions of gambling even without cards. At one point Genet even concedes that his having ended up with the Palestinians is the result of purest chance – a stroke of gambler's luck. This theme of absence – an active, organizing absence that takes on moral and esthetic and psychological weight, like emptiness in Sung landscape painting – moves in every direction. Genet sees blacks as the letters struck on the empty white page of America. He compares the shapes of his own life to the process of metal-working called 'damascening', except in his case no gold had been poured into the hollows gouged out of the baser metal. The card game without cards is linked elsewhere to buffoonish Japanese rituals for propitiating (and amusing) the dead.

At one point Genet begins to wonder why he's been so courted by extremists. They must see him as someone who has suffered as they have. But then Genet asks himself whether he hasn't exaggerated his childhood misery, whether he isn't just a natural sham.

Abysses open up all around him. He wonders if the Palestinians aren't just a media event and the Panthers more an 'act' than a real threat to American institutions. He asks: 'By agreeing to go first with the Panthers and then with the Palestinians, playing my role as a dreamer inside a dream, wasn't I just one more factor of unreality inside both movements? Wasn't I a European saying to a dream, "You are a dream – don't wake the sleeper"?'

Such questions 'betray' the simple, heroic rhetoric of a revolutionary movement, but they are a way of staying 'faithful' to a private, multi-faceted vision of truth. They are also a part of Genet's investigation into the nature of propaganda and image-making. At one point Genet humorously remarks that the people we call compulsive liars are just those who fail to project their image with enough force.

There are many threads that run through this book, furnishing every page with a surprising toughness – surprising, given that there is no suspense, no plot, little history, and no straightforward chronology.

The characters Genet develops, however, are among his best and very much in his style – larger than life, mythic. Take Mubarak, the lieutenant from the Sudan who speaks French like Maurice Chevalier, who graduated from Sandhurst, whose cheeks are cicatrized with tribal scars, who reads Spinoza, dances to African rock music and who, when Genet dares to ape him, responds by cruelly imitating Genet imitating him – a *tour de force* as clever as it is unsparing of Genet's age and limp

Curiously Mubarak is also a sort of double for Genet, his younger version, black, virile, handsome, but just as playful and mercurial, just as cosmopolitan, disabused, philosophical and cultured – a man who strums an imaginary guitar.

But the true continuities of *Prisoner of Love* are the poetic figures that recur – Genet's admiration for those who risk sex-change operations, say. Genet's fluent mind permits him to associate the heroism of sex changes with the suicidal courage of Palestinian soldiers – or with the joy in the face of death expressed by Mozart's Requiem.

Death was always one of Genet's great themes. He thought a play should be performed just once, and that one time in a cemetery; he recommended that Giacometti's statues be buried in the ground as offerings to the dead. His first novel, *Our Lady of the Flowers*, ends with the death of Divine, the transvestite hero, and the condemnation to death of Our Lady, a young thug who has murdered an old man. Genet's first published work was a poem, 'The Man Sentenced to Death', which he had printed at his own expense while still in prison. All of his other novels celebrate death and murder. In his plays death is staged in many modes. *The Screens*, for instance, ends with most of the many characters, Algerians and French colonials alike, bursting through screens into the afterlife, where they laugh together with eerie complicity. Under the sign of eternity, everything becomes comic. As Genet once remarked, 'What is not futile in this world? I'm asking you: what is not futile in the last analysis?'

I've spoken of a few of the many contradictions in *Prisoner of*

Love, but perhaps the most obvious one is that it is a religious statement by a non-believer, a bible written by a devil. Genet always pursued his own peculiar destiny as a mystical atheist, a saint complete with miracles, ecstasies, visions and stigmata but no deity and precious few good works. Sartre may tend to dismiss Genet's claims of saintliness, but many pages in *The Thief's Journal* leave little doubt that Genet was perfectly serious:

> Though saintliness is my goal, I cannot tell what it is.
>
> My point of departure is the word itself, which indicates the state closest to moral perfection. Of which I have known nothing, except that without it my life would be in vain. Unable to arrive at a definition of saintliness – no more than of beauty – I want at every moment to create it, that is, to act so that everything I do may lead me to what is unknown to me, so that at every moment I may be guided by a will to saintliness until the time when I am so luminous that people will say, 'He is a saint,' or more likely, 'He was a saint.' I am being led to it by a constant groping. No method exists. It is only obscurely and with no other proofs than the certainty of achieving saintliness that I make the gestures leading me to it ... Like beauty – and poetry – with which I merge it, saintliness is singular. Its expression is original. Yet it seems to me that its sole basis is renunciation. But I wish to be a saint because, above all, the word indicates the loftiest human attitude, and I shall do all to succeed.

Prisoner of Love contains no statement quite so direct, but only because Genet assumes he's already become a saint. He talks of his complete renunciation of things – he aspires to own but one pair of trousers, one shirt, one pair of shoes, nothing more. He experiences a miracle in Istanbul when his body lights up from within. He speaks of himself almost offhandedly in tones usually reserved for God. In referring to why he lives amongst the Palestinians, he writes:

> I might as well admit that by staying with them I was staying – I don't know, how else, to put it – in my own memory. By that rather childish expression I don't mean I lived and remembered previous lives. I'm saying as clearly as I can that the

Palestinian revolt was among my oldest memories. 'The Koran is eternal, uncreated, consubstantial with God.' Setting aside the word 'God,' their revolt was eternal, uncreated, consubstantial with me.

Like a *marabout*, a Muslim saint, he seems to expect that his tomb will become an important shrine, and he finds nothing odd in a Palestinian soldier's wish to have his bones after his death and imagines them carried about by the Palestinians until they recapture their homeland and can bury them beside the Dead Sea. (Abdelkebir Khatibi recounts that he once captured Genet's imagination by telling him about the cult of Muslim saints who'd been born Portuguese but who'd betrayed their own people in order to lead the Moroccans against the Christians in the holy wars.)

Elsewhere Genet sees himself as a dwarf shuffling off towards the horizon, a derelict old holy man being absorbed into the elements, an entranced Sufi.

Genet's ideas of sanctity dovetail with his ideas of individual worth. When he first began writing, his sovereign imagination and his brand of romanticism (a sophisticated and highly philosophical reworking of decadence) blinded him to the existence of other people except as shadow puppets of desire. As the quotation from *The Thief's Journal* reveals, for the Genet of that period 'Saintliness is singular' and its expression original.

Then one day, during a train ride, Genet had a revelation. He was seated in a third-class compartment opposite a dirty, ugly little man – and suddenly Genet felt a strange exchange of personalities with this stranger. Genet flowed into the man's body at the same time as the man flowed into Genet's body. Genet suddenly realized that everyone is of the same value – Raskolnikov's revelation in *Crime and Punishment* – an idea that struck Genet with particular force because he'd never before considered such a possibility.

In *Prisoner of Love* the tension between the romantic cult of the unique individual and the Christian faith in spiritual equality is reconciled in the central quest of the book. In the early 1970s Genet spent just twenty-two hours in the house of a Palestinian soldier named Hamza and his mother. Ever after he was haunted by thoughts of them – of Hamza going off in the night on a mission, of the mother coming to Genet's bedside with a cup of Turkish coffee, as she must have come to her sleeping son many times to awaken him. In Genet's mind the mother and son become reworked as emblems of the *pietà* in which sometimes Genet himself figures as the son (he recalls certain sculptures in which Mary is represented as younger than her crucified son). The images of the *pietà* become stronger over the years when Genet hears rumors that Hamza has been tortured and killed. At last Genet, fourteen years later and towards the end of the book (and his own life), revisits the mother and learns that Hamza is living safely in Germany, but this information in no way weakens Genet's conception of the holiness of this couple.

Psychologically Genet's reverence for Hamza's mother resolves his own feelings of rage at his real mother for having abandoned him. Even when Genet was in his sixties he told someone that if he knew where his mother was buried he'd spit on the grave – a remarkable fury against an unmarried servant girl who'd kept her child with her for seven months until poverty had forced her to hand him over to public welfare. She died during the influenza epidemic of 1919 when she was thirty and Genet nine (Genet may never have known when and how she died).

Philosophically Genet recognizes that Hamza and his mother are simply two more people in an overpopulated planet. She may possess a rare natural courtesy and may speak the purest Arabic, but Genet doesn't prize her for these qualities. Rather, like a lover, he lists the beloved's virtues after the fact to justify (or elaborate) his love, which is as strong as it is inexplicable. Love is the form of captivity that permits us at one *and* the same time to see the universality and the particularity of a person. Love reconciles Genet's feelings that everyone is of equal value and that each person is priceless. As Genet puts it, emotions live on and only the people who entertain them die: 'The happiness of my hand in the hair of a boy another hand will know, already knows, and if I die this happiness will go on.'

Such is the wisdom of a book that the philosopher Gilles Deleuze compared recently in a seminar to the Bible. Like the Bible, *Prisoner of Love* is about chosen people (Panthers, Palestinians) without a homeland. Like the Bible, Genet's book is polyvalent, inconsistent, an invitation to exegesis. Like the Bible it is a book of memory, of names. It alternates serenity and bellicose hate, history and poetry, epic and lyricism. Like the Bible it is the Only Book, one meant to be read again and again and that is constructed canonically, as though the first-time reader has already read it. Indeed Genet has invented a new sort of book altogether – a new kind of prose and a new genre. The prose is sometimes ruminative, almost grumbling, like that of late Céline, the man most French critics believe is Genet's only rival as a stylist in the twentieth century after Proust. Like the Céline of *Castle to Castle* or *Rigadoon*, Genet backs into his subjects, starts talking around something long before he identifies it. Like Céline, Genet appears to be casual and conversational, but through recurrence he heightens each subject until it turns mythical. Genet always constructed his fiction like cinematic montage, alternating one story with one or two others.

In *Prisoner of Love* the intercutting becomes rapid, constant, vertiginous – a formal device for showing the correspondences between elements where no connection had been previously suspected. In two pages Genet can make unexpected links between Mozart's scatology, a desire for a house, the prudish way the early Church Fathers referred to the Virgin's breast, the invisible cell that glided about around Saint Elizabeth, Queen of Hungary, the words of a Sufi poet, and so on.

In Genet's novels the poet's urge to uncover correspondences is encoded in brilliant metaphors. In *Prisoner of Love* metaphors have been replaced by a different method – radical juxtaposition without copula, that is, the tight sequencing of different subjects without transition. This method emphasizes the sovereignty of the observer – makes him into a god.

The genre established by Genet is a curious mixture of memoir, tract, stylized Platonic dialogue based on actual conversation, allegorical quest, epic. Written when Genet knew he was already afflicted with terminal throat cancer, the book necessarily makes us think of Chateaubriand's *Memoirs from Beyond the Grave*. Like Chateaubriand, who wrote about his years of poverty in London when he was the overfed ambassador to Britain, Genet is careful to establish the conditions under which he is composing his book and to distinguish them from the circumstances he is narrating. Like Chateaubriand, who lived through many different regimes and who rose and fell in favor more than once, Genet is a non-aligned observer of political events. And like Chateaubriand, who could separate Napoleon's true genius from the idol people made of him after he was deposed, Genet is never taken in by legends.

But again even the persona of the narrator in *Prisoner of Love* is torn with contradictions. He may be a seer but he is also a sham, a naïve outsider, a burden, a big pink baby in the strong arms of black or tan fathers. He is also Homer, and the soldiers are his Hectors and Achilles. Chateaubriand quotes, in speaking of Napoleon, an imaginary epitaph from the Greek Anthology: 'Don't judge Hector by his small tomb. The *Iliad*, Homer, the Greeks in flight, there's my sepulchre: I am buried under all these great actions.' Homer may be a blind, weak, ancient poet, but the glory of even the wiliest warrior depends on his frail voice. Genet often makes explicit reference to his Homeric powers; in a thousand years people will know of the Palestinian exodus only in his version.

Straight Women, Gay Men

Written in 1991 and previously unpublished.

Straight women and gay men are natural allies now, but when I was a kid back in the 1950s, long before either women's liberation or gay liberation, the two oppressed populations despised each other. Gay men hated each other so much that they longed to seduce heterosexual men, 'real men', and they resented women as rivals with an obvious biological advantage. I remember the appalling aspersions gays cast on 'fish' (as they called women), their horrible smells and erotic incompetence. When women weren't fish, they were 'stupid cows'. Conversely, women didn't usually like each other very much and gay men were doubly deplored, since they were perceived as wanting to be women, a curious ambition at best, a perverse loss of their natural advantage as men. Why would men deliberately abandon their God-given prerogatives in order to sink to the inferior level of women? That was the twisted reasoning behind the question and the hostility. Simone de Beauvoir, in her letters of the 1950s to her macho lover, the writer Nelson Algren, refers with real disgust to the fluttering 'pansies' she keeps encountering.

After the 1960s all that began to change. Women began to like themselves and to seek each other's company, and they began to have doubts about the traditional hierarchy. At the same time gay men also began to affirm themselves. No longer was their fondest hope (a hope by definition always frustrated) to sleep with straight men. Now those gay men who prized rough-and-ready masculinity began to embody it. In droves gay men went to the gym, sprouted mustaches, took up such professions as truck driving, heavy construction and farming. Other gay men decided they liked – in themselves or in their partners – softer, less aggressive qualities.

The upshot was self-respect on both sides, which led to new friendships between gay men and straight women and shared doubts about male supremacy. Even those newly hatched gay clones who were starting to swagger couldn't help smiling at their recently acquired machismo. Masculinity seemed more like a costume than an eternal and natural privilege.

My best friend in Paris, where I live, is close to sixty, and she has just gone through a long, nasty divorce. After some thirty years of marriage her husband has left her for a younger woman – a banal story, but one that was specially painful to my friend (whom I'll call Hélène) since they had been intimate and loving partners for three decades. Even he had to admit it had been an exceptionally good marriage.

Although Hélène and I had known each other a long time, we became best friends only just as her world was falling apart. I suppose it was a good thing I was there. She and I speak on the phone at least once a day; we've traveled to Istanbul and the south of France together, and soon we're off to Naples for ten days. She has grown-up children with whom she spends the holidays and whom she sees all the time, but she wouldn't want to discuss with them all her fears.

More importantly, I'm a man who likes her and looks after her. At exactly the moment her confidence was shaken, I was someone there who was proud to take her out to dinner, to entertain her, to be seen with her at the opera. People who don't understand such relationships think, 'Well, yes, but of course she'd prefer a boyfriend,' or, 'I suppose he helps her choose her frocks.' But in truth I don't know much about clothes, and what we have together isn't a mock marriage, a make-believe romance, but a real friendship.

The nineteenth-century German philosopher Hegel thought that the highest human love is that of brother for sister, since it blends the reciprocity of two genders into a tender, sexless relationship in which neither partner has a motive. By that definition a gay male–straight female friendship approaches those disinterested heights. Or as long as we're being philosophical, the French Christian mystic Simone Weil (not the politician by the same name) thought that the only true friendships were the ones in which neither partner exercised any power over the other one. Manipulation is the opposite of friendship.

Of course the most human relationships fall short of that ideal, but even a failed friendship between a thoroughly weak gay man and an alcoholic straight woman can possess all the elements of love, concern and charm. Tennessee Williams describes such a relationship in one of his best stories, 'Two on a Party'. Billy and Cora are drifters, drunks and friends, each in search of men. They're also so full of love for each other they imagine they're attracted to each other:

> That night in the shared compartment of the Pullman was the first time they had sex together. It happened casually, it was not important and it was not very satisfactory, perhaps because they were each too anxious to please the other, each too afraid the other would be disappointed. Sex has to be slightly selfish to have real excitement. Start worrying about the other party's reactions and the big charge just isn't there, and you've got to do it a number of times together before it becomes natural enough to be a completely satisfactory thing. The first time between strangers can be like a blaze of light, but when it happens between people who know each other well and have an established affection, it's likely to be self-conscious and even a little embarrassing, most of all afterwards.
>
> Afterwards they talked about it with a slight sense of strain. They felt they had gotten that sort of thing squared away and would not have to think about it between them again. But perhaps, in a way, it did add a little something to the intimacy of their living together; at least it had, as they put it, squared things away a bit. And they talked about it shyly, each one trying too hard to flatter the other.

For almost everyone brought up in our society, the learned social reflexes are heterosexual. A man who discovers he's gay does so at age sixteen or sixty, but in any event long after he's been raised in a heterosexual world; whatever his sexual tastes may be, women remain his most comfortable social partners. In the same way even a woman who's just barely survived a catastrophic divorce may think a long time before entering into a new sexual relationship with a man, but all her habits incline her towards confiding in a man and going out with him. An additional, never-discussed benefit in such friendships is that they often cut across age demarcations. My mother, for instance, who is eighty-five, has a longstanding friendship with a young gay man of twenty-five. I first met him in Europe through friends, but when I heard he was moving to Chicago I suggested he look my mother up. They spent long hours together over little meals she prepared and talked about life and love and literature, assuring each other how wise they were. Now that he's moved back to Europe he writes her frequent letters, making her a witness to his life (friendship is a kind of witnessing).

The exact tone that must be struck in such a relation is very important. If a younger woman, for instance, falls in love with a gay man her own age and hopes to 'convert' him to heterosexuality, the friendship is doomed and she's headed for unhappiness. If he uses her as a heterosexual decoy – a way of convincing his colleagues or his family that he, too, is straight – then the woman may feel exploited. To be sure, many marriages, especially in highly visible professions such as the arts, politics and fashion, are fronts for gay men; if they're to be successful the wife must enter into the arrangement clear-eyed, knowing it's in part a business deal. She should be the sort of woman who prefers money and status to romance, or who doesn't mind seeking love from an outside lover. Not that such 'New York marriages', as they used to be called, can't be very close. A few years ago a famous conductor shocked everyone with the sincerity of his grief after his wife's death. Everyone had assumed the marriage had been cynical, but he was inconsolable and went to bed for a month.

Although some women complain about the one-track minds of heterosexual wolves, they're slightly bewildered when a gay male friend *isn't* susceptible to their erotic appeal. The reverse is also true – an attractive gay man who has not come out at work, say, may be used to manipulating women through his looks and sex appeal. He may find it unsettling that a woman friend who knows he's gay responds to him as a pal, not a potential partner in bed. We all depend on our sex appeal without being quite conscious of it; gay male–straight female friendships make us come to terms with those assumptions.

Which doesn't mean that such friends can't share obsessions – men, for instance. Gay men, by virtue of both being men and loving them, have a knowledge, at once subjective and objective, of their sex. They have seen male egotism at close quarters – in their partners and in themselves. They have been shoved around by overbearing men – and they've overborne others as well.

On the gay scene they've felt the double pressure to be as successful and assertive as a heterosexual man and as physically attractive and accommodating as the traditional woman. Whereas straight men as they age continue to appeal to women so long as they've accomplished something, aging gay men become as invisible as aging straight women, since both fall victim to the conventional male taste for youth and youthful beauty. Now that the generation of gay men who invented gay liberation and of women who forged women's liberation is hitting their fifties and sixties, I don't think either group will take old age lying down – or if so then it will be with a partner! These two groups, so closely allied, have already redefined powerful prejudices against them; it will be fascinating to watch them re-invent the aging crisis with the same aplomb. Because of the AIDS crisis, older gay men, of course, are something of a rarity and the few survivors must combat all sorts of wrong-headed assumptions.

If gay male life in one sense reflects the dynamics of heterosexuality, in another it provides an alternative to heterosexual attitudes. Take jealousy. Gay men, because they are men, understand that their partners may need to have outside sexual adventures. (In this plague era, to be sure, philandering may prove fatal; all the more reason that both partners in a relationship, either straight or gay, should know what risks they're running and make a decision together – a calm decision that the fury of jealousy prohibits.)

After a gay romance wanes, the partners are often capable of staying on together as friends and roommates, even when each of the ex-lovers takes up with a new man. This realism (for isn't it realistic to want to conserve an old love in some form or other?) is unthinkable to heterosexual women. They can't imagine staying around to watch another woman take their place; the very idea outrages them, and if it doesn't, they're branded by their women friends as 'masochistic'.

Of all differences between heterosexual and gay male couples, this one seems the most extreme, and I've often sought an explanation of it. Is it that gay male lovers are first and foremost friends, and that the friendship precedes, underlies and survives the love? Or is it that heterosexual relationships, even in their most apparently liberated forms, are still tinged with old marital ideas of partner-as-property, and that unforgiving jealousy goes along with the territory? My friend Hélène thinks that all straight marriages are power plays and that only in friendships between gay men and straight women is the question of domination eliminated. I wonder. I've seen plenty of marriages that appear to be warm and companionable. And surely a friendship between two women is free of oppression and submission?

'But not of rivalry,' a young gay male friend of mine who lives in England remarked. He is studying to be a nurse in a coastal town in the south of England, where a fellow student, a woman his age, is his best friend. They're both in their early thirties, a good ten years older than the other students. 'Betty says that women inevitably make comparisons. She claims she's less afraid to admit to me her romantic failures than she would be to another woman.'

'But is it girl talk you have, you and Betty?' I ask him.

'Does she treat me as another woman? Not at all. Perhaps because we're both in our early thirties and have each had several affairs, we feel our age gives us more in common than the shared professional goals we have with the other students. We tell each other everything and we give each other advice, but it's not girl talk, as you say, which I'd hate, nor does she flirt with me, treat me as an honorary heterosexual, which would make me uncomfortable. I think with me she can be more honest about her sexual appetite than she could be with other women.'

Perhaps it's true that if every same-sex relationship (at least among heterosexuals) is a rivalry and every heterosexual couple engages in a power struggle, then a friendship between a straight woman and a gay man is one of the few that is straightforward, amiable and totally disinterested. In such a friendship neither person stands to gain anything except companionship, support and simple fun.

Of course such friendships are always vulnerable to change,

even dissolution, especially if the straight woman finds a new heterosexual partner. He may not like his girlfriend's 'capon' or 'walker', to use two derogatory terms for the gay male escorts of heterosexual women. Worse, he may think the gay man is no threat at all since he's not a sexual rival. Many gay hairdressers, antique dealers, realtors or decorators play the *cavalier servant* to a bored, rich, married woman whose overly busy husband shares none of her interests, whereas darling Bruce . . . But such arrangements are the opposite of the disinterested friendships I've idealized.

And what about gay men and lesbians? Militant feminism and lesbian separatism created a distance in the 1970s between the two groups, but the AIDS epidemic of the 1980s brought them closer together. Many, if not most, queer political leaders are now lesbians, women who are speaking not only for their sisters, but also for their fallen brothers. The New Lesbian – sex-positive, practical, playful, compassionate, self-assertive – has become an ideal companion for younger gay men. Novelist and AIDS activist Sarah Schulman, for instance, embraces not only the entire gay community – male and female – but also the whole rainbow coalition and does so without a hint of self-importance or sanctimoniousness. English novelist Jeanette Winterson is typical of the frankly erotic tone among younger lesbians, a tone that provides a link with gay men who have fought hard not to lose touch with an eroticism that has become increasingly vexed and stigmatized.

Political complicity, compassion, and a drive to live freely in the otherwise lusterless 1990s are the forces that bring together young lesbians and gay men. And if I describe their relationship abstractly, I do so because I've observed rather than lived it.

Black Like Whom?: Darryl Pinckney

Review of *High Cotton*, *New York Times Book Review*, 2 February 1992.

This is the first novel by a 38-year-old writer whose essays and stories have been published in the *New York Review of Books* and *Granta* and who has studied at Columbia and Princeton – which is a way of saying that the beauty and intelligence radiating from *High Cotton* are not a lucky hit by a talented beginner, but rather the considered achievement of a seasoned mind. Seasoning, of course, is no guarantee of originality, but Darryl Pinckney also has a distinctive voice and vision.

When an African-American writer or a gay writer or a Native American writer publishes a novel, especially an autobiographical novel, it's always read as somehow representative of the whole minority group. It's also regarded as a testimony of the writer's own coming to terms with that minority status. This kind of attention automatically focused on such books explains the power they generate and the constraints that are imposed upon them.

Pinckney's unnamed hero and narrator (who, like him, was born in Indiana and attended Columbia) is black and belongs to the fourth generation of his family to earn a college degree. He himself, despite this elite status, feels empty, inauthentic, chameleon-like. He does not want to deal with color in any way, and much of this book is about resisting the very literary project it has undertaken. When the narrator is one of the handful of black students in the 1960s to attend a suburban white school, he refuses to feel grateful for the 'advantages' he's enjoying. He refuses to acknowledge, even to himself, that there is anything new or startling, much less enviable, in his initiation into a new world:

> I couldn't allow myself to look back, having presented myself to myself as one who had never been anywhere but where I

was . . . My appreciation was like the relief of someone who has crashed a party but isn't asked to leave, in gratitude for which and also from misplaced pride, he doesn't touch a bite.

This play-acting is of a piece with all the other daydreams and affectations of this young man with his thick glasses, incessant reading, Anglophilia – and with his fascination for the small-town life of his forebears in the South, which he refers to as the 'Old Country'. This is the almost mythical land inhabited by Aunt Clara, a 'high yellow' who is 'as obsessed as Thomas Jefferson with the "algebraical notation" of blood mixture'. According to the family memoirs, her grandfather was 'seven-eighths Caucasian and possibly one-eighth Negro'. She reads over and over again the autobiography of Marian Anderson, the great opera singer who 'traveled with an iron to press her own dresses'.

Out of the 'Old Country' emerges Uncle Castor, a jazz musician who once worked in Paris but has now fallen on such hard times that he's obliged to accept the long-term hospitality of the narrator's parents:

> Uncle Castor had brought his own sugar. He drank coffee with a cube between his teeth, wiped his hands with a soft handkerchief that he tucked up his left sleeve, and asked for toothpowder or dentifrice instead of toothpaste, all of which seemed to fit a man who dressed as flamboyantly and spoke as primly as George Washington Carver. Uncle Castor had sailed on the *Île de France*, traveled on the Flying Scotsman, and been on friendly terms with the head porter of the North British Hotel. He had seen gigolos in Nice and Cannes with a suggestion of rickets in their legs do the Buzzard Lope and the Walk the Dog. He had made the Dolly Sisters laugh. He promised to send me some of his clips, but he never got around to it.

The most intensely studied character in this novel of glowing portraits is the narrator's grandfather. A graduate of Brown and Harvard who becomes a Congregational minister, Grandfather frustrates his followers by not giving them the apocalyptic 'heart religion' they yearn for. Instead, he 'lectured his congregation on the vanity of piety, his posture announcing that he was as strict as his model, the old Harvard dean, Willard Sperry'. Like his grandson, he is obsessed with racial scenarios but does not want to conform to them.

For this is a novel neither by nor about sharecroppers or homeboys. Pinckney's turf is the black elite, which W. E. B. Du Bois called 'the talented tenth'. When the narrator turns in an astonishingly good paper in high school, his white teacher urges him to confess that he's copied it. When as an adult he lives in New York he discovers racism in another form:

Taxi drivers would not stop for me after dark, white girls jogged to keep ahead of my shadow thrown at their heels by the amber streetlamps. Part of me didn't blame them, but most of me was hurt. I carried props into the subway – the latest *Semiotext(e)*, a hefty volume of the Frankfurt School – so that the employed would not get the wrong idea or, more to the point, the usual idea about me. I did not want them to take me for yet another young black prole, though I was exactly that, one in need of a haircut and patches for my jeans.

At the same time he recognizes that in liberal political circles in New York and London he is able to use the prestige of his skin color. He can 'act black' with whites his own age, although with other blacks he invariably shuts down, 'as uptight as a slumming white'.

He may experiment with all the available images – including black militancy (he briefly becomes 'minister of information' of a splinter group, the Heirs of Malcolm), black separatism and even chic black escapism in Paris – but none of these masks fit him, this bookish, unambitious, mildly despairing observer. He cons everyone else, but in the end he is the loser. When he works one hot New York summer for a welfare agency, he often plays hooky and sticks close to his fan at home. 'Sunday conversations with my parents I padded with talk-show-level sincerity about how much I was learning about Black America through my job, yarns that had the self-sabotage of the patient in analysis who gets nowhere because he thinks he has to keep the therapist entertained.'

Whereas Ralph Ellison's hero was an invisible man to the whites around him, Pinckney's seems unreal even to himself. He has acquaintances rather than friends, observations rather than passions, few resentments, guarded enthusiasms and no sex life. No wonder he's drawn back again and again to the authenticity of the old-timers he meets in Harlem bars or at family funerals.

If Grandfather with his elegant diction and sudden urges to travel, with his veiled but intense love and wounded pride, is the presiding spirit of this rich, dense novel, the muse is Djuna Barnes, the eccentric author of *Nightwood* for whom the narrator does odd jobs for a while. Her novel – arguably the strangest of all American masterpieces – has provided Pinckney with a model for his own idiosyncratic book. In *Nightwood* the language is wrought with Elizabethan music and multiple meanings; each chapter is as free-standing, figured and isolated as Trajan's Column; the atmosphere is nervous and Gothic. Pinckney has adapted Barnes's high style to his own much more realistic needs, for unlike *Nightwood* his book has a subject, the American subject, race. Unsentimental, frank, cool but compassionate, Pinckney has turned this subject (as one of his old timers might say) 'every which way but loose'. At a time in our history when a puerile 'political correctness' imposes hypocrisy on most writers dealing with sensitive topics, Darryl Pinckney has dared to treat his theme with excruciating honesty and the total freedom from restraint that Schiller said we find nowhere else but in authentic works of art.

Southern Belles Lettres:
Cormac McCarthy

Written in 1992, this essay is previously unpublished.

Cormac McCarthy is at once carnally present and fastidiously invisible in his work – present through his distinctive voice and invisible because there is not a trace of autobiography in his novels, at least the pen never wavers like a divining rod over the waters of the Self.

His style is Classy Southern Gothic and has often been compared to Faulkner's. Certainly neither man is reluctant to deck drab characters out in purple prose. McCarthy alternates lines of Appalachian dialogue ('git!') with Maeterlinckian cadences ('a meniscus of pale brown froth'), just as Faulkner's convict shouts, 'Gimme that oar' and then rows off 'with a calculated husbandry of effort'. On the very first page of *Suttree*, one of McCarthy's later novels, he is capable of writing: 'wave on wave of the violent and the insane, their brains stoked with spoorless analogues of all that was, lean aryans with their abrogate semitic chapbook reenacting the dramas and parables therein and mindless and pale with a longing that nothing save dark's total restitution could appease'. The trick, apparently, is to juxtapose gritty anglo-saxon concreteness with refined latinate abstractions ('spoorless analogues', whatever that means).

Despite such occasional excesses, McCarthy is a more controlled and resourceful stylist than Faulkner. Although both McCarthy and Faulkner are given (as Mary McCarthy once observed of another Southern Gothic, Tennessee Williams) to dropping the needle down on their poetic LPs in order to break up an otherwise pedestrian page, the resulting 'poetic realism' is less jarring in McCarthy's fiction, especially in his most recent novels, *Blood Meridian* and *All the Pretty Horses*. But even in *Horses* (the first volume in a projected trilogy), McCarthy can get

LPish, as in this evocation of an old Comanche road in Texas: 'nation and ghost of nation in a soft chorale across that mineral waste to darkness bearing lost to all history and all remembrance like a grail the sum of their secular and transitory and violent lives'.

Of course it all depends on how much you can take. I can take this sentence fine up through 'waste'. I like the Poundian tone of 'nation and ghost of nation' (as in Pound's 'drums and kettle-drums') and even in the windy last bit I recognize it's not just all blarney but that a sort of intelligence animates the contrasts between 'all history' and 'transitory' or 'grail' and 'secular', but the grail does seem out of place on the Texas plains, and in general the periodic sentence structure and the overkill rhetoric are far less admirable than McCarthy's more usual dry eloquence, as when he notes 'the muted run of sand in the brainbox' when a character turns over a horse skull, or compares the glow of distant lightning to 'welding seen through foundry smoke'.

The rusting sadness of American trainyards, the melancholy pyrography of the bleak American landscape are as comfortably within McCarthy's register as they are in Pynchon's (or Kerouac's), and the scandalous rearing up of violence out of a banal nowhere is as much McCarthy's as Flannery O'Connor's subject. Indeed McCarthy is the chronicler who has shown us (in *Blood Meridian*) the ceaseless bludgeoning violence that must have been the reality of all those heroic legends about the Old West, just as he is the poet of male solitude in a lonely man's world of cowboys and Indians or half-sane drifters.

Critics used to praise writers for their 'range'. They probably had Tolstoy or Balzac or Dickens in mind, and no one was considered great if he or she didn't render at least one birth and one death, one miser and one spinster, a first ball and a last hurrah, war and peace. These literary occasions have come to seem less and less obligatory as the twentieth century wanes; what we *fin de siècle* readers prize is obsessiveness and fervor, rhetorical energy, passionate intensity – all necessarily narrow, I suppose.

Cormac McCarthy's forte is solitude. He's always written about it. His first novel, *The Orchard Keeper*, has but a ghost of a plot: a man kills a stranger and then unknowingly becomes a friend to his victim's son. The characters are hillbillies lost in the mists and drizzle of their mountain fastnesses. His second novel, *Outer Dark*, is out of print and I haven't read it, but his third, *Child of God*, is Southern Gothic at its creepiest, the sort parodied by Nabokov in the afterword to *Lolita* ('I'm crazy, you're crazy, I guess God is crazy'). In *Child of God* a half-wit ('child of God' is regionalese for people with a screw lose) loses his ancestral farm, becomes a forest hermit, discovers a naked couple asphyxiated in a parked car and soon develops a taste for dead women.

Although few of the man's thoughts are reported and there is no meretricious effort to pass necrophilia off as just one more delightful variation on the great human themes, nevertheless we understand the murderer's singlemindedness. Within a cavern he assembles his corpses like the members of the family he's lost. The writing is as hard and mineral as A. A. Ammons's poetry:

In the night he heard hounds and called to them but the enormous echo of his voice in the cavern filled him with fear and he would not call again. He heard the mice scurry in the dark. Perhaps they'd nest in his skull, spawn their tiny bald and mewling whelps in the lobed caverns where his brain had been. His bones polished clean as eggshells, centipedes sleeping in their marrowed flutes, his ribs curling slender and whitely like a bone flower in the dark stone bowl.

Suttree is a long, dense novel about outcasts who live on a polluted river, probably the Tennessee. There's a terrible scene in which a bum tries to drown his dead father in order not to pay the funeral expenses, but the cadaver surfaces. The style has become more layered and detailed: 'Beyond the counter ranged carboys and galleypots and stained glass jars of chemic and cottonmouthed bottles cold and replete with their parti-colored pills'. Again the mineral note is the purest McCarthy sound: 'the incessant drip of water echoed everywhere through the spelean dark like dull chimes'.

A trace of plot emerges only towards the end of the book when Suttree is briefly kept by a salty whore and the two of them live through Hopperesque scenes set in Tennessee, becoming sweaty nighthawks in diners with rusting chrome and smudged windows.

Up to this point McCarthy's books seem like pretexts for singing the songs of poverty, solitude and mineral hardness. The plots are dicey, story points are scattered here and there like insufficient clues and they rarely condense into anything so solid as a mystery. Characters are half-glimpsed through palimpsests of words, and motives are difficult to dope out. Of course, as Vereen Bell has argued in her excellent book *The Achievement of Cormac McCarthy*, these may all be strategies for de-centering his novels and people ('only the aimless can be adequately open to the saving rhythm of experience').

But with *Blood Meridian* McCarthy seems to have discovered that suspense and memorable characters are the best fictional structures for promoting a sense of duration in the reader's perceptions. Since fiction, like music, is primarily a temporal art, any device that inflects the reader's perception of time becomes crucial, not just as a hook for grabbing the reader's attention but as a strategy for modifying the very material out of which this art is composed: time. Plots generate suspense and characters promote a sense of identification, both elements that engender a taut awareness of duration that has little to do with clock time.

Blood Meridian may be episodic but it is filled with a gathering horror as the author recounts the bloody progress made by a group of American adventurers into Mexico in the 1850s. Here the Indians are no noble savages; they are as rapacious, drunk and debased as the white men they fight. Presiding over the ghastly revelries is Judge Holden: 'He was as bald as a stone and he had no trace of beard and he had no brows to his eyes nor lashes to them. He was close on to seven feet in height and he stood smoking a cigar even in this nomadic house of God.' A gifted gabber, a born charlatan, fiendishly cruel, the judge is a cross between Tennessee Williams's Big Daddy and William Burroughs's Doctor Benway copied out in brimstone.

A fourteen-year-old named The Kid is the other protagonist in *Blood Meridian*, and as in all of McCarthy's novels a young man is learning sorry lessons about a hostile world. In *All the Pretty Horses* that youngster is brought to the extreme foreground, which is probably what makes this newest book more touching, more accessible, even more interesting than the others. Once again a youngster has lost his family and home, this time because his mother, a talentless actress, is divorcing his dying father and selling off her unprofitable Texas ranch. John Grady, the youngster, lives for nothing but horses and open spaces. He and his best friend, Rawlins, head south of the border. There they come across a hapless, unlucky North American lad named Blevins, who from the first smells of trouble.

Trouble is quick to find them all, but throughout the book the reader is convinced of John Grady's integrity. If *Blood Meridian* blasted away our last illusions about the Old West, *All the Pretty Horses* restores some of them; McCarthy has rescued for us out of the debris of all those bad movies and hackneyed books the ideal portrait of the stony-faced, stoic, completely decent cowboy. Grady suffers a nightmarish sentence in a Mexican prison because he's befriended the hotheaded Blevins. And he suffers from a broken heart because he's fallen in love with a highborn Mexican young lady.

McCarthy has never been much good at portraying women. In any event his men are too poor, downtrodden, crazed or shy to attract women. But here he has exquisitely rendered a high-spirited maiden out of a fairy tale ('she came in past him all rustling of clothes and the rich parade of her hair and perfume'). That 'parade' is worthy of Sir John Suckling. The increased human warmth, fortunately, has done nothing to dispel the metaphysical chill so essential to McCarthy's art:

The fire had burned to coals and he lay looking up at the stars in their places and the hot belt of matter that ran the chord of the dark vault overhead and he put his hands on the ground at either side of him and pressed them against the earth and in that coldly burning canopy of black he slowly turned dead center to the world, all of it taut and trembling and moving enormous and alive under his hands.

In this book the lyricism is under control, it serves a purpose, the number of rare words is reduced, the sense of overall design is surer. Politically the book seems admirably even-handed; Mexicans are as virtuous or evil as North Americans – and as various and complex.

Nor has the world of horses ever been shown with more

knowledge or pleasure. Grady and Rawlins win over the Mexican ranch-hands by breaking in a whole troupe of wild horses. Blevins dies when he protests against the theft of his horse. The horses are felt as living, sensitive creatures. Even human beings are described in equine terms ('You look like you been rode hard and put up wet').

This is almost as hard and relentless a book as the others. Only this time McCarthy has shown everything through the eyes of a young man who has some illusions left. To be sure there are flaws in the novel; the Mexican maiden aunt is allowed to discourse on and on in an utterly unbelievable, heightened way for page after page. Grady wavers between being a wise, preternaturally adult aristocrat and a typical redneck kid. But these 'flaws' mark the suture points where McCarthy has tried to graft on a fairy tale to realism, and this strange admixture gives the book its darkly poetic majesty.

Two Princes

The article on the singer Prince appeared in *Parkett*, 1985, that on Richard Prince in *Parkett*, 1992.

Prince

Just as pop music has borrowed from, parodied and sometimes trivialized classical music, so the vernacular visual style often inhabits the deserted, burned-out mansions of high art. This kind of visual squatting can bring an unexpected vitality to an exhausted tradition. Examples spring up in every epoch. For instance, the Egyptian artisans who decorated the tombs in the Valley of the Kings did not understand the symbolism they were employing; they did as the priests instructed. But when these same workmen decorated their own tombs, they freely adopted the vocabulary they'd memorized but hadn't grasped. Into the scenes of the magical resurrection rites of Osiris they introduced thoroughly demotic portraits of their wives and friends as well as scenes of hunting, fishing, and banqueting – the *gemütlich* version of the Mysteries.

Similarly, the first cult images of the Buddha were sculpted in India by the artists of Gandhara who'd absorbed without comprehending the Greek style of rendering Phoebus (a manner picked up from Alexander the Great's conquering armies).

A strict iconographic analysis of such vernacular adaptations would be misleading, since the artist is frequently unaware of the original meaning of the visual (or aural or literary) vocabulary he is manipulating. A comparison of Renaissance mythographies will reveal that, far from there having been an agreed-upon universal interpretation of conventional symbols (the sphinx, the shield, the virgin), the local scholar in every duchy had a different explanation. Today this sort of splendid symbolic confusion can be seen in Brazil, where the adherents to Macumba have conflated Christian saints and African deities.

This creative ignorance occurs at the junctions of two cultures or two classes or two religions. Robert Graves has written about the way in which some Greek myths were, so to speak, 'back formations', i.e. latter-day efforts to make sense of older words and signs no longer understood. Similarly, the literal-minded Chinese, upon seeing the etherealized, apparently sexless Gupta statues of the male Buddha Avolakitesvara, assumed he must be a goddess – and came up with Kuan-yin.

Recently Prince has been accused of perpetrating a dangerous Messianism and eschatology in which he supposedly would like to figure as a latter-day Christ who stages a cleansing nuclear Armageddon, the 'Purple Rain' of the song and film (or so the theory goes). The evidence marshaled against him is that he has sometimes ended concerts as though crucified against a silhouette of the Cross. Or that 'Purple Rain' begins with phrases from a sermon: 'Dearly Beloved, we're gathered here today to get through this thing called life ... But I'm here to tell you that there's something else: the Afterworld ...'

Certainly Prince's stage appearances – with their spooky use of dry-ice smoke transected by bank upon bank of amber or mauve or cadmium-white lights, of flights of stairs leading up to improbable props (a bathtub, say), of dramatic moments of complete silence or darkness – these concerts do seem to project a creepy 'spirituality'.

But I would argue that such an interpretation of Prince regards the nature of his artistic personality, which plays with all the contradictions at his disposal, often without a thorough grasp of the historical resonance of the symbols he is wielding. I would add that precisely such contradictions, dramatically underscored and rapidly alternated, dispel the awesomeness, the elevated solemnity of the Fascist esthetic he has been accused of re-inventing. The Fascist esthetic, as exemplified by the films of Leni Riefenstahl, the operas of Wagner and the plays of Robert Wilson, overwhelms and tranquilizes the critical intelligence. These works exalt the spirit and preclude humor or irony. To the degree they summon erotic energies, they disguise or transcend them; this is the art of sublimation. They transport us to another world and lead us there seamlessly. Any shock, any laugh, any rupture would cause the hot-air balloon to deflate and hurl us back to earth.

By contrast, Prince's art thrives on shock, contrast, scandalous changes of direction, sudden hemorrhages of meaning. He draws on worn-out esthetic vocabularies (the historical costume drama, the political rally, the born-again Christian camp meeting, the medieval morality play) without taking responsibility for their separate ideological burdens. He is a scamp, a jester, a Peer Gynt, the proletarian 'prince', i.e. immoral trickster, who figures so often as a folk hero in the fairy tales of most cultures. Moreover, his eroticism, far from being sublimated, is as explicit as the burlesque dancer's bump-and-grind.

I'm not claiming that Prince is indifferent to the traditions he alludes to; I'm merely arguing that he borrows their prestige without preaching their sermons. Indeed, such collages of tradition are only one aspect of a sophisticated art founded on antinomy, a series of paired opposites that one could begin to suggest by listing a few: big/small, male/female, black/white, good/bad, rich/poor, acid rock/gospel.

Let me fill in. By big/small I mean that although he is tiny (just five feet two inches), he towers above his fans, raised high on a spotlit platform. When he appears as a client at a bar or disco, he arranges to have himself lifted over the other customers by his immense (white) bodyguard; Prince is a diminutive but all-powerful Aladdin who commands the huge, subservient genie.

By male/female I mean that his androgyny, unlike Michael Jackson's, is not a denial of adult sexuality nor a consecration of Peter Pan, the skinny, grinning, inoffensive *puer aeternus*. Prince is not a boy; he is all man and all woman. In his live performances he teases his fans by rubbing his crotch ('You think you'd know what to do with it?') and then pirouettes and presents his ass to them ('How's your new man? Is he fine? Does he have an ass like mine?'). Prince, lavishly made up with eyeliner, his legs and buttocks sheathed in see-through lace stockings, mounts his motorcycle, his shoulders festooned in chains – but gold, festive ones; he is the operetta version of Brando in *The Wild One*.

His race is ambiguous. In *Purple Rain* he played the son born of a mixed marriage, but Prince's real parents insist they both have always considered themselves to be black. The rumors have circulated that he's part-Indian, maybe-Mexican.

Just as ambiguous is his musical style. At times he plays his guitar and assaults and provokes his listeners as did Jimi Hendrix. Then again, in his latest album, *Around the World in a Day*, he evokes the acid visions of the Beatles' *Sergeant Pepper* record. But these synthetic, blissed-out fancies Prince juxtaposes with echoes of gospel music in the penultimate song, 'The Ladder'. Some listeners may imagine that the falsetto wails and shouted interjections that embellish Prince's songs are primeval cries of sex and sin, but admirers should recall that the style derives from sacred, not profane, black music. It was the gospel singer Mahalia Jackson who wailed, not the frankly erotic Ma Rainey or Bessie Smith.

Prince's rapid shifts of style are paradigmatic, not syntagmatic. His narrative line never falters or strays, although with each phrase he feels free to substitute one style for another. Normally he abides by a primitive disco beat; at critical moments, however, the beat is suspended and Prince improvises cadenzas of a dizzying freedom. Such musical license is matched by his quicksilver visual allusiveness.

Why has Prince devised such a virtuoso technique? What function does his referential esthetic, so rich and irreverent, serve?

Prince's technique enables him to delineate psychological complexities with great subtlety. For instance, in his film he portrays a hostile, mocking singer who, for the first three-quarters of the story, refuses the help of his fellow performers and alienates his audiences. But it is crucial that he does not alienate *us*. How can Prince repulse his fictional listeners while attracting his real ones? How can the same actions make us love him and prompt the other characters to despise him?

Prince's appeal in *Purple Rain* is the same as that of Milton's Satan; he is doomed, proud and overflowing with willed energy. Many characters in fiction, drama, film or opera who exhibit great force (Dostoevsky's madmen, Carmen, Othello) are people we love – though we'd surely hate them if we met them. Prince portrays just such a demon of force.

Now the *particular* force Prince exerts is that of choice. Schiller taught that art educates us in freedom since it alone shows the human spirit untrammeled by compromising circumstance; only art is pure play. Prince – this diminutive prankster, surrounded by half-menacing, thoroughly capricious throngs, impaled by floodlights and hooked up to miles of electric wire – has found a way of triumphing over technology. Indeed, his very triumph, so capricious itself and invariably solipsistic, depends on technology, for only in the modern studio is Prince able to command so absolutely his resources, to sing every voice, play every instrument and mix every effect. If his freedom, his playfulness, has taken on a sinister edge, should we be so surprised?

Richard Prince

The Europeans hate us because we've retired to live inside our advertisements, like hermits going into caves to contemplate. We sleep in symbolic bedrooms, eat symbolic meals, are symbolically entertained – and that terrifies them, that fills them with fury and loathing because they can never understand it. They keep yelling out, 'These people are zombies!' They've got to make themselves believe that, because the alternative is to break down and admit that Americans are able to live like this because, actually, they're a far more advanced culture – five hundred, maybe a thousand years ahead of Europe, or anyone else on earth, for that matter. Essentially we're creatures of spirit. Our life is all in the mind.

Christopher Isherwood, *A Single Man* (1964)

Richard Prince's jokes are empty shells, long since abandoned by the wit that once inhabited them. Jokes about psychiatrists and adulterers, two of his favorite genres, flourished in the 1950s, the period when the standards of normality were never more sacred and rigid and the status of the couple never more 'natural'. Although Prince's jokes may be more recent, they are simply degenerate forms of this once hardy breed.

As Roland Barthes argues in *Mythologies*, a book of the 1960s, the function of popular art which appears to ridicule middle-class institutions is really to re-inforce them. If members of a royal family are shown shopping in Antigua or sailing on the Mediterranean, the unspoken strategy underlying such magazine features is to demonstrate that even though the king and queen appear to be normal folks, in fact their sacred character remains intact even when (especially when) they are performing secular acts.

New Yorker jokes use a similarly paradoxical strategy to recuperate the very values they seem to be mocking. The inevitability of marriage is assumed in jokes about adultery; in a genuinely permissive society such jokes misfire. Individualism and antisocial fantasizing, when expressed on the psychiatric couch, are neutralized and subsumed under the implicit and unquestioned rule of conformity. The psychiatric hour is the only time when rebellious sentiments can be aired and they are in any event treated as problems requiring medical attention. (Prince's most repeated psychiatric joke seems to be a wink toward his own appropriations: 'I went to a psychiatrist. He said, "Tell me everything." I did, and now he's doing my act.')

But these cartoons, which once appeared to be rueful comments on conventional life, are now completely extinct and pathetically unfunny (the psychiatrist joke is a bad Henry Youngman Borscht-belt one-liner). Why has Prince decided to display these dead stars in the firmament of his art?

He has sometimes been discussed as a latter-day Warhol, elevating popular culture, especially magazine culture, to the status of high art, but there are important distinctions between them. As Corinne Diserens and Vicente Todolfi have pointed out in their introduction to Prince's *Spiritual America*, 'unlike the pop artists, Prince does not choose spectacular images or famous characters; in an important way, he is a documentarian of the strangely ordinary'.

Warhol worked with commercial images (the soup-can label, the dollar bill) that were never meant to be seen as expressions of an individual sensibility; Prince's cartoons, by contrast, were conceived as witty, sophisticated comments on society by artists whose signatures were well known to readers of the *New Yorker* (which makes plagiarism more shocking). Warhol appropriated images that were still potent (pictures of Mao or Marilyn); whereas Prince deliberately chooses material that has long since cooled off. Warhol made multiples out of images that already existed only in forms of mass reproduction and that were perceived as multiple by their very nature (photos of stars for fans, labels, money). Prince, by contrast, makes a unique work of art out of a

cartoon that itself exists in two distinct states, as an original drawing that can be displayed and sold in a gallery *and* as a
'reproduction' in a magazine. Warhol's images seldom use words
beyond names; whereas Prince works with both words and texts.
Warhol's manipulations are 'superficial' in the sense that he
applies various colors or silkscreen printing techniques to an
image that remains unvarying and that is true to the original.
Prince, by contrast, manipulates the fundamental image by
assigning written dialogue from one cartoon to another. For
example, a wife surprises her husband with another woman but
the words read: 'A husband came home and found his wife in bed
with his best friend. "Hey! What do you think you're doing?"
said the husband. "See?" she said to the man beside her. "I told
you he was stupid."' Irregularities in the punctuation are further
distortions that degrade the text from within.

In subsequent variations, three actors in the cartoon are women
(image manipulation) or the written gag is *totally* irrelevant (text
manipulation).

If Warhol's art makes its point simply by bringing into conflict
the banal sphere of mass culture with the elevated world of fine
art, Prince 'deconstructs' his far more complex but less lively
originals through combinatorial variations, i.e. image remains
constant but caption is rotated; or one or more images are superimposed on the original and the text is irrelevant to all but one; or
above the image is a handwritten slogan, and below is a printed
one, neither relevant; or the image is fragmented into details, each
framed separately, and the text is eliminated; or the text is printed
on a canvas without an image; or the text is fragmented and the
characters liberated from their original cartoon and superimposed
in a weightless space; all images are eliminated and the jokes are
printed one after another, etc. Sometimes the image is derived
from a sophisticated *New Yorker* cartoon and the text is a gag
from a prole rag or something on the level of the *Reader's Digest*.

In *Menthol Pictures* Prince writes, somewhat elliptically, referring to an old movie plot he has just retold: 'The material
formally appropriated was available to anyone who cared to use
it. The fact that the material had probably been observed or unconsciously collected by persons other than myself defined its
desire and threat. It was this "prior availability" that verified this

fictional transformation and helped cool down the references to observable reality.' In other words, images or texts that have already been experienced by a generation of consumers are sufficiently exhausted and removed from the original observed reality to make them suitable for appropriation.

Undeniably, Prince's jokes have 'cooled down' precisely because they are dated. With a distance in time each cartoon seems less an individual observation and more an item in a general series, a member of a genre, and the genre itself seems weirdly (even unpleasantly) arbitrary. The moment when individual statement begins to look like collective utterance (folk art) has been caught by Prince's sense of timing; his appropriated cartoons are no longer perky witticisms but rather old, nauseating group chatter, no longer stinging satire but rather melancholy and sometimes even loony assertions of yesteryear.

Robert Darnton, the historian of the French Revolution, once wrote that the best entry point into an alien culture is through its jokes, especially those that no longer seem funny. He, for instance, derived a whole book about the pre-Revolutionary period from an analysis of a mock trial of cats at their very real execution – a hilarious prank at the time that now seems revoltingly cruel.

Prince's jokes, because they're out of date, ignore the feminist and gay revolutions, the dissolution of the family, the advent of identity politics, the end of Communism and the collapse of any consensus about what constitutes normality. His jokes were, even when they appeared, rear-guard efforts to shore up values that were already caving in. Now that the Iron Curtain has melted down, Prince resurrects cartoons about nuclear holocaust; soon he'll be moving on to bomb shelters. Now that gays have become as touchy as women and blacks, he's turned to puns on the word *fruit*, soon he'll be telling coon jokes. Now that family values survive only in campaign rhetoric, he's trotted out all the old traveling salesmen stories. Even at the time these jokes evoked little beyond a wan smile; now they're archeological.

George Orwell, by studying 'penny dreadfuls', joke books for the poor, learned that in working-class humor the horny and curvaceous honeymooners became almost overnight, toothless old Mum and Dad; a prolonged youth existed only amongst members of the newly rich middle class and of course the upper class. Orwell's research is paralleled by Prince's, although Prince is reluctant to draw conclusions or to treat jokes as specimens. Prince is not a sociologist nor a philosopher and he isn't exactly studying anything, but he is holding up stone-cold folk art for our delectation.

And it is a dandy's delectation that he's after, more than a philosopher's disdain. The dandy *enjoys* things (the true legacy of Pop Art); he doesn't feel superior to this world nor does he assent to common hierarchies of value. The dandy levels all distinctions and then creates a new order out of the vagaries of his own taste. Prince anthologizes gags, book titles, snippets from newspapers ('boiler plate' as such filler items are called), names and dates of minor events, slogans ('No glove no love'), even potted summaries of movie plots from *TV Guide* listings. Unlike Joe Brainard's lists in *I Remember*, Prince's aren't expressive or personal. He hasn't remembered or written them, he has merely collected them. In Prince's lists low-level babble is juxtaposed with highbrow chat ('A surprising concurrence of events, perceived as meaningfully related, with no casual connection'), which is undermined because the phrases don't add up to a sentence and the word 'casual' replaced the expected 'causal'.

What keeps us poring through these lists? We're looking for a 'concurrence' between his selections and ours. Or we're hoping to intuit the dimensions of his taste. We're checking the range of our own cultural preferences against his and possibly hoping to pick up a few new names. But mainly we're trying to find a pattern, a basis for predictability. If we were to succeed, such closure would be both reassuring and disappointing – reassuring because the mind longs for closure, disappointing because one of the principal virtues of contemporary art is its open-endedness. We're not interested (we're not allowed to be interested) in Prince's sensibility except for our efforts to decode criteria of inclusion and exclusion. Since his material is almost entirely appropriated, we cannot indulge in the usual romantic speculations about the expressive Self. Since, however, we still live in the romantic age with its cult of the individual (a cult both boosted and undermined by the media), we cannot resist focusing on Prince as the Artist (and to be sure he signs his work, has one-man shows, allows photos of himself to be published, gives interviews). He is a 'personality'. As a result our fascination with the Artist has nothing to dwell on except his criteria of selection – the artist as connoisseur, paladin of a pure taste, the ultimate badge of the dandy as *arbiter elegantarium*. Our mind becomes an analogue computer trying to process all of Prince's choices in order to come up with a robot portrait of his sensibility.

An overview of his entire production (not just his jokes) reveals Prince's interest in series, in variations on a single theme, in comparisons of disparate things (metaphor), recuperation of luxury or mass advertising. His starting points are always appropriation but no act of citation is clearly satirical or affirmative. His eye doesn't go to the outrageous, the grotesque, the venal but rather to the bland, the worn-out, the sublimely banal. He sinks a probe into cultural codes, but only those that have stopped functioning. His work is coherent but not systematic, baffling but not capricious.

Of course if his jokes or ads or lists or fashions are dated, they're also relevant in a larger sense. Feminism hasn't uprooted sexism but simply driven it underground; Prince's old gays take us back to a more naïvely bigoted era. The end of Communism hasn't eradicated nuclear threat; Prince's cartoons just pinpoint fears of mass destruction in their most paranoid form. Health-consciousness hasn't ended addiction; Prince's hallucinatory drunks simply return us to an era when drunks were considered as lovable bums (now that New York has as many homeless people as Calcutta even the *New Yorker* dare not publish all those funny bum cartoons).

But as the Isherwood passage printed at the beginning of this essay suggests, if Prince has called one collection of his work *Spiritual America*, he has done so because he has recognized the way in which Americans 'retired to live inside our advertisements like hermits going into caves to contemplate'. His ghostly cowboys with their raised lariats, his phantom models with the lovely downsweeping curve of their lashes, his sepia-tinted joke collections all point to the beauty and the essentially mystic aspect of America, the land of Bugs Bunny *and* Jonathan Edwards, of Horatio Alger and Moby Dick. The spiritual side of life, to be sure, is diminished by jokes; as Henri Bergson argued humor reveals the triumph of the material over the spiritual. Humor is the enemy of lyric beauty and sadism (Jean Genet is never funny), but their friend – or at least their willing accomplice – is *wan* humor, *weak* jokes, *old* gags, tired one-liners. The wise-ass will never feel enough about anything to arrive at wisdom, but the failed comic, who bores others and embraces himself but can't shut up, is both the Fool and Lear. Prince's bad jokes are the truest expression we have of spiritual America.

Two Eulogies

These two eulogies were read at memorial services and are previously unpublished.

David Kalstone (1932–86)

Everyone talks about the art of letter writing, but David was a master of the art of the telephone call. He was so good at it – so amusing, so kind, so smart – that everyone wanted to talk to him at least once a day.

Like Mme de Sévigné, who could plunge headlong into a story in the first line of a letter, David would sometimes start off by singing the latest pop song or quoting the latest advertising jingle. Sometimes he'd pretend to be someone else. I'd have a mad Russian professor on the end of the line asking me indignantly how to join the New York Institute for the Humanities and denouncing all other Eastern Europeans as frauds and KGB agents; or a timid, high little voice would be saying, 'Hello, Mr White, I'm twelve years old and I've just read your *Joy of Gay Sex*...'

Or he'd start by quoting a really juicy academic absurdity he'd gone truffling for in a learned journal. Or he'd report what Lola was about to do on *The Guiding Light* or what someone below his window had already done. David's interests ranged from Frecerro on Dante, or Jacoff on Frecerro, to the latest Bibiena exhibit or Beverly Hills diet, from a new reading of 'The Auroras of Autumn' to brim width at his hatmaker, Gélot in Paris. For such an unworldly man he was terribly *mondain*.

If he was munching something he'd give the recipe; I placed several transatlantic calls to get the recipe for *penne all'arrabiata*, which I kept losing and now have lost for good. An eavesdropper might have been startled by his instructions for Julia Child's grated zucchini: 'First you peel and rape six courgettes...'

I suppose anyone who belongs to a circle as tight, as overbred as ours needs to complain; at least David and I felt our blood had been oxygenated after a good complaining session. And of course there was the debriefing, usually cheerful: 'That was fun last night, wasn't it?' Often, during the social segment of the phone call, we'd assume new characters, loosely based on our own but exaggerated toward archness. With strangers we sometimes impersonate adults; with lovers we often impersonate children; but with friends we – at least David and I – styled ourselves as fantasy versions of ourselves, ourselves as eighteenth-century fops, which would provoke astounded laughs from the thoroughly workaday twentieth-century Midwesterners in us. We were appalled and thrilled by our own excesses as we played at being Venetians or New Yorkers or Parisians before an audience composed of David Kalstone from McKeesport and Ed White from Cincinnati, those two rubes.

From gossip we'd pass on to the ballet. Since David's ballet culture was as deep as his enthusiasm, he never merely gushed. He could describe with hallucinatory precision exactly what Suzanne had done the night before in *Tzigane* or the last movement of the *Brahms–Schoenberg*. David had the capacity to admire other people, especially women; he admired the ardor and feistiness of Suzanne, of Maxine, of Rachel, of Adrienne, of Elizabeth Bishop – it's a quality that links him in my mind to the author of *Portrait of a Lady*, his favorite novelist. Nor must we forget that David wrote his master's thesis on James's *The American Scene*. As a critic, David had the good fortune to enjoy the intimate friendship of two of his poets, James Merrill and John Ashbery, and to be on terms of respectful cordiality with a third, Elizabeth Bishop. I suspect future ages will marvel at this rapport, this example of 'poetic friendship', the subject of David's posthumous study.

David had a Mozartian lightness of touch in conversation. He liked opinions, not pronouncements, jokes not theories, suggestions not statements. He could be so indirect, so tactful, that his ever-so-subtle point would be lost on me and, once I grasped it, I'd tease him for being like Proust's aunts, and over the years David would ask me, 'Is that clear, or am I being like Proust's aunts?' Any sort of pretentiousness or sloppiness embarrassed him. If I'd say I'd decided I didn't really like Goethe, David would say coldly, 'Goethe is not being judged,' or, 'Think again, dear,' with an ominous emphasis on *dear*, or, 'I'm glad you told me.' If a nervous young scholar started raving and preaching Derrida or Lacan, David had a graceful way of getting back to the basics – love, movies, or the seating plan for dinner.

David, who was almost blind, saw everything. His eye was satiric but gentle, acute in the notation of detail and avid in the search for understanding. His laugh – his great, head-thrown-back, all-out, unthrottled laugh – announced his forbearance and hilarity in the face of experience (he pronounced it 'high-larity' and certainly we all got high off it, as though it was a rare ether we were sniffing). If David turned himself into one of the most companionable men in New York, he did so in the face of his natural shyness and bookishness; his social being was an achievement, a work of art.

David was kind, too kind, to his friends, shamefully indulgent with me. If he was good counsel in private, in public he defended his friends even when they were wrong, espoused their views, no matter how cockeyed, befriended their lovers, no matter how impossible. He was the most loyal friend I ever had – I think his code of loyalty must have been something he worked out at Harvard with Stephen Orgel, who shares his impossibly high samurai standards. David would listen over the phone to every page I wrote seconds after I'd written it and ponder every variant, a service I performed for him as well.

David gave the best advice, usually over the phone, for that was the chief medium of our friendship. He had great good sense as to how to maneuver in the world. He knew how to write a grant proposal, conduct a meeting, round off an essay. He was charmingly collegial, as his colleagues at the New York Institute for the Humanities and Rutgers know. He was proud and dignified and sure of his worth.

I phoned him first thing in the morning and last thing at night, even after we'd just spent a long evening together. I had a second-by-second, heartbeat-by-heartbeat sense of how he lived his life for thirteen years.

I haven't chosen to speak today of David as a teacher, though I once heard him teach a class on *The Tempest* in which he posed the most elegant questions, provoked the most focused discussion and paraphrased the responses with the most perfect tact. I haven't spoken of *Five Temperaments* or *Becoming a Poet*, although they are essential studies of what David, following John Ashbery, called *forms* of autobiography, to suggest a new genre that falls between *concierge* gossip and impersonal analysis – 'examples', David wrote, 'of how individuality or temperament emerges as poetic form'. There are other people in this room who can speak of David as a brother, a lover, an erudite, a critic. I must confess I'm intimidated by the task of rendering even the roughest sort of justice to such a complex and civilized man.

That's why I've snapped him simply at a characteristic moment of his day, in his crackling silk dressing gown, surrounded by the litter of his tea tray and mail, a record of Teresa Stratas singing Kurt Weill songs in the background, sunlight touching the freesias in the silver bowl and refracted through the Venetian prisms, the *New York Review of Books* open on the couch beside him, the telephone cradled between shoulder and ear as he searches in a book for that miraculous passage from Merrill or Bishop ... For me the mornings can be dull and depressing, but David was always at his best then – bright, cheerful, full of hope, loving, by turns silly and serious, gossipy and philosophical, frivolous and wise. For me his death is as unacceptable as though he'd changed his number and not given me the new one.

Robert Mapplethorpe (1946–89)

When we first met, Robert Mapplethorpe and I went out on two assignments together. First we visited Truman Capote for *After Dark* and then William Burroughs for the *SoHo Weekly News*. I was to conduct the interviews and Robert was to do the portraits. In fact he shot Truman and me together on that boiling hot day when the air conditioning failed – me all dressed up in my one good suit, my shirt collar too tight, Truman languishing with a palmetto leaf fan.

The interview was disorganized, tragic. Truman had just published *Music for Chameleons*, which felt like a comeback, but if he'd come back, he'd already gone away. He deliberately avoided looking at Robert, which was hard to do, since he was

then as always a walking sex symbol – sexy if you knew his reputation, just as sexy if you didn't. Robert worked very hard in the
stifling heat. The windows couldn't be opened. It was his idea to
include me in the picture. He didn't explain why. He just
grinned, waved me into the frame, laughed, shot his picture.
Capote murmured to himself, raved, forgot who we were and
who he was, left the room for longer and longer intervals.

Then we were back on the street, Robert's only comment was a
lifted eyebrow, a grin, troubled eyes: a no-comment way of saying,
'That was a mess', 'Poor guy', and 'We did it!' He and I were just
young enough still to feel we belonged to the later, saner generation and just old enough to fear we might end up the same way.
Mainly we were glad to hide behind our masks as journalists.

Burroughs was just as strange, when he received us in his win-
dowless Bowery bunker, the former YMCA boys' locker room
complete with ancient graffiti on the toilet walls. He showed us
Brion Gysin's paintings, then fired a few weapons and flipped
through his scrapbooks of naked boys. I was glad to have Robert
at my side.

All the time Robert seemed to be guarding a big secret, an
amusing but tricky and intimate secret, just as he spotted in me a
secret that was equally amusing but that I wasn't aware of yet.
He'd sit forward in his chair and look me in the eye, his gaze un-
flinching and curious, his smile complicitous. When I say
'curious' I don't mean he was looking for new things to discover
in me. He already knew more about me than I did. No, he was
simply curious to see if I'd catch on. Sometimes when we were
walking down the street – he in his saturnine motorcycle leathers
with the blue seams, so much more elegant than the clunky Per-
fectos everyone else was wearing – he'd look at me sideways to
see if I'd caught on yet. He wasn't nasty or trying to put me on.

I never caught on. Nor did I understand his secret, which must
have been frustrating for him. He'd try to explain his sexual
obsessions, but he was so patient and precise and smiling that he
made them sound more like a technical photographic process than
an obsession. He'd want me to understand things in their exact
proportions, all nuances left in. But I'd always overshoot the
mark. I'd think it was a game of domination, but he'd insist that
it was neither a game nor about domination. I'd think it was all a

fantasy, but he'd say he never fantasized. Each time I'd try a new explanation for size it would be the wrong fit. And I never understood how he saw me, except he once took a shocking picture of me screaming, a portrait so painful that I've never looked at it since.

Once when Robert went out of town he confided to me the care of his boyfriend at that time, a sailor on AWOL, a simple country boy from down South who was afraid of the big city and would soon go mad and try to swim the Hudson. At every step in that impossible affair Robert was considerate, ruinously spendthrift, affectionate.

If his sexual tastes sometimes led Robert into the poorest sections of the city, his success carried him to the richest. I never knew whether I'd see him skulking off at two in the morning with his leather or catch him in black tie in Paris or Gstaad or London. His manner never changed, because it worked equally well wherever he found himself. With his rich friends his simplicity came off as a form of sophistication; with his poor friends it seemed like simplicity, which is what it was.

Once he brought Lisa Lyon to dinner. We were astonished how graceful her body looked clothed and how powerful when she pushed up her sleeves and bared her massive shoulders. She was very knowing and very droll, which tickled Robert.

He and Bruce Chatwin became great friends and they resembled each other in the pleasure they took in their adventures, though Bruce's were exotic and Robert's were urban. More than any other photographer Robert caught Bruce's beauty, just as I think Bruce's text on Robert is the most brilliant. In other ways they were quite different. Bruce was the lordliest raconteur in English in his day, whereas Robert was quiet, cool. Bruce was social in the old hand-kissing manner, whereas Robert was more original in his simplicity and made everyone adapt themselves to his way.

When he did talk Robert never gave a bravura performance, although he knew a lot about many subjects, especially his collections. Like Andy Warhol or Joe Brainard he had a fearless, childlike way of saying things so basic they were startling. Unlike most great men, he noticed the people around him. He was deeply observant. He was affectionate but cool. He was a teaser.

He didn't dominate situations but he was so handsome and so sharp-eyed and then later so famous that no one could ever forget he was present. He liked to sponsor other people, an extraordinary beauty or talker or freak or artist. Just as he collected furniture or photographs or ceramics, he collected people whom he'd present, though he never took responsibility for them.

People say he was a dandy, I suppose, because he appeared to put beauty before goodness, because his own look was studied, because he inhabited a nocturnal and highly artificial environment. But he was far from being a poseur. He never said or did anything that wasn't entirely natural and unaffected. Some artists experiment with their own personalities, adopt new ways that don't always go, sometimes get caught in an awkward transition, but Robert wasn't like that. Just as his artistic vision seemed fully achieved as early as his nude of Patti Smith or his picture of the tattered American flag and he would investigate new subjects with new techniques but not evolve a new sensibility, in the same way as a person he would grow in wisdom but not change in temperament.

What was dandified about him was his high-handed manner of disrupting traditional values or conventions and replacing them with a simple standard of beauty, the gold standard, whether the beauty was to be found in a navel, a bald head, an orchid or a tranquil scene of torture. The dandy levels all other distinctions in order to plant above them the single flag of beauty. That's what Robert did, which is both his glory and ours.

Pool in Rocks by the Sea: Isherwood and Bachardy

Review of *Last Drawings of Christopher Isherwood* by Don Bachardy, *Artforum*, February 1992.

Seeing of course is always perceiving – an imaginative integration of memory, feeling and anticipation all subsumed under the aegis of style, that haphazard collection of conventions and intentions. But Don Bachardy in his recent book *Last Drawings of Christopher Isherwood* gives the appearance of seeing simply and purely more than any draftsman I know, which is especially remarkable since what he is looking at is the man he has lived with for some thirty years. Isherwood, when the drawings were made, was in his last months of life, had for the most part stopped talking, and seemed scarcely conscious of anything beyond his bodily suffering. With a paradoxically vigorous line, Bachardy recorded this collapse. Looking at Isherwood cruelly, if cruelty means honestly, he made these drawings the most disturbingly transgressive images I've seen of a man, a beloved man dying and dead.

The pictures do little to remind me of any direct precedents. Their forerunners in practise, though hardly in visual look, might be the death masks, even casts of the dead person's hands made in the nineteenth century as pious mementos, like the snippet of hair you might carry in a locket. But Bachardy has given us a series of perceptions not fossils. As John Russell writes in his introduction to the book, 'Faced with a death mask – glad as we may be to have so exact a record – we feel above all that nobody's home. In these drawings we feel Isherwood is as much at home as a human being can be.' Other precedents might include Joseph Severn's drawing of his friend Keats in death, or, from between 1913 and 1915, the Swiss painter Ferdinand Hodler's repeated drawings of his mistress Valentine Gode-Darel in her gradual decline, showing her playing with their child for example though gaunt and ill and finally rendering her after death in murky paint tones with graphic underdrawing. But Severn's saccharine sketch suggests none of the agonies of the tubercular poet, and Hodler, despite the closeness of their relationship, always drew Valentine at a distance and seldom looking directly at him and at us. Bachardy's pictures on the other hand record all of Isherwood's distraction, pain, sullenness, disorientation and growing inwardness. Positively invasive, they demand our complicity and refuse us the security of a discreet unchallenged distance.

With nasty wit, a line drawing of Isherwood in profile juxtaposes his sagging chin, bushy eyebrow and downturned mouth with an inverted profile painted on his shirt of a young woman with fashionably plucked brows and luscious painted lips. On the facing page the symmetrical black brushstrokes describing his windbreaker suggest a bird's feathery cape below a face stormy with mental confusion. In the first picture everything is rendered with a thin, dry, bounding line and contained white space; in the second nothing is left blank except the surround. Elsewhere the humble patience of dying is epitomized by clasped hands in a useless lap.

The closest equivalent to drawings like these may not be visual at all: it may be the prose of Simone de Beauvoir, who recorded every moment of Jean-Paul Sartre's final decline in her 1984 book *Adieu: A Farewell to Sartre*. Childish drinking bouts, incontinence, memory-lapses, bedsores, false teeth, ridiculous errors in judgment – the woman who spent forty years with this century's best-known Western thinker leaves nothing out of her account of his moral and physical decay. Thus Bachardy in diary entries excerpted in *Last Drawings* worries about what he's doing, using words like 'ghoulish' and 'ruthless', but acknowledging Stephen Spender's comment on his pictures: 'They are both merciless and loving.' And he writes of his art, 'It is the most intense way I know of to be with Chris. It is the only situation now in which we are both truly engaged.' After Isherwood's death he adds, 'While Chris was dying, I focused on him intensely hour after hour. I was able to identify with him to such an extent that I felt I was sharing his dying just as I'd shared so many other experiences with him. It began to seem that dying was something which we were doing together.'

Bachardy met Isherwood when he was eighteen and the writer

was forty-eight, and they spent the next thirty-three years to-gether. An early photo of them is shocking since Don looks barely a teenager – real jailbait. But over the years a mysterious personality exchange took place: Don developed an Oxford stut-ter and Chris became more and more Californian. Don seemed friendly but formal, Chris casual and noticeably friendlier. In fact no one was better company than this man who had accumulated decades of extraordinary experience but lived entirely in the moment. He'd been a member of the gentry in England, had lived in Berlin in the 1930s, then had worked for Hollywood. A friend of W. H. Auden and Spender, he was a Hindu convert who'd translated the *Bhagavad-Gita*. Just as his *Berlin Stories* created the myth of Germany between the wars, just as his *Prater Violet* is the best novel I know about the movies, his *A Single Man* published in 1964 is one of the first and best novels of the modern gay liberation movement.

Bachardy did not regard as tragic the decline of this man's bril-liant mind or his terminal cancer. A strange tropism oriented Chris to Don and Don to Chris throughout the last months of Isherwood's life from August 1985 to 4 January 1986, when he died. With wide-open eyes Don *looked* at Chris who returned the gaze whenever he wasn't befuddled by the radiation and chemo-therapy treatments. In this way Bachardy's portraits penetrate a face known to a wide public – through book-jacket photos, post-cards of authors, David Hockney's paintings – and dissolve its exacerbated individuality into a kind of landscape.

Isherwood himself in *A Single Man*, wrote of the self as a part of the landscape, as a sea pool in the rocks:

Just as George and the others are thought of, for convenience as individual entities, so you may think of a rock pool as an entity; though, of course, it is not. The waters of its con-sciousness – so to speak – are swarming with hunted anxieties, grim-jawed greeds, dartingly vivid intuitions, old crusty-shelled rock-gripping obstinacies, deep-down sparkling un-discovered secrets, ominous protean organisms motioning mysteriously, perhaps warningly toward the surface light . . . And, just as the waters of the ocean come flooding, darkening over the pools, so over George and the others in sleep come the waters of that other ocean – that consciousness which is no one's in particular but which contains everyone.

This cosmic view of the self recalls the art that Bachardy's drawings do in fact remind me of the most – the paintings of the Chinese artists, especially the Buddhists who broke down the distinction between animate and inanimate and erased the differences amongst animal, vegetable and mineral. In Sang dynasty art of the eleventh to thirteenth centuries a gnat-sized pilgrim often stares into an immense void which is as charged with energy, as is his regard. Jointed bamboo in this art has all the calligraphic force and subtlety – and is evoked with the same brushstrokes – as the poem that may be written beside it. Three persimmons in a row, or a spider monkey with her babies in a tree, are the moral equivalents to the old man in the mountains in Liang K'ai's thirteenth-century *The Sixth Zen Patriarch Tearing up a Sutra*, who howls a laugh into the wind as he rips apart a sacred scroll, demonstrating the supremacy of sudden enlightenment over the useless accumulation of wisdom.

What is remarkable in this art is that individuals are rendered in all their peculiarity at the same time that they seem to be interchangeable, a sleight-of-hand made possible by the painter's calligraphic style in which strokes linked to drawing stone can also trace a nose or chin, and lines that classically render water, pines, or clouds can describe a robe, a wizard's eyebrows or a young woman's floating hair. Bachardy has no such vocabulary of recognized conventions to draw on, but with his powers of improvisation he finds the protean exchanges between disparate components of matter – finds the skull under the face, reveals the relationship between bloated body and bony head, changes the inspired gaze of a seer into the angry grimace of a ruined old baboon. The character-revealing line beside the mouth metamorphoses into the down stroke of a wing, the flowing creases in the forehead become a river, the light that bleaches out the fixed stare emanates from the mystic's morning sun.

And yet the drawings are so quirkily individuated. Looking at them, it's hard to remember Isherwood's Eastern view of the self as a rock pool, a nonentity. That paradox – between the impersonal forces of cosmic energy and the patterns, unique as fingerprint, through which that energy flows and that constitute what we call the individual – is the fertile contradiction that animates both Isherwood's fiction and the drawings of Don Bachardy.

Marguerite Yourcenar

Review of *Marguerite Yourcenar: Inventing a Life* by Josyane Savigneau, translated by Joan E. Howard, *New York Times Book Review*, 17 October 1993.

Marguerite Yourcenar (who was born in 1903 and died in 1987) was the last echo of a heroic chorus of European writers that included Thomas Mann and André Gide, older men whom she particularly admired and whose work influenced hers. Like them she was a philosophical writer with a deep and wide culture, a moralist with a taste for historical perspectives, and a virtuoso equally at home in crafting novels, stories and essays (she also wrote rather bad plays and poems).

Like them she joined a dignified, not to say marmoreal, manner to a penchant for shocking subject matter, for she was as fascinated as they were by sexual ambiguity. Mann explored incest in 'Blood of the Volsungs' and an exalted if overripe Platonic homosexuality in *Death in Venice*. Gide touched on bisexuality and reveled in hedonism in *The Immoralist* and avowed his own homosexuality in *If It Die*. In a daring if often over-the-top essay, *Corydon*, Gide defended homosexuality as natural and even useful to society.

Yourcenar in her very Gidean first novel, *Alexis*, showed how a young husband's homosexuality could compromise his marriage while in her masterpiece, *Memoirs of Hadrian*, she invented one of the great same-sex love stories of all time, the Roman emperor's passion for his Greek lover. In her splendid essays on the Alexandrian poet Constantin Cavafy and the prolific Japanese novelist Yukio Mishima she honored two of the remarkable talents of our epoch, each so different from the other but both homosexual. Indeed her critical introduction to Cavafy is a particularly acute evaluation; for instance, she remarks, 'We are so used to seeing in wisdom a residue of dead passions that it's difficult to recognize in it the hardest and most condensed form of ardor, the gold nugget pulled out of the fire, not the ashes.' This Nietzschean celebration of passion would mark her own fiction. In her essay she also contrasts Cavafy's 'exquisite freedom from posturing' about his homosexuality with Proust's dishonesty (which led him to give 'a grotesque or false image of his own tendencies') and with Gide's need 'to put his personal experience immediately in the service of rational reform or social progress'. In her own writing and conduct Yourcenar would avoid the Proustian and Gidean extremes and cultivate Cavafy's unemphatic self-acceptance.

Cavafy's honesty is also similar to that of the Emperor Hadrian in Yourcenar's brilliant recreation. As she explained, in giving the background to her most famous book and how she came to write it, she had been struck as early as 1927 by one of Flaubert's letters in which he observed, 'There was a unique moment between Cicero and Marcus Aurelius when the gods no longer existed and Christ had not yet emerged and humanity was all alone.' This was the supremely humanist moment that Yourcenar captured with such success.

Josyane Savigneau has constructed a scrupulously accurate, never inflated account of Yourcenar which is surely the best biography to be written in French in several decades, one that quietly and affectionately takes the measure of a woman who could be maddeningly pompous and egotistical but whose single-mindedness still commands respect. Savigneau has traced out every step in the life of this secretive woman who seldom doubted that she was destined for greatness.

Marguerite Yourcenar was born in Brussels to a Belgian mother and French father, whose name was Michel de Crayencour (Yourcenar, a pen name, is a nearly perfect anagram). Her mother, Fernande, died ten days after Marguerite's birth, and the child was watched over from afar by a woman whom Marguerite later imagined must have been her mother's lover. She was raised, however, by her father, a compulsive gambler (already fifty years old when Marguerite was born), who destroyed the family fortune but conferred on his brilliant daughter a love of travel and learning. She was not sent to school nor did she embroider or play with dolls. She had few toys and preferred reciting poetry to playing, which must have made her seem unbearably priggish to her friends. At a precocious age she developed a sense that she was 'important, even very important', as she later recalled.

She and her father spent the beginning of the First World War in England, where they studied Latin and Greek together but made little headway with English. They returned to Paris in 1915, where she was tutored at home. Her father passed on to the child his favorite books by Goethe, Tolstoy, Huysmans and the controversial (because pacifist) Romain Rolland. She and her father read out loud Virgil in Latin and Homer in Greek. At age sixteen Marguerite wrote a poetic drama, *Icarus*.

The young writer developed a deep complicity with her father, who paid to have her first two books published, who wrote and signed letters for her in her absence – but who expressed no warmth to her. Yet when he was dying he was pleased to have lived long enough to have read her first genuine literary achievement, *Alexis*. In the same year, 1928, she began to work on a first (and soon abandoned) version of the life of the Emperor Hadrian. She was twenty-four years old. The *Memoirs of Hadrian* would not be published until 1951.

Yourcenar had in fact already discovered in her twenties almost all the literary themes she would develop over the next sixty years. She belonged to that small tribe of artists (Dante is another) who don't evolve but simply explore their chosen subjects with ever greater intensity.

Yourcenar quickly forgot about her father after his death and thought about him only several decades later. Passionate and cerebral, Yourcenar spent the ten years after her father's death and before the outbreak of war in 1939 traveling, living in small hotels, reading, writing and seducing both men and women. She had an unhappy experience pursuing a man, a French writer who was homosexual; the suffering was indirectly expressed in *Coup de grâce*, the short 1939 novel that is perhaps her strongest piece of fiction.

The title also alludes to her meeting with Grace Frick, an American with whom she would live until Frick's death forty years later. Frick would help Yourcenar with her research, organize her social life, translate her books and sustain her financially over the decades. Because Frick was American, Yourcenar – the most thoroughly French of all modern French writers –

would spend the majority of her life in the United States and, from 1950 on, in Maine on the remote island of Mount Desert. Yourcenar was the first woman ever to be admitted to the French Academy and one of the first living French writers to have her complete works published in the prestigious Pléiade series, usually consecrated to classic authors of the past; how strange that this monument of French letters should have lived as a virtual recluse on an American island, where many of her neighbors assumed 'Madame' could not even speak English. Her American years, moreover, affected her only in minor ways. She translated African-American spirituals into French as well as a collection of Blues and a play by James Baldwin and she became a committed ecologist; otherwise her adopted homeland scarcely left a trace on her work.

Savigneau (who met Yourcenar) recounts every moment of this complex and ultimately triumphant destiny with a rare combination of tact and verve. She never pretends to know more than can be known (Yourcenar's private papers are sealed until 2037). Savigneau has a sharp sense of the anguish this solitary genius suffered when she taught at a chummy American college; Yourcenar's aloofness at Sarah Lawrence sounds remarkably like Nabokov's at Cornell. The comic behind-the-scenes maneuverings that led to her election to the French Academy (an honor she never sought) are rendered with abundant and amusing detail.

The intricate checks and balances in Yourcenar's long marriage to Grace Frick are presented with sympathy and equanimity. Frick was forced into playing the bad cop in order to scare off reporters, graduate students, editors and other time-wasters long enough for Yourcenar to get on with her work, but most of her victims never forgave her and wrote about her as a neurotic shrew. Yourcenar herself dismissed their relationship after Grace's death: 'Essentially it's very simple: first it was a passion, then it was a habit, then just one woman looking after another who was ill.'

Marguerite Yourcenar was entering her glory years of international fame in the 1970s at the same time that Frick was becoming terminally ill. This disparity produced considerable bitterness in both women. After Frick's death in 1979 Yourcenar was taken up by Jerry Wilson, a thirty-year-old American gay

man. They enjoyed a stormy relationship, during which Wilson
often reproached Yourcenar for being tired all the time (she was
in her eighties). Despite their fights and her weakness, Wilson
enabled Yourcenar to return to her greatest passion – travel. She
and he were in constant motion – Kenya, Japan, India, Europe –
until 1986 when Wilson died of AIDS. Despite her continuing
travels and honors, she lost the will to live and died on 17 December 1987.

Like several other lesbian writers (Mary Renault is the most
obvious parallel), Yourcenar wrote best when she projected herself into the mind of a male homosexual character. In a note
appended to *Memoirs of Hadrian* she said that it was impossible
to make a woman her main character since 'the life of women is
too limited or too secret'. Yourcenar's was far from limited,
though she did her best to keep it secret. Fortunately for us,
Savigneau has laid many of her secrets bare without violating
them.

Hervé Guibert: Sade in Jeans

Review of *To the Friend Who Did Not Save My Life*, translated by
Linda Coverdale, 1991, *The Man in the Red Hat*, and *The Com-
passion Protocol*, both translated by James Kirkup, 1993, in *The
London Review of Books*, 4 November 1993.

Hervé Guibert died on 27 December 1991 from complications resulting from an unsuccessful suicide attempt. He had been ill with
AIDS for several years and in 1990 had made a spectacular
appearance on French television during which he'd discussed his
illness and the book he'd written about it, *To the Friend Who Did
Not Save My Life*. The thousands of letters he received as a result
encouraged him to write another book, *The Compassion Protocol*,
and to participate in another prime-time interview. This time he
was wearing a red hat, the very one referred to in the title of a
subsequent work, *The Man in the Red Hat*. During his final year
of life he also made a home video, *La Pudeur et l'impudeur*,
which was screened on television a month after his death. Yet
another AIDS book, *Cytomégalovirus*, was published at this time
and a posthumous novel, *Le Paradis*, appeared at the beginning of
1993.

As an heir to Sade and Bataille, Hervé Guibert had never felt
squeamish about rubbing his reader's nose in all his bodily ex-
cretions. His very first 'text' (for once this pretentious term is
useful, since Guibert's writing often confounds genres) is unqual-
ifiedly disgusting. In fact *La Mort propagande* combines several
of the themes he would develop more extensively later on. First,
the desire evinced by Proust's character Mlle Vinteuil to humiliate
her father in Guibert's case becomes a nearly erotic pleasure in
spitting on his parents' image. Guibert has a grotesque flash to his
childhood, when his mother would become so excited chatting
with the butcher that a fluid would flow down her leg and mix
with the sawdust on the floor, a process the little boy beside her
would observe with fascination. Other tropes include sessions
during which he photographs his bodily wastes, which he's been

saving up for the occasion; cottaging, during which he's beaten up and repeatedly violated; and a concluding scene during which his dead body is dissected, a moment that mixes science with sexual frenzy. Later Guibert would become a well-known photographer and the photography critic for *Le Monde*. His taste for sexual masochism would produce a slim volume of out-and-out pornography, *Les Chiens*, in which a master treats his slaves like dogs, confining them to a kennel where they are allowed to lick and play with slabs of cooked meat but never to swallow them. He later claimed this volume had been inspired by Francis Bacon's paintings. The brutal way of regarding his own body, prefigured in the suggestively titled *La Mort propagande*, was fully developed only in his last AIDS books.

A collection of Guibert's photographs, *Le Seul Visage*, begins with a startling admission.

> In my writing there's no brake on what I do, no misgivings since I'm virtually the only one who counts (other people become abstract characters bearing just initials), whereas in photography there's the body of other people, relatives, friends, and I'm always a bit worried: am I not about to betray them by turning them in this way into visual objects?

What's arresting about this admission is that it suggests the very real betrayals in his fiction don't count for him since Guibert feels he alone fully exists on the page. Although his narcissism may give an antic energy to his prose, fortunately it does not hood his observing eye. His characters are very real indeed and his betrayals as succulent as those Genet promises but seldom delivers.

Among his photographs are portraits of his friends, many of whom also show up in his books: Gina Lollobrigida, Isabelle Adjani, the director Patrice Chéreau (with whom Guibert wrote the filmscript *L'Homme blessé*), the novelist Mathieu Lindon (book critic for *Libération* and son of Jérôme Lindon, publisher of Les Editions de Minuit, Guibert's first publisher), Guibert's parents and finally his mentor, Michel Foucault, shown in a dressing gown before a mirror and the multiplied, distorted reflections of lacquered doors.

I first met the hyacinthine, ringleted, foggy-voiced young Guibert through Foucault in 1983. He was perhaps Foucault's best friend. Although Foucault liked working with women (Arlette Farge was a favorite), he didn't like socializing with them; once I invited Susan Sontag to dinner and he hissed at me when she left the room for a moment: 'Why did you invite *her*?' He preferred all-male evenings, preferably with talented youths such as Jacques Almira (whose first novel he introduced), Gilles Barbedette (to whom he granted his last deathbed interview), Mathieu Lindon and Guibert – all novelists, all gay, all attractive in a slender, ambiguous way, a bit like the willowy ephebes gathered around Plato in the painting by Théodor Chassériau in the Musée d'Orsay. I hasten to add that these boys were the exact opposite of the men Foucault felt attracted to. Since his ephebes were neither intellectuals nor objects of desire but artists, they suited his love of beauty and his cult of friendship.

Guibert, who was only twenty-eight at the time, had an earnest, wide-eyed, almost somnambulistic manner, devoid of the irony and bitchiness characteristic of his extremely rude generation in Paris. He was polite, remote, abstracted, although the moment he drew Foucault aside he became hushed and serious, incandescent. Oh, and I forgot to mention he had the most arresting, angelic face I've ever seen, with his heavy down-turned lips, vast blue eyes, perfect skin, blond curls. Later he cut all his hair off, which only threw the beauty of his features into higher relief, freed at last from their conventional Burne-Jones frame.

The first good things he wrote were a story in *Les Aventures singulières* and a short novel, *Voyage avec deux enfants*, both published in 1982, the same year he brought out the pornographic *Les Chiens*. The last story in *Les Aventures singulières* is called 'Le Désir d'imitation' and is a heartless but moving account of his friendship with Gina Lollobrigida. He goes to visit her in Italy; her chauffeur picks him up at the train station and drives him to her house, where he is given her basement sex hideaway as his bedroom, decorated with Indian statues of lascivious goddesses and perfumed with clouds of burning incense. The rest of the house is lugubrious, the grounds guarded by savage dogs that can be called off only by shouting commands in German (*Sitz! Platz! Auf!*). Every night she lets her guest choose another of her films to watch; she keeps the reels in a frigidaire. In a safe beside her bed she hides her jewels, tapes of her telephone conversations with old lovers and nude photos of herself when young (no one has ever seen these pictures).

The old actress is in love with the narrator but he despises her and dreams of killing her. When he confesses his evil thought, she laughs a huge laugh, delighted by the idea of dying at his hands. They spend New Year's Eve together and she makes him a bizarre toast:

> You think my mouth smells of powder, that it smells of flesh, of mucus or rather that it smells of wine, that it smells of vagina, that it smells of death. You say my mouth disgusts you, that my mouth stinks, that it stinks of death. This house is like a bank. I don't sleep. I'm alone and the dogs roam around it. Don't leave. The champagne is warm, too bad. Cheers. Happy New Year. Stay a little longer with me, all right?

The beautiful young gay man and the aging star keep circling around one another. The story ends when she says: 'Even in our impossible love there is still a little bit of love.'

Voyage avec deux enfants is a very different sort of love story. The narrator leaves his real lover, a young man his own age, in order to make a trip through Morocco with another man, B., and two pubescent boys. The narrator isn't even attracted to the kids but talks himself into desiring them, almost as though he's submitting to a monastic discipline. Characteristically, he chooses to concentrate on the homelier of the two boys. Nothing much happens. They travel from one town to another, staying mostly at cheap camping sites but splurging on the Gazelle d'Or, a luxury hotel in Taroudant. The boys are wise to the fact that the men desire them but deny them, tease them, insist on their privacy. Only on the last night, before flying back to Paris, do the narrator and his chosen finally have some sort of drugged sex on the rooftop of their hotel, where no sooner does the night club next door at last turn off its rock music than the muezzin begins to chant his morning prayers. Guibert captures perfectly all the nose-picking tedium and jokey empty-headedness of paedophilia, the exhausting boredom of wasting so much time on idiotic brats just to secure a few seconds of bliss. Not since Humbert Humbert has anyone made this condition so crystal clear.

After the narrator returns to Paris he discovers that in spite of himself he's fallen completely under the boy's spell. He rejects his adult lover, daydreams about Morocco, forgets to bathe or eat. He persuades the boy to write him a letter, which the boy does: 'It contained no expected, conventional formula of tenderness, it didn't even say "I kiss you" at the end, still less "I love you," it made no allusion to a shared experience, to a memory, and yet its very structure emanated, like a watermark, a marvelous tenderness.'

Guibert's next novel, *Les Lubies d'Arthur*, was the first I read, soon after it was published in 1983. At the time I liked it enough that I felt moved to write in American *Vogue* that Guibert was one of the most promising new French writers, but now the novel strikes me as mannered, formless, misguided in its surreal high jinks. Two homosexual bums, glorying in their filth, wander all over the world performing disgusting, sadistic acts. Even here, however, Guibert's constant inventiveness, his ease and pleasure in writing, his *pétillant* style are present, as they are in all his texts, even the least successful. I doubt if a talent such as Guibert's would have prospered in the English-speaking world, where books are expensive, launched with fanfare and extensively reviewed. In France he was free to publish three or four books a year, they cost just forty francs or so each in the soft-cover Editions de Minuit format, and they were never taken too seriously. In fact they were read more as chapters in one long *œuvre* than as crucial, individual milestones.

Des Aveugles, which came out in 1985, was his first book to be published by Gallimard. Guibert had done a reportage on the Institut National des Jeunes Aveugles and later became a volunteer reader for the blind; his novel, which created a stir, was adapted for the stage. Less extravagant than *Les Lubies d'Arthur* but similarly imagined, *Des Aveugles* is about a young blind couple, Josette and Robert, who live in an institution for the blind. When another blind man, Taillegeur, falls in love with Josette, he sets up an elaborate series of obstacles designed to kill Robert, but Robert outwits him and uses the same pitfalls to engineer Taillegeur's death. The melodramatic plot is unconvincing, but once

again Guibert beautifully evokes an impossible love, a love between two unfortunates, a love that contains large measures of
need and hate – true love, in short.

This is the sort of love that circulates among the family members in Guibert's best book, *Mes Parents*. Pitilessly, Guibert
details his parents' rituals, their superstitions, their favorite magazines, their fears, the emotional blackmail they practise on their
children. First the narrator's sixteen-year-old sister becomes pregnant and refuses an abortion; then the parents discover their son's
homosexuality. The mother shouts: 'A daughter pregnant at sixteen and a son who's queer, what did I ever do to the good
Lord?' The parents begin to police their son. The father pretends
he could lose his job if his son's homosexuality becomes known.
The mother roots through the love letters her boy is receiving and
throws them hysterically in his face. The narrator coolly remarks:
'When I'll lean over your dead bodies, my dear parents, instead of
kissing your skin, I'll pinch it, I'll pull out a hank of your hair.'

And yet a curious sensuality circulates between the parents and
their handsome child. When the boy's foreskin becomes infected,
the father administers the treatment every evening and, at the
son's insistence, even shows him his own penis, which the boy
perceives as though it is an X-ray, a visionary phallus denuded of
its flesh. Years later, when the son is grown up and living in Paris,
the father comes to visit. He seems timid, provincial, and insists
that his son order for him in a restaurant. He tells his offspring
that he is *en beauté*, something he's never said to his wife, and remarks that he is sure he will like everything his son writes since it
is 'the voice of my blood'. On a holiday trip home the son
becomes more and more passive, fills his days with the leaden
performance of basic functions, longs to escape, doesn't, finally
bars his father from the room and photographs his mother, half-
undressed. Time, he notices, slows down, becomes festive; the
pictures don't come out but these phantom images point toward
something 'other than imagery – towards narrative'.

Having broken a taboo with his frank and sometimes repellent
account of his feelings for his parents, Guibert is now free to
launch into his most horrendous book, *Vous m'avez fait former
des fantômes*, a nightmarish, stomach-turning *récit* about captur-
ing and torturing children. The title comes from a passage in a

letter Sade sent to his wife: 'You've filled me with fantasies that now I must realize.' Guibert's fantasies run to boys, no longer invited on lovely trips to Morocco but branded, put into burlap sacks and hung from hooks. One of the adult men stabs a particular sack and sucks the fresh blood from the cloth. A sustained infamy, this novel has only one parallel in English today, Dennis Cooper's narratives about murdering boys, *Frisk* and *Closer*.

Two years later, in 1989, Guibert brought out his purest, most idiosyncratic love story, *Fou de Vincent*. It is the tale of an abortive affair with someone totally 'unsuitable'. When a friend meets Vincent he asks Guibert: 'Who's that?' On discovering the kid's name he says: '*That's* Vincent?' Vincent is a very young ne'er-do-well on a skateboard, half-wild, whose erotic fantasies are all heterosexual, who has an ugly face but a beautiful torso, a small penis, rough palms, who refuses his ass to Guibert ('that's for caca'), and when Isabelle Adjani asks if at least Vincent loves Hervé, all Hervé can do is blubber the non-committal Roman verbal shrug, 'Beuh . . .'

If the other characters in Guibert's previous autofictions were just initials, Vincent is named, has pride of place in the title and is studied in detail. For the first time one believes in Guibert's love, which is not an 'interesting' obsession he's talked himself into or a scary story he's cooked up to frighten himself. I own a Mapplethorpe photo of a French guy, a young white man, one of Mapplethorpe's lovers. The picture was taken in the mid-1970s, and it has the same density, the same specificity as *Fou de Vincent*. The man is as particularized, adored but not stylized, as Vincent, unlike Mapplethorpe's totemic blacks or Guibert's faceless initials. What lends an aura to Vincent is his particularity, the mole on his haunch, his severely infected foot, and his death, for at the very beginning of the book Guibert announces to us that Vincent is already dead, that he jumped to his death while stoned (there's a suggestion that Vincent knew he had AIDS). In this book Guibert has exchanged one Proustian theme (spitting on the beloved parent's photo) for another (passionate love for someone who isn't even one's type). The book is scarcely organized at all, just journal entries, some of them dated, though the years ascend and descend at random. Snapshots.

Guibert lived in Rome for two years (1987–9) at the Villa

Medici; he had won the modern equivalent to the Prix de Rome and wrote a bored, spiteful book about his sojourn, *L'Incognito*, named after a gay pick-up bar for gigolos. The tone is listless. He takes note of all the absurdities of the villa, which he calls the Spanish Academy. He has encounters with hustlers that go nowhere. Almost casually, at the end of this 227-page novel (published in 1989), Guibert mentions he has AIDS, which he jokingly tells the reader he contracted from reading the newspaper.

Quickly he must have realized that AIDS was not just a medical curiosity or a product of American hysteria but rather his destiny and his subject, one that would bring together his hatred of his own body, his taste for the grotesque and his infatuation with death, a subject that would also give him something new, a pressure of fate brought to bear daily, hourly, on his previously aleatory existence. Henceforth if he travelled, if he read a book, if he talked to a cute guy with crossed eyes, the comings and goings of his life would no longer extend towards a sickeningly indefinite horizon; now death, which he'd always flirted with, was immanent, and dying might at any moment lend a sense of order, ending, necessity, to his most random acts.

Or as Guibert himself put it in *To the Friend Who Did Not Save My Life* (1990):

> Jules had once said to me, at a time when he didn't believe we were infected, that AIDS was a marvelous disease. And it's true that I was discovering something sleek and dazzling in its hideousness, for though it was certainly an inexorable illness, it wasn't immediately catastrophic, it was an illness in stages, a very long flight of steps that led assuredly to death, but whose every step represented a unique apprenticeship. It was a disease that gave death time to live and its victims time to die, time to discover time, and in the end to discover life, so in a way those green monkeys of Africa had provided us with a brilliant modern invention.

Michel Foucault appears in this book under the name of Muzil. He tells no one he is ill, not even his lover. Guibert would have liked to be as discreet, 'allowing friendships to live as lightly as air, carefree and eternal'. But he needs the sympathy of his friends, starting with that of Jules, his lover, who is also married. The title of the book refers to a former friend who works for an American drug company and has promised to give the Salk AIDS vaccine to the narrator and to his lover Jules as well as to Jules's wife and children. The 'friend', however, keeps putting the narrator off, though he does manage to administer the vaccine to a casual sexual partner easily enough.

The novel begins with the narrator's announcement that he is not going to die, that he is going to be the first person to beat this disease. He vows not to tell his parents ('my chief concern, in this business, is to avoid dying in the spotlight of the parental eye'). When Muzil first hears of the disease he falls off the sofa laughing ('a cancer that would hit only homosexuals, no, that's too good to be true. I could just die laughing'). After the narrator suspects that he and Jules are infected, 'this certainty changed everything . . . sapped my strength while at the same time increasing it tenfold'. A large part of this new energy goes into writing: 'when I'd learned I was going to die, I'd suddenly been seized with the desire to write every possible book – all the ones I hadn't written yet, at the risk of writing them badly: a funny, nasty book, then a philosophical one . . . and to write not only the books of my anticipated maturity but also, with the speed of light, the slowly ripened books of my old age.' Guibert is even forced to admit that he is exhilarated by his new close proximity to death: 'Ever since I was twelve years old . . . I've had a thing about death.'

One of the successful aspects of this book is the portrait of Foucault – something new for Guibert, the observation of someone outside the orbit of his obsessions. The worst part is the recital of grudges, the settling of scores – against Adjani, because she lets her whims interfere with his chance to earn some badly needed money, and especially against Bill, the friend who did not save his life. The end of the book is devoted to hopes for the vaccine and efforts to corner Bill into delivering it, all to no avail. The narrator has been told that the vaccine is no longer effective if the patient has fewer than 200 T-cells; on the last page of the book the narrator has hit 200 and Bill has vanished. (The scandal caused by Guibert's novel apparently convinced the American drug company in question not to conduct a trial for the Salk vaccine in France, which was judged to be too disputatious a nation.

In any event the benefits of the vaccine are still in doubt and even its defenders now set the cut-off point not at 200 but at 600 T-cells.)

In *The Compassion Protocol* Guibert, energized by anti-viral pills his lover steals from the bedside of a dead ballet dancer, begins a new journal ('It is when what I am writing takes the form of a journal that I most strongly feel that I am writing fiction'). Beautifully translated by James Kirkup, the book brings together themes such as Guibert's intermittent fight to survive, his continuing struggle to write, to deal with his parents, to find the proper treatment, even to accept his rapid aging ('In 1990 I am ninety-five, although I was born in 1955').

Having dealt directly with the disease in *To the Friend Who Did Not Save My Life, The Compassion Protocol* and *Cytomégalovirus*, Guibert then wrote three fantasias, as one might call them, on his grim theme. *The Man in the Red Hat*, which is about the art world, recounts in a haphazard way: attempts to find a missing painter in Moscow during the last days of the USSR; a disastrously gloomy stay in Crete in the house of a rich Greek painter named Yannis; and the successful pursuit of the eccentric, reclusive painter Balthus. The effect of putting AIDS in the background of a cops-and-robbers tale of the art world is to make it all the more menacing. At the end of a long paragraph the narrator mentions he's in a café where he's served by a new waiter:

> He kept glancing sidelong at me from time to time, his innocent eyes wide with fright. I too was watching him sidelong. I was longing to lick his hole. But we were already in different worlds separated by an invisible glass which is the passage from life to death, and who knows, from death to life.

He mentions his unquenchable taste for work, just as at the end of *To the Friend Who Did Not Save My Life* he acknowledges that he prefers writing to living, that he so dislikes his fellow men that his only remaining companion is whatever book he happens to be working on. In *Mon Valet et moi* Guibert builds a short narrative on the idea that AIDS makes young people old. Without once mentioning AIDS, the book gives the thoughts of a very old millionaire (living in the next century) who becomes more and more a victim of his valet, a sort of fiendish secret sharer. After making himself indispensable, the valet, a former movie actor, pushes the master out of his bedroom and barricades himself inside. Behind closed doors he transforms the room into a Sioux teepee (a dim recollection of a similar scene in Cocteau's *Les Enfants terribles*). The valet even begins to avail himself of Monsieur's morphine. And yet the complicity between master and servant is loving if bizarre and violent, and the valet is willing to let his master dictate the very text we're reading, which is dated 'Kyoto–Anchorage–Paris. January–February 2036'. Throughout Guibert's eventful and rushed writing career he had regularly alternated surreal novels filled with invented characters and events with thinly disguised autobiography (often not disguised at all). *Mon Valet et moi* is perhaps his most successful invention, partly because it gives in such lip-smacking, shocking detail the truth of physical decline and of the humiliation of being dependent on a hired helper. It's also a very funny book. In one scene the master makes his valet drive him to the Rambouillet forest, where he's discovered a factory that does nothing but pulp the novels of Marguerite Duras, 'a writer of the eighties'. As he explains: 'This occupation doesn't amuse my valet, he thinks it's unhealthy, he says: "Why do you have it in for this poor woman?"'

Guibert's last book, *Le Paradis*, was written during the summer of 1991, a few months before his death. He is no longer escaping his destiny by projecting himself into the future. Now he's concocted an Other who is a contemporary, a hero who is Swiss, heterosexual, healthy, vacationing on a tropical island. But this 'paradise' is not immune from the author's fears, since the story begins with the narrator's girlfriend's death. Jayne has gone swimming where she shouldn't have, and her body has been dragged by the tide across a coral reef, which eviscerated her.

Although the first two-thirds of this narrative are coherent, the last third is a delirious confusion. Sometimes the character is the heterosexual Swiss, but at other times he is Hervé Guibert. Sometimes Jayne is dead, but at others alive. Real events in Guibert's life impinge on the action. He loses his memory temporarily. He travels to Africa against his doctor's advice (an accident first recounted at the end of *The Man in the Red Hat*.) He remembers

Muzil-Foucault, who never properly understood that his philosophical works were really novels. His lover Jules tells him he looks like a zombie. He is haunted by his mad heroes – Artaud, Strindberg, Nietzsche. (At the beginning of the book Jayne is writing a thesis on Nietzsche, Strindberg and Robert Walser.) But Rimbaud is his true model, the Rimbaud who traveled to Africa and staked everything on earning a fortune so that he could marry a respectable woman and return to his village in glory, the Rimbaud who died of a wound contracted in Abyssinia. The narrator has installed a stuffed green African monkey on his desk, the very monkey that he claims transmitted AIDS to the human race.

Despite attacks of delirium and amnesia, despite a loss of motor control, Guibert continues to write. He knows that he has become old like a thousand-year-old iguana, its hide tanned by the sun. He takes note of Rimbaud's remark in a letter from Africa that he has aged five years in one. He contemplates suicide. But until the final moment he will continue to write, this man who, like Cocteau, can say he has turned his body into a fountain pen. 'When I no longer write I start to die,' he remarks near the end of *Le Paradis*.

Guibert placed himself in a tough Continental line of writers. He himself cites Sade, Nietzsche, Rimbaud, Strindberg, Artaud, Bataille and Thomas Bernhard (Guibert admired Bernhard for his tenacity and autobiographical honesty). Because of his heritage and a natural inclination towards the sordid, he approached AIDS with a lot less charity and emotion than such American writers as Larry Kramer and Paul Monette, and with less of a turn for psychological realism and moral exactitude than the English novelist Adam Mars-Jones. And yet this very taste for the grotesque, this compulsion to offend, finally affords Guibert the necessary rhetorical panache to convey the full, exhilarating horror of his predicament.

The Personal is Political: Queer Fiction and Criticism

A speech given at the Center for Lesbian and Gay Studies at New York University, 12 November 1993, and first published in *Brick*, 1994.

In one sense, most of the fiction I like and all the fiction I write is political. If I sometimes sound like an apostle of art for art's sake, this esthetic bias should be judged against an endless fascination with politics. The power dynamics between populations, the jousting for position within a group, the struggle for dominance in a couple, even the empowering awareness of individual oppression – by all these definitions, politics has been a constant theme in my work, even or especially in my novels of pure fantasy, *Forgetting Elena* and *Caracole*.

I hope you'll forgive me for speaking so much about my own work. I am certainly aware of its limitations, and I by no means want to disguise my naïveté and shortcomings as a political commentator or activist. For instance my nearly total silence in the face of AIDS, with the exception of my stories in *The Darker Proof*, I consider reprehensible, a lapsus I'm trying belatedly to fill with the novel I'm writing now, *The Farewell Symphony*, the sequel to my earlier autobiographical novels, *A Boy's Own Story* and *The Beautiful Room is Empty*.

If I speak so much of my own books, I do so because I know the ins and outs of their publishing history. And since my career happened sometimes to parallel the birth and growth of the modern gay publishing movement, my story may be of some general interest.

In *Forgetting Elena*, my first published novel, which came out in 1973, I tried to put into practice an observation I'd made about the work of writers I'd admired. I'd realized that they were at their best when exploring themes about which they themselves were of two minds. A thesis novel that propounds an idea the author has completely mapped out in advance is not one I want to read or write. I prefer a book in which the writer sinks a probe into a question that is difficult to resolve but urgent to consider.

When I was a student Saul Bellow spoke to us along these lines about *The Brothers Karamazov.* He said that in a letter written to a friend during the composition of the novel, Dostoevsky complained that in 'The Legend of the Grand Inquisitor' he'd so convincingly repudiated God's world that in the next section he feared he couldn't conjure up equally favorable arguments on behalf of his real credo – of universal harmony and the ascendancy of heart, feeling and faith over mind. Dostoevsky's dramatization of ideas struck me as the very way to stage my own political concerns. Proust had demonstrated the shortcomings of snobbism because he knew so intimately all about its allure, just as Elizabeth Bowen could write about the tragic conflict between unruly passion and crushing social convention in *The Death of the Heart* because she'd succumbed to passion and been impressed by the lustre convention gives to society.

Forgetting Elena is, among other things, a fantasy novel about the charm – and repulsiveness – of a closed society that has allowed the cult of beauty to replace genuine moral concerns. The denizens of my island kingdom, which sometimes resembles Fire Island, never stop to question if an act is good or bad so long as it is beautiful.

This estheticism produces sinister, even tragic, consequences. And yet I lavished on those rituals and dances and costumes and nature worship all the affection I myself felt for the shimmering, ephemeral, erotically charged drama and decor of the Pines at the end of the 1960s, when gays were crowding out straights in the beach community and when, in the rest of the United States, the new gay movement was generating a fresh take on gender politics. Simultaneously, the new gay sensibility was concocting extravagant inventions in the ephemeral arts of fashion, lighting, flower arranging, party design, window dressing, disco dancing, drug sequencing and sexual performance. I was attracted to both gay politics *and* the gay sensibility, two very different entities; the tension humming under every page of *Forgetting Elena* was born out of this conflict.

Perhaps for all writers, but certainly for us lesbian and gay writers in the 1970s, every artistic decision we made had its political aspect. Should we write gay fiction at all? At that time there was no known market for our work, few bookstores that would carry it, precious few editors who would even read our manuscripts. Literary friends told us that we were betraying our high calling by ghettoizing ourselves. After all, the argument ran, many great writers had been lesbian or gay, but Willa Cather and Virginia Woolf and Elizabeth Bishop wrote for all humanity and would have found any minority label demeaning. It would be absurd to call them lesbian writers, just as it would be grotesque to call E. M. Forster or Henry James gay writers.

Since I'd had my first breakthrough with *Forgetting Elena* – a novel that no critic had identified as gay and that a notorious heterosexual, Vladimir Nabokov, had singled out for praise – my timorous friends were all the more insistent that I should not come out in print or, as they put it, 'limit' myself.

Oddly enough Saul Bellow once again guided me. I read in his *Paris Review* interview that when he'd first started writing about the Jewish experience he'd been warned not to give up the writer's proudest birthright – his claim to universality (I say 'his' advisedly). Fortunately Bellow had ignored the warnings.

Anyway, ever since I was a teenager I'd been writing unpublished and unpublishable gay fiction, not out of an enlightened or campaigning spirit but because I felt driven to exorcize my demons and establish my right to exist, on the page if not yet in society. At age fifteen I'd already written a coming-out novel, *The Tower Window*, never published, of course, and not even read in manuscript. Now, after *Forgetting Elena*, the very next book I wrote (in collaboration with Dr Charles Silverstein) was *The Joy of Gay Sex*. In retrospect this book may look reckless (because of the subsequent AIDS crisis) or cynically commercial (because presumably we earned a lot of money) or blandly assimilationist (since the book appeared as a sequel to *The Joy of Sex*, a hugely successful guide for heterosexuals).

Queer history moves so quickly that even sixteen years later (*The Joy of Gay Sex* was published in 1977) that past moment is difficult to reconstruct. Needless to say, in 1977 no one could have foreseen the AIDS crisis of 1981 and at the time Dr Silverstein and I were often criticized by people in the gay community for being conservative because we labeled certain sexual practises dangerous. We certainly didn't get rich, since we were paid a flat fee and a miserable percentage. The publishers told me I could write the book under a pen name; at that time my name was virtually unknown in any event. If this project now seems assimilationist, at the time assimilation itself seemed a provocative and progressive idea. There were so few openings in the united front against homosexuality that only the sexual revolution seemed a possible point of entry.

Our book, moreover, was much more a guide to gay practical problems (for instance, how to write a will in favor of a lover) or psychological hurdles (how to come out at work, for example) than a sex manual, which we knew from Masters and Johnson's findings was far less a problem for gays than for straights. We felt courageous signing our real names to a book that would be sold across the country over the counter in major bookstores – a book that attempted to assuage fears, diminish guilt, combat puritanism, sanction sex. After 1981 we were naturally distressed that the book was still in print, but our efforts to revise it were ignored by the publishers, who had now been absorbed by American Express. Recently Dr Silverstein and Felice Picano were at last able to bring out a safe-sex version, for which I wrote an introduction.

In my next novel, *Nocturnes for the King of Naples*, my narrator writes a long love letter to an absent beloved who might, depending on one's interpretation, either be an older man or God. Mary Gordon, the then newly discovered Catholic novelist, gave me a blurb saying my novel had re-invented 'devotional literature'. Although I wrote the book out of my private poetic obsessions, I was certainly aware that in a country like the United States where homosexuals have suffered so much at the hands of organized religion, it was a useful literary act, if only for my 5,000 readers, to place an overtly gay love story in a mystical tradition that blends the carnal with the spiritual, a tradition that includes St John of the Cross, the Sufi poet Rumi and Baroque poets such as John Donne.

But perhaps the most dramatic choice was the decision not to explain gay lives but simply present them. In the novel I'm writing now, which starts in the late 1960s, before Stonewall, I have a passage that reads:

Back then I was anything but an objective observer. I was a

moralist, if that meant I wanted to suggest new ways of acting through examples and adjectives that were subtly praising or censorious. I knew as well as anyone else that homosexuality was an aberration, a disease, but in my fiction I pretended otherwise. I gave my characters problems, minor problems that struck me as human, decorous, rather than the one irrevocable tragedy of being blasted from the start. I showed my homosexual characters living their lives openly and parallel to those of their heterosexual friends: pure fiction. I pretended the homosexual characters had homes, loves, careers if not exactly the same at least of a similar weight and dignity. But my greatest invention was that I let my queers think about everything except the one subject that obsessed them: how they came to be this way, how they could evince the world's compassion rather than hate, and how they could be cured of their malady. I knew I didn't have the equilibrium or self-acceptance of my characters, but I thought by pretending *as if* (hadn't a whole German philosophy been based on the words 'as if'?) this utopia already existed I could authenticate my gay readers if not myself.

Curiously even *The Joy of Gay Sex* had advocated a warmer, more sensual view of sex than I myself could muster. This hortatory and utopian aspect of gay writing sometimes vexed straight readers. I remember that John Gardiner, the author of *On Moral Fiction*, told me that he considered *Nocturnes* immoral because in it the father breezes right past his son's confession of homosexuality. The father, if anything, seems *relieved* that his son won't be competing with him for women. Gardiner thought such broad-mindedness (or egotism) was unrealistic, hence immoral. He didn't understand I was trailblazing.

States of Desire: Travels in Gay America, published in 1980, took a half-admiring, half-castigating look at the triumphant clone culture that was about to be transformed beyond recognition by AIDS. As a socialist I was worried by the materialism, selfishness and racism I detected among successful white clones, but at the same time I had to admire the in-your-face confidence of this group in confronting Christian fundamentalist Anita Bryant, for instance. The most obvious political agenda of the book was to show the wide variety of gay lives. I also turned the travel-book format into a platform for writing mini-essays about man–boy love, racism, sado-masochism, agism and so on.

Perhaps the least obvious but most telling political decision was to address a sophisticated gay reader. If previously I'd written for an older European heterosexual woman, an ideal reader who helped me to screen out in-jokes and preaching to the converted, I now pictured my reader as another gay man. Up until now many gay non-fiction books had been pleas for compassion or primary guides to gay folklore addressed to an open-minded if uninformed straight audience. I decided to work on the principle behind the *New Yorker* that pretends all readers are Manhattanites, a policy that flatters even Iowans. I thought by writing for other gays I could get beyond the See- Dick-Run level and apologetic tone of most gay commentators, a tone that had begun to bore me.

If *A Boy's Own Story*, published in 1982, was my best received book, it succeeded partly because it seemed to fill an empty niche in the contemporary publishing ecology, the slot of the coming-out novel. What I wanted to show was the harm psychotheraphy had done to homosexuals and the self-hatred that was forced on a young gay man by a society that could conceive of homosexuality only as a sickness, sin or crime. What allowed me to write it and its sequel, *The Beautiful Room is Empty*, was the conviction I'd picked up in consciousness-raising groups in the early 1970s that the personal is political. This simple phrase, more than any other, opened the way to a genuine feminist and queer literature. We learned that what we'd endured and survived was not too subjective or peculiar to be of interest to readers. We also learned that what we'd lived through was not a neurosis in need of treatment but a shared experience that called for political action. My strategy in *The Beautiful Room is Empty* was to present a gay hero so self-hating that even the most retrograde reader would become impatient with his inner torment and welcome with relief the Stonewall Uprising, which is the concluding scene of that novel. I felt my strategy had worked when Christopher Lehmann-Haupt, an avowed heterosexual, wrote in his *New York Times* review that he found himself longing for the hero to settle down and get on with his life, even if it was gay.

The consciousness-raising group seemed not a bad model for the queer artistic and critical community. During a typical session we took a single theme – gays and religion, say – and each person was asked to give a personal testimony bearing on the subject. No one was permitted to advise another person or interpret her or his testimony – practices more appropriate to group therapy, which assumed the individual was out of step, than to the CR group, which was convinced society needed to be reformed. Only after everyone had spoken did we seek to find certain common themes, if there were any, and to envisage a remedial political action. For instance, if everyone, in speaking about coming out, testified to the blackout of information about homosexuality in the schools while growing up, we might plan actions that would provide it now.

The part of the formula that seems important to recall today is that no one had the right to challenge the political correctness of another person's story. Politics entered the process only after all the stories were told. Political correctness is a matter for criticism, not creativity.

Neither Marxist nor Freudian nor deconstructionist arguments have persuaded me to abandon the romantic creed that art is an expression of human freedom at its highest, virtually the only arena not subject to compromise, fear, contingency and accommodation. Fiction is based on human feelings, including those of hate, lust, greed and self-pity, and no one has the right to deny another person's emotions or to correct her or his account of them. To say, 'I know what you're feeling or what you *should* be feeling better than you yourself know' is redolent of the psychotherapeutic Fascism we queers have done so much to combat.

In recent years I've had the occasion to reread the novels of Jean Genet. They are genuinely perverse, often infantile, always shocking. They glorify passion and crime and exalt treachery. In my analysis of Genet's defiant satanism I never let myself lose sight of the fact that he, like me, like every homosexual before gay liberation, could choose only amongst the same three metaphors for homosexuality – as sickness, crime or sin. Almost all other homosexual writers chose sickness as their model since it called for compassion from the heterosexual reader. Genet chose the other two, sin and crime, which turned out to define the fiercer, prouder position. Genet wants to intimidate and alternately to seduce his heterosexual reader, not beg him for forgiveness. Instead of tea and sympathy, Genet offers vitriol and impudence.

A political analysis of Genet's fiction must recognize that regardless of his explicit message or his stated provocations, he invented the drag queen for literature with Divine in *Our Lady of the Flowers*, a novel that also gives us the most detailed picture we have of the slang and customs of the gay community in Montmartre just before the war. In a similar fashion *The Miracle of the Rose*, although anything but a work of realism, gives us the most detailed picture we have of sex and love at Mettray, the reform school Foucault also discusses in *Discipline and Punish*, just as *The Thief's Journal* is the most complete record that exists of the Barrio China in Barcelona, the stronghold of marginal Spain during the years of anarchy and civil war. The point is that we may feel uncomfortable when Genet relentlessly endorses male–female role-playing or equates homosexuality with treachery, but if we, first, acknowledge that his sexuality was formed by prison and, second, look beyond his attitudinizing to the actual content of his books, he is as useful a writer today as he was fifty years ago.

In interpreting Genet I'd learned a lesson from the struggles over Larry Kramer's *Faggots* in the 1970s. American gay commentators had mostly denounced the book for daring to criticize gay promiscuity, then considered a cornerstone of gay freedom. However, an important socialist review in Britain, *Gay Left*, took a very different stand and praised *Faggots* because it was set in the heart of the gay community and showed how gay people interact, not just as lovers but also as friends. This interaction was to be contrasted with the supposedly affirmative books and films of the period that invariably placed a loving lesbian or gay couple in an idyllic bucolic setting far from a gay social or cultural context, thereby covertly suggesting once again that only the alibi of love redeems a queer and that love can flourish only outside the supposedly neurotic and hostile ghetto.

Today many of the attacks staged by the Left on books are launched in the name of the politics of identity, the principle that each minority can and should speak only for itself and that outsiders should be banned from doing so. Much can be said in favor of this position and each of us can attest that we've learned more about African-Americans from Toni Morrison than William Faulkner, that we feel Andrew Holleran understands gays better than Norman Mailer does, and that Maxine Hong Kingston knows more about China than does Pearl Buck. These preferences, however, are esthetic and need no defense. Readers are naturally attracted to versions of an experience that are more detailed, more convincing, veristic, shaded. Yet we resist having this preference codified into a policy. Can only Salman Rushdie write about India? Most Indians agree that *Kim* is the best book about nineteenth-century India, despite Kipling's imperialist politics. I once asked one of my writing students, an African-American lesbian, what she thought about the politics of identity. With a little smile and a verbal shrug she said that after she heard Ishmael Reed say that black women didn't have the right to write about black men, she had decided to throw in the towel.

Many of the current battles over literature are being fought in the universities and are an effort to insert gay books or feminist books or African-American books or the books representing other minorities into the canon.

When I published three years ago an article in the *New York Times* magazine about the current state of gay fiction, I received dozens of letters from teachers asking me for a reading list, including the list I was using in a lesbian and gay literature course I was teaching at Brown that I'd mentioned. Some people seemed uncertain about which lesbian and gay books should be considered classics. Others had made their pick and wanted to introduce their favorite titles into the canon, the reading list of introductory literature courses.

I myself am in favor of desacralizing literature, of dismantling the idea of a few essential books, of retiring the whole concept of a canon. A canon is for people who don't like to read, people who want to know the bare minimum of titles they must consume in order to be considered polished, well rounded, civilized. Any real reader seeks the names of more and more books, not fewer and fewer.

The notion of a canon implies that we belong to something called Western Civilization that is built on a small sacred library and that that library is eternal and universal and important in the way no individual reader can ever be. I would say that every part of such an assumption is misguided. The United States is no more Western than Eastern, no more English than Spanish, no more Christian than Jewish or Buddhist. We must accept the full implications of pluri-culturalism. We must no longer attempt to introduce a few gay titles or a Chinese-American title into a canon that begins with Aristotle and Plato or the Bible. Even the hierarchy inherent in the concept of a canon must be jettisoned. In Latin a canon is a ruler, a rule or a model and the relevant primary meaning of the word is 'an authoritative list of books accepted as Holy Scripture'. No matter that the canon, even among the most conservative readers, shifts from one generation to the next. Look at the Harvard Five-Foot Shelf of Classics, once considered definitive. Few people today read Charles Dana's *Two Years Before the Mast* or Whittier's poetry, but for my grandparents such books were unquestionably canonical, as was *The Pilgrim's Progress* or William Dean Howell's *The Rise of Silas Lapham*.

Literature courses should teach students *how* to read, not *what* to read. Students can acquire from teachers the rigorous pleasure of close reading, of comparison and analysis, of broadened sympathies and finer moral discrimination. Students can be taught to be skeptical, to label rhetorical strategies, to uncover political subtexts, to spot allusions, to recognize the anxiety of influence and to detect the function of such fictional structures as mystery, suspense and characterization. They can't be taught to like or even finish *The Nicomachean Ethics*. Our reading lists should be long, heterodox, seductive and they should include many contemporary works; as John Ashbery once said, 'We should begin at the beginning, that is, the present.' The mind of a particular student, far from being just one more vessel into which the divine liquor of canonical wisdom is poured, is, at the moment of reading, the *unique* theater on which Shakespeare's plays are staged or the *only* altar where Bacon's Idols are overturned. A book exists only when a living mind recreates it and that recreation comes into being only through the full imaginative participation of a particular sensibility.

I've tried to show, in taking the example of my own work, the political assumptions I had to make in order to write some of my books. From there I've grazed past such explosive current questions as political correctness, artistic freedom and canon formation. I've suggested that whereas criticism can be correct, fiction itself is immune from such a judgment. Whereas criticism can discuss the political dimensions of fiction, in a novel whose dimensions are always richer and more subtle than at first one might suspect, less a question of explicit authorial message and more a matter of the milieu represented, the ideal reader addressed, the utopia adumbrated.

That our feelings run high when we discuss queer fiction only attests to the central role it plays in the formation of our new culture. It sometimes seems more people discuss fiction than read it, but this intense scrutiny, even anxiety, reveals that for us, perhaps more than for any other group, fiction is a way of preserving the past, recording the present, creating the future. Until recently there were few openly queer political leaders, social philosophers, literary critics, outspoken celebrities willing to take stands on important questions. When such stands do get taken, all too often they sound narrowly polemical and divisive. Philosophy is too abstract, history too circumstantial, politics too peremptory to show in precise, glowing detail the way an individual lives through a particular moment. To use the philosopher Richard Rorty's terms, only fiction does equal justice to private irony and public liberalism. Or to come back to our own vocabulary, only our fiction fully demonstrates how the personal is political.

Index